Latin American and US Latino Religions in North America

BLOOMSBURY RELIGION IN NORTH AMERICA

The chapters in this book were first published in the digital collection *Bloomsbury Religion in North America*. Covering North America's diverse religious traditions, this digital collection provides reliable and peer-reviewed articles and eBooks for students and instructors of religious studies, anthropology of religion, sociology of religion, and history. Learn more and get access for your library at www.theologyandreligiononline.com/bloomsbury-religion-in-north-america

BLOOMSBURY
RELIGION IN
NORTH AMERICA

Also available:
Islam in North America, edited by Hussein Rashid, Huma Mohibullah, and Vincent Biondo
Christianity in North America, edited by Dyron D. Daughrity
Religion, Science, and Technology in North America, edited by Lisa L. Stenmark and Whitney A. Bauman
Religion and Nature in North America, edited by Laurel D. Kearns and Whitney A. Bauman
Secularity and Nonreligion in North America, edited by Jesse M. Smith and Ryan T. Cragun
Judaism in North America, edited by Gary G. Porton
New Religious Movements in North America, edited by Lydia Willsky-Ciollo

Latin American and US Latino Religions in North America

An Introduction

EDITED BY LLOYD D. BARBA

BLOOMSBURY ACADEMIC
LONDON • NEW YORK • OXFORD • NEW DELHI • SYDNEY

BLOOMSBURY ACADEMIC
Bloomsbury Publishing Plc
50 Bedford Square, London, WC1B 3DP, UK
1385 Broadway, New York, NY 10018, USA
29 Earlsfort Terrace, Dublin 2, Ireland

BLOOMSBURY, BLOOMSBURY ACADEMIC and the Diana logo are
trademarks of Bloomsbury Publishing Plc

First published online 2022
This print edition published 2024

A catalogue record for this book is available from the British Library.

Library of Congress Cataloging-in-Publication Data
Names: Barba, Lloyd Daniel, editor.
Title: Latin American and US Latinx religions in North America :
an introduction / edited by Lloyd Barba.
Description: London : Bloomsbury Academic, 2024. | Series: Bloomsbury religion in
North America | First published online in 2021. | Includes bibliographical references and index.
Identifiers: LCCN 2023059756 | ISBN 9781350420489 (paperback) |
ISBN 9781350420472 (hardback)
Subjects: LCSH: North America–Religion. | Latin America–Religion. |
Hispanic Americans–Religion. | Religious pluralism–North America.
Classification: LCC BL2520 .L38 2024 | DDC 200.89/6807–dc23/eng/20240226
LC record available at https://lccn.loc.gov/2023059756

ISBN: HB: 978-1-3504-2047-2
PB: 978-1-3504-2048-9

Series: Bloomsbury Religion in North America

Typeset by Integra Software Services Pvt. Ltd.
Printed and bound in Great Britain

Contents

Illustrations

List of Contributors

Lloyd D. Barba (PhD American Culture, University of Michigan, Ann Arbor) is Assistant Professor of Religion and Core Faculty in Latinx and Latin American Studies at Amherst College. He is the author of *Sowing the Sacred: Mexican Pentecostal Farmworkers in California* (2022) and co-editor (with Andrea Johnson and Daniel Ramírez) of *Oneness Pentecostalism: Race, Gender, and Culture* (2023). His next monograph is *Cesar Chavez: A Catholic Social Prophet* and he is working on several projects pertaining to the US Sanctuary Movement from the 1980s to the present day.

Tatyana Castillo-Ramos (PhD candidate Religious Studies, Yale University) is completing a dissertation titled *Border Faith, Border Fields: Religion and Immigrant Rights Activism at the San Diego-Tijuana Border.* It focuses on the history of faith-based activists in the region and how religion has been performed to counteract the militarization of border enforcement.

João B. Chaves (PhD Religion, Baylor University) is Assistant Professor of the History of Religion in the Américas at Baylor University, Department of Religion. He is the author of several books, including *Migrational Religion*, *The Global Mission of the Jim Crow South*, and *Remembering Antônia Teixeira*, co-authored with Mikeal Parsons.

Ken Chitwood (PhD Religion, University of Florida) is a Senior Research Fellow with the Muslim Philanthropy Initiative at Indiana University-Purdue University Indianapolis (IUPUI). Chitwood is the author of *The Muslims of Latin America and the Caribbean* (2021) and his second book, *AmeRícan Muslims: The Everyday Lives of Puerto Rican Converts to Islam,* is forthcoming.

Robert A. Danielson (PhD, Intercultural Studies, Asbury Theological Seminary) is the Director of Strategic Collections and Scholarly Communications Librarian at Asbury Theological Seminary, where he is also a Faculty Associate and Affiliate Faculty member. His current research is on early Holiness/Pentecostal missions in Central America and the Caribbean.

Alejandro S. Escalante (PhD Religious Studies, University of North Carolina, Chapel Hill) is Lecturer in Social Anthropology at the University of Edinburgh. His work focuses on theories of subjectivity and the ways they integrate with the study of gender, race, and religion.

David Flores (PhD, Chicana/o and Central American Studies, University of California, Los Angeles) is Assistant Professor of Ethnic Studies at Sacramento State University. Flores is an East Los Angeles native and his research examines the intersection of religion and social movements, specifically the Chicana/o Civil Rights Movement in Los Angeles. Flores recently co-edited a dossier on Christianity and Chicana/o/x Latina/o/x Studies in *Aztlan: A Journal of Chicana/o Studies*.

Ángel J. Gallardo (PhD, Religion and Culture, Southern Methodist University) is Assistant Professor of Church History at Austin Presbyterian Theological Seminary in Austin, Texas. His forthcoming book, *Mapping the Nature of Empire*, narrates how, in the wake of 1492, a scholastic view of the natural order informed and contested the racial and geographic hierarchies that emerged in the early modern world.

Carlos Garma (PhD Anthropology, Universidad Autónoma Metropolitana-Iztapalapa) is Research Professor at Universidad Autónoma Metropolitana-Iztapalapa, in Mexico City. He is the author of numerous books, including *Mexico: Religious Tensions in Latin America's First Secular State* and *Buscando el Espíritu, Pentecostalismo en Iztapalapa y la Ciudad de México*.

Jacqueline M. Hidalgo (PhD Religion, Claremont Graduate University) is Professor of Theology and Religious Studies at the University of San Diego. She is the author of *Revelation in Aztlán: Scriptures, Utopias, and the Chicano Movement* (2016) and *Latina/o/x Studies and Biblical Studies* in *Brill Research Perspectives in Biblical Interpretation* (2020); she is also co-editor with Efraín Agosto of *Latinxs, the Bible, and Migration* (2018).

Laura Limonic (PhD Sociology, City University of New York) is an Associate Professor of Sociology at the SUNY Old Westbury. Her research is in the area of Latinx Jews with a focus on immigrant populations. Limonic's current work examines the rise of Chabad-Lubavitch communities in Latin America and among Latin American immigrants in the United States.

Alyssa Maldonado-Estrada (PhD Religion, Princeton University) is Assistant Professor of Religion at Kalamazoo College. She is the author of *Lifeblood of the Parish: Men and Catholic Devotion in Williamsburg, Brooklyn* (2020).

Néstor Medina (PhD Interdisciplinary Studies, St Michael's College, University of Toronto) is Associate Professor of Religious Ethics at Emmanuel College, University of Toronto. He engages ethics from contextual, liberationist, intercultural, and post/decolonial perspectives. He is the author of *Mestizaje: (Re)Mapping "Race," Culture, and Faith in Latina/o Catholicism* (2009), a booklet *On the Doctrine of Discovery* (2017), and *Christianity, Empire and the Spirit* (2018).

Francisco Peláez-Díaz (PhD Religion and Society, Princeton Theological Seminary) is Assistant Teaching Professor in Latinx Studies and Ministries at Drew Theological School. His current project is a book chapter titled "The Church at the Crossroads of Migrants, Trauma and Hope: A Healing Centered Approach." This project seeks to contribute to a deeper understanding of the ecologies of migrant care in the United States, particularly those linked to religious institutions.

Daniel Ramírez (PhD American Religious History, Duke University) is Associate Professor of American Religions at Claremont Graduate University and past president of the American Society of Church History. He is the author of *Migrating Faith: Pentecostalism in the United States and Mexico in the Twentieth Century* (2015) and co-editor (with Lloyd D. Barba and Andrea Johnson) of *Oneness Pentecostalism: Race, Gender, and Culture* (2023). His current monograph project is titled "Pentecostalisms of Oaxacalifornia."

Erica Ramirez (PhD Religion, Drew University) is a sociologist of religion and Director of Research at Auburn Theological Seminary in Manhattan. Her first book, *Rise of the Lamb's Queen: Pentecostalism as Carnivalesque,* uses ritual theory to chart the politics of American Pentecostal altar practices.

Aida Isela Ramos (PhD Sociology, University of Texas, Austin) is a sociologist and the Dean of the College of Education and Social & Behavioral Sciences at John Brown University. Her research lies at the nexus of race/ethnicity, sociology of religion, and first-generation student success. She is writing her next book, *Faith on the Frontera: Religion and Racialization in the Texas-Mexico Borderlands.*

Daisy Vargas (PhD History, University of California, Riverside) is Assistant Professor in the Department of Religious Studies & Classics at the University of Arizona. Her current book project traces the history of Mexican religion, race, and the law from the nineteenth century to the contemporary moment.

Preface

Lloyd D. Barba

The chapters in this volume came together as part of a series of seventeen articles I edited from 2021 to 2023 for the online platform *Bloomsbury Religion in North America*. In addition to the seventeen articles, I wrote an overview article which serves as the first chapter in this volume. That chapter is not an overview of this volume but rather of the broader world of Latin American and US Latino religion as well as the connections between the two. Too often, definitions of "North America" only include the United States and Canada. Mexico might sometimes be included, but far too frequently Central America and the Caribbean are left out. This volume includes these regions in its analysis of North America, recognizing them as vital components of the Latinx religious world.

To be sure, "Latin American Religion" and "US Latinx Religion" constitute separate fields of study. However, given the increased connections brought on by social media, expedited travel, and migration networks (even amidst increased border security in the United States), we have more reason than ever to consider the links between Latin America proper and its diasporic populations in the United States. As is often the case, what happens in Latin America impacts its diasporic populations in the United States and vice versa. According to the 2020 US Census, Latinos comprise nearly 19% (that is, almost one in five) of the overall population. Furthermore, consider how the US Latino population in 2020 (at over 62 million) alone outnumbered the total population of all Latin American countries, save Brazil (approximately 212 million) and Mexico (approximately 128 million) and also comprised more than double the entire population of Canada. *Latinidad* signals a modus vivendi across borders in the Americas. These statistics and adjustments in the immigrant experience do not erase important differences between the US Latinx populations and their compatriots in Latin America. But given the extent of the Latin American diaspora in North America, this volume compels readers to consider the dense connections across the Americas and the role of religion in various communities.

Latin American and US Latino Religions in North America is primarily geared toward students new to these fields of study, but even researchers well acquainted with these fields stand to learn much from novel connections drawn by the authors, methodology, and new insights. All the authors in this volume have deep connections with Latinx communities, either having grown up in these contexts or from years of research and a variety of life experiences. When I initially recruited authors for this project, I sought to cast a wide net in terms of geography, history, and methodology. No single volume can account for all experiences, but this volume has sought to bring out major trends via established scholarship as well as new research projects debuted here.

This volume is divided into five parts. Part I introduces readers to "origins," focusing in large part on colonial histories of Latin America. Chapter 1 offers a sweeping historical overview that focuses on continuities and contrasts across the Latinx Americas. The following two chapters trace theological and racial concerns during the colonial period. Chapter 2 discusses Spain's religious and geopolitical colonial mapping projects in the Americas, and Chapter 3 addresses the development of the *mestizaje* (intermixture) of European, African, and Indigenous peoples.

Part II provides broad overviews of particular religious traditions across different contexts. Chapters 4 through 7 examine Christian traditions while Chapters 8 through 10 survey vibrant but numerically smaller traditions. Chapter 4 explores Christianity in Central America, discussing both Catholicism and more recent Pentecostal developments. Chapter 5 takes up the long history and intricate hierarchy of Catholicism in Mexico. Chapter 6 details a history of Latinx Catholicism in the United States from its Mexican origins to present-day expression from people of various Latinx nations. Chapter 7 offers an interpretation of the history of US Latino Pentecostalism, one of the fastest growing movements in the Americas. Chapter 8 examines Black Atlantic Religions such as Candomblé, Espiritismo, Ocha, and Palo. Chapter 9 delves into the numerically small but deeply historical and growing community of Muslims in Latin America and US Latinx communities. And in the final chapter of Part II, Chapter 10 lays out a history Latino Jewish communities and discusses the ways in which they are redefining Judaism in the United States. Together, these seven chapters cover a vast geographical area and account for many of the various religious communities that Latinx people across the Americas inhabit.

Part III is comprised of four shorter chapters that draw our attention to the material and textual worlds Latino Americans inhabit. Chapter 11 offers readers various frameworks through which to interpret the dense world of "devotional stuff." Drawing out the importance of texts in religious communities, Chapter 12 introduces readers to the Bible's use in the colonization of the Americas as well as its historical and modern receptions in Latinx communities. In a similar manner of a colonial symbol that was later reinterpreted, Chapter 13 takes up the most ubiquitous religious symbol across the Latinx Americas, the Virgin of Guadalupe, and shows how a symbol of colonization has long been mobilized in service of political and social movements. In recent years, the devotion to another female saint has grown exponentially in Mexico and the United States: *Santa Muerte* (Saint Death), a topic taken up in Chapter 14.

The majority of US Latinos are not immigrants; nevertheless, immigration remains central to many communities. Thus, many academic studies of US Latinx communities continue to focus on the importance of immigration. And while there exists a variety of ways to study immigrant communities, the two chapters in Part IV emphasize transnationalism, that is, the connections between a country of origin and destination. Chapter 15 offers a snapshot into a community of Oaxacan (Indigenous Mexican) Pentecostals in California's Central Coast. Chapter 16 provides a window into how

Brazilian Christianity constitutes a type of "migrational" religion, owing in no small part to the dense transnational connections that the faithful from the Baptist tradition have forged in the United States. In this sense, a Brazilian migrational religion has become a North American phenomenon.

The fifth and final part offers the reader overviews of current and future trends in the field as observed in recent survey data. Chapter 17 surveys broader patterns of conversion and shifts in religious affiliation among US Latinos, noting the most common reasons for change. Speaking to these changes in religious affiliation, the final chapter describes the rapid increase of US Latino "Nones," those who check off "none" when asked about religious affiliation.

With the exception of the lengthier overview in Chapter 1, there are three kinds of chapters presented in this volume. There are ten chapters (originally written as 5,000-word Main Articles), which provide broad overviews of traditions. These chapters comprise most of Part I and all of Part II of this volume. Then, with one exception (Chapter 16), the remainder of the chapters are shorter. Chapters 12 and 15 originally appeared as Case Study Articles (approximately 2,000 words each), and the rest were initially published as Hot Topic Articles (just over 1,000 words). With little time separating the digital availability of these articles and the publication of the subsequent volume, the various types of articles (now chapters) still represent new and cutting-edge scholarship in the field. To promote comprehension of foreign and/or academic terms, each chapter also includes a section outlining glossary terms.

Authors in this volume have employed a variety of terms to describe the Latin American population in the United States. Some of these terms include the more traditional use of Latino as well as Latina/o and Latinx. The term Latine or Latiné has gained more (yet still limited) traction in the last year both in academic and media circles, but authors sparingly employed either term in this volume, owing to the fact that Latinx and Latina/o were still primarily used by the time these chapters were originally written. The variety of terms highlights the ongoing discussions in the field about which terms to use. The term Hispanic fails to capture the breadth of people included in this volume, as it is a designation that excludes people from Brazil, which was not colonized by the Spanish (Hispanics) but rather by the Portuguese. "Latin Americas," as well as variants of that term, offers a far more capacious framing. Future studies will further test the strengths and limitations of these terms and will no doubt offer new ones.

To bring alive the vibrant world of Latin American and US Latino religions, the authors in this volume have provided numerous images of rituals, religious sites, texts, and various elements of religion as well as statistical graphs and tables. Some of the photographs capture more formal "institutional" aspects of religion while others beckon readers to regard dimensions of "popular" religion, that is, religion as practiced by everyday people and not necessarily with formal approval of a religious authority. Together, these chapters offer snapshots into the lively world of *Latin American and US Latino Religions in North America*.

–Lloyd D. Barba
November 2023

PART I

Origins

1

Introduction to Latin American and US Latino Religions in North America

Lloyd D. Barba

Introduction: Commonalities and Contrasts

The study of religion in Latin American and Latinx contexts of North America necessarily pushes against fixed boundaries of nation, language, class, race, and culture. In these contexts, Catholicism continues to be the single most influential force. Nevertheless, even within Catholicism, various devotions have flourished. An interpretation of historical trends that centers on commonalities and contrasts allows us to better discern how different institutions, ideas, and people maintained dominance and how everyday people, in turn, responded to that domination. This chapter posits the importance of diversity because doing so offers us a more complete—thus more accurate—history.

Cultural historian Edwin Aponte argues that virtually all Latinx communities have some "sense of spirituality and a quality that may be considered *sagrada* (sacred) or *santo* (holy)" (2012: 9–10). Aponte uses the term "*santo*" to encompass "Hispanic spirituality widely conceived" and as a "collective concept [that] includes Latino and Latina perspectives on traditional religion, life interpretation and explanations (sense-making), healing, health, wholeness, understandings of existence and the future, and balancing relationships at all levels of existence" (2012: 10). These aspects took deep root during and after Catholic colonialism (Bingemer 2016: 16). Aponte's framing of *santo* situates common practices such as folk medicine and places like botánicas as religious. The *santo* manifests itself both in and between institutional religion and popular religion. The former encompasses officially approved beliefs and practices, while the latter refers to those that the Church may (or may not) officially sanction. The temptation to draw too firm of a line between them should not ensnare readers. As seen below, the two often exist in productive tension.

A historical overview of religious traditions offers a chance to examine commonalities that link Latin Americans to the US Latinx population. To be clear, US Latinx and Latin American Studies are distinct fields of scholarship. Nevertheless, the United States has played an outsized role in the influence and control of markets and governments in Latin American nations. As a result of destabilized economies and governments, Latinx migration is a North American story. In 2020 Latinos/Hispanics accounted for over 60 million or 18.3 percent of the overall US population. "Hispanics" constitute the largest ethnic minority in the United States. The total Latinx population of the United States is larger than the entire population of Canada and trails behind only two Latin American counties (Mexico and Brazil). Essays on topics pertaining to "North America" often discuss only the United States, sometimes including Canada and Mexico. This chapter calls for a broader scope and includes Central American nations and the Hispanophone islands of the Caribbean in its discussion.

This chapter offers historical perspectives and periodizations, paying special attention to origins and key developments. It outlines three areas of study: (1) Indigenous Roots and Persistence; (2) Transgressive Sites of Religious Mixing and Minority Religious Traditions; and (3) Christianity. The chapter concludes with consideration of religious activism on the border of labor and immigration rights which are core issues affecting Latin American and Latinx communities.

Indigenous Roots and Persistence

My flowers will not come to an end,
My song will not come to an end,
I, the singer, raise them up,
They are scattered, they are bestowed.
—Nezahualcóyotl, fifteenth-century Texcoco ruler and poet

Nezahualcóyotl painted pictures of human completeness in his poems. Using a poetical expression, "*in xochitl in cuicatl*" ("*flor y canto*" in Spanish or "flower and song" in English), his words sought to capture truth through the completeness of two complementary ideas. In hindsight, the words of the poet prove eerily prescient as they prefigured the roots and persistence of their sacred truths. To grasp a sense of these roots and their persistence, this section draws on the religions of Mesoamerica, the region where Nezahualcóyotl composed his musings.

The term "religion" ought to be understood in this section with a few caveats in mind. Indigenous views of what the West has called religion typically involves a much more totalizing system in which mytho-histories, omens, and deity-like figures pervaded everyday consciousness, civic practices, and organization of social and political bodies (Tavárez 2016). Indigenous religion posed **incommensurabilties** to Catholicism. Historian Tzevetan Todorov's remarks about Euro-Indigenous encounters are particularly illuminating. He argues that in human history, "We do not have the same sense of radical difference in the 'discovery' of other continents and of other peoples: Europeans have never been altogether ignorant of the existence of Africa, India, or China" (Todorov 1992: 4). The radical sense of difference is especially notable in the vastly different conceptions of what constitutes religion. Perhaps the Lakota scholar Vine Deloria Jr. best delineated the core incommensurabilty between Amerindian and European religion and systems of thought. He argued that, whereas Western societies and religions privileged temporal (time-based or chronological) understandings of the sacred past and the world, Indigenous people understood their place in the world primary in spatial (place) terms. So rather than caring, for example, that God created the world in six days, Amerindians were concerned more with their place in the world according to the land they came from (Deloria 1994). In many of their creation stories, Native groups belong to the land from whence they were created, and life-creating forces such as water, corn, caves, and mountains hold special significance. The importance of time and/or space, to be sure, varies across Indigenous societies. The Aztecs and Maya, for example, placed great importance on time as evidenced by their intricate calendar systems replete with cosmological meaning.

For this survey, we return to temporal conceptualizations to periodize Indigenous history. After the "Hunter Gatherer Archaic Societies" (8000–1600 BCE), the more familiar elements of Mesoamerican religions emerged during the "Formative Period" (1800 BCE–200 CE), "Classical Period" (200–900 CE), and "Postclassical Period" (900–1521 CE). Mesoamerican societies built up impressive ceremonial centers as early as the Formative Period (Carrasco 2014: 44; Tavárez 2016: 22). Although temporally linear, these periodizations caution against assumptions of "timelessness" often imputed to non-Western Indigenous societies by Westerners. Such periodization, however, should not flatten out the vast diversity of the at least 250 different Indigenous ethnocultural groups in the Americas (Medina 2009: 395).

The hundreds of archaeological sites in Mesoamerica attest to both commonalities and contrasts between disparate societies. Pyramids, tombs, ballcourts, and other ritual buildings fill these sites. Rituals at these sites included elaborate dances involving people dressed as animals (e.g., birds and jaguars) and sacred ball games (which climaxed with human sacrifice). These rituals reflected a greater cosmic drama of war and conflict and were necessary to appease deities. Archaeologist Davíd Carrasco offers the term "cosmovision" to describe "how cultures combined their cosmological notions relating to time and space into a structure and systematical whole" (2014: 69). Nowhere was such a totalizing view of place, myth, history, and the present more on display than in hundreds of ritual centers, such as Chichén Itzá (Mexico), Copán (Honduras), and Tikal (Guatemala). The ritual center of Teotihuacán held such widespread influence as a cosmic place of origins that people came from Tikal, Copán, and Piedras Negras for rituals of royal legitimation (Carrasco 2014: 52–70). In fact, the full meaning of these ceremonial centers as well as the precision and symmetry with which Natives built them in relation to celestial bodies, continues to elude clear explanation to outsiders today and occasions much speculation. (For example, in 2012 the Mayan Long Count calendar, which begins in 3114 BCE and ends in 2012 CE, stirred panic about the end of the world) (Carrasco 2014: 56.)

Codices such as the *Popol Vuh* (discovered in 1701 in Guatamala), *The Book of Chilam Balam of Tizimin* (Yucatan Maya), and the *Florentine Codex* (compiled by Bernardo de Sahagún) detail ideas of cosmovision in pictograms and writings. Celebrations on the Day of the Dead also offer glimpses into the power of Mesoamerican rituals to integrate the past and present and the dead and the living.

Native Americans retained whatever they could during European colonization, often resorting to methods of resistance for survival. A few decades ago, scholars began to study the highly asymmetrical Spanish-Indian relations through a lens of "native agency." In this framework, "natives are active agents in their own lives, not simply

FIGURE 1.1 *The temple of Kukulcan at Chichen Itza, Yucatan, Mexico.* Source: *Photo by Lloyd D. Barba.*

FIGURE 1.2 *Day of the Dead celebration with kites in Guatemala.* Source: *Johan Ordonez/ AFP via Getty Images.*

passive in the face of the European cultural onslaught" (Schwaller 2011: 6). Such agency ranged from outright resistance, such as uprisings and violence, to the more covert forms, such as slight modification to rituals and secrecy. But resistance, to be sure, is not the only form of agency. Our understanding of agency should also include how Amerindians incorporated Catholic traditions in ways that were advantageous to them. These incorporations of Catholicism sometimes included church-sanctioned practices as well as those that fell outside any sense of **orthodoxy**. Anthropologist Andrew Orta details an approach of conceptualizing Christianity "less as an index of degrees of assimilation or change, and more as a dynamic cultural resource and frame of continuing encounter that remains a generative component of an emerging Indigenous modernity" (Orta 2020: 83). This interpretation challenges the flattened binaries of timeless Indigenous practices versus modernity and converts versus resistors. Because Catholicism has so deeply insinuated itself into Latin America over the course of more than 500 years, "indigeneity and Christianity in Latin America are inconceivable apart from one another" (Orta 2020: 83–9). "Traditionalist" Catholics in the highlands of southern Mexico (Chiapas) and Guatemala, for example, continue to fuse traditional religious folkways with Catholicism (Kovic 2007: 199–215; Orta 2020). With greater geographical distance from populous European settlements came better preservation of Indigenous culture. Today, Indigenous societies throughout Latin America continue to reclaim the once-condemned traditions of their ancestors. For example, since the 1990s Maya Christians have incorporated the *Popol Vuh* into scriptural readings (Medina 2009: 398–9).

Latin American Indigenous populations continue to shape the landscape of US Latinx religion. Religious Studies scholar Natalie Avalos points out how, despite a half millennium of colonialism:

> Indigenous religious lifeways from Latin America continue in diaspora, often in conversation with Native North American religious lifeways in the United States because these religious traditions are not just isolated religious practices but holistic metaphysical systems, replete with medicinal practices of the body, sets of ethics, and unique conceptualizations of self in relation to the cosmos… For Latinx communities in the United States, these rhythms continue in unique ways. They may constitute the metaphysical foundation from which this population draws in order to make sense of the world; they may constitute features of religious practice, conceptualizations of the soul, sacred relationships to the land and to community.
> (2022: 298)

These diasporic religious lifeways develop out of back-and-forth migration.

In the 1980s, civil wars in Central America uprooted thousands of Indigenous Guatemalans, many of whom fled north to Mexico and the United States. And in the 1990s, Mexicans, especially Indigenous people from Mexico's southernmost states, followed suit after the North American Free Trade Agreement (NAFTA) adversely impacted the market price of crops and goods. Some of them joined the ranks of existing Catholic communities in the United States, but others established their own Evangelical/Pentecostal churches in which Mixtec and Zapotec are the linguae francae (O'Connor 2016: 91–114; Ramírez 2023).

Latin American Indigenous religions garnered increasing popularity in the United States beginning in the late twentieth century. Most recently, movies such as *The Book of Life* and *Coco* shed light on Day of the Dead rituals. Mestizos, many of whom are unable to pinpoint the Indigenous nations from which they are descended, also participate in the recovery of Indigenous religions. *Danzantes* (dance societies) perform dances as acts of cultural preservation in many US urban centers. During the Chicano Movement of the 1960s and 1970s, activists extensively drew upon Indigenous imagery and myths to stake their claims of belonging in the US Southwest. As an extension of the Mexican arts movement known as *Indigenismo*, Chicano artists decorated stores, apartments buildings, churches, and civic centers with art portraying pre-Columbian temples and warriors alongside labor and civil rights leaders such as Cesar Chavez. (Critics of *Indigenismo* readily pointed out how the movement invoked the image of the Indian to celebrate the country's strength and unity while simultaneously neglecting Indigenous communities and their modern, real-life problems.) Champions of the Chicano Movement invoked the idea of Aztlán, a mythic homeland of Mexicans, to assert their rightful place in the US Southwest. Some pointed to the 1704 Gemelli Map as evidence of their claim regarding Aztlan's location in the US borderlands. Platforms such as *El Plan Espiritual de Aztlán* sought liberation and solidarity for Chicanos (Sagarena 2014: 129–58; Hidalgo 2016).

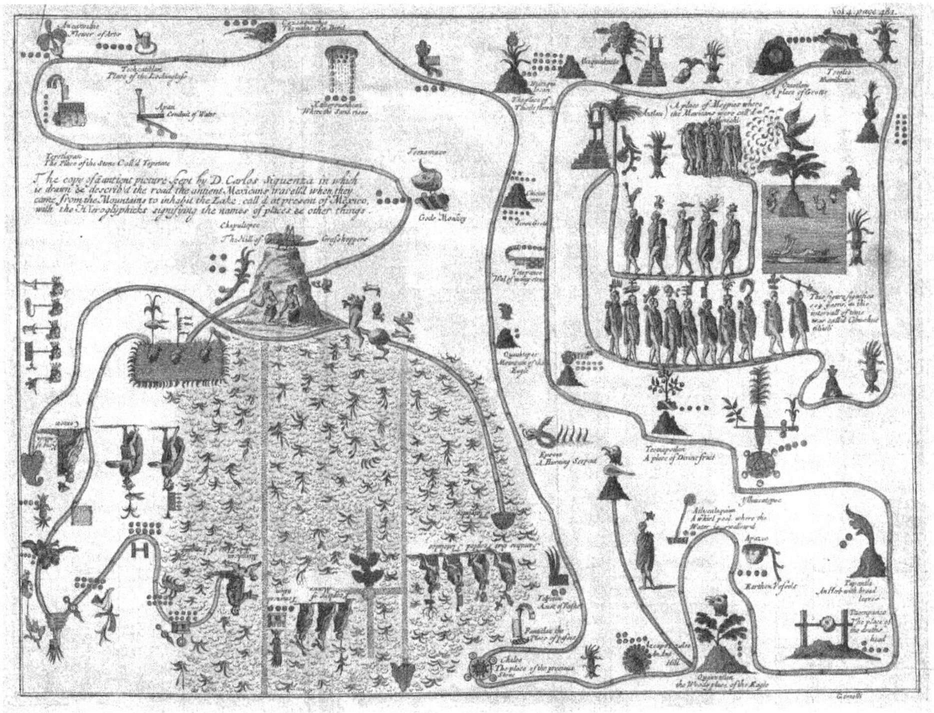

FIGURE 1.3 *1704 Gemelli Map showing the Aztec migration from Aztlán.* Source: *Gemelli Careri, G. F.,* A Voyage Round the World. In Six Parts, viz. I. of Turky. II. of Persia. III. of India. IV. of China. V. of the Philippine Islands. VI. of New Spain. Written originally in Italian, Translated into English *(Printed for Awnsham and John Churchill at the Black Swan in Pater-noster-Row, London) 1704.*

No figure or symbol, however, articulated a diasporic sense of indigeneity and racial mixing more than that of the Virgin of Guadalupe.

Transgressive Sites of Religious Mixing and Minoritized Traditions

Thus reprimanding him for the evil thing he had done, he answered me: Father, do not be frightened because we are still *nepantla*, and since I understood what he meant to say by that phrase and metaphor, which means to be in the middle, I insisted that he tell me in what middle it was in which they found themselves. He told me that since they were still not well rooted in the faith, I should not be surprised that they were still neutral, that they neither answered to one faith or

> the other or, better said, that they believed in God and at the same time keep their ancient customs and demonic rites.
>
> —Diego Durán, late sixteenth century

A definition to describe the process by which religious traditions come into contact and form new phenomena eludes scholarly consensus. For years scholars have used the term "syncretism." But even that term presented its own set of limitations, as it arose out of debates which assumed that such syncretic products constituted corruptions of "pure" originals. More recently, terms from Latin American and US Latinx contexts have offered helpful alternatives to understand the process of mixing, crossing, and transgressing what are often assumed to be normative lines of religion. One alternative is "*nepantla*" from the Nahuatl term meaning "in the middle." As described by the Indigenous man to Diego Durán in the opening quote of this section, the term reflects a period of time when the Aztec's religious system was caught in the middle (Medina 2006: 248–66). Relatedly, the term "mestizaje" enjoys widespread use by the scholarly community and beyond as a metaphor of religious and racial mixing (Elizondo 2000; Vásquez 2006; Medina 2008). *Mulatez* similarly describes racial mixing but more specifically refers to African and Indigenous peoples in the Caribbean and among Honduras' Garifuna populations (De La Torre 2006: 158–75).

Every religious system is itself a blending of some sort. Even Iberian Catholicism emerged from a crucible of Islamic, Jewish, and Christian cultural and intellectual traditions, marking it as distinct from other forms European Catholicism. Scholars' attempts to offer either Indigenous- or Spanish-based terms reflect a desire to decolonize Western Anglophone methods of conceptualizing religion as a dualistic phenomenon. The non-English terms especially convey the sense that so much religious practice exists "in the middle," neither here nor there.

In a world where so much of Indigenous religious culture faced swift destruction, dissimulation and covert practices became key methods of Indigenous persistence and resistance. Latin America's most popular symbol, the Virgin of Guadalupe, offers a prime example of mestizaje. According to Catholic tradition, in 1531 Guadalupe (Mother of God) appeared to Juan Diego, a recent Indigenous convert. Speaking in Nahuatl, Guadalupe commanded him to build her a chapel on the Tepeyac, a hill where Indigenous people worshiped Tonantzin (Our Revered Mother). The renowned linguist and friar Bernardo de Sahagún grumbled in 1576 that the Guadalupan devotion cloaked pre-Columbian rituals of Tonantzin (Peterson 1992: 39–40). Other scholars question the actual affinity between Tonantzin and Guadalupe (Poole 1995: 8–10). In recent years, artists have gradually darkened Guadalupe, whom many affectionately call *La Morenita* (the little brown-skinned one) (Ehrenberg 1996; Pérez 2007: 257–96; Peterson 2014: 17–68). Guadalupe's racial nepantla is not simply reflective of competing claims of her pigmentation. Her in-betweenness and racial mixture as *La Morenita* offer apt metaphors to understand theological and cultural mestizaje (Elizondo 1980). Mexican

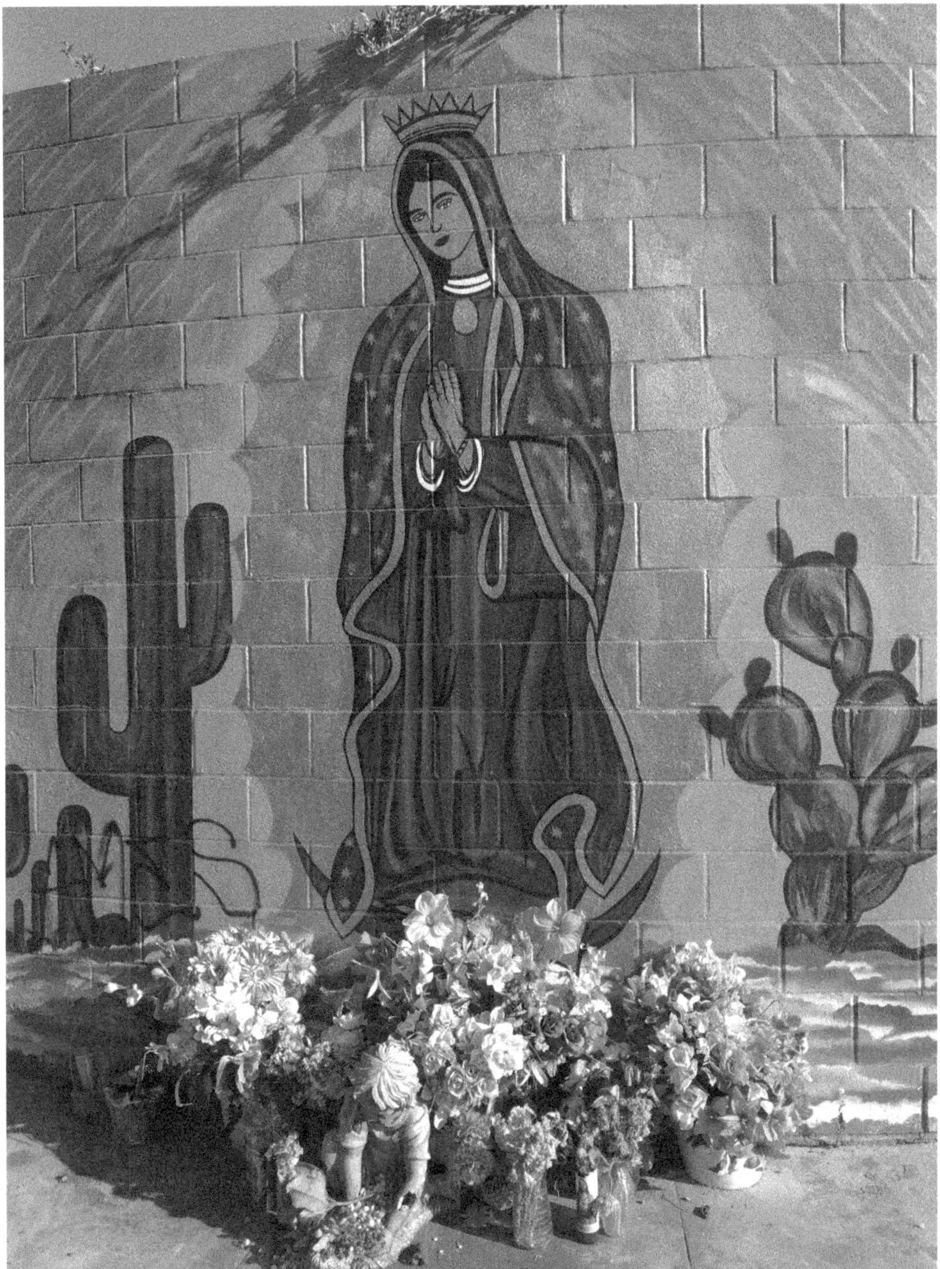

FIGURE 1.4 *Murals of Guadalupe often turn into shrines as devotees bring flowers, votive candles, and petitions before her likeness as shown here in Lamont, California, a predominantly Latinx community.* Source: *Photo by Lloyd D. Barba.*

and Latinx political and immigrant rights movements also adopted Guadalupe as a symbol of resistance because of her ability to bring various groups into solidarity (Castillo-Ramos 2023). From gracing the banner of the Mexican War of Independence (1810–21) to being crowned Queen of Mexico and Empress of the Americas in 1945, Guadalupe has enjoyed adoration for centuries and from all classes. Her widespread devotion persists irrespective of popular or institutional forms of religion. To this day, devotees very well may pray to her in church as well as at their home altars or at public murals (Matovina 2019; Barba 2024).

Santería (the way of the saints) is the popular term for a creole West African and Caribbean tradition known formally as Regla Lucumí (the Rule of Lucumí) or Regla de Ocha (Rule of Orishas). Santería assumed various forms in Cuba, but West-African Yoruba religion constitutes its main elements, with Catholicism blended in. The Afro-Cubanism movement of the 1920s and 1930s revitalized Santería, which originally arose in the sugar plantation colonies in the Caribbean. Enslaved Africans outnumbered free Europeans on the sugar plantations, resulting in less direct oversight. And in this arrangement *cabildos* abounded. A cabildo refers type of *cofradía* (confraternity or sodality) or mutual aid society for African descended people. Cabildos afforded many spaces to combine African deities with Catholic saints, thereby reinterpreting both Yoruba and Iberian Catholicism. For example, the spirit beings (Orishas), who act as intermediaries to the higher deity Oludamare, could be disguised behind or strategically mixed with the notion of the Catholic saints who mediate between humans and God (Edmonds and González 2010: 94–102; Escalante 2023). The Orisha Shangó/Changó and the Catholic saint Santa Barbara offer a striking example of mixing. Both can be found cloaked in red and wielding the power of lightning and fire. The lyrics of Cuban duo Celina y Reutilio's song "A Santa Barbara (Que Viva Chango)" express these similarities and mixings. The role of *Babalawos* (ritual specialists) in some ways is analogous to that of Catholic priests in that both preside over rituals and formally invoke the presence of deities. It is not uncommon for individuals and families to follow both religions. Santería continues to flourish between Cuba and the United States with new initiates seeking to connect to the Yoruban tradition in West Africa (De La Torre 2004; Edmonds and González 2010).

In sugar colonies across the Caribbean and mainland New Spain, non-sanctioned healing practices, labeled by the Church "magic" and "witchcraft," took deep root. In Mexico, Blacks drew on Indigenous know-how of peyote for healing purposes and fashioned talismans that reflected West African traditions of root medicine and conjuring. These practices converged as a sort of bricolage, drawing and transmitting expertise from disparate parts of the coast of sub-Saharan Africa (Bristol 2016: 203–4). African, Amerindian, and Iberian Catholic folk healing traditions converged and gave rise to the *curandero* (healer) tradition. *Curanderismo* encompasses a constellation of healing traditions whose practitioners use herbs and folk remedies. The Mexican *curanderos* Niño Fidencio, Teresa Urrea, and Don Pedrito Jaramillo stand out as luminaries of this tradition (Seman 2021).

FIGURE 1.5 *Santa Barbara at the Museum of the Orishas in Havana, Cuba.* Source: *Burkhard Mücke/Wikimedia Commons.*

The devotion to *La Santa Muerte* (Holy Death) has soared in popularity in recent years. Films and media outlets mostly highlight the array of unsavory rituals and imagery of La Santa Muerte associated with the rise of narco violence in Mexico and the borderlands. To be sure, the nacro saint is far more than just a narco saint. Santa Muerte is among the fastest growing religious traditions in the Mexico. The rise of this unofficial saint likely owes to her ability to offer protection and intervene in hopeless love relationships and legal battles (Perdigón Castañeda 2008; Chesnut 2017; Peláez-Díaz 2023).

Devotees of Guadalupe, Santería saints, and Santa Muerte purchase much of their ritual paraphernalia at botánicas. These shops sell religious wares both sanctioned by and antithetical to the institutional Church. Beyond acting as a main retailer, botánicas themselves constitute sites of devotion since most are operated by ritual specialists who offer formal consultations on matters of love, money, and spiritual direction. Botánicas are a mainstay in Latin America and many Latinx neighborhoods in the United States as commercial retail shops (Murphy 2015). Aponte describes them as sites of "metaphysical blending" and as "spiritual meeting places" (2006: 46–63). Botánicas offer a vast array Latin American Amerindian ritual items and figurines (i.e., the "stuff of material Latinx religion") (Maldonado-Estrada 2023). Similarly, items used in rituals of *Espiritismo*, curanderismo, Candomblé, and other "creole devotions" can be found next to or mixed among those for use in sanctioned Catholic rituals. The abundance of devotional wares at botánicas exemplifies religious mixing with various commonalities and contrasts.

To be sure, religious mixing occurred but not exclusively with Christian, African, and Indigenous traditions in Latin America. In fact, Iberian Catholicism was shaped in the context of flourishing (and at times suppressed) Islamic, Jewish, and various European Christian traditions (Gallardo 2023). A brief note on minority religious traditions is in order before proceeding in the continent's most popular religion, Christianity.

The stories of Jews and Muslims in Latin America summon themes of migration, feigned conversions, and expulsions. The dispersion of Jews in North America cannot be separated from a broader history of facing persecution especially evident in the Alhambra Decree, which called for the expulsion of Jews from the Iberian Peninsula in 1492. Some Jews converted in name only and later sought to take their ancient tradition to the far reaches of New Spain. Records from the Inquisition Court of the Indies show that Jewish practices persisted in the New World but not without heavy surveillance. In the far-flung reaches of New Spain (e.g., present-day border states of Mexico and the United States), Jewish families were determined to carry out their practices in covert ways. **Crypto Jews** practiced a wide variety of disguised rituals (Hordes 2008). Many of the customs did not survive the test of time and posterity. In a perhaps unexpected turn, the rise of DNA testing and access to robust genealogical records has prompted many individuals and families of Mexican descent to trace their Jewish roots. Aside from these Jewish roots that stretch back into Mexico across many generations, recent immigration of Latin American Jews to the United States continues to shape internal dynamics within both Jewish and Latinx communities.

As Jews, they face uneven assimilation among the Christian majority of Latinos, and, as Latinos, they often do not readily fit in with the majority Ashkenazi European Jews (Limonic 2019).

Muslims faced a similar fate of forced conversion beginning in 1499 and expulsion from the Spanish Empire in 1609. The **Reconquista** aimed to not only takeover land but also to subjugate people (Gallardo 2023). Though a small minority in Latin America, Muslims have greatly shaped Latin American societies as they have pushed for religious tolerance. At the same time, those in the region maintain a sense of belonging to the Umma, the global Muslim community (Chitwood 2021). Modern-day Latinx Muslims who did not grow up in the faith claim that they did not undergo conversion but rather, reversion because Islam's ties to Spain and New Spain stretch back several centuries (Morales 2018).

Christianity

> Death to the *Gachupines*! Long live the Virgin of Guadalupe!
> —Father Miguel Hidalgo y Costilla

We do not know the exact words of Father Miguel Hidalgo y Costilla's famous *grito de Dolores* (cry of Dolores), the proclamation that heralded the Mexican War of Independence. But the spirit of his cry captured the deep animosity toward the *Gachupines* (a pejorative for "Spaniard") and a profound admiration for Guadalupe. After various revolutions swept the Americas during this period, the Spanish Crown's empire lay decimated, but Catholicism remained. For over half a millennium, the Catholic Church is the only institution that "has remained central to most people's lives" (Schwaller 2011: 1).

In its broadest terms, Latin American history can be broken up into two larger periods since European arrival: the colonial and the modern. The colonial period begins with the arrival of the Spanish and ends with the independence of various nations from Spain. The colonial period can be further divided as conquest and settlement (sixteenth century); productivity and production (seventeenth century); and the era of reforms (eighteenth century) (Schwaller 2011: 2–3). The modern refers to the time since independence. Catholicism firmly established itself during the colonial period and continued to flourish after independence. Protestantism arrived in Latin American countries unevenly, largely depending on the national government's reception of Protestants and their attendant "Americanness." Pentecostalism, as a largely grassroots movement free from larger ecclesial bureaucracy, erupted onto the scene by the early twentieth century and quickly indigenized in most countries. Its spread across North America emerged from a three-year revival in Los Angeles hosted by the African American preacher Williams Seymour and attended by whites, African Americans, Latinos, and people from across the globe (Espinosa 2014b).

Catholicism's Arrival and Order in the Sixteenth and Early Seventeenth Centuries

Ironies abound in the Catholic origins of North America, a continent accidentally happened upon by Europeans en route to India. Christopher Columbus himself embodied these ironies: as ardently Catholic, apocalyptic, and bent on evangelization. In 1492, even before he knew the extent of the Americas, he declared to the Spanish Crown that the profits of his enterprise should be spent on the conquest of Jerusalem (Todorov 1992: 11). His goals of spreading Catholicism to the known world, re-discovering the Garden of Eden, and conquering Jerusalem played no small part in his wanderings and writings. The irony in Columbus' conquest was that he, a rather Medieval man fueled by futuristic apocalyptic desires, effectively ushered in the modern era (Todorov 1992: 12). Although the Spanish Crown never conquered Jerusalem, nor was the Garden of Eden found, his apocalyptic vision of the widespread evangelism of the Catholicism would come to fruition in an unknown world. Soul by soul, the Crown would expel, exploit, and exterminate most of the original inhabitants of the Americas, and mine by mine extract gold, silver, and natural resources. Spain's ascendancy as the most powerful monarchy and leader in world exploration came as a direct result of its plunder of the Americas. Catholicism arose hand in hand with the Crown.

Patterns of conquest, settlement, and evangelization mostly characterized the first full century of the colonial era. First, a series of 1493 **papal bulls** (*Inter Caetera* and *Dudum Siquidem*) portrayed the conquest as evangelization. In 1504, over a century before any permanent English settlement in the Americas, the Spanish monarchy established the diocese of Santo Domingo on the island of Hispaniola. Few documents better evidence the twin forces of religion and conquest than the *Requerimento*, a legal pronouncement that the Spanish would declare to Natives (in Spanish, a language they did not understand) upon arrival to their land. It offered Natives an ultimatum to convert to the new royal and religious order or face the ramifications of conquest. Even before Hernán Cortés landed in Mexico in 1519, the Indigenous populations of Hispaniola, Puerto Rico, Cuba, and Jamaica faced decimation and deracination at the hands of the Spanish. With fewer natural resources left to extract on the islands, the work turned to plantations, along with which came a steady flow of slaves, troops, and priests. As plantation islands, the Spanish Catholic colonies of the Caribbean followed a different trajectory than the mainland settlements. Hernán Cortés' 1521 overthrow of the Aztecs in Mexico and Francisco Pizzaro's 1532 conquest of the Inca in Peru shifted the center of Spain's interest from the Caribbean to the two viceroyalties: New Spain (established in 1535 and based in Mexico City) and Peru (established in 1542 and based in Lima). The former oversaw the Crown's interest in North America while the latter (later joined by the viceroyalties of the Río de Plata and New Granada) did so for South America (González and González 2008: 40–63; Schwaller 2011: 52–70). Due to this chapter's focus on North America, discussions of colonial Latin American will stick to the Viceroyalty of New Spain.

By the end of 1511, Dominican priest Antonio de Montesinos had famously condemned settlers' wholesale exploitation of Hispaniola Natives. His pleas for reform to officially recognize the humanity of Natives influenced the Crown's passage of the Law of Burgos in 1512. The calls for reform culminated in the Valladolid debates from 1550 to 1551 in which Bartolomé de Las Casas, later dubbed the patron saint of the Indians, argued that Indians were fully human and thus made in the image of God. De Las Casas' reforms came to fruition, but the decline of reliance on enslaved Indigenous people directly resulted in the importation and enslavement of Africans to work the plantations (Romero 2020: 48–69). By the end of the 1500s, the Indigenous population, already entirely wiped out in some settlements, had suffered severe overall loss. Some estimates suggest a 75 percent population reduction by the late sixteenth century. Perennial epidemics, forced labor, and displacement collectively accounted for most of the devastation. Meanwhile, the Catholic Church grew rapidly, resulting in "five archbishops, twenty-seven bishops, two universities, four hundred priories and

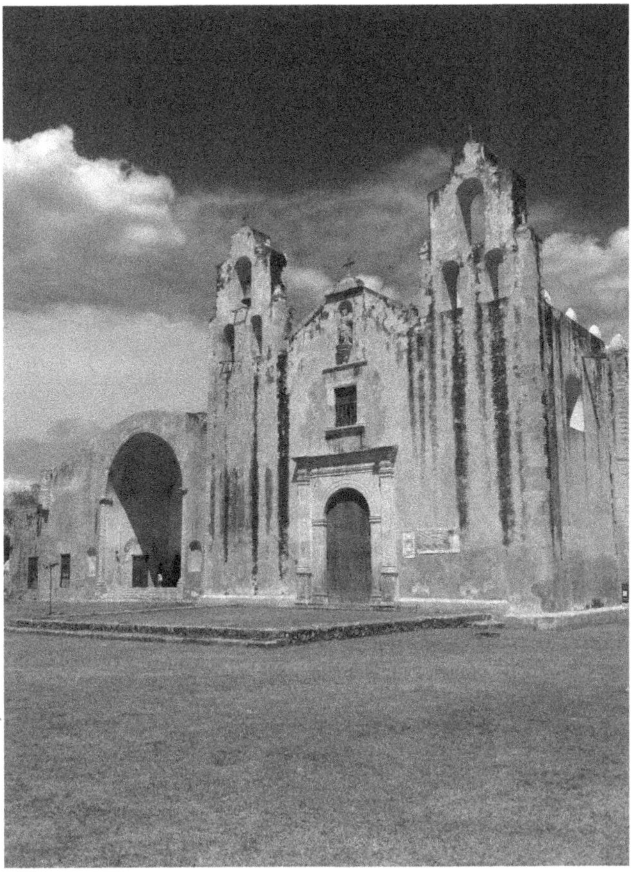

FIGURE 1.6 *In 1562 Diego de Landa, bishop of Yucatan, called for an auto-de-fé in Maní, Yucatan, to burn dozens of codices and upwards of thousands of "idol" images.* Source: *Photo by Lloyd D. Barba.*

colleges of religious orders" and parishes that served nearly every Spanish settlement (Hastings 1999: 332–3). With the growth of the Church came the suppression and destruction of Indigenous religious shrines, codices, and images in *auto-de-fé* (act of faith) public penance ceremonies.

The Vatican initially sanctioned the taking of land shortly after reports of Columbus' voyage arrived. But the Spanish Crown swiftly assumed control over the affairs of the Catholic Church in Latin America in an arrangement known as ***El Patronato Real*** (the Royal Patronage). (In fact, it was not until the twentieth century, after bouts of anti-clerical governments, that the Vatican more fully regained control) (Schwaller 2011: 8, 41–8). The Crown largely controlled the affairs of the Church in New Spain and the Holy Office of the Inquisition through the Council of the Indies located in Spain. The Church's persistent evangelization also betokened strict governmental enforcement.

The records of the Inquisition open up opportunities to read against the grain of institutional church history and better sense the texture of popular religion and resistance. Take, for example, Carlos Ometochtzin, a Native ruler of Texcoco who stood accused of apostacy and idolatry after his baptism. Having been convicted, he was burned at the stake in 1539, a punishment that drew swift criticism. The outcry altered the rules of the Inquisition for Natives as the Spanish conceded that Natives did not necessarily fully understand foreign religious concepts (Schwaller 2011: 86).

The writings of early missionaries decried the widespread violence in New Spain. These writings unintentionally gave rise to Black Legends, popular sentiments and writings that sought to demonize the Spanish Catholic empire in the Americas. Such tales, whether exaggerated or not, lent settlers of the Protestant Anglo-Americas a sense of moral superiority and benevolence. The rhetoric of Black Legends denigrated the Spanish and seemingly justified Anglo settlements, thus portraying the Americas as if they were in need of Protestant colonization in order to undo or redeem the harm brought about by Catholicism. A temptation then arises to label Catholicism in the Inquisition era as "medieval" for its repressive aspects. Such an appellation, however, might be a misnomer, for "medieval Spain quite lacked the systematic intolerance of sixteenth century Spain," whose Inquisition fell under the direct control of the monarchy (Hastings 1999: 329). The threat of the Inquisition became a key way for the Catholic Church to root out popular beliefs and practices.

Both the timing and the kind of Catholicism brought to New Spain greatly influenced the sorts of popular religion that arose in the Americas. Latin America (and thereby Latino Catholicism) absorbed and reflected a Catholicism that was "planted in the Americas approximately two generations before Trent's opening session" and thus was more characteristically Iberian, medieval, and **pre-Tridentine** (Espín 1995: 117–19). Over the centuries, this pre-Tridentine nature of popular Mexican Catholicism, still extant to various degrees today, has manifested itself in a host of rituals, songs, dances, pilgrimages, shrines, objects, and trinkets (i.e., a heavy material and performance culture). Cofradías emerged as important social spaces to preserve popular Catholicism steeped in these practices (Espín 1995: 136–44; Goizueta 2004: 258–62; Peterson and Vásquez 2008: 56).

Popular devotions honoring many different saints flourished throughout New Spain. According to historian Frances Ramos, religious orders wished to "Europeanize the American landscape" by installing a visual culture of relics, retablos, and paintings in newly acquired territories. For example, in 1578 the Jesuits of Mexico City hosted "elaborate festivities" celebrating the arrival of 214 relics honoring saints that had been sent to the colony by Pope Gregory VIII. These highly celebrated relics enjoyed the adoration of locals and amounted to "sources of civic pride." Inquisition records indicate that locals championed an array of local saints, such as Juan de Palafox y Mendoza, a priest who, after death, attracted veneration. Virtually every community had its own *cofradía*, with larger cities having multiple. These devotions led by confraternities cropped up in hospitals, chapels, convents, and parishes. When the founding of a town coincided with the feast day of a saint, he or she often assumed the status as the community's patron saint (Ramos 2016: 148–53). Churches named after that patron saint were commonly built in the center of town, adjacent to the plaza.

Popular religion thrived especially in places outside of the main cities, as the Church often faced a shortage of priests to attend to rural flocks. In such sites, cofradías greatly shaped the social fabric of Catholicism, weaving into it popular customs and rituals. Members paid dues and, in turn, received mutual aid benefits such as burial services for the dead and indulgences. Because of the collective buy-in, cofradías in some communities wielded immense power and elevated the leader's social standing. Against the wishes of parish clergy, cofradías often elected their leaders, thus opening up opportunities for Native leadership (Schwaller 2011: 84–5).

The history of Black Catholics in Latin America demonstrates how, even in the most acutely asymmetrical power relations, **subaltern** populations found ways of refashioning religion to address their own needs. After the immense decline of Native populations in the Caribbean islands and the passage of laws that prohibited the enslavement of Natives, European colonial powers forcibly brought in millions of West Africans and kept their descendants in bondage. While some Africans who were forced onto slave ships were already Catholic, most "became" Christians (at least nominally according to the Church) at trading posts or after arriving in the Americas. Enslaved people hailing from Muslim backgrounds (as opposed to those who practiced Indigenous African ancestral religions) would have been more familiar with Catholicism. For many (such as those in cabildos), Catholicism proved significant to their daily lives. In general, the priesthood remained off limits to non-Europeans for the majority of Latin American history, but Black leadership thrived in cabildos. In some cases, members of cabildos even pooled their resources to purchase a member's freedom. Church authorities regarded the fraternal orders with suspicion and at times suppressed them outright (Bristol 2016: 201–3).

FIGURE 1.7 *A statue of Antonio de Padua, patron saint of Dorado, Puerto Rico, stands in front of the church dedicated to him.* Source: *Eva Marie Photography.*

Baroque Era of the Seventeenth Century and Bourbon Reforms of the Eighteenth Century

Seventeenth-century New Spain witnessed the Baroque Era in all of its lavish, pious expressions of larger-than-life religious processions and grandiose architecture. The Church grew immensely in terms of economic, political, and social power, also increasing the relevance of the *cofradía* system. Moving into the century, a robust hierarchy of Church officials (backed by the Crown) rendered the Catholic Church the most powerful institution across Latin America. The Church owned large swaths of land and collected various taxes from locals. And it earned its income in the form of tithe, rent, interest from liens and mortgages, parochial dues (that is, service charges), alms, and first fruits. Elite families realized the prestige of having a family member in the clergy and often pushed to have at least one male member among the secular order (Jesuits, Dominicans, and Franciscans) or the religious order (priests who took vows of poverty, chastity, and obedience). Women, many of whom sought some semblance of autonomy, joined cloisters and convents, as did women who simply wished to live a more devoted life, among other reasons (Schwaller 2011: 71–104). Sor Juana Inés de la Cruz exemplifies the women who became nuns in order to assert autonomy and critique patriarchal norms (Romero 2020: 90–7).

The reform and enlightenment era of eighteenth- and early nineteenth-century Latin America ushered in drastic changes during the Bourbon Reforms. Proponents of the reforms maintained the position that colonies primarily existed to benefit the mother country. As one might suspect, this position resulted in a gradual souring of the relationship between Spain and its colonies. Costly eighteenth-century wars compelled the monarchs to shore up losses by exacting an exorbitant amount of taxes on the colonies. The Crown especially targeted the Church's deep coffers and at times confiscated properties and investments while placing a moratorium on the construction of new convents and monasteries. Further, the government "secularized" the lands, buildings, and holdings of the religious orders, so the orders could not collect their usual dues from taxes. Finally, in 1767, the Crown expelled the Jesuits from New Spain. The Jesuits had proven the most successful of the orders throughout Latin America, to the extent that the Crown viewed their autonomous work as a challenge to the social order. Furthermore, given the Crown's weakening position in the eighteenth century, it could not tolerate the many exceptions and exemptions made for the wealthy religious order. The Crown seized the Jesuit's massive estates, colleges, houses, and land from South America to California. The Crown gave Jesuits the option of leaving New Spain, recanting their vows, or transferring to a different order. The Jesuits' resentment remained and swelled, as former Jesuits constituted a fair number of independence leaders in the early 1800s (González and González 2008: 104–30; Schwaller 2011: 97–9, 108–19).

Modern Period Revolutionary Change and Church Conflict

Beginning in the late 1700s, independence movements swept across the Americas. As new nations emerged during the first quarter of the 1800s, their leaders faced the challenge of dealing with the most influential remaining institution: the Catholic Church. At the most general level, a basic division emerged between two major factions: conservatives and liberals. Conservatives fought to maintain close relations with the Church, with most advocating to keep it as the official church of the state. Liberals, meanwhile, spelled out various measures to attenuate the Church's influence on civil affairs, asking primarily whether or not the Church should be separate from the state. All the while, the papacy insisted that the new states needed to negotiate a legal relationship with the Vatican in order to enjoy its established patronage.

After independence, Mexican Liberals crafted a series of anticlerical constitutions, which met major resistance from the Church. Constitutions from 1824 to 1917 laid the anti-clerical groundwork that boiled over into conflicts between the Church and the state. In a series of moderate to liberal constitutions—varyingly and sparingly enforced—the anti-clerical measures spelled out the criminalization of holding outdoor church services and wearing the clerical collar in public. In accordance with the 1857 Constitution, the Mexican government abolished the **fuero** and prohibited social corporations from holding more land beyond that deemed necessary for a central purpose. These changes targeted the Church. New laws also regulated how much priests could charge for the exercise of their offices; this included baptisms, marriages, and funerals. The Constitution drew stern rebuke from Pope Pius IX. Longtime Mexican president Porfirio Díaz restored much of the Church's power. But he was ousted in the Mexican Revolution (1910–17), widening the rift between the Church and state. And the government's expropriation of Church lands exacerbated matters further (Schwaller 2011: 189–99). The enforcement of the 1917 Constitution's anti-clerical laws came to a head during the Cristero War, the standoff between militaristic Catholics and the regime of Plutarco Elías Calles (Schwaller 2011: 130–50). The war grabbed international attention, and exiled priests and Catholics in the United States financially supported their Catholic compatriots (Young 2015).

Popular religious movements boomed at the turn of the twentieth century. Healing traditions of curanderismo and *Espiritismo* (Spiritism) worked alongside, and in some cases despite, the Catholic Church and liberal reforms of the day. Francisco Madero, who ousted the dictator Porfirio Diaz and became president of Mexico in 1911, was a Spiritist medium and transmitted messages of the dead. In a perhaps somewhat unexpected episode, in 1928 President Calles sought out the healing power of curandero Niño Fidencio and claimed that he healed him of a chronic skin condition (Seman 2021: 61–5, 133–15).

A different trajectory played out in Central America following the Mexican War of Independence. Central America initially fell under the authority of Mexico until 1823. The Constitution of the new Federation of Central America established Catholicism as the official religion of all member states. But dissention boiled over. On the one hand,

Liberal governments sought to temper the power of the Church while, on the other hand, member states such as El Salvador and Costa Rica swiftly broke away from the diocese of Guatemala. Beginning in the 1830s, while Mexico dealt with the breakaway Republic ofTexas in its northern reaches, Central American states to the south dissolved and regrouped. With the Church's backing, the mestizo General Rafael Carrera led the dissolution of the federation. He restored various Church privileges and welcomed the Jesuits back to Central America. Carrera later led the newly independent state of Guatemala, where the 1851 Constitution granted the Church two seats in Congress. Much more liberal governments followed Carrera's regime in Guatemala. This back and forth continued for decades in most of the republics. By the 1850s, the new Central American nations established concordats with the papacy that "granted the right of patronage to the government in return for a declaration that the official religion of the country was the Catholic Church" (Schwaller 2011: 164). The institutional Church as well as local sodalities and cofradías had an interest in preserving a relationship with the state. For example, members of cofradías in Guatelmala (comprised of many Indigenous people and Ladinos) risked losing significant wealth and power if the state took over the Church's lands. Moving into the last quarter of the nineteenth century, Guatemala provided only tepid support for the Church while supporting liberal measures. Perhaps most notably, several Central American states invited Protestant missionaries. Many viewed missionaries as agents of US progress and heralds of a Protestant work ethic. With the exception of Nicaragua and Costa Rica, which did not mount anticlerical challenges against the Church for any sustained period of time, the other Central American nations in large part witnessed a similar trajectory to that of Guatemala described above (Schwaller 2011: 162–3, 178–81).

From the early to mid-twentieth century and onward, Catholics maintained social dominance. Lay groups such as Catholic Action played an important role in preserving the influence of the Church. Together, the laity and clergy offered new responses to an increasingly globalizing world. Lay networks such as the Cursillo movement took spiritual and pastoral roles into their own hands. Political and economic upheavals gave rise to a new kind of theological praxis: liberation theology. This new theological paradigm responded to the orders the Church made during the Second Vatican Council (1962–5) to empower the laity to carry out the work of the Church and for the Church to better address the needs of the poor (Schwaller 2011: 213–30). Liberation theology has been at the root of much religious activism since the 1960s. Its fundamental question asks: "what does it mean to be a Christian in continent of poor and oppressed people?" (Bingemer 2016: 18). Contrary to the notion that Marxism and religion are fundamentally incompatible, proponents of liberation theology turn to the economic exploitation of Latin America as a key interpretive lens to understand what the role of the church should be. Latin American theologians discussed how to carry out this task in a series of conferences held throughout Latin America. The CELAM (*Consejo Episcopal Latinoamericano* or Latin American Episcopal Conference) in Medillin, Colombia in 1968 offered concerned church leaders clear marching orders as to how to activate theologically driven justice. Three years later, the Peruvian theologian Gustavo

Gutiérrez published his world-famous book *Teología de la Liberación* (Theology of Liberation). While rooted in the Catholic tradition, it has had major reverberations in the larger religious world, inspiring Protestants to forge their counterpart, *Misión Integral* (Integral Mission), in Latin America (Kirkpatrick 2019). US Latinx theologians and churches, Catholic and Protestants alike, have drawn inspiration from these liberationist teachings (González 2014; Romero 2020: 142–62).

Protestantism in Latin America

In many Latin American nations, the invitation to Protestant missionaries was indeed a twofold move: solicitation of US interests and a rebuke of the hegemony of the Catholic Church. The Church's standing in the government and in popular opinion dictated responses to Protestantism's arrival. In Cuba, deep anti-Spanish sentiments surfaced in the form of anti-Catholicism, and many welcomed Protestants soon after independence from Spain in 1898. But in Mexico, Catholicism remained deeply rooted. In general, it has been only since the 1900s that Protestants have established a significant presence in the various Spanish-speaking countries of North America. Mainline Protestants established comity agreements with various countries. These agreements outlined the geographical jurisdiction of each denomination. Such accords tempered potential competition and streamlined missionary efforts.

Before proceeding further, one should note the variegated nomenclature applied to Protestants in Latin America. Generally speaking, Protestants (even mainline Protestants) in Latin America use the Spanish term "*Evangélico*" in lieu of the cognate "*Protestante*." The term *Evangélico* does not fit hand in glove with the US English term "Evangelical." The vast majority of Latin American and US Latinx *Protestantes* or *Evangélicos* have undergone or at least witnessed "the Pentecostalization of Latin American and U.S. Latino Christianity" (Espinosa 2004).

As a grassroots movement that claimed no authority or leader other than the Holy Spirit, early Pentecostalism operated its missionary endeavors outside of mainline Protestant comity agreements. Pentecostals, while categorically under the Protestant umbrella, emphasize the charismata, that is, the gifts of the Holy Spirit. These include speaking in tongues, engaging in spiritual warfare, praying for divine healing, and practicing various other modern-day miracles; Pentecostals also maintain a steadfast belief in the second coming of Jesus. In more recent years, many have championed a prosperity or health and wealth gospel (Lin 2020). The movement has thrived across the Americas among independent churches as well as in formal US denominations. In the US mainland, the Assemblies of God (Latino), Apostolic Assembly of the Faith in Christ Jesus, and Church of God lead the way as the largest Latino denominations. They have faced increased competition in recent decades from Latin American-based denominations such as *Iglesia de Dios Pentecostal Movimiento Internacional* (Puerto Rico), *Misión Cristiana Elim* (El Salvador), and *Igreja Universal do Reino de Deus* Universal Church of the Kingdom of God (Brazil) (Barba 2022a).

Pentecostalism insinuated itself rather quickly and deeply throughout Latin America both because of its commonalities to Catholicism as well as its contrasts. Its reception in large part owes to the fact that the Pentecostals' emphasis of the Holy Spirit animating the daily lives of the faithful through signs and miracles dovetailed with popular Catholic feasts, music, sacralization of the body, and miraculous workings (Ramírez 2014: 113–14). In many cases, fellow Latin Americans introduced Pentecostalism to their compatriots. And. in cases of US missionary efforts, the movement typically indigenized rather quickly. But Pentecostalism also departs from Catholicism in important ways. A majority of converts to Pentecostalism often point out the differences between the two, citing "a more personal relationship with God" as a chief reason for conversion while also noting differences in worship, music, and emphasis on the Holy Spirit (Pew Research Center 2014a; Ramos 2023). Yet the more recent rise of **Charismatic Catholics**, who in large part incorporate Pentecostalism's emphasis on the Holy Spirit, calls for further examination of similarities between the two (Chesnut 2003; Espinosa 2004; Cleary 2011).

Protestants have made significant inroads into the various majority-Catholic nations. In some countries, such as Guatemala, El Salvador, and Nicaragua, Catholics now account for only half of the population, whereas in Honduras they comprise even less (Pew Research Center 2014b: 14). Some of these changes reflect the kind of Protestantism that arrived as well as the process through which it arrived. Swiss sociologist Christian Lalive d'Epinday outlined five types of Protestant churches in Latin America: immigrant or diaspora churches; ethnic; mainline Protestants; Holiness churches; and indigenous Latin American Protestant churches (1981). This last category largely includes Pentecostals, whose rapid rise was facilitated by the change of leadership into the hands of locals.

Scholars Ennis Edmonds and Michelle González aptly outline the broad trends of the growth of Protestantism in the Caribbean. They note "the arrival of North American cultural values with evangelization; an alienation from Spanish colonial Catholicism; and the incorporation of indigenous leadership into the evangelization process" (2010: 158). The uneven reception of Protestantism in Latin America owes to the timing of events in the Caribbean versus those of mainland Mexico and Central America. For example, independence from Spain in the case of Cuba and Puerto Rico did not come to fruition until the Spanish-American War of 1898, over 75 years after the independence of several other North American nations. The Monroe Doctrine, driving so much of United States' nineteenth-century expansion, guided how the United States asserted its power on the Caribbean. To a greater extent than in Mexico, the United States sought economic control and social influence, relying upon religious institutions as agents of cultural change. Black Legends led US Protestants to view Latin American Catholicism as a brutal religious system whose allegiance to the Vatican was fundamentally antithetical to democracy. Religion and empire worked symbiotically in this era. Immediately after the Spanish-American War, state-backed US missionary programs established comity agreements to divide Puerto Rico into areas to be evangelized by Presbyterians, Baptists, Congregationalists, Disciples of Christ,

TABLE 1.1 *A 2014 Pew Research Center table showing the religious affiliation of Latin Americans by nation*

	Catholic	Protestant	Unaffiliated	Other
Predominantly Catholic				
Paraguay	89%	7%	1%	2%
Mexico	81	9	7	4
Colombia	79	13	6	2
Ecuador	79	13	5	3
Bolivia	77	16	4	3
Peru	76	17	4	3
Venezuela	73	17	7	4
Argentina	71	15	11	3
Panama	70	19	7	4
Majority Catholic				
Chile	64	17	16	3
Costa Rica	62	25	9	4
Brazil	61	26	8	5
Dominican Rep.	57	23	18	2
Puerto Rico	56	33	8	2
US Hispanics	55	22	18	5
Half Catholic				
El Salvador	50	36	12	3
Guatemala	50	41	6	3
Nicaragua	50	40	7	4
Less than half Catholic				
Honduras	46	41	10	2
Uruguay	42	15	37	6
Regional total* (adjusting for each country's population size)	69	19	8	4

* Regional total does not include US Hispanics.

Percentages may not add to 100 due to rounding.

Source: *Pew Research Center.*

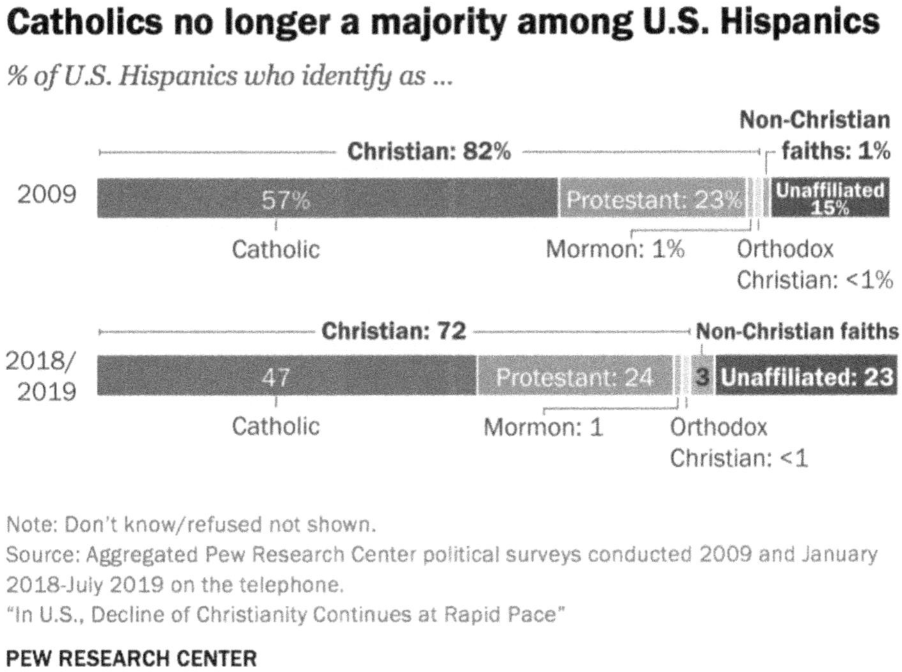

FIGURE 1.8 *A 2019 Pew Research Center graph showing that Catholics are no longer the majority among "US Hispanics." Further note that the vast majority of Latinx Protestants are Pentecostal and Evangelical. The unaffiliated group has shown the greatest growth from 2009 to 2018/2019.* Source: *Pew Research Center.*

Brethren, and Methodists (Vendrell 2021: 1–2). But even these strategically planned evangelization campaigns could barely compete with the Pentecostal movements that swept across the Caribbean islands in the following decades.

From its start, Pentecostalism came to Puerto Rico by way of returned Puerto Rican missionaries. Foremost among these was Juan Lugo, who converted while working on the sugar cane plantations in Hawaii. Lugo proved instrumental in the founding of the Assemblies of God in Puerto Rico and the island's own *Iglesia de Dios Pentecostal, Movimiento Internacional*. The Mexican-born US evangelist Francisco Olazábal held massive revivals there in the 1930s, working signs and wonders and converting multitudes (Espinosa 2014a: 192–232). Well into the twenty-first century, nearly a quarter of Puerto Ricans identified as Pentecostal (Edmonds and Gonzalez 2010: 158–9). As in Puerto Rico, mainline Protestants arrived in Cuba in limited numbers during the last quarter of the nineteenth century. But unlike their Puerto Rican counterparts, Cuban missionaries were in large part locals of the island. A stronger anti-Spanish sentiment pervaded Cuba than Puerto Rico, turning many against Catholicism and toward Protestantism. This pattern continued well into the twentieth century until Protestants, like all established religious groups, faced hostility from Fidel Castro's regime. Many churches shuttered during this time (Edmonds and González 2010: 163–6).

Even after the turbulent years of independence, the Catholic Church remained a mainstay and the official religion of the Dominican Republic. But Protestants, comparatively speaking, arrived early on and with methods different from those used in nearby Latin American nations. African American immigrants to the Dominican Republic brought Protestantism while the country was still under Haitian rule (1822–44), and in 1824 the president of Haiti welcomed 2,400 Protestant missionaries. For much of the nineteenth century, missionaries largely ministered to Anglophone immigrant communities residing on the island for business. More Protestant missionaries arrived with the US occupation of the island and sought to spread US ideas among residents. Because of the close association between missionaries and the occupation, locals largely resisted missionization (Edmonds and González 2010: 161–2). Protestants did not make significant inroads until Pentecostalism's arrival in the twentieth century (Thornton 2016).

The history and trajectory of Protestantism in Latin American and Latino USA since the twentieth century point to a broader pattern of conversion. The dynamics at the heart of these conversions have been studied more thoroughly in Latin America (Martin 1990; Stoll 1990; Garrard-Burnett and Stoll 1993; Chesnut 2003; Garma 2004; Steigenga and Cleary 2007; Hartch 2014) than in the United States (Mulder, Ramos, and Martí 2017; Calvillo 2020). Catholicism in Latin America has declined from about 90 percent of the population in the mid-twentieth century to about 70 percent by the late 2010s (Thornton 2018: 858). This decline largely owes to conversion to Pentecostalism. The rise of Charismatic Catholicism has helped to stave off further attrition (Cleary 2011). Conversion from Catholicism, especially in times of social, political, and civil unrest proved important to the success of Pentecostalism. This has been the case in the Dominican Republic, Honduras, Nicaragua, Guatemala, and El Salvador (Garrard-Burnett 1998; Wadkins 2017). As the United States attempted to protect its capitalist interests in Central America and the Caribbean, white US missionaries preached a gospel of anti-communism. Conversion to Protestantism also has impacted Catholicism's stronghold among US Latinos. One recent study revealed for the first time that Catholics account for less than 50 percent of the US Latinx population (Pew Research Center 2019). This change owes mostly to increased Latinx conversion to Protestantism and the disaffiliation of the so-called religious "nones" (Flores 2023).

US Latinx Catholicism

Whereas the story of Catholicism in Latin America is clearly over half a millennium old, its US Latinx counterpart invites a rather complicated origin story. Do we begin with Juan Ponce de Leon's 1513 landing in present-day Florida, which eventually led to Spanish settlements throughout the Southeast? Or do we begin with the US annexation of over half of Mexico in 1848? Regardless of where we start, any origin point summons some sense of "in betweenness," eluding clear-cut boundaries.

For chronological purposes, we will begin in 1848. Arguments over whether the United States should incorporate much of then northern Mexico involved spirited debates about the status of Mexicans as a Catholic and non-white "mongrel race." In mid-nineteenth century America, either of those characteristics alone posed a serious problem; combined (as many regarded race and religion operating hand-in-hand), they exceeded the tolerance of many (Martínez 2006). Reminders of the Catholic past survived in the landscape. Spanish missions cropped up all across the Southwest. By the late nineteenth and early twentieth centuries, Protestant boosters rebranded this Catholic past, emphasizing the European Spanish aspects of the missions as a way to ideologically whitewash the region's history of its Mexican (Brown) characteristics (Sagarena 2014). The reinterpretation of Spanish missionary history notwithstanding, no one could ignore the presence of former Mexican nationals now on US soil. Because of the annexation of northern Mexico and well over a century of subsequent immigration, some of the nation's largest parishes are located in the Southwest and tend to Latinx populations.

The history of Latinx Catholics in the United States is intimately tied to US empire, both because of the incorporation of new territories, such as Mexico and Puerto Rico, and the United States' role in foreign governments and economies, such as Cuba, the Dominican Republic and Central American states. For much of the twentieth century, North American Latinx arrivals to the United States have shared struggles around (im)migration to the US mainland (Barba 2021). While annexed people strive to maintain whatever they can hold on to, immigrants bring their religion with them. Mexican and Puerto Rican Catholics faced similar struggles with the US Catholic Church, which sought to fast track their assimilation into US society and denied them priests from their communities. Mexicans and Puerto Ricans largely arrived as a labor diaspora, and many thought they would only stay in the United States for a short while. For decades now, they have comprised a staying force of US Catholicism (Hinojosa 2021).

Cubans, Dominicans, and Central Americans arrived relatively later and thus faced different processes of incorporation. Cubans came in large numbers as exiles from communism during the Cold War and thus enjoyed different treatment. The Cubans arriving in the United States at the outbreak of the Cuban Revolution mostly hailed from better socio-economic classes and quickly transplanted educational, civic, and fraternal institutions, with Miami serving as a main hub. The devotion to Our Lady of Charity was among the important cultural and religious institutions they quickly set up in Miami. Our Lady of Charity continues to play a prominent role in centering diasporic nationalism with religion (Pérez 1994; Tweed 1997). Because many Cubans today lived under the atheistic Castro regime, over one-quarter are religiously unaffiliated (the highest of any Latinx group) and only 49 percent in the US identify as Catholic (see Figure 1.8). Dominican Catholics began to arrive to the United States in increasing numbers after 1965. Thus, their immigration has had only a limited impact on the US religious landscape. Like Puerto Ricans and Central Americans, many Dominicans engage in economic and religious transnational networks. This transnationalism has increased more in recent years with the rise of social media platforms. Dominicans have settled mostly in the US Northeast and have brought devotions to Our Lady of Altagracia with them (Figueroa 2009). At 59 percent, Dominicans are second only to Mexicans as the highest percentage of Latino national groups who identify as Catholics.

Meanwhile, Catholicism has faced a rapid decline in Central America for the past half century. Only Costa Rica and Panama remain Catholic-majority countries (Pew Research Center 2014b). Less politically stable Central American nations have witnessed much larger exoduses to the United States. Because Central American immigrants are relative newcomers compared to their other Latin American counterparts, much of their Catholic devotions have been incorporated into existing Latino parishes. Every Latin American country boasts a national Marian devotion. But in El Salvador and Guatemala, the most prominent national devotions honor Christ, not Mary. The devotion to *El Divino Salvador* enjoys hearty celebration in Los Angeles in an annual festival that coincides with the Day of the Salvadoran (Reedy Solano 2004). Guatemalan devotion to the Black Christ of Esquipulas inspires the faithful to retain a diasporic religious sensibility. Catholicism, as in Latin America, is the most unifying social force among Latinos in the United States. In all, Latinos account for 40 percent of all US Catholics (Pew Research Center 2014a).

US Latinx Protestantism

The Protestantization of the US Latinx population started inauspiciously for missionaries. Protestant missionaries focused on inculcating American values and breaking the dominance of Catholicism in the US Southwest. But they had only minimal success in the nineteenth and early twentieth century (Martinez 2006). In the past several decades, however, Latin American immigrants along with second- and third-generation Latinos have joined the ranks of mainline Protestant denominations. Yet the number of these conversions pales in comparison to those joining the ranks of Pentecostals (Mulder et al. 2017).

Overall, the Pentecostalization of Christianity across the Latinx Americas bears major importance in the story of conversion. Even when a Latinx church is not necessarily Pentecostal in name or confession, it adopts many Pentecostal or Charismatic aesthetics and practices (Espinosa 2004; Medina and Alfaro 2015). The development of global Pentecostalism has had far reaching effects on the broader world of Protestantism. In more recent years, historians have identified how Pentecostalism spread from Los Angles to surrounding Mexican-American communities and shortly thereafter to Mexico via Mexican, Mexican-American, and Euro-American missionaries (Sánchez-Walsh 2003; Espinosa 2014a; Ramírez 2015; Barba 2022b). Over the course of the twentieth century, Latino Pentecostalism has developed over three stages: Foundation (1906–29), when it spread to California, Texas, Puerto Rico, and Mexico; Building (1930–65), when leaders and laity faced a host of external social, economic, and political challenges but despite initial setbacks continued to build the movement; and Expansion (1966–2006), when Latino Pentecostals made inroads in the US mainstream and sent missionaries to Central America. This last period also included the arrival of missionaries from Latin American denominations to the United States, effectively bringing the diasporic experience full circle as a reverse mission (Barba 2022a). The diversity within Latin American Pentecostalism alone compelled one Mexican historian to call the movement "a mosaic within a mosaic" (Gaxiola-Gaxiola 1991).

The cultural hegemony of Catholicism in Latin American and the United States tends to overshadow other global religions that have flourished in the broader Latinx context. Like Pentecostals of the twentieth century, Mormons have been a major religious competitor, attracting converts away from Catholicism. Mormonism has realized its greatest growth in colonies and particular regions of Latin America (Grover 2016). When Mormons first settled in what is now Utah, their trek constituted an exodus beyond US border as they had entered northernmost reaches of Mexico. Although this arrangement proved short lived, Mormonism planted itself deeply in the US-Mexico borderlands and continues to thrive among Latinos (Dormady and Tamez 2015; Vega 2022).

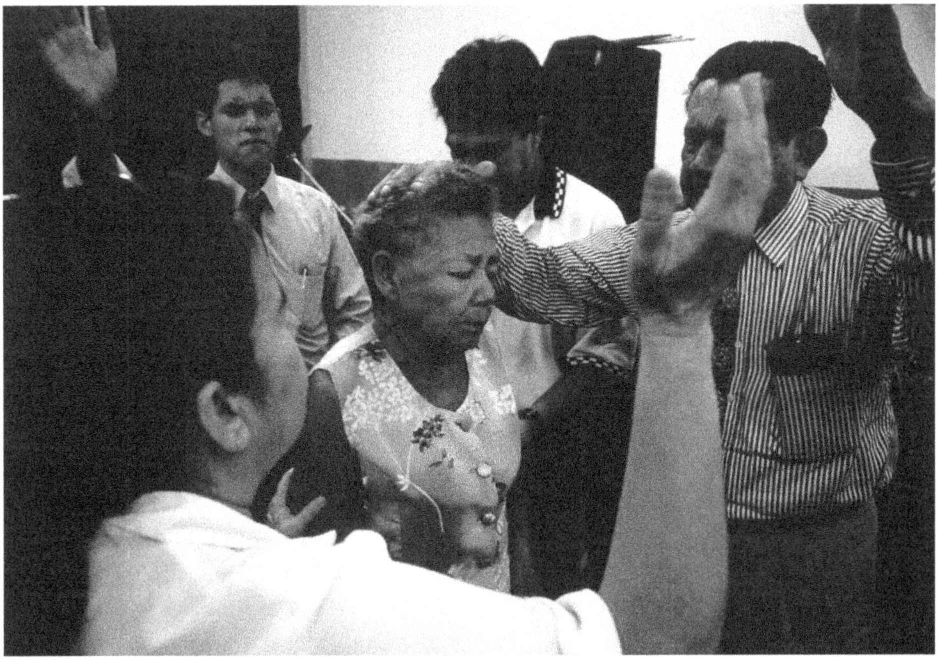

FIGURE 1.9 *Woman seeks healing at a Latino Pentecostal church in East Los Angeles, California.* Source: *Photo by Gilles Mingasson/Getty Images.*

Conclusion: Religious Activism on the Border of Labor and Immigration

This is the Sanctuary of God for the oppressed of Central America.
—Declaration of Sanctuary at Southern Presbyterian Church in Tucson, Arizona.

Latino faith politics have long been concerned with systems of political power, such as housing, labor, immigration, education, and healthcare (instead of presidential or electoral politics) (Hinojosa, et al. 2022: 4). In these arenas, justice and liberation can be more readily discerned and demanded. Historian Roberto Chao Romero has recently developed the concept of the "Brown Church" to describe how, for the past 500 years, religious figures from the Latin American (and later in US Latinx contexts) cultivated a social justice tradition. The messages of the Brown Church's prophets easily cross borders.

Included among Romero's prophets of the Brown Church is the lay Catholic and civil rights figure Cesar Chavez. During the civil rights era, Chavez drew national attention to the plight of farmworker by drawing upon overt Catholic symbols and relying upon Protestant and Jewish networks to mobilize the farmworkers' cause. Farmworkers protested across the country and called for an international boycott of grapes grown by the companies and farm cooperatives most responsible for suppressing the movement's call for better working conditions and wages and the right to unionize (Watt 2011; Romero 2020: 120–41). The struggle in the fields soon expanded to urban centers, where groups such as the Young Lords Organization occupied church buildings to fight urban renewal (Hinojosa 2021; Hinojosa 2022: 166–87).

Just over a decade later, the US-Mexico border became ground zero of the Sanctuary Movement and the larger immigration crisis. On March 24, 1982, a day commemorating two years since the assassination of Brown Church prophet Oscar Romero, the members of Southside Presbyterian Church, pastored by John Fife, declared their church a "Sanctuary for the oppressed of Central America," effectively spurring a movement of civil disobedience across the United States. Two decades later, the New Sanctuary Movement emerged while US Congress attempted (but ultimately failed) to pass comprehensive immigration reform. As deportations increased after 9/11, the New Sanctuary Movement became a broader movement for immigration rights. Trump's election set into motion a renewed wave of sanctuary activism (Barba and Castillo-Ramos 2019). Because of unsolved immigration crises, the US-Mexico border continues to constitute a key site for prophetic activist movements and organizations that call for a more just immigration system (Menjívar 2007; Sostaita 2020).

The religious work at the border led by immigrant justice coalitions reminds us of the thin space that exists between US Latinx and Latin American identities. In a world of increasing **transnationalism**, it is perhaps best to understand the two identities as distinct but not necessarily separate from one another. To be sure, studies of US Latinx and Latin American religion are discrete undertakings and specializations. Even so, this chapter has provided contextualization to understand the relationship between the two. Various metaphors such as border, syncretism, and *nepantla* all generally point to the contradictions enveloped in Latinx identity: some Laitnos have been in the United States for multiple generations, others are immigrants, still others had the border cross them. Whatever the attendant circumstances might be, we find that religion in Latin American and Latinx contexts of North America indeed pushes against any fixed boundaries of nation, language, class, race, and culture.

Further Reading

Aponte, E.D. 2012. *¡Santo! Varieties of Latino/a Spirituality*. Maryknoll, NY: Orbis Books.

Edmonds, E.B. and M.A. González. 2010. *Caribbean Religious History: An Introduction*. New York: New York University Press.

González, O.E. and J.L. González. 2008. *Christianity in Latin America: A History*. New York: Cambridge University Press.

Hartch, T. 2014. *The Rebirth of Latin American Christianity*. New York: Oxford University Press.

Mulder, M., A. Ramos, and G. Martí. 2017. *Latino Protestants in America: Growing and Diverse*. Lanham: Rowman and Littlefield.

Schwaller, J.F. 2011. *A History of the Catholic Church in Latin America: From Conquest to Revolution and Beyond*. New York: New York University Press.

References

Aponte, E.D. 2006. "Metaphysical Blending in Latino/a Botánicas in Dallas." In *Rethinking Latino(a) Religion and Identity*, edited by M.A. De La Torre and G. Espinosa, 46–68. Cleveland: Pilgrim Press.

Aponte, E.D. 2012. *¡Santo! Varieties of Latino/a Spirituality*. Maryknoll, NY: Orbis Books.

Avalos, N. 2022. "Latinx Indigeneities and Christianity." In *The Oxford Handbook of Latinx Christianities in the United States*, edited by K. Nabhan-Warren, 296–315. New York: Oxford University Press.

Barba, L. 2021. "Latinx Christianities in North America." In *Bloomsbury Religion in North America*, edited by D.B. Daughrity. London: Bloomsbury Academic. DOI: http://dx.doi.org/10.5040/9781350971073.0023

Barba, L.D. 2022a. "Latina/o Pentecostalism." In *The Oxford Handbook of Latinx Christianities in the United States*, edited by K. Nabhan-Warren, 130–50. New York: Oxford University Press.

Barba, L.D. 2022b. *Sowing the Sacred: Mexican Pentecostal Farmworkers in California*. New York: Oxford University Press.

Barba, L.D. 2024. "Guadalupe Represents La Cultura: A Mexican-American Mural-Shrine in California." In *American Patroness*, edited by K. Dugan and K. Park, 44–66. New York: Fordham University Press.

Barba, L. and T. Castillo-Ramos. 2019. "La Migra No Profana El Santuario: The Sanctuary Movement from Reagan to Trump." *Perspectivas* (16): 11–36.

Barton, P. 2006. *Hispanic Methodists, Presbyterians, and Baptists in Texas*. Austin: University of Texas Press.
Bingemer, M.C. 2016. *Latin American Theology: Roots and Branches*. Maryknoll, NY: Orbis Books.
Bristol, J. 2016. "The Church, Africans, and Slave Religion in Latin America." In *The Cambridge History of Religion in Latin America*, edited by V. Garrard-Burnett, P. Freston, and S.C. Dove, 198–206. New York: Cambridge University Press.
Calvillo, J. 2020. *The Saints of Santa Ana: Faith and Ethnicity in a Mexican Majority City*. New York: Oxford University Press.
Carrasco, D. 2014. *Religions of Mesoamerica*. Long Grove, IL: Waveland Press.
Castillo-Ramos, T. 2023. "Guadalupe as a Symbol of Resistance." In *Bloomsbury Religion in North America*, edited by L.D. Barba. London: Bloomsbury Academic. DOI: http://dx.doi.org/10.5040/9781350898813.003
Chesnut, R.A. 2003. *Competitive Spirits: Latin America's New Religious Economy*. New York: Oxford University Press.
Chesnut, R.A. 2017. *Devoted to Death: Santa Muerte, the Skeleton Saint*, 2nd edn. New York: Oxford University Press.
Chitwood, K. 2021. *The Muslims of Latin America*. Boulder, CO: Lynn Reinner Publishers.
Cleary, E.L. 2011. *The Rise of Charismatic Catholicism in Latin America*. Gainesville: University Press of Florida.
d'Epinday, C.L. 1981. "Dependance sociale et religion: pasteures et protestantismes latino-americains." *Archives de sciences sociales de religions* 26: 85–97.
Danielson, R.A. 2015. "Transnationalism and the Pentecostal Salvadoran Church: A Case Study of Misión Cristiana Elim." In *Pentecostals and Charismatics in Latin American and Latino Communities*, edited by N. Medina and S. Alfaro, 111–24. New York: Palgrave Macmillan.
Danielson, R.A. 2023. "Central American Christianity." In *Bloomsbury Religion in North America*, edited by L.D. Barba. London: Bloomsbury Academic. DOI: http://dx.doi.org/10.5040/9781350915824.001
De La Torre, M.A. 2004. *Santeria: The Beliefs and Rituals of a Religion in America*. Berkeley: University of California Press.
De La Torre, M.A. 2006. "Rethinking Mulatez." In *Rethinking Latino(a) Religion and Identity*, edited by M.A. De La Torre and G. Espinosa, 158–75. Cleveland: Pilgrim Press.
Deloria Jr., V. 1994. *God Is Red: A Native View of Religion*, 2nd edn. Golden, CO: Fulcrum.
Dolan, J.P. and J.R. Vidal, eds. 1994. *Puerto Rican and Cuban Catholics in the U.S., 1900–1965*. South Bend: University of Notre Dame Press.
Dormady, J.H. and J.M. Tamez, eds. 2015. *Just South of Zion: The Mormons in Mexico and Its Borderlands*. Albuquerque: University of New Mexico Press.
Edmonds, E.B. and M.A. González. 2010. *Caribbean Religious History: An Introduction*. New York: New York University Press.
Ehrenberg, F. 1996. "Framing an Icon: Guadalupe and the Artist's Vision." In *Goddess of the Americas La Diosa de las Américas*, edited by A. Castillo, 170–7. New York: Riverhead Books.
Elizondo, V. 1980. *La Morenita: Evangelizer of the Americas*. San Antonio: Mexican American Cultural Center.
Elizondo, V. 2000. *The Future Is Mestizo: Life Where Cultures Meet*, revised edn. Boulder: The University Press of Colorado.
Escalante, A. 2023. "Black Atlantic Religions." In *Bloomsbury Religion in North America*, edited by L.D. Barba. London: Bloomsbury Academic. DOI: http://dx.doi.org/10.5040/9781350898806.001
Espín, O. 1995. "Pentecostalism and Popular Catholicism: The Poor and Tradition." *Journal of Hispanic/Latino Theology* 3 (2): 14–43.

Espín, O. 1997. *The Faith of the People: Theological Reflections on Popular Catholicism*. Maryknoll, NY: Orbis.
Espinosa, G. 2004. "The Pentecostalization of Latin American and U.S. Latino Christianity." *Pneuma: The Journal of the Society for Pentecostal Studies* 26 (2): 262–92.
Espinosa, G. 2014a. *Latino Pentecostals: Faith and Politics in Action*. Cambridge, MA: Harvard University Press.
Espinosa, G. 2014b. *William J. Seymour and the Origins of Global Pentecostalism*. Durham: Duke University Press.
Espinosa, G., V. Elizondo, and J. Miranda, eds. 2005. *Latino Religions and Civic Activism*. New York: Oxford University Press.
Figueroa, A.M. 2009. "Dominicans." In *Hispanic American Religious Cultures*, edited by M.A. De La Torre, 205–7. Santa Barbara: ABC-CLIO.
Flores, D. 2023. "Latinx Religious Nones." In *Bloomsbury Religion in North America*, edited by L.D. Barba. London: Bloomsbury Academic. DOI: http://dx.doi.org/10.5040/9781350898806.004
Gallardo, A. 2023. "Mapping the Transatlantic Origins of Latin American Christianity." In *Bloomsbury Religion in North America*, edited by L.D. Barba. London: Bloomsbury Academic. DOI: http://dx.doi.org/10.5040/9781350898813.005
Garma Navarro, C. 2004. *Pentecostalismo en Iztapalapa y la Ciudad de México*. Mexico, DF: Universidad Metropolitana, Iztapalapa.
Garrard-Burnett, V. 1998. *Protestantism in Guatemala: Living in the New Jerusalem*. Austin: University of Texas Press.
Garrard-Burnett, V. and D. Stoll, eds. 1993. *Rethinking Protestantism in Latin America*. Philadelphia: Temple University Press.
Gaxiola-Gaxiola, M.J. 1991. "Latin American Pentecostalism: A Mosaic within a Mosaic." *Pneuma: The Journal of the Society for Pentecostal Studies* 13 (1): 107–29.
Goizueta, R.S. 2004. "The Symbolic Realism of U.S. Latino/a Popular Catholicism." *Theological Studies* 65 (2): 255–74.
González, M.A. 2014. *A Critical Introduction to Religion in the Americas: Bridging the Liberation Theology and Religious Studies Divide*. New York: New York University Press.
González, O.E. and J.L. González. 2008. *Christianity in Latin America: A History*. New York: Cambridge University Press.
Grover, M. 2016. "Mormons in Latin America." In *The Oxford Handbook of Mormonism*, edited by T.L. Givens and P.L. Barlow. New York: Oxford University Press. DOI: https://doi.org/10.1093/oxfordhb/9780199778362.001.0001
Hartch, T. 2014. *The Rebirth of Latin American Christianity*. New York: Oxford University Press.
Hastings, A. 1999. "Latin America." In *A World History of Christianity*, edited by A. Hastings, 328–68. Grand Rapids: William B. Eerdmans Publishing Company.
Hidalgo, J.M. 2016. *Revelation in Aztlán: Scriptures, Utopias, and the Chicano Movement*. New York: Palgrave.
Hinojosa, F. 2021. *Apostles of Change: Latino Radical Politics, Church Occupations, and the Fight to Save the Barrio*. Austin: University of Texas Press.
Hinojosa, F. 2022. "From the Fields to the Cities: The Rise of Latina/o Religious Politics in the Civil Rights Era." In *Faith and Power: Latino Religious Politics Since 1945*, edited by F. Hinojosa, M. Elmore, and S.M. González, 166–87. New York: New York University Press.
Hinojosa, F., M. Elmore, and S.M. González. 2022. *Faith and Power: Latino Religious Politics since 1945*. New York: New York University Press.
Hordes, S. 2008. *To the Ends of the Earth: A History of Crypto Jews in New Mexico*. New York: Columbia University Press.
Horton, S. 2009. "The Latino Springtime of the Catholic Church: Lay Religious Networks and Transnationalism from Below." In *Religion at the Corner of Bliss and*

Nirvana: Politics, Identity, and Faith in New Migrant Communities, edited by L.A. Lorentzen, J.J. Gonzalez, K.M. Chun, and H.D. Do, 243–62. Durham, NC: Duke University Press.

Hurbon, L. 2001. "Pentecostalism and Transnationalisation in the Caribbean." In *Between Babel and Pentecost: Transnational Pentecostalism in Africa and Latin America*, edited by A. Corten and R. Marshall-Fratani, 124–41. Bloomington: Indiana University Press.

Kirkpatrick, D.C. 2019. *A Gospel for the Poor: Global Social Christianity and the Latin American Evangelical Left*. Philadelphia: University of Pennsylvania Press.

Kovic, C. 2007. "Indigenous Conversion to Catholicism: Change of Heart in Chiapas, Mexico." In *Conversion of a Continent: Contemporary Religious Change in Latin America*, edited by T.J. Steignega and E.L. Cleary, 199–217. New Brunswick: Rutgers University Press.

Limonic, L. 2019. *Kugel and Frijoles: Latino Jews in the United States*. Detroit: Wayne State University Press.

Lin, T.T.R. 2020. *Prosperity Gospel Latinos and Their American Dream*. Chapel Hill: University of North Carolina Press.

Maldonado-Estrada, A. 2023. "Latinx Devotional Stuff and Material Religion." In *Bloomsbury Religion in North America*, edited by L.D. Barba. London: Bloomsbury Academic. DOI: http://dx.doi.org/10.5040/9781350898806.003

Martin, D. 1990. *Tongues of Fire: The Explosion of Protestantism in Latin America*. Cambridge: Blackwell.

Martinez, J. 2006. *Sea la Luz: The Making of Mexican Protestantism in the American Southwest, 1829–1900*. Denton, TX: University of North Texas Press.

Matovina, T. 2019. *Theologies of Guadalupe: From the Era of Conquest to Pope Francis*. New York: Oxford University Press.

Medina, L. 2006. "Nepantla Spirituality: Negotiating Multiple Religious Identities among U.S. Latinas." In *Rethinking Latino(a) Religion and Identity*, edited by M.A. De La Torre and G. Espinosa, 248–66. Cleveland: Pilgrim Press.

Medina, N. 2008. *Mestizaje: Remapping Race, Culture, and Faith in Latina/o Catholicism*. Maryknoll, NY: Orbis Books.

Medina, N. 2009. "Native Americans." In *Hispanic American Religious Cultures*, vol. 2, edited by M.A. De La Torre, 395–403. Santa Barbara: ABC-CLIO.

Medina, N. 2022. "Retracing Intermixture/Mestizaje in Latin America and among Latinas/os/xs." In *Bloomsbury Religion in North America*, edited by L.D. Barba. London: Bloomsbury Academic. DOI: http://dx.doi.org/10.5040/9781350926882.001.

Medina, N. and S. Alfaro, eds. 2015. *Pentecostals and Charismatics in Latin American and Latino Communities*. New York: Palgrave Macmillan.

Menjívar, C. 2007. "Serving Christ in the Borderlands: Faith Workers Respond to Border Violence." In *Religion and Social Justice for Immigrants*, edited by P. Hondagneu-Sotelo, 104–21. New Brunswick: Rutgers University Press.

Morales, H.D. 2018. *Latino and Muslim in America: Race, Religion, and the Making of a New Minority*. New York: Oxford University Press.

Mulder, M., A. Ramos, and G. Martí. 2017. *Latino Protestants in America: Growing and Diverse*. Lanham: Rowman and Littlefield.

Murphy, J.M. 2015. *Botánicas: Sacred Spaces of Healing and Devotion in Urban America*. Jackson: The University Press of Mississippi.

Orta, A. 2020. "Indigenous Christianities: Commensuration, (De)Colonization, and Cultural Production in Latin America." In *The Oxford Handbook of Latin American Christianity*, edited by D.T. Orique, S. Fitzpatrick-Behrens, and V. Garrard, 83–97. New York: Oxford University Press.

O'Connor, M.I. 2016. *Mixtec Evangelicals: Globalization, Migration, and Religious Change in a Oaxacan Indigenous Group*. Boulder: University Press of Colorado.
Peláez-Diaz, F. 2023. "Santa Muerte, Holy Death." In *Bloomsbury Religion in North America*, edited by L.D. Barba. London: Bloomsbury Academic. DOI: http://dx.doi.org/10.5040/9781350898813.001
Perdigón-Castañeda, J.K. 2008. *Santa Muerte: Protectora de los hombres*. Mexico D.F.: Instituto Nacional de Antropología e Historia.
Pérez, L. 1994. "Cuban Catholics in the United States." In *Puerto Rican and Cuban Catholics in the U.S., 1900–1965*, edited by J.P. Dolan and J.R. Vidal, 147–207. South Bend: University of Notre Dame Press.
Pérez, L. 2007. *Chicana Art: The Politics of Spiritual and Aesthetic Altarities*. Durham: Duke University Press.
Peterson, A.L. and M. Vásquez. 2008. *Latin American Religions: Histories and Documents in Context*. New York: New York University Press.
Peterson, J.F. 1992. "The Virgin of Guadalupe Symbol of Conquest or Liberation?" *Art Journal* 51 (4): 39–47.
Peterson, J.F. 2014. *Visualizing Guadalupe: From Black Madonna to Queen of the Americas*. Austin: University of Texas Press.
Pew Research Center. 2014a. "The Shifting Religious Identities of Latinos in the United States." May 7. https://www.pewresearch.org/religion/2014/05/07/the-shifting-religious-identity-of-latinos-in-the-united-states/
Pew Research Center. 2014b. "Religion in Latin America: Widespread Change in a Historically Catholic Region." November 13. https://www.pewresearch.org/religion/wp-content/uploads/sites/7/2014/11/Religion-in-Latin-America-11-12-PM-full-PDF.pdf
Pew Research Center. 2019. "In U.S., Decline of Christianity Continues at Rapid Pace: An Update on America's Changing Religious Landscape." October 17. https://www.pewforum.org/2019/10/17/in-u-s-decline-of-christianity-continues-at-rapid-pace/
Poole, S. 1995. *Our Lady of Guadalupe: The Origins and Sources of a Mexican National Symbol, 1531–1797*. Tucson: University of Arizona Press.
Ramírez, D. 2014. "Pentecostalism in Latin America." In *The Cambridge Companion to Pentecostalism*, edited by Cecil M. Robeck Jr. and Amos Yong. New York: Cambridge University Press.
Ramírez, D. 2015. *Migrating Faith: Pentecostalism in the United States and Mexico in the Twentieth Century*. Chapel Hill: University of North Carolina Press.
Ramírez, D. 2023. "Oaxacan Religious Transnationalism." In *Bloomsbury Religion in North America*, edited by L.D. Barba. London: Bloomsbury Academic. DOI: http://dx.doi.org/10.5040/9781350890244.002
Ramos, A. 2023. "Latinx Conversions & Religious Change in the United States." In *Bloomsbury Religion in North America*, edited by L.D. Barba. London: Bloomsbury Academic. DOI: http://dx.doi.org/10.5040/9781350898813.003
Ramos, F.L. 2016. "Saints, Shrines, and Festival Days in Colonial Spanish America." In *The Cambridge History of Religion in Latin America*, edited by V. Garrard-Burnett, P. Freston, and S.C. Dove, 143–59. New York: Cambridge University Press.
Reedy Solano, J. 2004. "The Central American Religious Experience in the U.S.: Salvadorans and Guatemalans as Case Studies." In *Introduction to the U.S. Latina and Latino Religious Experience*, edited by H. Avalos, 116–39. Boston: Brill.
Romero, R.C. 2020. *Brown Church: Five Centuries of Latina/o Social Justice, Theology, and Identity*. Downers Grove, IL: Intervarsity Press.
Sagarena, R.L. 2009. "Making a There There: Marian Muralism and Devotional Streetscapes." *Visual Resources* 25 (1): 100–4.

Sagarena, R.L. 2014. *Aztlán and Arcadia: Religion, Ethnicity, and the Creation of Place.* New York: New York University Press.
Sánchez-Walsh, A. 2003. *Latino Pentecostal Identity: Evangelical Faith, Self, and Society.* New York: Columbia University Press.
Schwaller, J.F. 2011. *A History of the Catholic Church in Latin America: From Conquest to Revolution and Beyond.* New York: New York University Press.
Seman, J.K. 2021. *Borderlands Curanderos: The Worlds of Santa Teresa Urrea and Don Pedrito Jaramillo.* Austin: University of Texas Press.
Sostaita, B. 2020. "Water Not Walls: Towards a Religious Study of Life that Defies Borders." *American Religion* 1 (2): 74–97.
Steigenga, T. and E.L. Cleary, eds. 2007. *Conversion of a Continent Contemporary Religious Change in Latin America.* New Brunswick: Rutgers University Press.
Stoll, D. 1990. *Is Latin America Turning Protestant? The Politics of Evangelical Growth.* Berkeley and Los Angeles: University of California Press.
Tavárez, David. 2016. "Religion in the Pre-Contact New World: Mesoamerica and the Andes." In *The Cambridge History of Religion in Latin America*, edited by V. Garrard-Burnett, P. Freston, and S.C. Dove, 22–33. New York: Cambridge University Press.
Thornton, B.J. 2016. *Negotiating Respect: Pentecostalism, Masculinity, and the Politics of Spiritual Authority.* Gainesville: University Press of Florida.
Thornton, B.J. 2018."Changing Landscapes of Faith: Latin American Religion in the Twenty-First Century." *Latin American Research Review* 53 (4): 857–62.
Todorov, T. 1992. *The Conquest of America.* San Francisco: Harper Perennial.
Tweed, T. 1997. *Our Lady of Exile: Diasporic Religion at a Cuban Shrine in Miami.* New York: Oxford University Press.
Vásquez, M. 2006. "Rethinking Mestizaje." In *Rethinking Latino(a) Religion and Identity*, edited by M.A. De La Torre and G. Espinosa, 129–57. Cleveland: Pilgrim Press.
Vega, S. 2022. "Latina/o/x Mormons." In *The Oxford Handbook of Latinx Christianities in the United States*, edited by K. Nabhan-Warren, 151–68. New York: Oxford University Press.
Vendrell, S.A. 2021."Give Them Christ: Native Agency in the Evangelization of Puerto Rico, 1900 to 1917." *Religions* 12 (3). DOI: https://doi.org/10.3390/rel12030196
Wadkins, T.H. 2017. *The Rise of Pentecostalism in Modern El Salvador: From the Blood of the Martyrs to the Baptism of the Spirit.* Waco: Baylor University Press.
Watt, A.J. 2011. *Farmworkers and the Churches: The Movement in California and Texas.* College Station: Texas A&M Press.
Young, J.G. 2015. *Mexican Exodus: Emigrants, Exiles, and Refugees of the Cristero War.* New York: Oxford University Press.

Glossary Terms

Charismatic Catholics Catholics who partake in Pentecostal-influenced practices involving the Holy Spirit and its various gifts.

Crypto Jews Jews who practiced or retained their religious customs in secret.

Fuero A legal system that established various privileges (especially monetary) for the Catholic Church in Latin America.

Incommensurabilities This describes large-scale and fundamental differences in worldview.

Orthodoxy The correct teaching as defined and enforced by a religious institution.
Papal Bulls Official decree issued by the pope.
Patronato Real A patronage system whereby the Spanish Crown exercised considerable control over the Catholic Church's affairs in its colonies.
Pre-Tridentine Traditions defined before the Council of Trent 1545–63.
Reconquista Spanish for "reconquest," this term refers to the Catholic struggle to reconquer the Iberian Peninsula, which had been under Muslim rule for nearly 800 years.
Subaltern The people under domination in a system of immense power imbalance.
Transnationalism The phenomena in which people and institutions maintain ties and share ideas and commodities across nations.

Time Line

Date	Event
1492	Expulsion of Jews from Spain and the Spanish arrival in the Americas See chapter by Gallardo
1531	According to Catholic tradition, Our Lady of Guadalupe appeared to Juan Diego. This marks the origins of the most popular Marian devotion in the Americas See chapter by Castillo-Ramos
1550–1	Bartolomé de Las Casas defends Amerindians in the Valladolid debate. The consequent reduction of Amerindian enslavement resulted in the importation of enslaved Africans including Muslims See chapters by Medina; Chitwood; and Escalante
1600–early 1700s	During the Baroque Era, the Catholic Church amasses vast wealth from Latin America and thoroughly establishes itself throughout Latin America See chapters by Garma and Barba
1700s	Bourbon Reforms put a major strain on the relationship between Spain and its colonies See chapters by Garma and Barba
1800s	Black Atlantic religions concretely organize in the Caribbean See chapter by Escalante
1821	Various Latin American nations declare independence from Spain. The role of the Catholic Church in the new states is heavily debated See chapters by Barba; Garma; Escalante; and D. Ramírez

Date	Event
1848	The United States annexes over half of Mexico thus marking the beginning of US Manifest Destiny in Latin America See chapters by Barba and Vargas
Post 1965	Latin American immigration significantly increases after passage of Immigration and Nationality Act of 1965. In the 1980s, Central American refugees arrived to the US; Latinx religious diversity greatly increases
2001	9/11 terrorist attacks result in a fundamental changes for Muslim and Latin American immigrants See chapters by Chitwood and Barba.

2

Mapping the Origins of Christianity in the Americas

Ángel J. Gallardo

Introduction

This chapter maps the origins of Christianity in the Americas by showing how theological ideas about nature informed Spain's religious and geopolitical projects and subsequently galvanized the Columbian Enterprise. Section I situates Christopher Columbus within the fifteenth-century Iberian context. Section I shows how discourse about blood purity (*limpieza de sangre*) began racializing religion by reconfiguring Christian and Jewish identity as a "natural" condition determined through reproduction. This section discusses how Spanish royals expelled the Jewish and Muslim populations in an effort to forge a "pure" Christian empire. Section II explores the colonial impact of medieval theology by considering how scholastic ideas about the natural order informed the Columbian Enterprise. It examines how Columbus, and the Iberian cosmographers that followed, employed a scholastic vision of nature to transform the southern hemisphere into colonial space. Section III discusses the life and legacy of Bartolomé de Las Casas. It outlines how Las Casas undermined Spain's claims of dominion by developing a *theological geography* that affirmed the natural sovereignty of Indigenous people.

Late Medieval Iberian Context

From the ninth to the fifteenth century, Iberia exhibited one of the most diverse populations in western Europe. In general, scholars have characterized relations between the peninsula's Abrahamic traditions as harmonious with occasional episodes of conflict (Baer 1961; Glick 1979: 6–13; Nirenberg 8–9). Advocates of this view underscore the long periods of cultural exchange enjoyed by Muslims, Jews, and Christians, an approach known as *convivencia* (living together) (Castro 1983: 200–9; Sánchez-Albornoz 1956; Roth 1992; Chazan 2010). In addition to lauding a Jewish "Golden Age," *convivencia* proponents also represent **Al-Andalus** under the Islamic Umayyad dynasty as a place where "people of the Book" (*dhimmi*)—meaning Jews and Christians—could peacefully co-exist along with Muslims (Roth 1992: 19–20; Burns 1973: 157). Yet whatever harmony existed in the Middle Ages radically shifted at the start of the fifteenth century.

Castilian and Aragonese writers, legislators, and ecclesial authorities began using notions of purity to conceptualize social deviants: heretics, witches, Jews, Muslims, prostitutes, homosexuals, and lepers (Richards 1994). Eventually, this discourse encompassed recent Jewish converts (*conversos*) and Muslim converts (*moriscos*) to Christianity. David Nirenberg observes that by "the early fifteenth century 'raza,' casta,' and 'linaje' were part of a complex of interchangeable terms that linked both behavior and appearance to nature and reproduction" (2007: 77). And so, purity discourse would emerge from this cultural milieu steeped in the scholastic tradition. "This naturalization of a religious-cultural identity," as Maria Elena Martínez argues, "coincided with the emergence of a lexicon consisting of terms such as race (*raza*), caste (*casta*), and lineage (*linaje*) that was informed by popular notions regarding biological reproduction in the natural world and, in particular, horse breeding" (Barnes 1984: 1111–219; 2000; Covarrubias Orozco 2006: 824; Martínez 2008: 28; Nirenberg 2008: 78–9). Iberian Christians would conceptualize religious identity as an immutable condition transmitted through blood. According to Nirenberg, "words like *raza* and *linage* (and their cognates in the various Iberian romance languages) were already embedded in identifiable biological ideas about breeding and reproduction in the first half of the fifteenth century" (2008: 79). In this way, this religious understanding of nature informed the racial hierarchies that materialized in colonial Spanish America. Since birth ultimately determined caste, status was ascribed rather than earned. In the colonial context, terms such as *generación* or *calidad* were oftentimes used in place of *raza* or *casta* (Lewis 2012: 104).

Religious tensions escalated when Christian residents in Castile and Aragon began protesting what modern historians consider a rebellion against the Crown's centralizing policies (Nirenberg 1996: 43–51). Jews who worked in the financial sector were responsible for collecting taxes on behalf of the Crown. And after a wave of anti-Jewish persecution, monarchs would oftentimes lay claim to the debts owed to local moneylenders (Menache 1987). In turn, Christians from the urban upper classes expressed frustration, claiming that Jews unfairly benefitted from royal protection, access to circles of power, and control over financial institutions. Responding to pressure from social elites, King of Castile Enrique II (1334–79) granted monarchical support to "a series of anti-Jewish lawsuits in the *cortes* of Burgos" (Hering Torres 2012: 15).

The year 1391 marked a pivotal moment as popular segments began expressing anti-Jewish sentiment through public violence. Large crowds rioted in Sevilla, Córdoba, Valencia, Toledo, Ciudad Real, and Barcelona; protestors destroyed Jewish property and, in some cases, even executed residents in public space (Kamen 2014: 28–65). It is unclear who incited the masses. Clear it is, however, that by the turn of the century, Iberian Jews inhabited a paradoxical state of existence. They had become targets of systemic exclusion and popular violence while at the same time remaining necessary to the social order.

Iberian efforts to remap religious boundaries occured within broader geopolitical shifts. After the advance of North African Berbers into Al-Andalus and the collapse of the Umayyad Caliphate, Jews and *mozárabes* (Christians residing in Islamic territories) migrated into historically Christian provinces where they were to a certain degree accepted by Castilian and Aragonese authorities (Nirenberg 1996: 37; Greer, Mignolo, and Quilligan 2007: 11). This dynamic imploded with the Decree of Expulsion of 1492. In it, the Catholic kings "ordered the separation of those Jews in all the cities, towns, and places in our kingdoms and domains, creating separate places for the Jews, hoping that with this separation the problem [of apostasy] would be solved" (Cowans 2003: 21). This decree illuminates the extent to which the Crown sought to configure its body politic around distinct religious identities (Glazier and Hellwig 2004: 256–63, 855–62). Although the Spanish Crown and its allies took deliberate steps to demarcate religious difference and to expunge the "Jewish trace," they were not alone. The executive council of the Roman Catholic Church also contributed to the racialization of religious difference.

In the late fifteenth century, the Spanish Crown orchestrated the overthrow of Al-Andalus in what became known as the **Reconquista** (Elliott 1977; Ladero Quesada 1989). The Reconquista, as Ramón Grosfoguel notes, signified an "ethnic cleansing of the Andalusian territory," which "produced a physical genocide and cultural genocide" because "Jews and Muslims who stayed in the territory were either killed (physical genocide) or forced to conversion (cultural genocide)" (2013: 78). While the capitulation of Alhambra in 1491 dealt Islam an existential blow, the Reconquista would symbolize the natural superiority of Western Christianity in the modern world (López-Baralt 1989: 32). In 1487, Muslims residing in the city of Málaga eventually succumbed to military attacks despite a prolonged resistance. And as "a punishment for their defiance," historian Michael Carr points out, "virtually the entire population was sold into slavery or given as 'gifts' to other Christian rulers" (2009: 7). In fact, the Catholic kings designated ten large ships to deport Muslim insurrectionists to the Berber lands in Northern Africa (Ladero Quesada 1967; Ladero Quesada 1993). Muslims could also leave voluntarily. If Muslims submitted requests fifty days in advance, then Castilian authorities guaranteed a "safe and free passage" at any point during a three-year period (Cowans 2003: 17). Jews suffered a similar fate. As in the northern kingdoms, Jews were banned from assuming high-ranking positions. According to the Surrender Treaty, the royals "shall not permit Jews to have any power or authority over Moors, nor shall they be allowed to collect any kind of rent from them" (Cowans 2003: 17). Moreover, Jewish "natives of Granada and the Albaicín and its surrounding areas" who refused conversion had to "leave for the Berber lands within three years" (Cowans 2003: 19). In this way, the Reconquista enacted physical and epistemic violence.

March 1492 marked a watershed moment. Two months after the overthrow of Granada, the Catholic kings eradicated Jews from their territories by signing the Expulsion Decree. In this decree, the Spanish Crown "order[ed] all of the Jews and

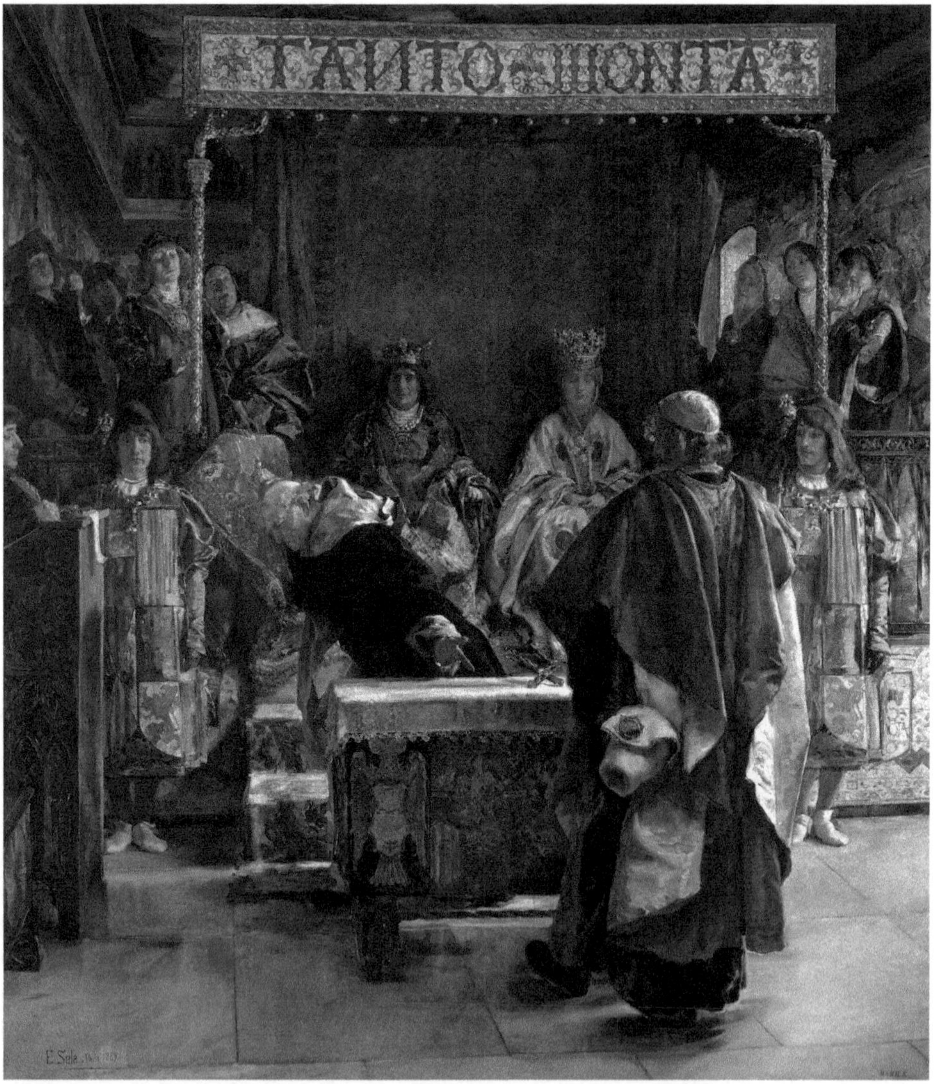

FIGURE 2.1 *Expulsion of the Jews from Spain (Expulsión de los judíos de España)*, c. *1889*. Source: *Oil on canvas painting by Emilio Sala/Wikimedia Commons.*

Jewesses of any age who live and reside and are in our kingdoms and domains, including natives as well as those who are not natives, and who for whatever reason or purpose may have come here or are here, to leave all of our kingdoms and domains along with their sons and daughters and male and female servants and Jewish family members small and large of any age by the end of this coming July of the present year" (Cowans 2003: 22). The authorities would execute Jews who remained and harshly punish Christians who provided refuge. Jews who remained risked death; they lived in a state of illegality. Castilian authorities deported thousands of families to Portugal, Italy, and northern Africa in what became known as the Iberian Exodus. The Expulsion Decree furthered an imperial Christian identity.

In this section, we discussed how theologically informed discourses of blood purity racialized religious identity in late medieval Iberia. By implementing purity statutes, Spanish rulers, in conjunction with their allies and the Holy Office of the Inquisition, consolidated power around natural Christian bloodlines. Only Iberians who offered proof of genealogical purity could hold governmental, financial, or ecclesial positions of authority. In the end, by defining Old Christian status an outcome of reproduction, *limpieza de sangre* (purity of blood) reconfigured Jewish and Muslim blood as an insurmountable impediment to genuine conversion. Moriscos and conversos embodied a noxious threat to the social order.

After the Reconquista, Fernando and Isabel would turn their focus abroad. They established two objectives: recuperate Jerusalem from the Muslims and secure economic advantages over Portugal. Fortunately for the Catholic kings, a Genoese

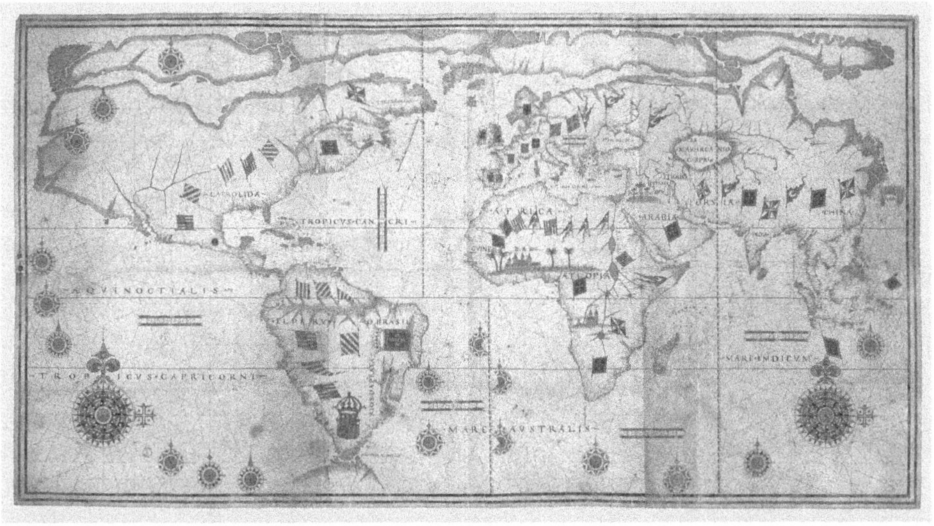

FIGURE 2.2 *In this Lemos Planisphère map by Pedro de Lemos, one can see the Global Lines of Demarcation as established by Alcáçovas (1480), Tordesillas (1494), and Zaragoza (1529).* Source: *Public Domain original in Bibliothèque nationale de France/Wikimedia Commons.*

sailor by the name of Cristobal Colón promised to fulfill both by establishing a lucrative trading route to Asia. This project would not only require fortuity but also considerable resources. If achieved, however, it would enable Spain to accomplish its global ambitions. Columbus would extend imperial dominion into the tropics by sailing "*south* to the Indies" (Wey Gómez 2008: 4). Within a few years, Spain and Portugal would carve up the Atlantic world and, by the end of the century, divide up the rest of the globe (see Figure 2.2). The next section analyzes this process by exploring the ways in which aspects of the **scholastic tradition** informed the Columbian Enterprise.

The Columbian Enterprise

The year 1492 introduced the modern/colonial world by igniting the African slave trade, dispossession of land, and destruction of Indigenous ecologies (Wallerstein 1983: 11–44; Quíjano 2000; Mignolo 2005). Imperial maps illustrate this process by showing how Christian empires transformed the southern hemisphere into colonial space. Columbus, and the Iberian cosmographers that followed, employed a scholastic vision of nature to map the tropics. This section examines key primary sources that reflect how Iberians conceptualized global expansion through the dispossession of space.

The Treaty of Alcáçovas, signed in 1480, resolved fifteenth-century disputes between Spain and Portugal (Gardiner Davenport and Paullin 1917: 33–48). From 1475 to 1479, Iberian empires had engaged in military conflicts over the northwestern coast of Africa and its surrounding islands. Intending to reach a diplomatic truce and define commercial terms of ownership, the Portuguese royals, King Alfonso V (1432–81) and Prince João II (1455–95), convened a meeting with the Catholic kings of Spain (Prieto Yegros 2006: 38–43). The Treaty of Alcáçovas, moreover, received approval the following year from Pope Sixtus IV (1414–84), who had just commissioned the Spanish Inquisition. Through the papal bull *Aeterni regis* (1481), Sixtus IV validated the agreement on behalf of the Roman Catholic Church (Gardiner Davenport and Paullin 1917: 49–55).

Alcáçovas deserves careful analysis because its theological discourse provides the framework for imperial expansion. The treaty begins by equating adherence to its terms with Christian obedience. Signatories claim to emulate Christ's "infinite goodness and clemency" by entering into this agreement (Gardiner Davenport and Paullin 1917: 43). After all, Christ "ordered that peace be procured," thus instituting the legal precedent for imperial dominion (Gardiner Davenport and Paullin 1917: 43). Spain and Portugal swear before God and the Virgin Mary to uphold the agreement, making its terms "firm and valid forever" (Gardiner Davenport and Paullin 1917: 46). Alcáçovas, therefore, grounds imperial dominion on Christ's identity as the Prince of Peace. Serving more than a formality, theological considerations also appear in Isabel and Fernando's concessions. The Spanish monarchs "renounced all rights, laws, customs, usages, actions, and opinions of doctors" (i.e., theologians) that could be invoked to claim Portuguese territories. These terms restricted scholastic theology from justifying Spanish incursions into Africa. In this way, the theological discourse of Alcáçovas "opened for the first time in history a distinct perspective that enabled Iberian kingdoms to henceforth allocate dominion" of territories outside Christendom (Prieto Yegros 2006: 39; translation by the author). In subsequent years, imperial and ecclesial authorities would have to configure global expansion in accordance with these terms.

Alcáçovas geographic demarcation reveals the way in which Iberian empires mapped space and race together. The Portuguese Cantino Map, produced around 1502 (see Figures 2.3 and 2.4), depicts imperial mastery over space by inserting Spanish and Portuguese flags throughout the northwestern African coast and its surrounding islands. Notably, by awarding Portugal exclusive rights over "all the trade" east of the dividing line, Alcáçovas grants legitimacy to the transatlantic slave trade. Furthermore, the Cantino Map also exhibits a racial imaginary, as evidenced by the depiction of Black bodies in the southern hemisphere (Harley 2001: 76). Iberian empires linked spatial dispossession to racial commodification.

Alcáçovas would galvanize Columbus expeditions by granting Spain exclusive rights over the Canary Islands—located at approximately 28° north of the equator and directly west of Cape Bojador. Sailor-merchants from Catalunya entered this archipelago in the late 1300s (Phillips and Phillips 1992: 55–60). And although Castile did not fully subjugate the native Guanche people until 1496, Alcáçovas transformed this group of islands into colonial space. Atlantic historians William and Karla Rahn Phillips indicate that countless "enslaved Guanches were taken to be sold in Spain or in the Madeira Islands settled by the Portuguese" while "other slaves remained in the Canaries to work for European settlers" (Phillips and Phillips 1992: 59). By confirming the lucrative possibilities of tropical climates, the Canaries provided the conceptual and literal "point

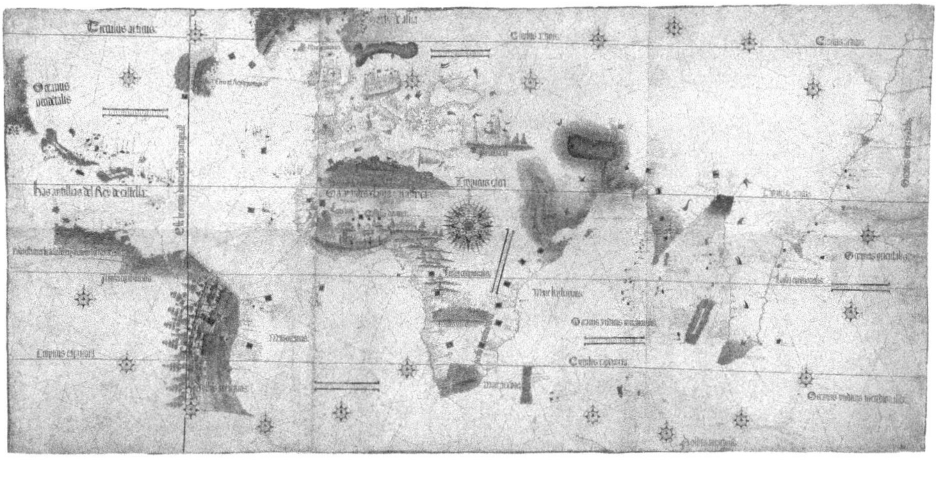

FIGURE 2.3 *Line of Demarcation after Tordesillas, Portuguese Cantino World Map, c. 1502.* Source: *Public Domain original in Biblioteca Estense Universitaria, Modena, Italy/Wikimedia Commons.*

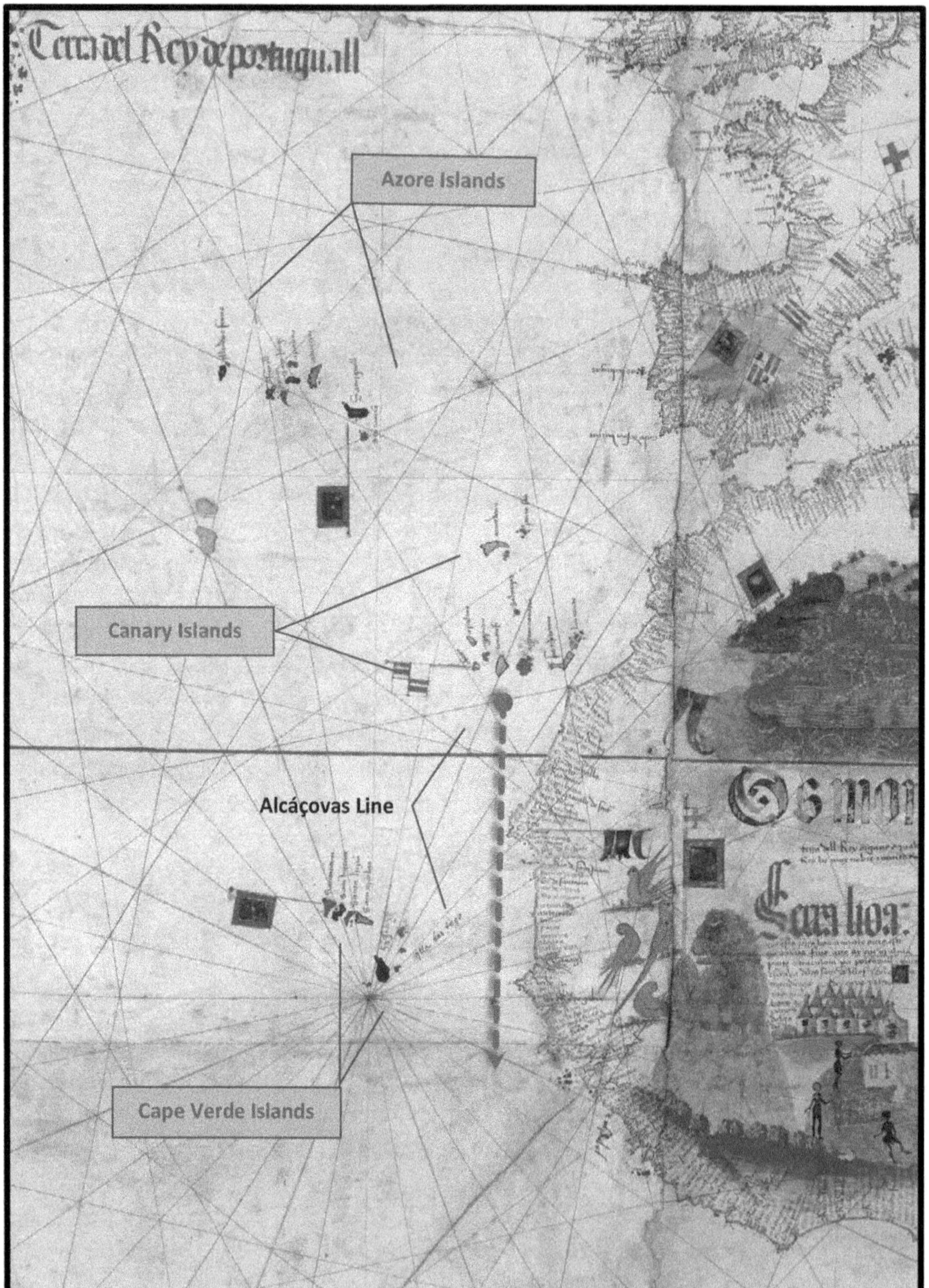

FIGURE 2.4 *Details of Portuguese and Spanish territories along the West African coast. Portuguese Cantino Map. Superimposed location points marked by the author.* Source: *Public Domain original in Biblioteca Estense Universitaria, Modena, Italy/Wikimedia Commons.*

of departure" for Columbus enterprise (Phillips and Phillips 1992: 145). Apparently, the Canaries incited the first "shock of discovery." According to Mediterranean historian David Abulafia, Iberian colonialists who crossed the Atlantic were surprised to see that Amerindians were

> isolated, simple, living unadorned lives, more like the "Stone Age" Canary islanders than like the silk–clad natives of the Far Eastern empires. Not for nothing did the earliest printed accounts of Columbus' first voyage to the Caribbean refer to his discoveries as the "New Canaries."
>
> (2008: 5)

Alcáçovas repercussions reverberated across the Atlantic. After 1492, Iberian merchants would begin transferring manufacturing techniques and systems of labor from sugar plantations (*ingenious de azúcar*) in the Azore, Madeira, and Canary Islands "to the newly discovered Caribbean Islands early in the colonizing process" (Phillips and Phillips 1992: 59). In fact, "Columbus had come from the Canary Islands on his second voyage in 1493 when he introduced sugar cane into Haiti" (Verlinden 1995: 244). Less than two decades later, colonialists would transform the Caribbean basin, and eventually Mexico, Peru, and later Cuba, into the global center of sugarcane production.

The Catholic kings inscribed official terms for the Columbian Enterprise in the Capitulaciones de Santa Fe, signed in Granada on April 17, 1492. In five short articles, this charter outlines Columbus objectives and lists the rights and privileges of both parties. From the outset, the royals direct Columbus to "discover" and thereby "acquire" new "mainlands and islands" on behalf of Spain (Jara and Spadaccini 1989: 383–5). From its inception, the enterprise intended to fulfill an imperialist desire for expansion.

The charter's terms also foreground capitalist accumulation. Using generic terms such as "islands and mainlands," which function as "empty signifiers constituting a semantic void," the text leaves the places "unnamed and undefined," or as *terra nullus* (Abufalia 2008: 155). Literary scholar Evelina Gužauskytė describes this silence as "a work of true craftsmanship of diplomacy and intuition" (Gužauskytė 2014: 3). She maintains that it laid the "ground for naming as an instrument for announcing territorial claims" (Gužauskytė 2014: 3). In stark contrast to this silence, the text identifies Columbus as the one who fills this semantic void. As the 1510 map of Juan de la Cosa displays, the words, memories, and interests of colonialists would reconfigure the tropics. Rather than using generic terms, the charter refers to Columbus specifically as "Admiral of the Ocean." In turn, this title authorizes him to name the anonymous islands and mainlands (Gužauskytė 2014: 170–95). Upon conferring the titles of "Viceroy" and "Governor General," the text establishes political order by authorizing Columbus to name "three persons for each [government] office" (Jara and Spadaccini 1989: 381). He embodies imperial authority. The charter also delineates the commodification of natural resources. According to the agreement, the Crown would retain ninety percent of all commodities, leaving Columbus with ten percent of any "goods, whether they be pearls, precious stones, gold or silver, [and] spices" (Jara and Spadaccini 1989: 384). Columbus charter, therefore, initiates a political-economic-legal apparatus, which would come to define the modern world-system.

In his journal's prologue, Columbus outlines the religious ideology undergirding imperialist expansion. Columbus begins by extoling the Crown's success in "combating the religion of Mahomet and all idolatries and heresies" and subsequently "expelling all the Jews from your kingdoms and territories" (Gužauskytė 2014: 81). Columbus identifies three main objectives in Al-Andalus: (1) to meet their rulers; (2) to ascertain the distribution of towns and lands; and (3) to determine how they could be converted to the Holy Faith. Mapping political, geographic, and religious landscapes was a central function imperial expansion.

In the wake of the Reconquista, Columbus sees the defeat and deportation of non-Christians as directly related to his enterprise. According to Columbus, the Crown first had to bring "to an end the war against the remaining Moorish kingdom on European soil, terminating the campaign in the great city of Granada" (Keller 1994: 81). Only after doing so, was the Crown able to commission "me to sail to those regions of India" (Dunn and Kelly Jr. 1989: 81). Columbus believes his enterprise could help fund Christendom's wars against Islam. In fact, in the March 4 letter, Columbus promises to help finance the liberation of the Holy Lands from Muslim control (Dunn and Kelly Jr. 1989). He assures the Crown that "in seven years from today I will be able to pay Your Highnesses for five thousand cavalry and fifty thousand foot soldiers for the war and conquest of Jerusalem, for which purpose this enterprise was undertaken" (Zamora 1993: 181–97). As postcolonial theologian Catherine Keller remarks, "the crusades, as apocalyptically inspired movements against dark unchristian peoples, had already provided the transitional inversion of the apocalypse into imperial aggression" (Columbus 1992: 67). And so, the persecution of Muslims and Jews in the conquest of Al-Andalus functions as both the precondition and the purpose for Columbus's enterprise.

Bartolomé de Las Casas and Christianity's Birth in the Americas

Historical records indicate that Bartolomé de Las Casas participated directly in the early Spanish conquest. Although details about his nascent years are scant, it is clear that Las Casas held a front row seat to the Columbian Enterprise. Bartolomé's father, Pedro de Las Casas was among the first **encomenderos** in the New World. Pedro, in fact, accompanied Columbus on his second voyage and in 1498 returned to Seville on a ship carrying over three hundred enslaved Amerindians. The Admiral rewarded Pedro with a young Amerindian slave named Juanico, whom he gave to his adolescent son, Bartolomé, as a gift (Wagner and Parish 1967: 12–13; Clayton 2012: 21).

Bartolomé de Las Casas completed his first transatlantic venture in 1502, just ten years after Columbus's initial voyage. At the age of 18, Las Casas, along with his father, sailed with Nicolás de Ovando, a Cistercian friar and member of the military order of Alcántara. The Spanish monarchs commissioned Ovando, who commanded thirty-two ships and 2,500 men, to replace the unruly Francisco de Bobadilla as Governor of Santo Domingo, and he served in this official capacity for 8 years (Clayton 2012: 23). Las Casas set foot on Hispaniola (modern-day Haiti/Dominican Republic) for the first time on April 15, 1502. Besides managing the agricultural production on his father's encomienda, located near the city of La Vega, Las Casas also traveled throughout the island. He partook in (or heard about first hand) several excursions in which Ovando's army forced the Taínos, the Indigenous people of the Caribbean, into submission. He was thus aware of how military interventions, under the pretext of just war, served to procure slaves. These experiences went on to inform his *Brief Account* (1542), the well-known text that would fuel the infamous Black Legend (de Las Casas 1992a). After this four-year venture, he returned to Iberia in 1506 and soon thereafter arranged to take holy vows; Las Casas entered the priesthood the subsequent spring (Clayton 2012: 50).

Las Casas crossed the Atlantic a second time in 1509. This time, as a 26-year-old priest, he arrived in Santo Domingo with members of the nobility and Columbus immediate family (de Las Casas 1992a: 51). As before, Las Casas oversaw the Amerindians held at his father's encomienda based along the Yanique River (de Las Casas 1992a: 56). In 1512, Las Casas accepted Panfilo de Narváez's invitation to join Diego de Velásquez in the conquest of *Juana* (Cuba). Las Casas would continue participating in such Taíno raids until 1515. In doing so, he acquired more slaves who, by working the mines or fields, generated additional wealth for Las Casas. Years later, he "acknowledged that he took more care of this [business] than of teaching them the faith" (Wagner and Parish 1967: 7; Las Casas 1994a). Bartolomé directly participated in what he would later denounce as the "destruction of the Indies."

The arrival of the Dominicans—the Order of Preachers—would lead Las Casas down a path of resistance. Under the leadership of Fray Pedro de Córdoba, the first Dominican missionaries disembarked on Hispaniola's shores in 1510 (Hernández 1986: 317–42). Hailing from the priory of San Estebán in Salamanca, they were sent by the Master General Cajetan (Tommaso de Vío) to start a convent. During this period, Iberian universities and monasteries were undergoing theological reform. The scholastic ideal of *contemptus mundi* ("the fullness of life") would define the "mentality of the Spanish renaissance" (Fernández Rodriguez 1994: 19; translation by the author). Salamanca apparently embodied the highest virtues of the Catholic reformation (Brufau Prats 1989: 33). Steeped in this religious and intellectual milieu, Dominicans combined practices of austerity, devout spirituality, scholasticism, and a missionary impulse. All these would shape Las Casas's identity.

The Dominicans would shift Las Casas' social location. Like other Mendicant orders, Dominicans made vows of chastity, obedience, and poverty. Lantigua explains that

FIGURE 2.5 *Bartolomé de Las Casas with Amerindian, an 1876 painting in the Senate Wing of the US Capitol building.* Source: *Oil on plaster painting by Constantino Brumidi/ Wikimedia Commons.*

these missionaries spurned personal wealth and decided to live among the Indigenous people. Inhabiting a marginal location, Lantigua suggests, allowed these friars to perceive and eventually criticize their inhumane treatment (2015: 216). And so, when confronted by the systemic violence of the encomienda, this ethical impulse led Fray Antón Montesinos to preach a scathing condemnation. On the Fourth Sunday of Advent in 1511, Montesinos famously asked the encomenderos: "by what right and with what justice do you so violently enslave these Indians?" (de Las Casas 1994c: 1761–5; translation by the author). Risking personal harm, Dominican friars persisted in their critique of Indigenous exploitation and, in some cases, withheld the Eucharist from encomenderos. In the end, their prophetic witness compelled Las Casas to join the Order in 1522.

Direct exposure to the systems of labor had a profound impact on Las Casas. After becoming a Dominican friar, Las Casas renounced all personal property. Doing so would alter his relationship to the Amerindians, since he no longer benefitted from their labor. Living in close proximity to Indigenous people made Las Casas aware of their suffering. This enabled him to perceive the unethical nature of the encomienda and to reevaluate the method of evangelism. A reconfigured doctrine of Christ (Christology) spurred this transformation. Rather than seeing God on the side of the powerful, he began to see Christ—the embodiment of God—on the side of the poor and the oppressed. Las Casas drew on first-hand experience and from the Salamanca School to reconceptualize the spread of Christianity in the New World. He dedicated several years to writing the influential text *De Único Modo* (1534) (Parish and Weidman 1992: 36). In it, Las Casas persuasively argued that evangelization of the

FIGURE 2.6 *Bartolomé de Las Casas baptizes Indian prisoners in Cuba in 1511.* Source: *Public Domain uploaded by Biblioteca Rector Machado y Nuñez/Wikimedia Commons.*

Indies must be based on Christ's teachings and example; as such, it may be carried out only through non-violent means (de Las Casas 1992b). In retrospect, Las Casas attributes his transformation to the Dominicans' prophetic witness; they shifted his theological imagination by altering his social location.

From its inception, Christianity in the Americas was inextricably linked to systems of production. Labor and religion were configured together. After subjugating the Taíno and Arawak Natives of the Caribbean islands, Governor Ovando introduced a system of labor called the *encomienda* in 1502. Under this system, the crown awarded conquistadores who had faithfully completed their military service with land and with Amerindian workers. Historian Lawrence Clayton explains how the encomienda, as "the central instrument of Indian despoliation and exploitation" was "later exported to other islands and finally to the mainland as the Spanish conquest proceeded in the next half century" (2012: 28). The encomienda would, in effect, introduce a system of exploitation that would enslave vast segments of the Indigenous population (van Deusen 2012; Reséndez 2016). In fact, historian Nancy van Deusen "discovered that in the sixteenth century at least 650,000 Indigenous people were enslaved and forced to relocate to foreign lands throughout the inter-American and transatlantic Iberian world" (van Deusen 2015: 2). In the Americas, encomenderos were also expected to educate their subjects in the Christian faith. But rather than functioning as faithful conduits of Christianity, conquistadores-turned-encomenderos would focus on extracting tribute from their subjects (Tutino 2011: 72). For this reason, Las Casas proclaimed that in "the nine years of his government of this island, [Ovando] was no more interested in the indoctrination and salvation of the Indians than if they were stick and stone, or cats and dogs" (de Las Casas 1994a: 1345–55; translation by the author). The encomienda would simultaneously generate revenue for Spain and produce new converts for the Church. This system of labor became an integral part of the disciplinary practices through which Native peoples would acquire a colonial identity.

During the sixteenth century, the Spanish Crown established colonial hegemony by creating organs of governance throughout the Atlantic world. Historian C. H. Haring characterizes the first period of political organization (1492–1530) as the age of the *adelantados* (1985: 69–81). Immediately after Columbus first voyage, Charles V appointed Juan Rodríguez de Fonseca, "archdeacon of the cathedral of Seville and the queen's chaplain, to take care of all matters relating to the newly discovered lands" (Haring 1985: 94). And in 1503, at the behest of Queen Isabel, Fonseca founded the House of Trade (*Casa de Contratación*), which regulated travel and commerce to and from the Indies and oversaw the production of maps and cosmographic guides for navigation. After Fonseca's death in 1524, Charles formed the Council of the Indies (*El Real y Supremo Consejo de Indias*) to oversee juridical administration and provide the royals with counsel on colonial affairs (Olson 1991: 146, 211). The Crown also asserted jurisdiction over what became the southwestern United States, Mexico, Central America, and the Caribbean by forming the Viceroyalty of New Spain upon the ruins of the Aztec capital Tenochtitlán.

The system of repartimiento scattered Amerindians among the colonialists to labor in private estates or on public projects. Theoretically, they were supposed to receive wages and to be protected from slave raids (Olson 1991: 515–16). It was hardly a new system. "[M]odeled on the long conquest of the Canary Islands over the course of the fifteenth century," it was conveniently applied when manual labor became scarce or encomenderos faced legal opposition (Clayton 2012: 41). In the Americas, this division of labor would entail the racialization of *Indios*; for only their bodies were conscribed to forced labor. Las Casas describes this arrangement in *Historia de las Indias*, declaring that

> even the beasts usually have some liberty to go graze in the pastures, a liberty which our Spaniards denied the poor miserable Indians. And so, in truth, they were in perpetual slavery, for they were deprived of their free will to do anything other than what the cruelty and avarice of the Spaniards desired, not like prisoners but like beasts whose owners keep them tethered.
>
> (de Las Casas 1994b: 1353; translation by the author)

As historian Laura Lewis indicates, all "'race' based classifications nevertheless satisfied the need for different kinds of labor, became the basis for rules about individual privileges and obligations, and helped to maintain the fiction of the religious and ancestral 'cleanliness' (*limpieza*) of Spaniards" (2012: 101). Yet racial classification of entire populations was part of Spain's broader reconfiguration of local ecologies, which entailed mastery over space. Historian Alejandro Cañeque explains how the repartimiento transformed Indigenous "principles of rotation and compulsion," such that "community work that had characterized the pre–Hispanic modality rapidly disappeared" and matured into a "system of exploitation of native labor for the benefit of the population of European descent" (2004: 201). By mid-century, colonial authorities began engineering the displacement and relocation of Indigenous people throughout central Mexico. In doing so, administration officials filled the swelling demand for agricultural labor, urban construction, and mineral extraction in surrounding regions. Colonialist exploitation presupposed the racial inferiority of Amerindian peoples.

From the outset, the encomienda and repartimiento subsumed local ecologies within transatlantic networks of production and consumption. The circulation of New World commodities—sugar, tobacco, and silver—would ignite a racialized labor market that began with the commodification of Brown Indigenous bodies and soon thereafter Black African bodies. In turn, incorporation of the Americas into a global market would present investment opportunities for financial institutions in Europe (Wallerstein 1974; Smith 2010). The colonial matrix of power came to undergird a capitalist world-system (Quijano and Wallerstein 1992: 553). However, the colonial violence that generated such wealth remained largely hidden. Across the Atlantic, Amerindians and Africans were forced to labor in the fields, mines, estates, and bedrooms of their "natural" lords. Their labor not only yielded return on investment; it also generated taxes for the Crown and tithes for the Church (Ricard 1966). Las Casas would inhabit and benefit from, but ultimately seek to reform these colonial structures. And as the ensuing debates reveal, Las Casas and his fellow scholastics would deploy a theological geography to either to justify or to scrutinize the nascent colonial order.

Las Casas evaluates native societies through the lens of natural law. He claims that Amerindians live according to Aristotle and Augustine's definition of what constitutes a rational society (de Las Casas 1994c: 1792–3; translation by the author). In what undoubtedly surprised Iberian audiences, Las Casas contends that Amerindians "run their governments according to laws that are often superior to our own" (de Las Casas 1992b: 64). Many Native customs, he says, surpass those of the "English, the French and some groups in our native Spain" (de Las Casas 1992b: 66). Even some Roman and Greek customs are inferior when compared to Amerindian practices, he says (de Las Casas 1992b: 65–6; translation by the author). This rhetorical move reveals Las Casas subversive disposition. He essentially uses the scholastic tradition to classify Amerindian societies as superior to Christian empires. A colonial logic, however, upholds this argument. Las Casas presupposes the universal scope of northern systems of knowledge. This assumption enables him to use Aristotle and Augustine in order to evaluate civilizations across the Atlantic world. In doing so, Las Casas leaves his epistemic authority intact. He, like his opponents, could properly discern the order of things.

Las Casas relies on medieval cosmology to bolster Native sovereignty. He claims that Amerindians "are not servants by nature; and neither due to the *nature of the earth nor the effect of the heavens*" as "Father Bernaldo O.P. affirmed in his second proposition" (de Las Casas 1994c: 1793; translation by the author). In essence, Las Casas insists that Indigenous peoples' natural capacity "comes from the fostering influence of the heavens, from the kind conditions of the places God gave them to live in, the fair and clement weather" (de Las Casas 1992b: 63).

Amerindians are capable in all matters of government, Las Casas assert, because of how the cosmic order effects their bodies. He elaborates by writing:

> Due to all these influences—the broad/celestial, the narrow/terrestrial, the essential/accidental—the Indians come to be endowed, first by force of nature, next by force of personal achievement and experience, with the three kinds of self–rule required: (1) personal, by which one knows how to rule oneself, (2) domestic, by which one knows how to rule a household, and (3) political, knowledge of how to set up and rule a city.
>
> (de Las Casas 1992b: 65)

The hierarchical role of causation in this extended passage reflects the influence of Aristotelian physics. Note how Las Casas emphasizes the way in which higher elements affect lower ones: heavenly ("celestial") motion affects the earth ("terrestrial"), which in turn, shapes human ("accidental") bodies. On such grounds, tropical habitats provide the proper conditions for human flourishing. The "forces of nature," however, do not negate human agency. Rather, Amerindians acquire the ability for self-rule "by force of personal achievement and experience." In the end, "even without Christian faith and knowledge of the true God," Amerindians are the rightful lords of the Indies (de Las Casas 1994c: 1793). Las Casas proclaims that they "have and hold their realms, their lands, by natural law and by the law of nations," and hence, "owe allegiance to no one higher than themselves, outside themselves, neither de jure nor de facto" (de Las Casas 1992b: 66). Through God's providential design, their sovereignty is conferred by nature itself. In Aristotelian terms, they actualize their God-given capacity because of the quality of the tropics.

Las Casas life and legacy testify to the subversive capacity of the Christian faith. In following the early Dominican missionaries, Las Casas enacted an ancient Christian principle: solidarity with the poor and oppressed. Solidarity with the Indigenous people compelled him to confront the evils of colonialism. In the end, Las Casas summoned resources from the history of Christian thought to articulate and uphold the religious freedom, human dignity, and political sovereignty of Amerindian people.

Conclusion

In this chapter, I mapped the origins of Christianity in the Americas by analyzing key primary sources that elucidate the role of scholastic theology in the racial and geographic hierarchies that emerged in the early modern world. As one of the first trained theologians to reside in the Americas and seriously grapple with the ethical and intellectual dilemmas triggered by the so-called Discovery, Las Casas introduced many of the terms that continue to inform contemporary debates about slavery, human rights, land ownership, and environmental justice. The historic Valladolid debate of 1550–1 between Las Casas and the jurist-theologian, Juan Gínes de Sepúlveda (1494–1573) was a prime example. Close analysis of the geographic dimensions of Las Casas thought, which have been widely ignored, could expand our understanding of how his legacy can continue to speak to us today.

Further Reading

Clatyon, L.A. 2012. *Bartolomé de las Casas: A Biography.* New York: Cambridge University Press.

Clayton, L. A., and D. M. Lantigua, eds. 2020. *Bartolomé de Las Casas and the Defense of Amerindian Rights: A Brief History with Documents.* University of Alabama Press.

de Las Casas, B. 1992a. *A Short Account of the Destruction of the Indies.* New York: Penguin Books.

Hering Torres, M.S., M.E. Martínez, and D. Nirenberg, eds. 2012. *Race and Blood in the Iberian World.* Zurich: LIT Verlag.

Martínez, M.E. 2008. *Genealogical Fictions: Limpieza de Sangre, Religion, and Gender in Colonial Mexico.* Stanford: Stanford University Press.

References

Abulafia, D. 2008. *The Discovery of Mankind: Atlantic Encounters in the Age of Columbus.* New Haven: Yale University Press.
Baer, Y. 1961. *A History of the Jews in Christian Spain*, trans. Louis Schoffman, 1st ed., 2 vols. Philadelphia: Jewish Publication Society of America.
Brufau Prats, J. 1989. *La Escuela de Salamanca ante el descubrimiento del Nuevo Mundo.* Salamanca : Editorial San Esteban.
Burns, R.I. 1973. *Islam under the Crusaders: Colonial Survival in the Thirteenth-Century Kingdom of Valencia.* Princeton: Princeton University Press.
Cañeque, A. 2004. *The King's Living Image: The Culture and Politics of Viceregal Power in Colonial Mexico.* New York: Routledge.
Carr, M. 2009. *Blood and Faith: The Purging of Muslim Spain.* New York: The New Press.
Castro, A. 1983. *España en su Historia: Cristianos, Moros y Judíos*, 2nd edn. Barcelona: Grijalbo Mondadori.
Chazan, R. 2010. *Reassessing Jewish Life in Medieval Europe.* New York: Cambridge University Press.
Clatyon, L.A. 2012. *Bartolomé de las Casas: A Biography.* New York: Cambridge University Press.
Columbus, C. 1992. *The Voyage of Christopher Columbus: Columbus's Own Journal of Discovery*, trans. J. G. Cummins, Newly Restored Edition. New York: St. Martin's Press.
Cowans, J., ed. 2003. *Early Modern Spain: A Documentary History.* Philadelphia: University of Pennsylvania Press.
de Covarrubias Orozco, S. 2006. *Tesoro de la Lengua Castellana O Española.* Pamplona: Universidad de Navarra.
de Las Casas, B. 1992a. *A Short Account of the Destruction of the Indies.* New York: Penguin Books.
de Las Casas, B. 1992b. *The Only Way*, ed. H.R. Parish, trans. F.P. Sullivan. Mahwah, NJ: Paulist Press.
de Las Casas, B. 1994a. *Historia de las Indias*, ed. Paulino Castañeda Delgado, Jesús Ángel Barreda, and Isacio Pérez Fernández, vol. 1. Madrid: Alianza Editorial.
de Las Casas, B. 1994b. *Historia de las Indias*, ed. Paulino Castañeda Delgado, Jesús Ángel Barreda, and Isacio Pérez Fernández, vol. 2. Madrid: Alianza Editorial.
de Las Casas, B. 1994c. *Historia de las Indias*, ed. Paulino Castañeda Delgado, Jesús Ángel Barreda, and Isacio Pérez Fernández, vol. 3. Madrid: Alianza Editorial.
Dunn, O.C. and J.E. Kelley Jr., eds. 1989. *The Diario of Christopher Columbus's First Voyage to America, 1492–1493.* Norman: University of Oklahoma Press.
Elliott, J.H. 1977. *Imperial Spain, 1469–1716.* New York: New American Library.
Fernández Rodríguez, P. 1994. *Los Dominicos en el Contexto de la Primera Evangelización de México, 1526–1550*, vol. 3. Salamanca: Editorial San Esteban.
Gardiner Davenport, F. and C.O. Paullin, eds. 1917. *European Treaties Bearing on the History of the United States and Its Dependencies*, vol. 1. Washington, DC: Carnegie Institution of Washington.
Glazier, M. and M. Hellwig, eds. 2004. *The Modern Catholic Encyclopedia.* Collegeville, MN: Liturgical Press.
Glick, T.F. 1979. *Islamic and Christian Spain in the Early Middle Ages.* Princeton: Princeton University Press.
Greer, M.R., W.D. Mignolo, and M. Quilligan. 2007. "Introduction." In *Rereading the Black Legend: The Discourses of Religious and Racial Difference in the Renaissance Empires,*

edited by M.R. Greer, W.D. Mignolo, and M. Quilligan, 1–24. Chicago: University of Chicago Press.
Grosfoguel, R. 2013. "The Structure of Knowledge in Westernized Universities Epistemic Racism/Sexism and the Four Genocides/Epistemicides of the Long 16th Century." *Human Architecture: Journal of the Sociology of Self-Knowledge* XI (1): 73–90.
Gužauskytė, E. 2014. *Christopher Columbus's Naming in the Diarios of the Four Voyages (1492–1504): A Discourse of Negotiation*. Toronto: University of Toronto.
Haring, C.H. 1985. *The Spanish Empire in America*. San Diego: Harcourt.
Harley, J. B. 2001. *The New Nature of Maps: Essays in the History of Cartography*. Baltimore: Johns Hopkins University Press.
Hering Torres, M.S. 2012. "Purity of Blood: Problems of Interpretation." In *Race and Blood in the Iberian World*, edited by M.S. Hering Torres, M.E. Martínez, and D. Nirenberg, 11–38. Zurich: LIT Verlag.
Hernández, R. 1986. "Primeros Dominicos del Convento de San Esteban en América." *Ciencia Tomista* 113 (1986): 317–42.
Jara, R. and N. Spadaccini, eds. 1989. *1492–1992: Re/discovering Colonial Writing*. Minneapolis: Prisma Institute.
Kamen, H. 2014. *The Spanish Inquisition: A Historical Revision*. New Haven: Yale University Press.
Keller, C. 1994. "The Breast, the Apocalypse, and the Colonial Journey." *Journal of Feminist Studies in Religion* 10 (1): 53–72.
Ladero Quesada, M.A. 1967. *Castilla y la conquista del Reino de Granada*. Valladolid: Universidad de Valladolid, Secretariado de Publicaciones.
Ladero Quesada, M.A. 1989. *Granada: Historia de un País Islámico (1232–1571)*, 3rd edn. Madrid: Gredos.
Ladero Quesada, M.A. 1993. *La Incorporación de Granada a la Corona de Castilla: Actas del Symposium Conmemorativo del Quinto*. Granada: Diputación Provincial de Granada.
Lantigua, D.M. 2015. "The Freedom of the Gospel: Aquinas, Subversive Natural Law, and the Spanish Wars of Religion." *Modern Theology* 31 (2): 312–37.
Lewis, L. 2012. "Between Casta and Raza: The Example of Colonial Mexico." In *Race and Blood in the Iberian World*, edited by M.S. Hering Torres, M.E. Martínez, and D. Nirenberg, 99–123. Zurich: LIT Verlag.
López-Baralt, L. 1989. *Huellas del Islam en la Literatura Española: de Juan Ruiz a Juan Goytisolo*, 2nd edn. Madrid: Hiperión.
Martínez, M.E. 2008. *Genealogical Fictions: Limpieza de Sangre, Religion, and Gender in Colonial Mexico*. Stanford: Stanford University Press.
Menache, S. 1987. "The King, the Church, and the Jews: Some Considerations on the Expulsions from England and France." *Journal of Medieval History* 13: 223–36.
Mignolo, Walter D. 2005. *The Idea of Latin America*. Malden, MA: Wiley.
Nirenberg, D. 1996. *Communities of Violence: Persecution of Minorities in the Middle Ages*. Princeton: Princeton University Press.
Nirenberg, D. 2000. "El Concepto de la Raza en la España Medieval." *Edad Media: Revista de Historia* (3): 39–60.
Nirenberg, D. 2007. "Race and the Middle Ages: The Case of Spain and Its Jews." In *Rereading the Black Legend: The Discourses of Religious and Racial Difference in the Renaissance Empires*, edited by M.R. Greer, W.D. Mignolo, and M. Quilligan, 71–87. Chicago: University of Chicago Press.
Olson, J.S., ed. 1991. *Historical Dictionary of the Spanish Empire*. Westport, CT: Greenwood Press.

Parish, H.R. and H.E. Weidman, eds. 1992. *Las Casas en México: Historia y obra desconocidas*. Mexico City: Fondo de Cultura Económica.
Phillips, W.D. and C.R. Phillips. 1992. *The Worlds of Christopher Columbus*. Cambridge: Cambridge University Press.
Prieto Yegros, M. 2006. *El Tratado de Tordesillas*. Asunción: Intercontinental.
Quijano, A. 2000. "Coloniality of Power and Eurocentrism in Latin America." *International Sociology* 15 (2): 215–32.
Quijano, A. and I. Wallerstein. 1992. "Americanity as a Concept, or the Americas in the Modern World-system." *International Social Science Journal* 44 (134): 549–57.
Reséndez, A. 2016. *The Other Slavery: The Uncovered Story of Indian Enslavement in America*. Boston: Houghton Mifflin Harcourt.
Ricard, R. 1966. *The Spiritual Conquest of Mexico: An Essay on the Apostolate and the Evangelizing Methods of the Mendicant Orders in New Spain, 1523–1572*. Berkeley: University of California Press.
Richards, J. 1994. *Sex, Dissidence and Damnation Minority Groups in the Middle Ages*. New York: Routledge.
Roth, N. 1992. "The Jews of Spain and the Expulsion of 1492." *Historian* 55 (1): 17–30.
Sánchez-Albornoz, C. 1956. *España, un Enigma Histórico*, 2 vols. Buenos Aires: Editorial Sudamericana.
Smith, J. 2010. *Europe and the Americas: State Formation, Capitalism and Civilizations in Atlantic Modernity*. Leiden: Brill.
Tutino, J. 2011. *Making a New World: Founding Capitalism in the Bajío and Spanish North America*. Durham: Duke University Press.
van Deusen, N.E. 2012. "Seeing Indios in Sixteenth-Century Castile." *William and Mary Quarterly* 69 (2): 205–34.
van Deusen, N.E. 2015. *The Indigenous Struggle for Justice in Sixteenth-Century*. Spain, Durham: Duke University Press.
Verlinden. 1995. "The Transfer of Colonial Techniques: from the Mediterranean to the Atlantic." In *The European Opportunity*, edited by F. Fernández-Armesto, 225–54. New York: Routledge.
Wagner, H.R. and H.R. Parish. 1967. *The Life and Writings of Bartolomé de Las Casas*, 1st edn. Albuquerque: University of New Mexico Press.
Wallerstein, I.M. 1974. The Modern World-System I: *Capitalist Agriculture and the Origins of the European World–Economy in the Sixteenth Century*. New York: Academic Press.
Wallerstein, I. 1983. *Historical Capitalism*. London: Verso.
Wey Gómez, N. 2008. *Tropics of Empire: Why Columbus Sailed South to the Indies*. Cambridge: The MIT Press.
Zamora, M. 1993. *Reading Columbus*. Berkeley: University of California Press.

Glossary Terms

Al-Andalus Al-Andalus refers to a region of southern Spain that encompassed the Muslim-dominated kingdom of Andalusia. With the city of Granada as the capital, Al-Andalus served as the Iberian epicenter of Islamic power for over six centuries.

Encomenderos Encomenderos were colonial settlers who were granted dominion of land and Indigenous slaves for their service. The Spanish Crown "commandeered," or rewarded colonialists with dominion over the empire's newly acquired territories and subjects.

Reconquista The term "Reconquista" (or reconquest) refers to King Ferdinand and Queen Isabella's defeat of Islamic dominion over the kingdom of Al-Andalus in southern Spain.

Scholastic tradition This refers to the medieval theology that developed in western universities from 800 to 1400. Influenced by the newly discovered works of Aristotle, scholasticism is associated with figures such as Peter Abelard, Anselm of Canterbury, Duns Scotus, Albert the Great, and, most importantly, Thomas Aquinas.

3

Retracing Intermixture/*Mestizaje* in Latin America and Among Latinas/os/xs

Néstor Medina

Intermixture: Origins

Whether called *mestizaje, métissage, metissagem, creolization*, or other labels, the phenomena of intermixture have shaped the world in many ways. By intermixture, I mean the complex processes of biological, cultural, and religious exchange, sharing, and adoption that take place as ethnocultural groups collide or interact with each other within specific social contexts. In the context of Latin America and among Latinas/os/xs, these complex processes are commonly understood as part of the five-centuries-long story of *mestizaje*.

Most scholars begin studies of intermixture in Latin America and among Latinas/os/xs from 1492, when the Western European colonial project first emerged. In the violent Western European encounter with the Indigenous peoples of Abya Yala/Aztlán/Turtle Island (today's Americas), they projected onto Indigenous peoples—and the rest of the Indigenous world for that matter—their sense of racial superiority and supremacy. Indeed, *Los archivos generales de las Indias* (the General Archives of the Indies) show that cataloging people's level of intermixture based on their ancestral ethnic parents (European, African, and Indigenous) was indeed practiced in social and religious institutions from very early on, immediately after the arrival of the Spanish (and other Europeans) to the lands of Abya Yala/Aztlán/Turtle Island.

However, other earlier events took place in the Iberian Peninsula that provoked a heightened attention to levels of intermixture there which also impacted the formation of Latin American colonial societies. These modes of thinking about intermixture are important to consider as well. The Spanish Catholic Inquisition, established in 1478, for instance, deployed the language of purity of blood, which later became of common use in Spanish colonial societies in the Americas (Kaplan 2012). It is worth noting that the original ideas of "pure" or "impure" blood were not associated with racialization as it is commonly understood. Rather, in its original expressions and in connections with the activities and goals of the Inquisition authorities, purity of blood had religious overtones.

It is important to note that these changes were taking please at two levels. At the social level, the Spanish were trying to reconquer the Iberian Peninsula by battling the Arab Islamic presence. At the religious level, the Spanish monarchs, Queen Isabel de Castilla and King Fernando de Aragón, who succeeded in unifying the kingdom of Spain, sought to spread their commitment and devotion to Catholicism over the entire kingdom. During this time of heightened tensions, ideas of purity of blood served to distinguish between those whose Christian faith could be traced generations back and those who had just recently converted. This strategy helped those in power to expose those Jews and Muslims who had just recently converted to Christianity with no intention of abandoning their own religious traditions and practices. In other words, when someone was able to demonstrate their long Christian ancestral line, they were considered old Christians and were deemed to have pure blood. Conversely, those who had recently converted, who quite often were Jews or Muslims, regardless of their ethnoracial background, were deemed to have impure blood and were under general suspicion by local authorities (Böttcher, Hausberger, and Hering Torres 2012).

Intermixture: First Encounters

As the Spanish and Portuguese arrived to the Americas, they carried with them their anti-Muslim sentiments. Many of these sentiments were projected onto the Indigenous peoples of the region. At the same time, as Western Europeans arrived and invaded the lands and conquered the Indigenous peoples, they also began intermixing with them. Spanish and Portuguese women only arrived years after the initial conquest and invasions. As a result, Spanish and Portuguese males initially began mixing with Indigenous women. But this **miscegenation** took place in large part because of the raping of Indigenous women by Spanish and Portuguese males. The descendants of these intermixtures came to be known as *mestizos/as*, mixed children with ancestral Indigenous and Spanish blood. By the same token, when Spanish women arrived to the Americas, some were kidnapped and raped by the Indigenous men. Their offspring were also known as *mestizos/as*. It is important to note that in the first Spanish and Portuguese conquests, many Europeans from many regions also arrived to the Americas; French, British, Dutch, and German, among others, were among the conquistadors. Thus, though I focus on the Spanish and Portuguese, my chapter also applies to other Western Europeans who participated in the destruction of Indigenous peoples, traditions, and cultures.

These mixed children were caught in a social, emotional, and spiritual liminal space; they bore the brunt of the Spanish discriminatory sentiments, carried the Catholic Church's stigma of "spiritual decadence," and suffered the mistrust of the Indigenous peoples. As *mestizos/as* grew up, they were objects of suspicion for the Spanish because they were afraid *mestizos/as* would join their Indigenous parents in a revolt against the Spanish. The Church condemned *mestizas/os* for their perceived "immoral" state because they were the result of relations out of wedlock. Further, the Indigenous peoples rejected them, for they were the material reminder of their despoliation, the raping of Indigenous women, and the loss of their lands and customs at the hands of the Spanish (and other Europeans). Many Spaniards deluded themselves into believing that Indigenous women were attracted to them because of their physical features and masculinity, and as a result wanted to have sex with them. At the end of the day, these women were considered libidinous. As a result, the violent rape of Indigenous women and the feminization of Indigenous males simply went unregistered in the consciousness of colonial societies and continues unregistered in many contexts even today. We see the internal conflict wrought by these sociocultural tensions in Garcilaso de la Vega's own reclaiming of his identity as a *mestizo*; he lived with and was educated by the Spanish but deeply longed to reconnect with his Inca ancestral line (1996).

The complicated nature of intermixture increased upon the arrival of African peoples and their descendants. Some arrived to the Americas with conquistadors and aided in the conquest. Most arrived as slaves to replace the millions of Indigenous peoples dying because of European illnesses and because of exhaustion from working in the mines and plantations. As with intermixture between the Indigenous and the Spanish, the Africans, whether free or enslaved, also mixed with Europeans and resulted in the birth of the new group of mixed children called *mulatos/as*. The Africans also mixed with the Indigenous peoples, with their children becoming known as the *zambos/as*. Within a very few years after establishing colonial encampments and subsequent societies, the mixed population had grown exponentially.

It is within the ferment of initial invasion and conquest, as well as the resulting intermixture between Europeans (in this case Spanish), Indigenous, and African peoples, that the Western European sense of superiority and supremacy over other peoples solidified. This sense of the superiority of the Western Europeans emerged simultaneously with the sense of inferiority of the Indigenous and Africans peoples. These were two sides of the same invention of white supremacy. The idea of Western Europeans as being civilized was complemented with the ideas that Indigenous peoples were lazy and deceitful, and that African peoples were arrogant, lascivious, and inclined to evil doing (Medina 2018: 98–150).

Not surprisingly, these same moralized character-defects were projected onto the generations of mixed children. Because of this projection, along with their concrete connections to their Indigenous and African parents, mixed children (*mestizos/as* and *mulatos/as*) were also suspect. To repeat, the Europeans were afraid that the mixed population would join their Indigenous and African parents to get rid of the Europeans

FIGURE 3.1 *Andrés Sánchez Galque,* Los Tres Mulatos de Esmeraldas/The Three Mulattos of Esmeraldas *(Ecuador), 1599, oil on canvas, Museo del Prado, Madrid, Spain. The painting reveals the African presence in colonial Latin America since early in the sixteenth century.* Source: *Prado Museum/Wikimedia Commons.*

in a rebellion. To ameliorate their fears, the Spanish created vagrancy laws to regulate social gatherings. A detailed system of fines, imprisonment, and corporal punishment was devised to prevent Blacks, mulattos, and *mestizos* from meeting publicly in groups of more than two. They were also prevented from going into the *reducciones*, the areas designated for the Indigenous populations. Additionally, mixed children were deprived of key social privileges, including access to university education and specific careers such as doctors, priests, soldiers, notaries, among others. These careers were reserved for the European population and their descendants who became known as *criollos*.

Intermixture/*Mestizaje*: The Caste System

Because of the emergence of many mixed children, the safeguarding of the social privileges of the white European population gained prominence. Notions of purity of blood resurfaced, this time with racialized overtones. As the mixed children further mixed among themselves, new mixtures emerged. Spanish colonial society devised a sophisticated system of castes through which the populations of the colonial societies were cataloged according to the percentage of European, Indigenous, and African blood they carried. The names of the castes put on display a range of names from zoology, particularly for those castes with predominant Indigenous and African bloods, namely, *lobo* and *coyote* (wolf and coyote) (Rosenblat 1954). All kinds of negotiations and maneuverings were made to ensure and protect the "purity" of Spanish blood and social status. With the dearth of Spanish "civilized" women in some places, many orphan mestiza girls were put into convents to ensure they received the proper "Spanish" and Christian training to become fit wives for young Spanish conquistadors and those seeking to settle in the lands newly acquired by the Spanish Crown (Burns 1998). After all, by mixing with Europeans, two generations later, the children could once again be considered "white."

The development of the castes contributed enormously to the formation of ethnic identities among the various groups that made up the colonial societies, but they were certainly not culturally nor socially neutral. The castes also functioned as mechanisms of population control, as effective ways to establish social ranking, and as protection for the social privileges of the "white" population (García Sáiz 1989). By the middle of the eighteenth century, wealthy patrons commissioned paintings of the castes to display in their homes. It is very likely that these painting were used to affirm the patrons' self-understanding of being close to or being direct descendants of white Europeans. The paintings included sixteen frames of different castes outlining the names ascribed to the children of the original parental mixtures between Spanish (European) and Indigenous; Spanish and African; and Indigenous and African as well as subsequent intermixtures up to a fourth generation, though not always very easy to discern on the basis of color of skin alone (Katzew 2004). As miscegenation among castes continued, the system of castes became unwieldy, to the degree that, at one point, there were well over 120 identifiable castes (Rosenblat 1954).

Their complexity notwithstanding, it is very evident that the caste system and the *castas* paintings (see Figure 3.2) engendered a different understanding of racialization. In the alchemy of intermixture, "whiteness," "blackness," and "Indianness" were not understood as fixed in the ways that they are in contemporary understandings of race. There was much mobility and fluidity between the castes. Quite often, marital unions, having children, and getting married were considered in light of the social benefits they brought to individuals and their potential offspring. For example, some African slave women preferred to be a white man's concubine because their children would be born free. The same thing happened if these slave women had children with someone of Indigenous background—their children would be free. But if they had children with Black men, their children would be born into slavery (Twinam 2015). The Spanish Crown sought to stop this level of intermixed marriage by proclaiming laws that threatened to punish those who married "below" their caste—with Indigenous or African people—through the loss of their parental inheritance (Meléndez Obando 2003).

Many others, particularly of African descent, sought to purchase their whiteness at the cost of abandoning their inherited African customs and practices. Facing the disarray that the caste system had caused, the Spanish Crown also created opportunities for people to request being exempted from their African ancestral stain. "*Gracias al sacar*" (literally "thanks for taking me out") was the 1795 royal decree that exempted individuals from the social restrictions their caste placed on them and enabled them to purchase whiteness and be free from the caste system. As Ann Twinam masterfully documents, there were a good number of families, primarily Quarterones—those

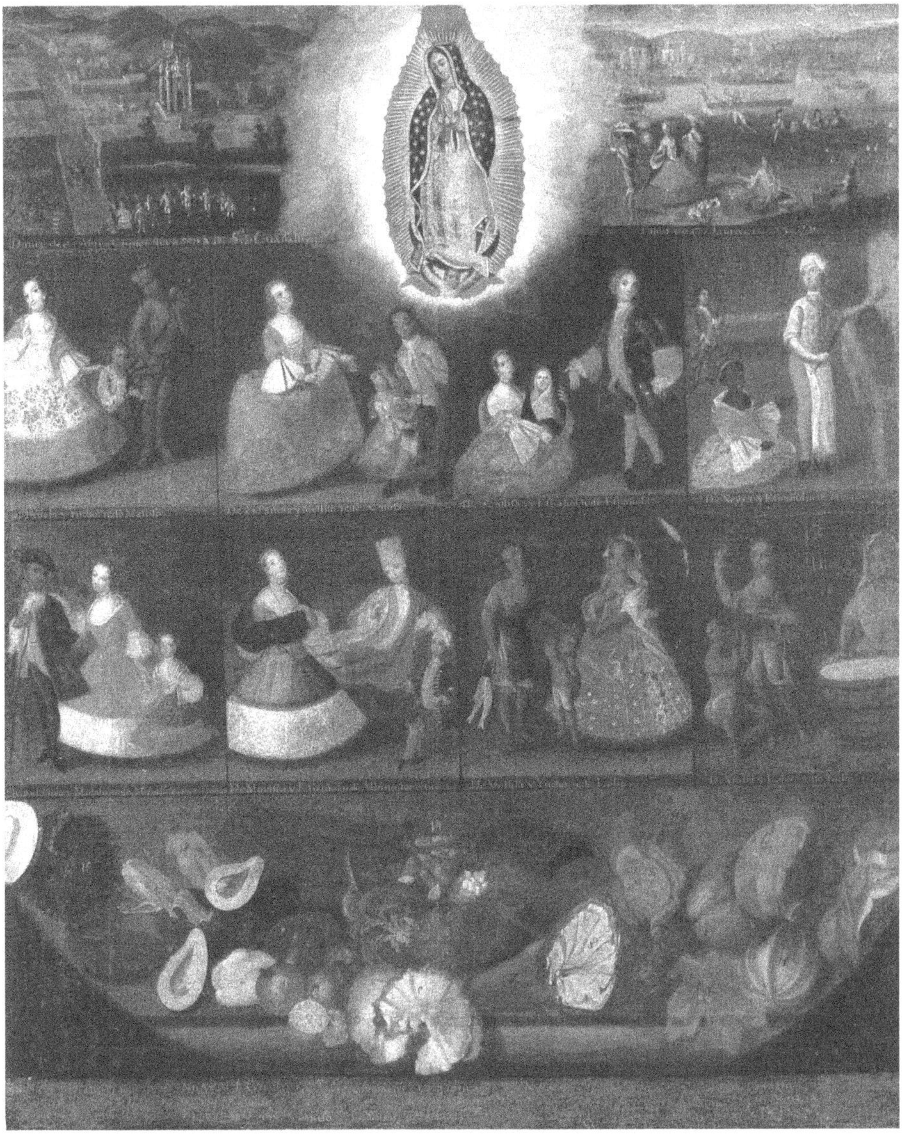

FIGURE 3.2 *Luis de Mena,* The Virgin of Guadalupe Stands Above Las Castas, *1750, oil on canvas, Museo de America, Madrid, Spain. The painting displays the intimate connection between religious faith and questions of racialization and identity.* Source: *Wikimedia Commons.*

who could trace African ancestry four generations back—who sought such exemption and in fact obtained it. Meanwhile, those who could pass as "white" descendants of Europeans affirmed their whiteness and claimed social privileges (Twinam 2015). Quite often, claiming those privileges came at the cost of severing their relationships with their Indigenous and African blood connections.

FIGURE 3.3 Sixteen categories of las castas, *eighteenth century, oil on canvas, Museo Nacional del Virreinato, Mexico. Frame reveals the three main groups that intermixed during colonial Latin America, Spanish (Europeans), Indigenous, and Africans.* Source: *Wikimedia Commons.*

By the end of the eighteenth century, the caste system had become so cumbersome that identifying the caste to which individuals belonged based on physical features and color of the skin was next to impossible. What followed was the emergence of what Alejandro Lipschutz coined as pigmentocracy; that is, the shaping and organizing of society and social structures around people's skin color and features, and their perceived ancestry (1967). The effects of the porosity of caste boundaries ensured that intermixture, which was central to the formation of colonial social structures, later became the very reason for the collapse of the caste system. By the end of the eighteenth century, in an attempt to regain control over the affairs of colonial societies, the caste system was no longer used and all castes were lumped together under a single label, *mestizaje*. Quite quickly, *mestizaje* became the single most important aspect in the building of identity of the populations that later came to be called Latin American.

The "castes" had not really come to an end; they were simply reduced to four key categories: "white," *mestizo/a*, Indigenous, and African-Black, in that ranking and order. As *mestizaje* assumed center stage, the labels Indigenous and African-Black were generally set aside and the peoples from these communities were occluded from public attention. White or Criollos had not disappeared as categories, however, and were at the top of the social ladder. During the first quarter of the nineteenth century, the label *mestizaje* gained ideological currency whereby the entire population of Latin America was affirmed as being *mestiza*.

Intermixture as Social and Political Ideology and Ethos

Politically, *mestizaje* was also deployed as a rallying point when Latin Americans sought to obtain their independence from the Spanish colonial powers. For example, among Mexicans, the Lady the Guadalupe and *mestizaje* were the two key symbols that brought the people together. Many *mestizos/as* participated in Mexican struggles for independence, most prominently José María Morelos. Similarly, as Father Hidalgo y Costilla prepared to lead the first uprising toward independence on September 16, 1810, he commended their cause under the protective mantle of Our Lady of Guadalupe, the *mestiza* Virgin. As a result, the Virgin became the most recognizable symbol of the quest for an independent Mexican nation and remains a vital cultural and religious symbol today. Banners and signs with the images of Our Lady of Guadalupe printed on them were carried by the *independendentista* rebel forces.

The wars of independence contributed greatly to *mestizaje* emerging as the single most important descriptor in the formation of people's ethnic identity in the newly formed nations of Latin America. Crucial here are the efforts both of José de San Martín and Simón Bolívar. Both leaders sought to bring unity to today's South América. The *mestizo* San Martín approached the independence of today's Argentina, Chile,

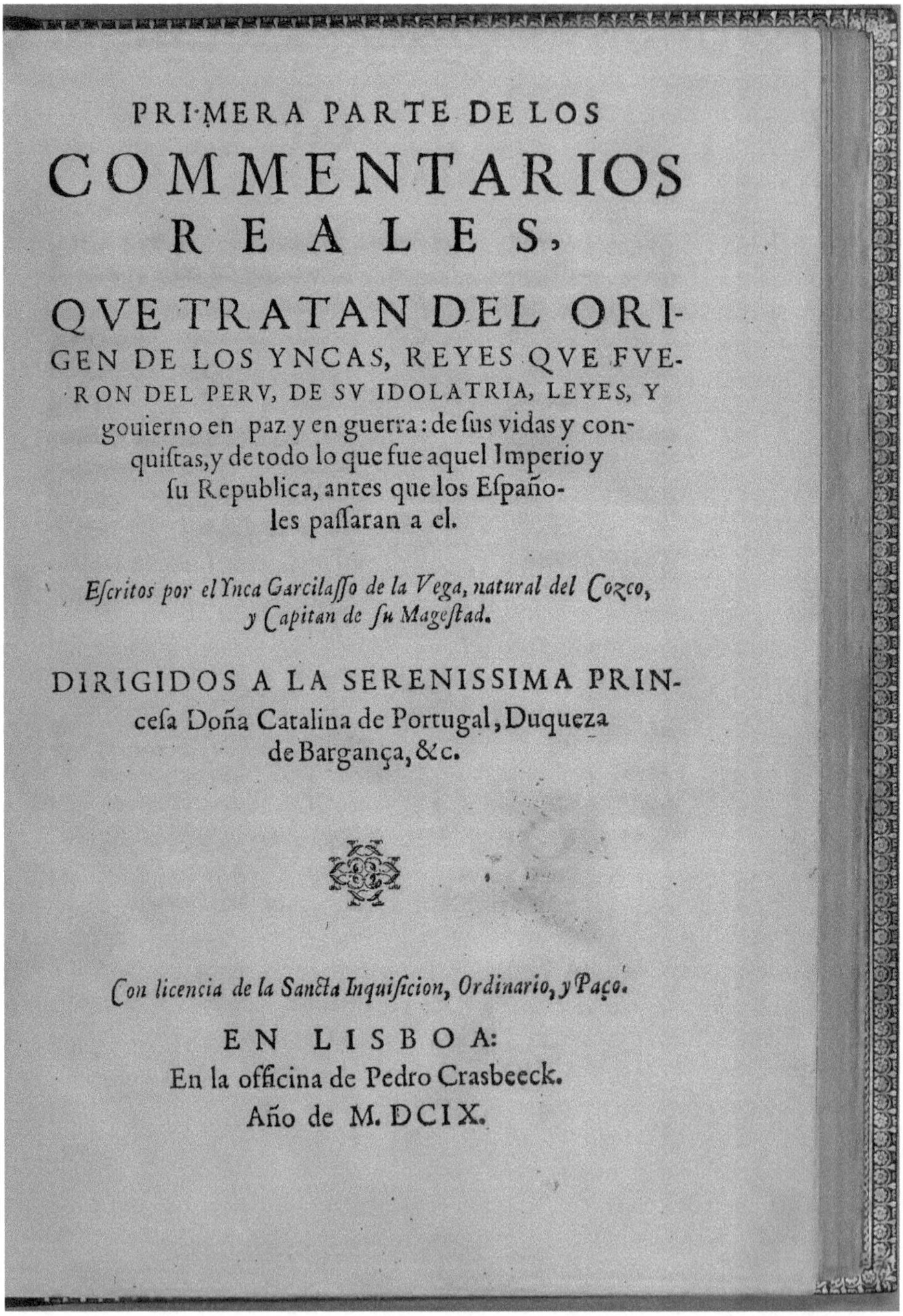

PRIMERA PARTE DE LOS
COMMENTARIOS
REALES,
QVE TRATAN DEL ORIGEN DE LOS YNCAS, REYES QVE FVERON DEL PERV, DE SV IDOLATRIA, LEYES, Y gouierno en paz y en guerra: de ſus vidas y conquiſtas, y de todo lo que fue aquel Imperio y ſu Republica, antes que los Eſpañoles paſſaran a el.

Eſcritos por el Ynca Garcilaſſo de la Vega, natural del Cozco, y Capitan de ſu Mageſtad.

DIRIGIDOS A LA SERENISSIMA PRINceſa Doña Catalina de Portugal, Duqueza de Bargança, &c.

Con licencia de la Sancta Inquiſicion, Ordinario, y Paço.

EN LISBOA:
En la officina de Pedro Crasbeeck.
Año de M.DCIX.

FIGURE 3.4 *Garcilaso de la Vega's magnum opus* Comentarios Reales *(1609), a commentary on the history, culture, laws, and customs of the Inca.* Source: *John Carter Brown Library/ Internet Archive.*

FIGURE 3.5 *Juan O'Gorman,* Retablo de la Independencia, *mural, 16 m × 4.5 m, Museo Nacional de Historia, Ciudad de México, México. The mural highlights the racial mixing of Mexico and the religious origins of the War of Independence.* Source: *Danita Delimont/Alamy Stock Photo.*

and Peru as an opportunity to celebrate the identity of the people. Greatly inspired by Garcilaso de la Vega's proud claiming of his *mestizo* identity, he quickly moved to prohibit the labels "negro" (Black) and "Indio" (Indian) and highlighted their common experience of conquest by emphasizing *mestizaje* (Chumbita 2001).

Aware of racialized divisions in the regions, vestiges from the Spanish colonial times, Bolívar sought to further articulate and build on his project for independence by highlighting *mestizaje* as the unique feature that connected all the inhabitants of today's Venezuela, Colombia, Bolivia, Panama, and Ecuador. His *Carta de Jamaica* (Letter from Jamaica)—which he wrote while he was planning his campaign for independence—and is also known as his manifesto of independence—grounds his cry of independence on the affirmation that the entire population is *mestiza*. It is important to note that Bolívar had no intention of relinquishing his own status and social privileges as "white" born in the Americas, after all he was a *criollo*. Moreover, unlike San Martín, he continued to utilize the labels for Black and Indigenous peoples to describe these two sectors of the population, and not usually in a positive light. His use of *mestizaje* in the Letter of Jamaica, and later expanded on in his *Discurso de Angostura* (Discourse in Angostura), was a strategic rhetorical move to provide people with a sense of common cause and shared history against the imperial forces of Spain (Miller 2004).

Whether in Spanish North America (Mexico) or Central and South America, the struggles for independence took on *mestizaje* as a critical rallying point, a national identity descriptor and symbol, and a social and historical imaginary for giving this entire region a sense of coherence. Through the adoption of *mestizaje*, these countries succeeded in creating a collective national and regional building project. Still, *mestizaje* remained a contested term and reality. At the same time, it also experienced a resurgence from the first quarter of the twentieth century onward to which we now turn.

On the Theorization of Intermixture/*Mestizaje*

The twentieth century saw a proliferation of theoretical articulations of *mestizaje* from multiple camps: idealists, detractors, and challengers. From among the idealists, some thought that *mestizaje* reflected the shared experience and history of the peoples in Latin American nations. Though he had his reservations because of his socialist commitment with the Indigenous peoples of Peru, José Carlos Mariátegui expressed support of a national agenda of *mestizaje* (1991). Along similar lines, his countryman, José María Arguedas wrote some of his most celebrated novels using *mestizaje* to encompass the possibilities of recognizing the many peoples that made up the population of Peru (1987). Others went so far as to imagine the divine providential hand behind the Latin American reality of intermixture. Among proponents of this idea was José Vasconcelos. He adopted a Hegelian aestheticism to explore the potentialities of Latin America's *mestizaje*, which, he insisted, would result in the creation of a final *quinta raza* (fifth race) which would be the synthesis of the best aspects of all the other races of the world (Vasconcelos 1983: 1925).

In this second camp with Vasconcelos of adopting *mestizaje* for the purpose of national unification, though with a different agenda, were those who saw *mestizaje* as an opportunity to promote inherited Eurocentric ideas and cultural traditions. Their goal was to effectively remove the Indigenous presence from Latin American identity altogether. Following are some of the ways this removal was enacted: national policies of education that emphasized de-Indigenization of the social landscape as it happened in Mexico and Guatemala (Gamio 1930); the emphasis on a united national identity to undermine the African presence in Cuba (Duno Gottberg 2003); the development of a systematic agenda of displacement of Indigenous peoples in northern Nicaragua (Gould 1998); and the required replacement of Indigenous last names with Spanish ones as in the case of Bolivia (Sanjinés Casanovas 2004).

A third group were those inspired by Western European ideas of positivism and who adopted Herbert Spencer's (and later Adolf Hitler's) rejection of miscegenation. This group was convinced that miscegenation resulted in weak offspring. As Alberto Wagner de Reyna argued, the Indigenous and African peoples were in fact inferior, and the intermixture between Indigenous and Africans and Europeans had produced inferior stock; *mestizaje* was therefore responsible for Latin America's inability to progress (Wagner de Reyna 1954). Similarly, as Domingo Sarmiento put it, the *mestizo/a* population were barbarians, and the only solution to get them from out of their barbarism was to promote a eugenics kind of *mestizaje*. His proposal was to import the best stock from Western Europeans and have them mix with the current population with the goal of undoing the "contamination" of Indigenous and African peoples (Sarmiento 2001).

By the time of the quincentenary of the Spanish (and European) invasion of Abya Yala/Aztlán/Turtle Island, it became evident that the most affected peoples—the impoverished, marginalized, and disenfranchised Indigenous and African masses in Latin America—had their own interpretations of *mestizaje*. Some of the expressions were very positive, others were very negative. Generally, they fall into four camps. In the first camp, Otto Morales Benítez sought to find ways for carving a social space for AfroColombians by affirming Africa as the crib of civilization millennia ago (1984). As he saw it, since the emergence of humanity in Africa intermixture has been a part of the human experience. As a result, *mestizaje* creates space for the inclusion of the diverse groups that make up Latin America (in his case Colombia), and especially the African presence. In the second camp, we find the Indigenous communities of Peru, who have now adopted the language of *mestizaje* not as a mechanism for abandoning people's Indigenous roots, but as a key cipher to identify those people of Indigenous background who are able to speak their native Quechua or Aymara and can also navigate the dominant social context and structures because they also speak Spanish (de la Cadena 2000). Though they are derogatorily called *cholos* (people of mixed-blood) in parts of Ecuador and Peru, these cultural border people are celebrated and have gained a high social status among the Indigenous peoples in the markets of Peru.

In the third camp are those Indigenous thinkers who reject *mestizaje* as self-descriptor or as part of their identity (Bonilla 2002). Not falling into any type of ethnic purism, they opt to reject *mestizaje* as part of the dominant social and cultural ethos because it was designed to erase their Indigenous identities and to eradicate their Indigenous customs, practices, and spiritualities. Fourth, *mestizaje* has been reinterpreted by some thinkers and social activists in Latin America as a way to carve out social spaces for those ethnic groups not often accounted for in the Latin American ethnic landscape. For example, Breny Mendoza argues for *mestizaje* as the legitimate frame for the inclusion of the Arabic population in Honduras (2001). Richard Feierstein has also shown how the notion of *mestizaje* resonates with the experience of Jews in Argentina (1996). More recently, Hanna Kang has also drawn on *mestizaje* to affirm and celebrate the Asian (Chinese, Korean, and Japanese) presence in Latin America (2021).

In sum, this centuries-long, complex ferment of intermixture/*mestizaje* as a historical imaginary includes its uses as: a descriptor for the biological reality of miscegenation; a social construct for organizing and controlling the population; a symbol of collective national identity; a mechanism for whitening of the population, and a cipher for reclaiming Indigenous and African voices. *Mestizaje* also found particular expression among Latinas/os/xs and Chicanoas/os/xs in the United States. In some important ways there are overlaps, but there are also important differences.

Intermixture/*Mestizaje* among Chicanas/os/xs and Latinas/os/xs

In 1967 as the civil rights movement was in full swing in the United States, the unification of Chicana/o/x and Mexican American youth and student movements formed the MEChA (Movimiento Estudiantil Chicano de Aztlán). Inspired and empowered by the civil rights movement, this movement sought to promote Chicana/o/x unity and political action on behalf of their communities. They saw themselves as members of *la raza* (the race) and claimed *mestizaje* as their key identifier. Resonating with notions of intermixture as characteristics of their ethnicity, an idealized interpretation of *mestizaje* undergirded their understanding of themselves (Pérez-Torres 1998). Other thinkers from that generation also drew on *mestizaje* to articulate their experiences and grievances and proposed using it to refresh the theoretical frames for understanding the reality of Chicanas/os/xs and Latinas/os/xs. Gloria Anzaldúa is one such thinker. She propelled the Chicana/o/x and queer movements to reclaim *mestizaje* as a critical theoretical framing and vantage point of **liminality** from which to understand Chicana/o/x experiences (1987; Barnard 1997; Aigner-Varoz 2000).

Within that same generation of inspired Mexican Americans who struggled for social justice were theologians including Virgilio Elizondo, who sought to rethink the experiences of Mexican Americans in the United States using *mestizaje* as critical hermeneutical and theological framework (1989). As one of the original founders of the Latina/o/x theological school, he deployed *mestizaje* to uncover the history of colonization experienced by Mexican Americans, including their experience of double marginalization, and to affirm their ethnic, cultural, and faith traditions. Taking their cue from Elizondo and in close conversation with Latin American Liberation Theology, Latina/o/x theologians began to rethink the religious experiences of their communities. They too found *mestizaje* to be a fruitful framework for articulating the experiences of faith, the customs, and the spiritualities of Latina/o/x communities (Medina 2009). Through the lenses of *mestizaje*, these scholars proposed that Christian theology, history, spirituality, and biblical studies, including worship could be reformulated (Elizondo and Matovina 1998; Rodríguez 2004; Delgadillo 2011). By drawing on *mestizaje*, they exposed the Eurocentric nature of Christian theology and history. They also showed how the framework *mestizaje* helped to reinterpret the biblical text in ways that are relevant to the history and experiences of Latinas/os/xs.

There is no doubt that the language of *mestizaje* did provide a wide range of theological and hermeneutical insights. More recently, however, the use of *mestizaje* has come under criticism because of the romantic ways in which some Latina/o/x theologians first articulated it. It has become evident that earlier theological perspectives of *mestizaje*, including the works of Anzaldúa and Elizondo, among others, were influenced by the romantic proposal of Vasconcelos's fifth race mentioned above (Aquino 2015). Of course, such a powerful symbol of the identity, history, and collective imaginary of Latin Americans and Latinas/os/xs cannot simply be dismissed, despite these concerns. *Mestizaje* continues to offer important insights on how to articulate the experience of intermixture in its multifaceted expressions by these diverse communities.

Intermixture/*Mestizaje* Interdisciplinarily

The inspiration and rich insights provoked by the reality of intermixture have spilled over to various disciplinary fields. Here I only mention a few, as the reinterpretation of intermixture/*mestizaje* continues to grow exponentially. Katherine Jamieson, for example, discusses the strategic importance for considering the role of Latina/o/x *mestizo* ethnicities for sport studies (2003). Carolina Prieto Molano has also engaged the question of *mestizaje* from the perspective of the intersection of culture, folklore, and food (1994). Similarly, foregrounding Chicana cultural traditions, practices, and spiritualities in academia, Amanda Jo Córdova draws on a Chicana Feminist Epistemology to articulate a *mestiza* approach to research methodology (2021). And in an exploration of politics through the eyes of *mestizaje*, John Burke proposes a border crossing approach to constructing democracy (2002). Finally, Brian McNeill and José Cervantes remind us of the unique approaches to healing among Indigenous peoples from Latin America and among Latinas/os/xs (2008).

These multiple strands show how intermixture/*mestizaje* has been understood, articulated, and reinterpreted in multiple fields of study and its continuing relevance for people in Latin America as well as among Latinas/os/xs. Though the condition of biological, cultural, and religious intermixture/*mestizaje* has shifted significantly since the heyday of colonial societies, its social, political, religious, and theoretical epistemological implications continue to help Latin American and Latinas/os/xs interpret their past and forge a strong future.

Further Reading and Online Resources

Anzaldúa, G. 1987. *Borderlands / La Frontera: The New Mestiza*, San Francisco: An Aunt Lute books.

Aquino, J.A. 2015. "*Mestizaje*: The Latina/o Religious Imaginary in the North American Racial Crucible," in O. Espín (ed.), *The Wiley Blackwell Companion to Latino/a Theology*, 283–311, Chichester, UK: Wiley Blackwell.

Delgadillo, T. 2011. *Spiritual Mestizaje: Religion, Gender, Race, and Nation in Contemporary Chicana Narrative*, Durham, NC: Duke University Press.

Miller, M.G. 2004. *Rise and Fall of the Cosmic Race: The Cult of* Mestizaje *in Latin America*, Austin: University of Texas Press.
Medina, N. 2008. "The Religious Psychology of *Mestizaje*: Gómez Suárez de Figueroa or Garcilaso de la Vega," *Pastoral Psychology*, 57 (September): 115–24.
Medina, N. 2009. *Mestizaje: (Re)Mapping "Race, Culture, and Faith in Latina/o Catholicism*," Maryknoll, NY: Orbis Books.

References

Aigner-Varoz, E. 2000. "Metaphors of a Mestiza Consciousness: Anzaldúa's Borderlands / La Frontera," *MELUS*, 25 (2), Latino Identities (Summer): 47–62.
Anzaldúa, G. 1987. *Borderlands* / La Frontera: *The New Mestiza*, San Francisco: Aunt Lute Books.
Aquino J., A. 2015. "*Mestizaje*: The Latina/o Religious Imaginary in the North American Racial Crucible," in O. Espín (ed.), *The Wiley Blackwell Companion to Latino/a Theology*, 283–311, Chichester, UK: Wiley Blackwell.
Arguedas, J.M. 1987. *Todas las sangres*, compiled by S. de Arguedas, Peru: Editorial Horizontes.
Barnard, I. 1997. "Gloria Anzaldúa's Queer Mestizaje," *MELUS*, 22 (1) (Spring): 35–53.
Bonilla, R.P. 2002. *Los intelectuales y la narrativa mestiza en el Ecuador*, Quito, Ecuador: Universidad Andina Simón Bolívar, Ediciones Abya Yala, Corporación editora nacional.
Böttcher, N., B. Hausberger, and M.S. Hering Torres 2012. "Introduction: Sangre, Mestizaje y Nobleza," in N. Böttcher, B. Hausberger, and M.S. Hering Torres (eds.), *El peso de la sangre: Limpios, mestizos y nobles en el mundo hispánico*, 9–27, Mexico City: El Colegio de Mexico.
Burke, J.F. 2002. *Mestizo Democracy: The Politics of Crossing Borders*, with a foreword by V. Elizondo, College Station: Texas A&M University Press.
Burns, K. 1998. "Gender and the Politics of *Mestizaje*: The Convent of Santa Clara in Cuzco, Peru," *The Hispanic American Historical Review*, 78 (1): 5–44.
Chumbita, H. 2001. *El secreto de Yapeyú*, Buenos Aires: Emecé Editores S.A.
Córdova, A.J. 2021. "Mestiza Methodology: Research as a Site of Healing," *Journal of Women and Gender in Higher Education*, 14 (1): 40–58.
de la Cadena, M. 2000. *Indigenous Mestizos: The Politics of Race and Culture in Cuzco,* Peru, *1919–1991*, Latin American Otherwise: Languages, Empires, Nations, Durham, NC: Duke University Press.
de la Vega, I.G. 1996. *Diario del Inca Garcilaso (1562–1616)*, ed. F.C. Espejo. Lima: Editorial Horizonte.
Delgadillo, T. 2011. *Spiritual Mestizaje: Religion, Gender, Race, and Nation in Contemporary Chicana Narrative*, Durham, NC: Duke University Press.
Duno Gottberg, L. 2003. *Solventando las diferencias: La ideología del mestizaje en Cuba*, Madrid: Iberoamericana.
Elizondo, V.P. and T.M. Matovina, eds. 1998. *Mestizo Worship: A Pastoral Approach to Liturgical Ministry*, Collegeville, MN: Liturgical Press.
Elizondo, V. 1989. "Mestizaje as a Locus of Theological Reflection," in M.H. Ellis and O. Maduro (eds.), *The Future of Liberation Theology: Essays in Honor of Gustavo Gutiérrez*, 358–74, Maryknoll, NY: Orbis Books.
Feierstein, R. 1996. "Todas las culturas, la cultura," in *Contraexilio y Mestizaje: Ser judío en latinoamerica*, Colección Ensayos, 109–59, Buenos Aires: Editorial Milá.

Gamio, M. 1930. "El mestizaje eugenésico en la población de la América Indoibérica," *Anales de la Sociedad de Geografía e Historia de Guatemala*, 6 (3): 333–7.
García Sáiz, M.C. 1989. *Las castas mexicanas: Un género pictórico americano*, trans. J. Escobar, Milan: Olivetti.
Gould, J.L. 1998. *To Die in This Way: Nicaraguan Indians and the Myth of Mestizaje*, Durham, NC: Duke University Press.
Jamieson, K.M. 2003. "Occupying a Middle Space: Toward a Mestiza Sport Studies," *Sociology of Sport Journal*, 20: 1–16.
Kang, H. 2021. "Mestizos/as with an Asian Face," *Perspectivas*, 18: 43–60.
Kaplan, G.B. 2012. "The Inception of *Limpieza de Sangre* (Purity of Blood) and Its Impact in Medieval and Golden Age Spain," in A. Aronson-Friedman and G.B. Kaplan (eds.), *Marginal Voices: Studies in Converso Literature of Medieval and Golden Agen Spain*, 19–41, Leiden: Brill.
Katzew, I. 2004. *Casta Paintings*, New Haven, CT: Yale University Press.
Lipschutz, A. 1967. *El problema racial en la conquista de América y el mestizaje*, 2nd edn., Santiago, Chile: Editorial Andres Bello.
Mariátegui, J.C. 1991. "El problema del Indio," in *7 Ensayos de interpretación de la realidad peruana*, vol. 4: *Pensamiento Peruano*, 45–57, Lima: Editorial Horizonte.
McNeill, B. and J.M. Cervantes, eds. 2008. *Latina/o Healing Practices: Mestizo and Indigenous Perspectives*, London: Routledge.
Medina, N. 2009. *Mestizaje: (Re)Mapping "Race, Culture, and Faith in Latina/o Catholicism,"* Maryknoll, NY: Orbis Books.
Medina, N. 2018. *Christianity, Empire, and the Spirit: (Re)Configuring Faith and the Cultural*, Leiden: Brill.
Meléndez Obando, M. 2003. "Estratificación socio-racial y matrimonio en la Intendencia de San Salvador y la Alcaldía mayor de Sonsonate," in A.M. Gómez and S.A. Herrera (eds.), *Mestizaje, poder y sociedad*, 29–46, San Salvador: FLACSO Programa El Salvador.
Mendoza, B. 2001. "La desmitologización del mestizaje en Honduras: Evaluando nuevos aportes," Denison. Available online: http://istmo.denison.edu/n08/articulos/desmitologizacion.html (accessed January 15, 2006).
Miller, M.G. 2004. *Rise and Fall of the Cosmic Race: The Cult of* Mestizaje *in Latin America*, Austin: University of Texas Press.
Morales Benítez, O. 1984. *Memorias del mestizaje*, prologue by J.C. Higgins, Bogotá: Plaza y Janes, Editores-Colombia Ltda.
Pérez-Torres, R. 1998. "Chicano Ethnicity, Cultural Hybridity, and the Mestizo Voice," *American Literature*, 70 (1) (March): 153–76.
Prieto Molano, C. 1994. *Hasta la tierra es mestiza*, Historia Colombiana, Bogotá: Colección Bibliográfica Banco de la República.
Rodríguez, J. 2004. "Mestiza Spirituality: Community, Ritual, and Justice," *Theological Studies*, 65 (2): 317–39.
Rosenblat, Á. 1954. *La Población Indígena y el Mestizaje en América*, vol. 2: *El mestizaje y las castas coloniales*, Buenos Aires: Editorial Nova.
Sanjinés, C.J. 2004. Mestizaje *Upside-Down: Aesthetic Politics in Modern Bolivia*, Pittsburgh, PA: University of Pittsburgh Press.
Sarmiento, D.F. 2001. *Facundo*, Buenos Aires: Grupo Editor Altamira.
Twinam, A. 2015. *Purchasing Whiteness: Pardos, Mulattos, and the Quest for Social Mobility in the Spanish Indies*, Stanford, CA: Stanford University Press.
Vasconcelos, J. 1983. *La raza cósmica: Misión de la raza iberoamericana*. Asociación Nacional de Libreros, Mexico City: Litografía Ediciones Olimpia, S.A.
Wagner de Reyna, A. 1954. *Destino y vocación de Iberoamérica*, prologue by G. de Reynold, Madrid: Ediciones Cultura Hispánica.

Glossary Terms

Liminality In identity debates, it corresponds with the experience of in-betweeness experienced by people who are ethnoracially mixed. It is that sense of not belonging fully to either one of the original ancestral ethnoracial strands.

Miscegenation This refers to the process of interbreeding between people from different ethnoracial groups. In colonial Latin America it refers to the process of intermixture between Spanish (Europeans), Indigenous, and African peoples, and their mixed offspring.

PART II

Traditions

4

Central American Christianity

Robert A. Danielson

Introduction

Geographically, Central America can be defined as the seven nations which bridge North and South America, including the nations of Belize, Guatemala, El Salvador, Honduras, Nicaragua, Costa Rica, and Panama. Yet despite its close geographical proximity, this region represents great cultural diversity. In this brief examination of the history of Christianity in Central America, Belize will be largely excluded. Since 1840, Belize was mostly under British colonial control, first as British Honduras and then as the nation of Belize. Due to this historical relationship, its religious history diverges from the rest of Central America and holds more in common with the British Caribbean. Likewise, Panama primarily aligned itself politically and culturally with the South American nations of Colombia, Ecuador, and Venezuela after it split from Spain in 1821. Even though it shares a history of Spanish colonialism and the common official language of Spanish, its historical development is more closely tied with South America. For the purposes of this chapter, Central America will be defined as Guatemala, El Salvador, Honduras, Nicaragua, and Costa Rica, five nations that share a common history, culture, language, and religious development.

Indigenous Influences

Culturally, the five Central American nations are not completely homogenous. They can be divided into three broad cultural areas. Most of Guatemala and western Honduras (as well as Belize) were part of the Mayan Empire, with a complex hierarchy, grand temples, and a culture which included writing and complex astronomy. The Pacific coast of Guatemala, western El Salvador, and Nicaragua have long contained cultures connected to the Nahuatl-speaking people of southern Mexico, which also had developed a complex civilization, most frequently known through the Aztecs of Mexico. These groups had taken over these areas of Central America from previous Mayan populations or other tribes and they included the Pipil of El Salvador and the Nicarao of Nicaragua. Eastern Honduras, eastern El Salvador, parts of Nicaragua, and Costa Rica were inhabited by different tribal groups, including the Lenca, the Chorotegas, the Subtibias, the Bribri, and the Boruca. With this ethnic and cultural diversity, each region has subtle religious and cultural differences based on how much influence the Indigenous people maintained throughout the subsequent years of conquest and colonialism.

The Spanish Conquest and Early Roman Catholicism (1520–1850)

It did not take long for the Spanish conquistadors in Mexico to find their way south after defeating the Aztecs in 1521. After landing in Panama in 1520, Gil González Dávila entered what is today Costa Rica in 1522 with little resistance after first moving through Nicaragua. A follow-up expedition by Francisco Hernández de Córdoba concluded the conquest of what is today Nicaragua in 1524. Also in 1524, Gil González Dávila moved into Honduras, followed by Hernán Cortés, but due to fierce resistance from the Lenca tribe, it was not completely conquered until about 1539. By 1528, Pedro de Alvarado had defeated most of the Mayan kingdoms of Guatemala and the Pipil of El Salvador. By 1543, the Spanish Crown had created the *Audiencia y Cancillería Real de Santiago de Guatemala* (Royal Appellate Court and Chancellery of St. James of Guatemala), an official jurisdiction which included most of what is now Central America, including the Mexican state of Chiapas (but excluding Panama and Belize). In 1609, this region would become the Captaincy General of Guatemala, also referred to as the Kingdom of Guatemala.

Roman Catholicism came with the Spanish conquest and would become the dominant religion in the region. The mission work was often accomplished by Dominicans or Franciscans, and the oppression of the Native people was usually the rule. Especially noteworthy was a Franciscan, Diego de Landa Calderón, a Spanish bishop of the Yucatán who notoriously destroyed most of the books of the Mayan culture in 1562 and brought the Spanish Inquisition to root out idolatry. One exception to this brutal history of repression was the noted missionary Bartolomé de las Casas, who volunteered to help Christianize the Tezulután region of Guatemala after the conquistadors had failed (Grubb 1937: 55–7). Las Casas and the Dominicans were given charge of the region and were allowed to Christianize the area by using the Quiché language to compose a poem of the history of the Bible. Their work was successful enough to keep out Spanish soldiers for a lengthy time.

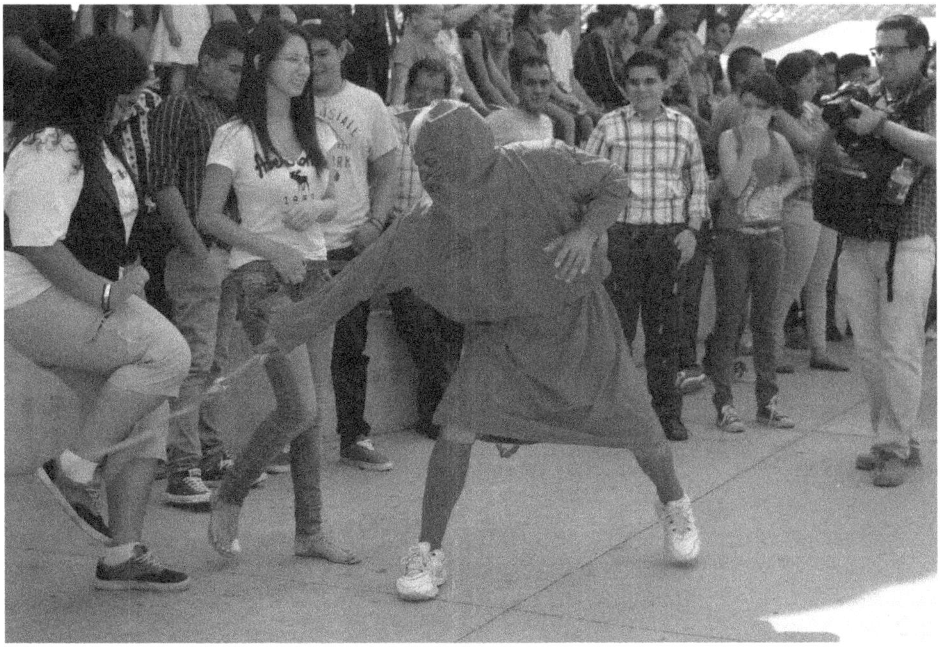

FIGURE 4.1 *The Talcigüines of Texistepeque, El Salvador use pre-Hispanic images in traditional Catholic dramas still performed today. Photo by Kelly Godoy de Danielson.*

For the most part, Catholic efforts were often superficial and only masked ongoing Indigenous beliefs. Baptized Natives often combined some Christian ideas with their own traditional religions. Saints, such as the Black Christ of Esquipulas in Guatemala, similar to the Virgin of Guadalupe in Mexico, took on characteristics of local traditional gods, and local fiestas were celebrated for these patron saints. According to some views, the Black Christ is connected with Mayan symbolism of caves and mountains, and the cross and may be connected to the worship of Ek Chuah, a Black Mayan god perhaps worshiped in Copan, Honduras (Kapusta 2016: 86–7).

A similar case also included pre-Hispanic images in performances like the Talcigüines of El Salvador, performed on the Monday of Holy Week in the town of Texistepeque. In this performance, men in jaguar-like costumes whip local inhabitants until a Christ figure emerges from the local church to defeat them. This is thought to possibly be a remnant of Nahuatl religious dramas, which were common in early mission work in Mexico (Danielson 2017). Such early accounts of contextualization were common and included training young Indigenous men for the priesthood and the composition of the syncretistic Books of Chilam Balam, which blended Christian and Indigenous religion together in the seventeenth and eighteenth centuries, usually in areas outside firm Spanish control. The perceived failure of these forms of contextualization led Roman

Catholic missions in other parts of the world to stick closely to untranslated Latin texts as Catholic missions progressed.

As the influence of the US Revolution against Britain (1776) and the French Revolution (1789) began to spread, and as Spain was weakened by the Napoleonic Wars (from 1807 to 1814), the Spanish Empire in the New World began to dissolve. The Captaincy General of Guatemala was part of a movement that included Mexico (1810–21), Argentina (1816), and Simón Bolívar (who helped liberate Venezuela, Colombia, Panama, Ecuador, Peru, and Bolivia from 1808 to 1824). On September 15, 1821, the Central American nations declared their independence from Spain. While briefly a part of the First Mexican Empire, the Federal Republic of Central America was declared on July 1, 1823. In 1840, the Federal Republic dissolved into the independent nations of Guatemala, El Salvador, Honduras, Nicaragua, and Costa Rica. As the ties with Spain were broken, the monopoly of the Roman Catholic Church over the region also began to weaken. Anticlerical movements often accompanied these independence movements and opened the way for Protestants to enter Central America, in part by curtailing the numbers of priests and the political power of the Catholic Church (Schwaller 2011: 162–5).

With this shift in regard to Catholic clergy, the focus moved more strongly to the role of lay people, especially in terms of local religious festivals and fiestas (Cleary 2011: 244–7). These became quite elaborate over time, and each local town has its patron saint and special days for religious processions and festivals. Often in Central America, these fiestas include tasks for lay Catholics or special groups, often called a **cofradía** (brotherhood), which organized the processions, the care of the church and statues of the saints, and even the making of elaborate carpets in the streets for the annual processions which are made of colored sawdust, flowers, and other natural elements.

Early Protestantism in Central America (1850–1960)

There were a few early efforts to bring Protestantism into Central America, mostly from British controlled regions. The Moravian mission in Nicaragua, which started in 1849, and the work of Anglicans, Methodists, and some Baptists entering from Belize into Guatemala as early as the 1820s are some examples. Belize would also become a center for the early work of the British and Foreign Bible Society in the 1830s. In Costa Rica, the Jamaican Baptist Missionary Society arrived in 1887, and the British Methodists arrived in 1894. The Presbyterians would enter Guatemala in 1882 at the invitation of President Justo Rufino Barrios. But most of this early pioneer work was fragmentary and not influential in spreading the Protestant faith. This work often focused on expatriates or English-speaking people living in Central America and expanded very little into Spanish-speaking areas.

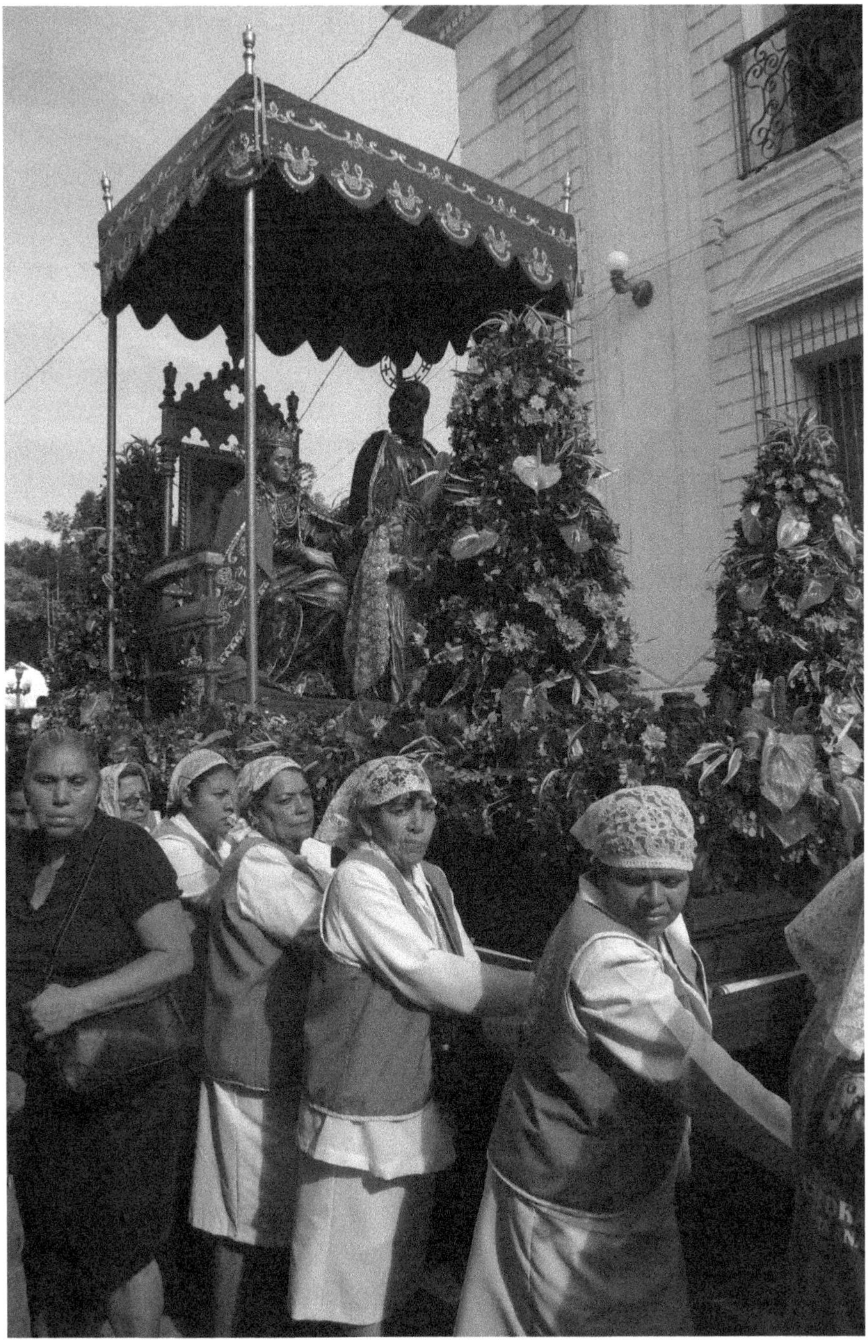

FIGURE 4.2 *The procession of the image of Saint Anne, the Patron Saint of Santa Ana, El Salvador during the fiesta held every July. Photo by Kelly Godoy de Danielson.*

Francisco G. Penzotti (1851–1925)

One of the most important influences on the start of Protestant work in Central America was Francisco G. Penzotti. Penzotti had been born in Italy but became an immigrant to Uruguay at 13 years old. He was converted at a Methodist mission in 1876 and then became a worker for the American Bible Society. He worked as a **colporteur**, selling Bibles and religious literature while preaching in South America. In 1890, he was arrested in Peru and his trial and imprisonment would become international news, referred to as the Penzotti Affair. He was released in 1891 and by 1894 he was sent to open branch work of the American Bible Society in Central America. Penzotti worked in Central America for about fifteen years and, by the time he left, he had organized branches of the American Bible Society in all of the Central American nations (Dwight 1916; Penzotti 1914).

Penzotti's key effort in bringing Protestant Christianity to Central America was by developing networks of local colporteurs, who were the very first evangelists in the region. They took the brunt of anti-Protestant attacks and traveled constantly, selling Bibles and other Christian literature. The use of colporteurs in Latin America reflects a key question about mission in Latin America: should Roman Catholics be considered Christians by Protestants? Some mainline Christian groups argued that Latin America had already been evangelized and so the mission focus should be on Africa and Asia. For more conservative Protestants, this argument was not valid since the reading of scripture in Catholicism was mostly limited to the Latin Mass. This is why groups like the American Bible Society set out to make Bibles in Spanish available to the general public. Colporteurs carried the scripture and sold it, but they also preached and planted churches when possible. Many of their names are unknown, but these organized networks of local colporteurs would be the primary source for native pastors as Protestant groups continued to grow.

Central American Mission

One of the most important early influences on Protestantism in Central America can be linked to an independent mission organization called the Central American Mission (CAM). Founded by Cyrus I. Scofield, best known for his influential reference Bible, this group was a conservative religious effort centered in Texas with a special passion to reach Central America. In 1891, their first missionaries arrived in Costa Rica, followed by missions in El Salvador and Honduras in 1896, Guatemala in 1899, and Nicaragua in 1900. The early missionaries from CAM were guided by Penzotti, who helped their missionaries plant missions in Nicaragua, El Salvador, and Honduras. He even helped lead services in CAM churches in El Salvador (Spain 1954).

The Central American Mission provided the first focused Protestant mission in the region to Spanish speakers. They organized churches and provided resources to help local colporteurs become established pastors. CAM groups still exist in Central

America, including the *Iglesia Evangélica Centroamericana en Guatemala* (Central American Evangelical Church in Guatemala), Costa Rica's *Asociación de Iglesias Evangélicas Centroamericanas* (Association of Central American Evangelical Churches), El Salvador's *Iglesia Evangélica de El Salvador* (Evangelical Church of El Salvador), and Honduras's *Camino Global* (Global Way). CAM provided the foundational work from which most other Protestant work would grow in the region as well.

Holiness/Pentecostal Mission Work

At about the same time as CAM, independent missionaries from Holiness churches and early Pentecostal groups began to arrive in the region. In 1896, two members of the Salvation Army from the United Kingdom, Mr. and Mrs. Fred Moules, settled in San Pedro, Costa Rica. They were joined by another worker and in 1907 a Peruvian, Captain Eduardo Palaci, and a Jamaican, Lieutenant George Stewart, officially opened the mission in Port Limón, but this remained primarily an English-language work.

In 1898, the Christian Brethren (a branch of the Plymouth Brethren) began a small effort in San Pedro Sula, Honduras with Christopher Knapp. Later joined by Alfred Hockins of the British and Foreign Bible Society, it would become part of Christian Missions in Many Lands in 1919. But this mission work also remained rather isolated.

Guatemala was the site of several small independent Holiness missions. In 1902, two workers from the Boyle Heights Training School for Christian Workers in California arrived in the capital to learn Spanish and soon founded a mission work in Chiquimula, Guatemala. They returned with reinforcements in 1903, and the mission was eventually taken over by the Californian Yearly Meeting of Friends (a group of Quakers with a Holiness orientation) who had provided most of the workers (Enyart 1970). By 1912, the Quakers had spread their mission to Honduras. In 1903, the Pentecostal Mission entered the nation and would end up becoming the foundational work for the Church of the Nazarene in Guatemala.

A little-known Canadian missionary, Frederick Ernest Mebius, seems to have arrived between 1904 and 1907 in the area of Santa Ana, El Salvador. He had a background with the Christian and Missionary Alliance in Bolivia but was independent at this time and may have had associations with the Quakers in Guatemala. He established a small group of believers and returned to the United States, where he became Pentecostal. He returned to resume his mission work in El Salvador in 1910, and his churches would become an important foundation for independent Pentecostals in El Salvador (sometimes referred to as the Free Apostolic Churches), the Assemblies of God (1927) in El Salvador, and the Church of God (Cleveland) (1941 or 1942) in El Salvador. In 1931, Mebius is also credited with traveling to Honduras and establishing the first Pentecostal churches there which joined with the Assemblies of God around 1940.

Venus Shoneckey and his family came to Nicaragua in 1911 and founded a Pentecostal mission which joined with the Assemblies of God in the 1930s. These

FIGURE 4.3 *The Holiness missionaries of the California Yearly Meeting of Friends sent to Guatemala in 1903. Photo courtesy of Azusa Pacific University Special Collections.*

small Pentecostal movements would often join traditional Pentecostal groups later, but many also remained independent, and it is not uncommon to find small independent Pentecostal churches in Central America.

In this early period of time, Holiness/Pentecostal missions were often small, faith-based efforts led by motivated individuals. They built off of the previous work of colporteurs from the Bible Societies and Central American Mission but introduced theological ideas that would take root in the Central American people and eventually emerge in indigenous Pentecostal movements, and so these early efforts are particularly worth noting.

Mainline Protestants and Comity Agreements

Mainline Protestant groups followed CAM and the early Holiness and Pentecostal missionaries into the region. Presbyterians were already present in Guatemala in 1882, Methodists entered Costa Rica in 1894, and Baptists had entered Honduras in

1846 (via work from Belize) before entering El Salvador in 1911 and Nicaragua in 1917. Traditionally at that time, mainline Christian groups would divide up mission territory through **comity agreements**. These agreements were an informal (and sometimes formal) division of political territory among various religious organizations. The principle was to reduce the costs of Christian mission and to spread out resources without duplicating work or needless competition. This idea seldom worked well.

Central America was formally divided by comity agreements at the Panama Congress of 1916, one of the first major ecumenical mission conferences held as an offshoot of the Edinburgh 1910 conference. CAM did not attend the Panama Congress because it was seen as being too friendly to Roman Catholicism. As a result, in the formal division, the American Baptists were assigned El Salvador, Honduras, and Nicaragua as their territory. The Presbyterians were assigned Guatemala, and the Methodists were assigned Costa Rica and Panama (Hallum 1996: 29). CAM and Holiness/Pentecostal groups simply ignored these divisions.

The rise of Protestant Christianity in Central America occurred alongside the rise of American imperialism in the region as well. The wealth of cash crops such as sugar, coffee, bananas, and cacao attracted a great deal of investment from the United States, and military control of the various nations seemed to mark this period. While Costa Rica was rather peaceful, the nation experienced the military dictatorship of General Federico Tinoco Granados (1917–9) and a brief civil war in 1948 after a disputed election. El Salvador experienced various changes in government, often with military coups. The administration of General Maximiliano Hernández Martínez led to a revolt in 1932 in which tens of thousands died, mostly Indigenous people. Guatemala likewise experienced multiple changes in leadership. Perhaps one of the most infamous being that of Estrada Cabrera, who turned over large amounts of land and control to the United Fruit Company in 1904 for their banana business. In 1952, the United States would orchestrate a coup to remove Jacobo Árbenz Guzmán when the fortunes of the United Fruit Company were threatened. Likewise, US fruit companies, including the United Fruit Company, Cuyamel Fruit Company, and Standard Fruit Company, would control the politics of Honduras, which was invaded by US troops in 1903, 1907, 1911, 1912, 1919, 1924, and 1925. The United States also supported the overthrow of José Santos Zelaya in Nicaragua, occupying the country from 1909 to 1933. This situation tended to relate imperialism and Protestantism in many minds and often in the church's relationship to military dictatorships as well.

During this period of time, sharp divisions arose between Roman Catholics and Protestants, who are traditionally referred to as *Evangélicos* (Evangelicals). This term has come to be applied to members of both traditional mainline Protestant denominations as well as Pentecostals and newer independent Neo-Charismatic groups (discussed below).

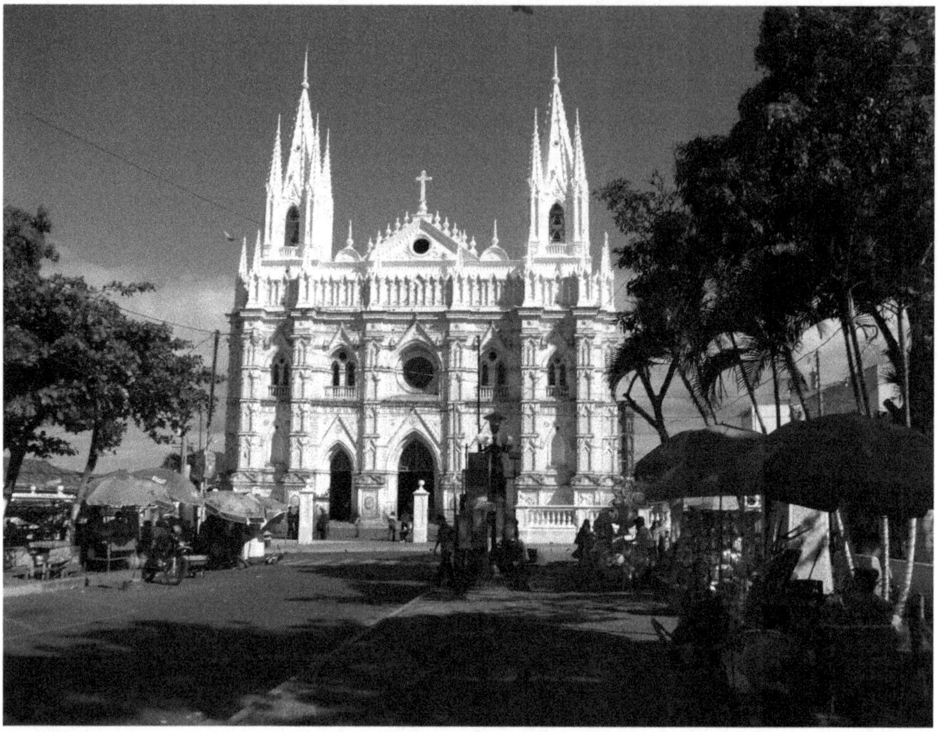

FIGURE 4.4 *The Roman Catholic Cathedral in Santa Ana, El Salvador. Despite the rise of Protestantism, Catholic churches still dominate the urban centers. Photo by Kelly Godoy de Danielson.*

Rise of Liberation Theology and Civil War (1960–2000)

While the vast majority of the people still saw themselves as Roman Catholics during the period of imperialism, the Roman Catholic Church itself did little to encourage people to move toward political action. This began to change with the Second Vatican Council from 1962 to 1965. There was a renewed interest in reading scripture, in ecumenism, moving the Mass from Latin to local languages, and eventually in political and social concerns. This later movement was especially influential in Latin America, where the Second Episcopal Conference of Latin America in Medellín, Colombia solidified Liberation Theology in Latin America. Many leaders came out of South America, with Leonardo Boff (Brazil), Gustavo Gutiérrez (Peru), and Juan Luis Segundo (Uruguay) frequently earning mention in historical writings. However, this movement also influenced Central America, in particular El Salvador, where Jon Sobrino, Ignacio Ellacuría, and Óscar Romero became well-known figures in the Catholic movement for liberation from poverty and oppression. In Costa Rica, Chilean-born Pablo Richard Guzmán was also associated with this movement. The movement frequently led to division within Catholic leadership between more conservative, traditional leaders and those impacted by the new thinking emerging from Liberation Theology (Schwaller 2011: 250–8).

This development led to a volatile period of time in Central America as civil wars shook the region and the nations struggled to form democratic governments. From 1960 to 1996, Guatemala fought a violent civil war between the US-backed government and leftist rebels. After periodic fighting in the 1960s and 1970s in Nicaragua, leftist rebels, called the Sandinista National Liberation Front, overthrew the Somoza dynasty in 1979. The United States backed the right-wing Contras against the Sandinistas in a civil war which lasted until 1990. In 1979, violence broke out in El Salvador, and the assassination of Archbishop Óscar Romero helped send the nation into civil war between the US-backed government and leftist rebels until the 1992 peace accords. The United States maintained a military presence in Honduras during much of this same time in order to support fighting against the Sandinistas of Nicaragua, so it was spared similar civil upheaval, but the Honduran army maintained an ongoing effort to put down leftist movements involved in kidnappings and other attacks. Only Costa Rica managed to sustain a strong stable democratic government and economy through this period of time.

While it is not accurate to say that Liberation Theology was the only reason for this intense period of fighting and violence (there were other social and economic inequalities and political forces at work as well), it was a contributing cause, as it encouraged the poor and oppressed to see liberation as a part of God's action in the world. Through Liberation Theology, **Ecclesial Base Communities** sought to educate, organize, and empower people who had previously been economically and socially oppressed. This helped motivate the poor to rally against injustice and fight for better treatment. Liberation Theology particularly played an important role in Nicaragua and El Salvador and often resulted in divisions within the Roman Catholic Church itself.

Growth of Pentecostalism

As Roman Catholicism focused on the issues of social and economic liberation, the early work of the Holiness Movement, and the early Pentecostals which followed them, began to take root and grow rapidly in the context of increasing political and social violence. Pentecostalism offered a different type of liberation, which was spiritual and not political, but also helped to empower people who were usually left on the margins. While some of these movements were tied with traditional Pentecostal denominations, many of them are uniquely Central American, with local leaders and structures. Until the 1960s, around 90 percent of people in Central America considered themselves to be Roman Catholic. That number has dropped to around 69 percent, and most of those who have left the Roman Catholic Church have moved toward Protestantism, but primarily to Pentecostalism (Wormald 2014).

Part of the success of Pentecostalism in Central America was due to its being planted early among the people, primarily the poor, with their own Indigenous leaders and with worship styles that incorporated traditional music and rhythms. Pentecostalism also focused on faith healing and empowered people spiritually, when the society around them often kept them poor and marginalized. Unlike the Roman Catholic Church, men and women could become Pentecostal leaders through the gifts of the Holy Spirit and did not require special education or training. For those with limited educational opportunities and few social connections, Pentecostalism provided a faith that allowed people to move away from alcohol and drugs and into more healthy communities and relationships.

In large part, this movement has exemplified a rejection of Liberation Theology and the violence of the civil wars and political upheaval. One important exception was General Efraín RÍos Montt, who served as president of Guatemala after a military coup in 1982. Later found guilty of genocide in 2013, Montt was an Evangelical of the *Iglesia El Verbo* church, with connections to the Jesus Movement in California (Anfuso and Sczepanski 1983; Garrard-Burnett 2010). While not precisely Pentecostal, such evangelical churches were often influenced by the growing Charismatic Movement.

FIGURE 4.5 *A small Pentecostal church in rural El Salvador. Photo by Kelly Godoy de Danielson.*

As Pentecostalism has grown and the wars have ended, new problems have arisen. Violence from increased gang activity and the stresses of families broken by immigration to seek better opportunities, especially in the United States, has led to new problems, which Pentecostal leaders are seeking to respond to with new ministries and outreach. There has also been a growth in independent Protestant groups that do not profess to be Pentecostal but share many similar characteristics and are referred to as Neo-Charismatics. These churches have Pentecostal types of worship and ministries and may be tied to traditional Protestant denominations in some fashion but have often developed local leadership which is not under the control of outside denominations (Danielson 2013; Danielson and Vega 2014). All of these groups have grown during this particular period, while traditional Protestants have tended to decline or stay at a fairly small, constant number.

The Catholic Charismatic Movement as a Response

As Pentecostalism and the Neo-Charismatic groups began to grow in the 1960s and 1970s in Central America, the Roman Catholic Church also experienced a movement away from Liberation Theology and toward the Catholic Charismatic Movement. This movement in Central America is often traced back to a Dominican, Francis Scott MacNutt, who was influenced by the Charismatic Movement in the United States and later founded Christian Healing Ministries. He visited Costa Rica and Guatemala in 1972, conducting Life in the Spirit seminars (Cleary 2011: 30). Around the same year, the movement spread into Nicaragua, where it became tied up with politics, especially in conservative opposition to the Sandinistas, where Liberation Theology had been popular and maintained some political power. MacNutt influenced Father James Burke in Bolivia, who brought Charismatic seminars into Honduras through *Délegados de la Palabra* (Delegates of the Word), locally trained leaders of small communities. The movement would enter El Salvador later in 1983 from Costa Rica with Father Miguel Ángel Zamora, a critical figure for the movement in San Salvador.

While Guatemala became the first country in Latin America to officially approve of the Catholic Charismatic Movement, the movement tends to focus on lay leadership and especially empowers women within the Roman Catholic Church. The growth of this movement focused on evangelization through catechists with Catholic Action, the *Cursillos de Cristiandad* (Short Courses in Christianity), and similar groups of dedicated lay people (Cleary 2011: 243–4). This movement has done much to stem the tide of growing Pentecostal and Neo-Charismatic Protestant churches but has also faced some criticism for the "Pentecostalization" of the traditional Roman Catholic Church. Nevertheless, this significant movement has drastically changed the religious landscape of Central America without actually changing membership within the churches themselves.

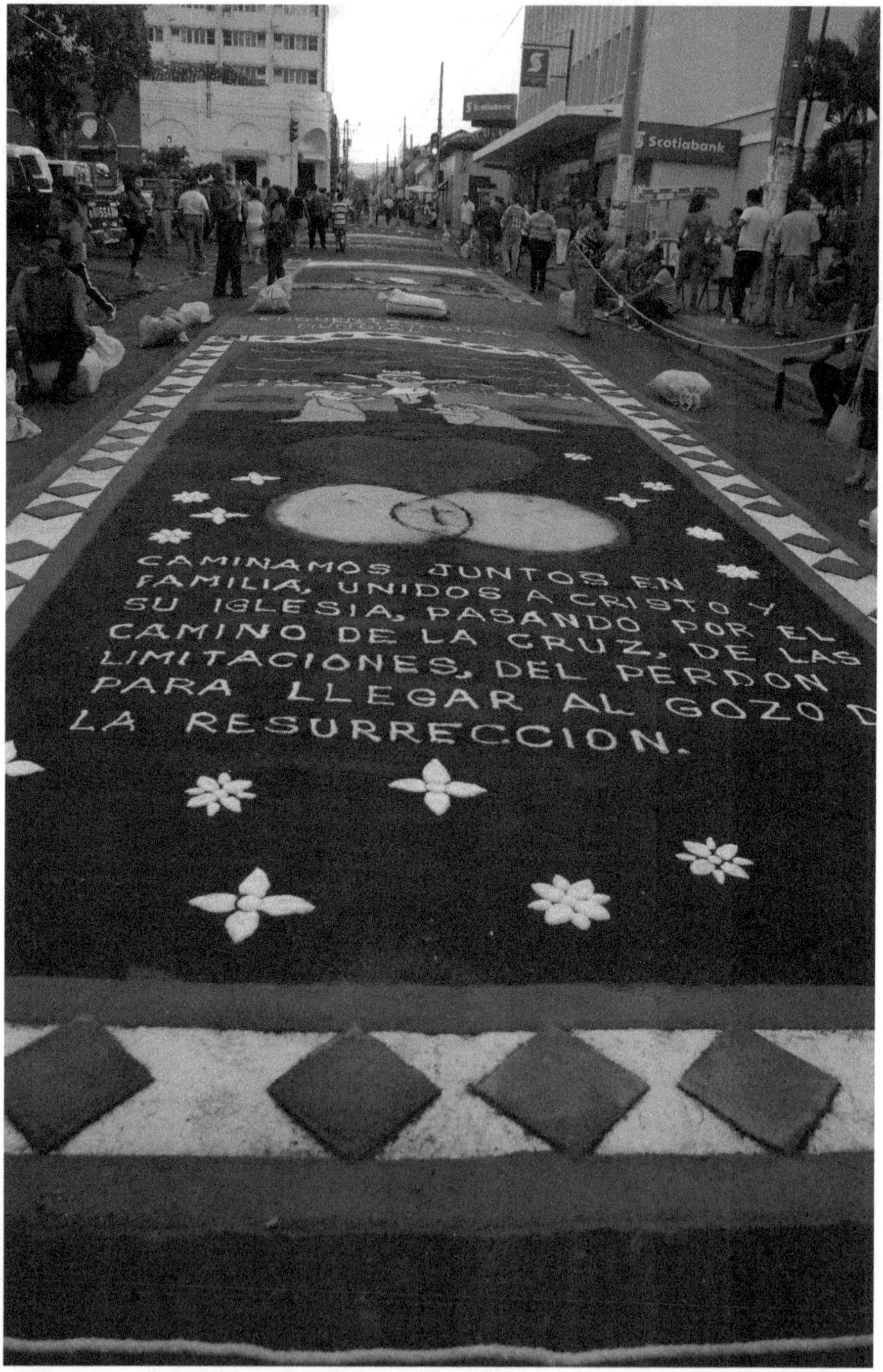

FIGURE 4.6 *The devotion of Roman Catholic lay people can be observed in the elaborate carpets they create for religious processions. Photo by Kelly Godoy de Danielson.*

Current Situation of Christianity in Central America (2000–Present)

Currently, Christianity in Central America is adjusting to many of these ongoing shifts. A 2014 survey of Latin Americans by the Pew Research Center (Wormald 2014) presented the statistical evidence for these shifts based on surveys of people's actual religious involvement. The numbers include the following data:

TABLE 4.1 *Results from the 2014 Pew Research Center Religion in Latin America survey.*

Nation	Roman Catholic (%)	Protestant (%)	Unaffiliated (%)
Costa Rica	62	25	9
El Salvador	50	36	12
Guatemala	50	41	6
Honduras	46	41	10
Nicaragua	50	40	10

Source: *Pew Research Center.*

According to 1970 figures, the average for Roman Catholic identification in Central America was roughly 93 percent compared to an average in 2014 of 52 percent, a decline of 41 percent in just 44 years. The shift to Protestantism is clear, but determining Pentecostal identification or Catholic Charismatic identification can be more complicated.

To accomplish an understanding of the influence of Pentecostal and Charismatic influence, the Pew Research Center asked two key questions based on key Pentecostal practices. The first asked if a person had witnessed divine healing in their churches. On average across Central America, 66.4 percent of Protestants and 41.6 percent of Catholics responded positively to the question. The second question asked how many had witnessed "speaking in tongues" at least occasionally in their churches. Across Central America, 89.4 percent of Protestants and 52.6 percent of Catholics responded positively. Most of the Pew numbers for the individual Central American nations are consistent with only minor variations.

From these figures, it is clear that Pentecostalism has had a major impact, with as many as 60–80 percent of the Protestant churches likely to be Pentecostal or Neo-Charismatic, and roughly 40–50 percent of Roman Catholics in Central America to be connected in some way to the Catholic Charismatic Movement and its influences. Protestants, especially Pentecostals, are growing in Central America, while the Roman Catholic Church is either shrinking or becoming more charismatic. New independent churches tend to be Neo-Charismatic with Pentecostal types of worship but with local leaders and authority structures (Danielson 2013). Some of these newer Neo-

Charismatic or Pentecostal churches are expanding outside of Central America due to immigration, many even being planted by immigrants in the United States and Canada or Europe, while Charismatic Catholics are likely making a similar impact on the Roman Catholic Church through immigration. Such movements are likely to continue, and if immigration trends continue, the impact of Pentecostal and Charismatic Christians from Central America is likely to be felt globally as well.

Further Reading

Alvarez, M, ed. 2016. *Reshaping of Mission in Latin America*, Regnum Edinburgh Centenary Series, Vol. 30. Eugene: Wipf and Stock.

Colón-Emeric, E. A. 2018. *Óscar Romero's Theological Vision: Liberation and the Transfiguration of the Poor*. Notre Dame: University of Notre Dame Press.

Hartch, T. 2014. *The Rebirth of Latin American Christianity*. New York: Oxford University Press.

Koll, K. A., ed. 2019. *Signs of New Life in Central America and the Caribbean: Christian Revitalization Amid Social Change*. Wilmore: First Fruits Press.

Wadkins, T. H. 2017. *The Rise of Pentecostalism in Modern El Salvador: From the Blood of the Martyrs to the Baptism of the Spirit*. Waco: Baylor University Press.

References

Anfuso, J., and D. Sczepanski. 1983. *Efrain Rios Montt: Servant of Dictator?* Ventura: Vision House.

Cleary, E. L. 2011. *The Rise of Charismatic Catholicism in Latin America*. Gainesville: University Press of Florida.

Danielson, R. A. 2011. "A Transnational Faith: El Salvador and Immigrant Christianity." *The Asbury Journal* 66 (2): 4–17.

Danielson, R. A. 2013. "Independent Indigenous Protestant Mega Churches in El Salvador." *Missiology: An International Review* 41 (3): 329–42.

Danielson, R. A. 2015. "Transnationalism and the Pentecostal Salvadoran Church: A Case Study of *Misión Cristiana Elim*." In *Pentecostals and Charismatics in Latin America and Latino Communities*, edited by N. Medina and S. Alfaro, 111–24. New York: Palgrave MacMillan.

Danielson, R.A. 2017. "The Talcigüines of El Salvador: A Contextual Example of Nahua Drama in the Public Square." In *Public Theology. Working Papers of the American Society of Missiology*, edited by R. A. Danielson and W. L. Selvidge, Vol. 3, 22–41. Wilmore: First Fruits Press.

Danielson, R. A., and M. Vega. 2014. "The Vital Role of the Laity in Revitalization: A Case Study of Misión Cristiana Elim." *The Asbury Journal* 69 (1): 64–73.

Dwight, H. O. 1916. *The Centennial History of the American Bible Society*, Vol. 2. New York: Macmillan Company.

Enyart, P. 1970. *Friends in Central America*. South Pasadena: William Carey Library.

Garrard-Burnett, V. 2010. *Terror in the Land of the Holy Spirit: Guatemala under General Efrain Rios Montt, 1982–1983*. New York: Oxford University Press.

Grubb, K. G. 1937. *Religion in Central America*. New York: World Dominion Press.

Hallum, A. M. 1996. *Beyond Missionaries: Toward an Understanding of the Protestant Movement in Central America.* Lanham: Rowman and Littlefield Publishers, Inc.
Holland, C. L. 2010. "Costa Rica." In *Religion of the World: A Comprehensive Encyclopedia of Beliefs and Practices*, edited by J. G. Melton and M. Baumann, Vol. 2, 798–810. Santa Barbara: ABC-CLIO.
Holland, C. L. 2010. "El Salvador." In *Religion of the World: A Comprehensive Encyclopedia of Beliefs and Practices*, edited by J. G. Melton and M. Baumann, Vol. 3, 954–966. Santa Barbara: ABC-CLIO.
Holland, C. L. 2010. "Guatemala." In *Religion of the World: A Comprehensive Encyclopedia of Beliefs and Practices*, edited by J. G. Melton and M. Baumann, Vol. 3, 1267–1279. Santa Barbara: ABC-CLIO.
Holland, C. L. 2010. "Honduras." In *Religion of the World: A Comprehensive Encyclopedia of Beliefs and Practices*, edited by J. G. Melton and M. Baumann, Vol. 3, 1345–1356. Santa Barbara: ABC-CLIO.
Holland, C. L. 2010. "Nicaragua." In *Religion of the World: A Comprehensive Encyclopedia of Beliefs and Practices*, edited by J. G. Melton and M. Baumann, Vol. 5, 2085–96. Santa Barbara: ABC-CLIO.
Kapusta, J. 2016. "The Maya Pilgrimage to the Black Christ: A Phenomenology of Journey, Sacrifice, and Renewal." *Anthropos* 111 (1): 83–98.
Nelson, W. M. 1984. *Protestantism in Central America.* Grand Rapids: William B. Eerdmans.
Penzotti, F. 1914. "The Bible in Latin America." *Missionary Review of the World* 37: 839–42.
Schwaller, J.F. 2011. *The History of the Catholic Church in Latin America: From Conquest to Revolution and Beyond.* New York: New York University Press.
Spain, M. W. 1954. *"And in Samaria": Story of More Than Sixty Years' Missionary Witness in Central America 1890–1954.* Dallas: The Central American Mission.
Wormald, B. 2014. "Religion in Latin America." Accessed March 20, 2022. https://www.pewresearch.org/religion/2014/11/13/religion-in-latin-america/

Glossary Terms

Colporteurs were local Protestant men who traveled into remote areas to sell Bibles and other Christian literature. They would also evangelize and preach to the people in the local language and organize local churches if possible. Many later became local pastors for emerging Protestant groups.

A cofradía (or confraternity) is a local Roman Catholic lay organization which often helps organize fiestas and processions for patron saints and also helps with the upkeep of the church buildings and the care of the statues of the saints.

Comity agreements were formal or informal arrangements formed mostly by mainline Protestant denominations to divide up territory for mission responsibility. This was done to reduce competition and maximize the use of available resources and missionaries.

Ecclesial base communities (or comunidades eclesiales de base) were locally run organizations of Roman Catholic lay people which emerged out of Liberation Theology. They were designed to teach and empower the poor and marginalized through theological study of the Bible and organize people for social reform on the local level.

5

Catholicism in Mexico

Carlos Garma Navarro

Introduction

Catholicism is still the principal religion in Mexico. According to the 2020 census, 97,864,218 persons consider themselves Catholic. This is 77.7 percent of the population of the country. It should be noted that these figures actually represent a decrease in the percentage of Catholics when compared to previous census information. In 2010, the national figures for members of this religion were higher at 83.9 percent. Yet, in 1960 the percentage of Catholics was 96.5 percent. There has been a gradual but continuous decline in the percentage of believers, a decline that became especially significant since 1970 (96.2 percent) to 1990 (89.7 percent) and again from 2000 (88.0 percent) to 2020 (77.7 percent) (it should be noted that these were periods of crisis and social transformation). During the same period other religious groups have grown consistently, most notably Evangelical Protestants, and to a lesser degree, Mormons, Jehovah's Witnesses, non-Christians such as Buddhists and Jews, and the "*no creyentes*" (nonbelievers), which includes agnostics and atheists. It should be noted that the decline of Catholicism is widespread in all of Latin America and that Mexico still has one of the largest total number of members in this faith for the region.

It is important to consider that there are significant regional variations regarding religious affiliation in Mexico. The western central states are often mentioned as the main core of Catholicism in the country. These states (Jalisco, Aguascalientes, Colima, Zacatecas, Michoacan, San Luis Potosi, and Guanajuato) all account for very high percentages of Catholic affiliation and participation. In this region, the percentage of Evangelical Protestants and nonbelievers is the lowest in the nation. In contrast, the southern states (Chiapas, Tabasco, Quintana Roo, and Yucatan) all show the lowest percentage of Catholic affiliation and participation. It is in this area where the presence of Evangelical Protestants and nonbelievers is highest. The influence of a growing religious diversity and the weakening of Catholic hegemony, a phenomenon that is prevalent in the countries of Central America (e.g., in Guatemala, El Salvador, Honduras, and Nicaragua) seems to have influenced Mexico's southernmost regions. Central Mexico (Mexico City, the State of Mexico, Puebla, Tlaxcala, Morelos, and Hidalgo) includes the largest metropolitan area of the country and important religious shrines. Until recently, Catholicism here was stable with high numbers, which have begun to decline quite recently due to the gradual growth of nonbelievers. The northern border states (Chihuahua, Sonora, Baja California, Nuevo Leon, and Tamaulipas) also show a decline in Catholic believers and growth of Evangelical Protestants but not as sustained as in southern Mexico. The two extremes can be seen if we compare the state with the largest percentage of Catholic believers—which is in Guanajuato, located in the Catholic core, with 90.8 percent of its population as Catholics according to the 2020 census—to the state with the lowest percentage of Catholic believers—which is Chiapas in the southern border, with 53.9 percent of its population as followers according to the 2020 census.

Organization of Catholicism

In Mexico, the term "Catholic Church" refers to the Roman Catholic Church, which considers the Pope as the highest spiritual leader and the successor of the apostle Peter as bishop of Rome. He is elected by the Sacred College of Cardinals, who are reunited after the previous Pope dies or resigns. In Mexico, there are some other Catholics such as members of the *Iglesia Católica Maronita* (Maronite Catholic Church), which is under the guidance of a patriarch in Beirut, Lebanon. However, this organization has very limited presence and only a small number of followers, most of whom are immigrants living in Mexico City.

The Catholic Church is organized in territorial units known as dioceses, each of which is under the spiritual jurisdiction of a bishop, who may eventually be promoted to archbishop or cardinal. The diocese itself is divided into parishes, which are administered by a particular priest who has been named by the bishop. In Spanish, these priests are called *curas*; in the United States, they are called pastors. The clergy who attend to parishes are priests and nuns who have made religious vows. Priests undergo training at seminaries such as those in Guadalajara, Puebla, Morelia, and Monterrey. There are also Catholic religious orders, which have male or female members. The persons in these associations are consecrated to a religious life and have made vows of loyalty to God, the Church, and the director of the order. There are actually over 500 religious orders in Mexico. Among the most important are Franciscans, Jesuits, Dominicans, Augustinians, Salesians, Marists, and Lasallists. A great amount of the social work of the Catholic Church is carried out by its religious orders.

Believers who are not clergy are considered laity. In Catholicism there are various lay movements, which may or may not be under the direction and guidance of the clergy, though the institution will try to assert certain control over them. In Mexico and Latin America, there is what experts and researchers have called "**Popular Catholicism**." It is based on practices carried out by **subaltern** sectors (peasants, Indigenous persons, urban lower classes, etc.), who often act with autonomy from the institutional Church's clergy. Popular religiosity is much more oriented to the worldly elements of survival (health and illness, drought or floods, situations of danger) than the spiritual aspects of persons. There is little interest in abstract theological matters. Rituals such as pilgrimages and visits to shrines and beliefs in the miraculous powers of sacred figures are important to these believers. Popular Catholicism is highly syncretic, with elements of Indigenous, African, and European cultures.

There are various Catholic lay movements and organizations in Mexico which are quite different in their social and spiritual orientations. Among the most important are the *Opus Dei* (Latin for "The Work of God"), *Movimiento Familiar Cristiano* (Christian Family Movement), *Comunidades Eclesiales de Base* (Ecclesial Base Communities), *Adoración Nocturna* (Nocturnal Adoration), and *Renovación Carismatica* (Charismatic Renewal). The flexibility that allows Catholic believers various options in their faith is part of the current strategy of the Catholic Church to confront the growing competition of other religions and spiritualties, and in particular Evangelical Protestantism.

Practices, Beliefs, and Social Attitudes

It is important to note that there are significant differences among Catholics in Mexico, particularly regarding how they practice their faith. The element that unifies them as members of this religion is baptism, a sacrament usually performed at infancy. Participation in the other sacraments is another matter. Receiving the First Holy Communion is common across urban Mexico and in rural communities staffed with priests. Yet, recent surveys (ENCREER/RIFREM 2016) have shown that many Catholic Mexicans do not attend weekly Mass, receive Holy Communion, or go to confession on a regular basis. Official marriage through the Catholic Church seems to be on the decline, and many young people prefer to simply have a civil matrimony ceremony. A religious burial, however, is still highly regarded and sought after by believers. Practicing Catholics who receive the sacraments regularly and follow religious rules and orientations carefully are still quite numerous in Mexico. However, there is a significant number of "nominal Catholics," those who are baptized but do not participate regularly in official religious services or receive the sacraments. Most of these nominal Catholics are practitioners of popular Catholicism.

Recent surveys show that one of the most favored religious practices of Mexican Catholics is not even an official sacrament recognized in church doctrine but instead is a popular activity: participation in religious pilgrimages and visits to shrines and holy sites. Throughout the country, pilgrims go to the many places of devotion, where they congregate to pray and visit the sacred images of popular devotion that represent Christ, the Virgin Mary, and diverse saints. The followers believe that these figures and representations have miraculous powers. Mexico can indeed be called a country of pilgrimage, as anthropologists Victor and Edith Turner once wrote (2011). There are many localities which have shrines and sanctuaries that receive pilgrims who travel distances to worship at the sites where the religious figures and representations are venerated. Among the most important shrines are those located in San Juan de Lagos in Jalisco, Chalma in the State of Mexico, Ocotlán in Tlaxcala, Cerro del Cubilete in Guanajuato, Fresnillo in Zacatecas, Ixamal in Yucatán, and Juquila in Oaxaca. The most important shrine of all is the Basilica of Guadalupe, located on the hill of Tepeyac on the outskirts of Mexico City. The Basilica of Guadalupe is actually tied with the Cathedral of Saint Peter in Rome as the two Catholic shrines that receive the greatest number of visitors.

Another activity that is related to pilgrimage, and that is often combined with it, is the participation in religious *fiestas* or feasts that celebrate the official date of the saints or the Virgin. The "fiesta system" involves the participation of the village or town, but often also relies on individual sponsors who must support a large share

FIGURE 5.1 Pilgrims *making their way to the shrine of San Juan de los Lagos in Jalisco.* Source: *Monica Guadalupe Delgado del Real/Wikimedia Commons.*

of the costs for food, musicians, shows, and even fireworks. These events are important in many communities which are often located in rural areas or in places where migrants from these localities have arrived. This has facilitated the feasts of the **patron saints** in some communities to amass a following across Mexico and internationally. For example, some rural communities in Oaxaca or Michoacan have sponsors for local fiestas who live in Mexico City, Tijuana, California, Illinois, or Texas and send their monetary support or remittances from distant areas, have set up their own Guadalupan shrines abroad, and will even travel to be present on the date of the communal event (Peña 2011).

Another special activity is putting up altars or small religious shrines that may be kept in a special place at home or in specific locations within the public space, such as street corners, markets, working venues, and even certain areas where special protection is required such as prisons. The altars are dedicated to images of Christ, the Virgin Mary, and different saints. The believer will strive to keep the altar in good condition and may go to great lengths and incur expenses to do so. The shrine is celebrated on a special date dedicated to the venerated religious figure or holy person, and often ritual festivities are carried out on that day.

Special mention should be made here of the altars for "*Dia de los Muertos*" (Day of the Dead), which is celebrated on the second of November. These shrines are made to remember specific deceased persons and hold objects related to them. Originally, they were temporary private shrines made in homes or sometimes placed on tombs in cemeteries. The elaboration of altars to the dead was once considered a practice that was mostly carried out in regions with a strong Indigenous influence like Oaxaca and Michoacan. Yet in the last decades, the "*altares de muertos*" have become enormously popular due in part to the influence of national and international promotions and campaigns. Elaborate altars can now be found in schools and other public buildings throughout the country. November 2 is now an official holiday and "Dia de los Muertos" has been labeled as an important part of Mexican national culture. It is interesting to note that this very syncretic practice of building shrines to the dead is reluctantly accepted by the Catholic Church authorities, who will admit that it is not officially a recognized Catholic ceremony. Evangelical Protestants by and large view "Dia de los Muertos" as a pagan practice.

Let us now consider beliefs. Most Catholic believers from this country venerate the Virgin of Guadalupe. Her devotees, in general, are certain of the existence of God and life after death. Nevertheless, there is a certain decline in the belief in the devil and hell among persons with a higher educational level. Yet the formal formation and knowledge about religion varies greatly according to different social groups and regions and sometimes even due to political persuasion. In fact, conservative families still favor a religious education for their children. The number of persons who attend catechism and religious classes is declining. Bible reading is practiced by various Catholics even though many followers do not even have a copy of the scriptures. Priests and members of religious orders continue to play a significant role in this matter. For example, religious education is rather limited in many rural areas that lack a resident member of the clergy or of a religious order.

The attitudes and beliefs of Mexican Catholics regarding matters of gender, sexual orientation, and abortion continue to attract much study. The public role of the Catholic Church is affected by its positions on aspects related to some of its beliefs on human life. According to recent surveys (ENCREER/RIFREM 2016), most Mexican Catholics do not favor the legalization of abortion, though a significant minority would accept it. According to the same sources, the majority of persons affiliated with the Catholic Church do not accept homosexual marriage, and an even greater percentage do not accept adoption of children by homosexual couples. Again, on both issues, a significant minority of believers disagree. Nevertheless, a very strong majority of Mexican Catholics favor the separation of church and state as well as favor education on sexuality in public schools. It is interesting that Catholic believers (or laity) in general are somewhat more liberal in these matters than the Catholic clergy themselves. Persons in certain social sectors (those who are younger and have a higher level of formal education) regard Catholic authorities with suspicion and mistrust due to knowledge of clerical abuse within the institution.

A Historical Overview

The Colonial Period

The presence of the Catholic Church in Mexico began when 12 Franciscan missionaries arrived at the port of Veracruz on May 13, 1524. Hernán Cortes, the Spanish *conquistador* whose armed forces defeated the Aztec empire on 1521, had requested of the Spanish Crown the participation of religious orders to carry out the swift evangelization of the Indigenous population. The conversion of the Native American population to the new faith was considered an important justification of the violent subordination carried out by the European imperial forces.

However, important regulations on religion in the New World had already been established by then. The Royal Agreement of 1501, made by Pope Alexander VI with the Spanish and Portuguese monarchies, established that Catholicism was the only religion allowed in the Americas. This was later organized as the "Patronato Regio" (Royal Patronage) in 1508, which formed a legal basis for the monopoly of Catholicism in the kingdom. All other forms of religious belief were prohibited, including Lutheran "heresy," Judaism, and traditional Native American practices. All persons who immigrated to New Spain had to be baptized as Catholics. This restriction was applied not only to the Spanish, Portuguese, and other European colonizers but also to all enslaved people brought from Africa. In order to carry out the surveillance and enforcement of religion, the high court and tribunal of the Inquisition was founded in Mexico City in 1572 (Schwaller 2011: 13–71).

FIGURE 5.2 *A mural at the Immaculate Conception Church in Ozumba, Mexico depicts Hernán Cortes greeting the twelve Franciscan "Apostles" upon their arrival.* Source: *Alejandro Linares Garcia/Wikimedia Commons.*

European missionaries carried out the evangelization of the Indigenous population, which resulted in the gradual adaptation of the new faith. The Spanish colonial authorities and members of the clergy committed many violent excesses and atrocities. So poor were conditions of colonization that some represented voices of dissent arose within the clerical ranks. The Dominican friar, Bartolomé de las Casas, Bishop of Chiapas, denounced the excessive exploitation and repression of Indigenous peoples. He participated in public debates and was the author of important essays, including his famous text, "Brevisma Relación de la Destrucción de las Indias" (Brief Account of the Destruction of the Indies) written in 1542 and published in Seville, Spain, in 1552 (Rivera 1992).

The Catholic Church enjoyed great economic and social power during Mexico's long colonial period (1521–1821), when the country was officially called el Virreinato de la Nueva España (Viceroyalty of New Spain). The Royal Patronage permitted a close collaboration between church and state. The Catholic clergy and religious orders gained many large properties and founded important institutions, including convents, seminaries, and schools. Cathedrals, sanctuaries, shrines, and churches were built with Indigenous and slave labor throughout the colony.

The Virgin of Guadalupe emerged as an important source of popular religious fervor and national identity. According to traditional sources, this Marian apparition transpired on the hill of Tepeyac, then outside of Mexico City, in December 1531, when the Virgin Mary appeared to Juan Diego Cuahtlatoatzin, a young Indigenous person, and asked him to build a shrine in her honor there. When this request was received with disbelief by the clergy, the Virgin miraculously appeared imprinted on the *tilma* (robe) used by Juan Diego. This relic is still shown publicly at the Basilica of Guadalupe, built on the site of the apparition. The first historical account of the event is believed to be the text known as the "Nican Mopohua" (thus it is written), composed in the Nahuatl language by Antonio Valeriano in 1556. However, some discrepancies appeared. The Franciscan friars were critical of the veneration to the image because the hill of Tepeyac had been the site of pre-Hispanic rites offered to Tonantzin, a female Aztec deity related to the earth and fertility. The friars considered this veneration a situation where different cultural elements would be a source of confusion for Indigenous persons. But in the following years, the Virgin of Guadalupe became a symbol of God's love for all Mexicans. During various large epidemics during the colonial period, devotees used the image in public processions and they considered it to have miraculous powers. Different social movements with very different political orientations have also used the image on banners to ask for guidance and protection (Brading 2001).

FIGURE 5.3 *Juan Diego's tilma is displayed at the Basilica of Our Lady of Guadalupe in Mexico City.* Source: *Eman Kazemi/Alamy Stock Photo.*

Independence and Revolution

The War of Independence in Mexico (1810–21) saw Catholic clergy participate on both sides of the dispute. Two priests, Miguel Hidalgo y Costilla and José Maria Morelos y Pavón, were key military, leaders during the revolt. Both were captured and executed by the colonial military, which was entirely loyal to Spain. Church authorities in Mexico City, Madrid, and Rome condemned the actions of the rebel priests. After the consolidation of Mexico´s independence in 1821, however, ties between the Vatican and the new national government became strained. In just a few short years, the Royal Patronage was suspended, and the Inquisition and slavery were abolished.

In the mid-nineteenth century, Liberal anti-clerical leaders fought against Conservatives who supported the authorities of the Catholic Church and asked for a return to the colonial order. The Liberal victory culminated with the presidency of Benito Juárez (1857–71), an iconic figure in Mexican history, who is still until now the country's only president of Indigenous descent. Juárez separated church and state in 1875, establishing the first lay or secular state in Latin America and opening the door to Protestant institutions. The state confiscated and sold many rural properties belonging to clergy and religious orders. Later in that century, the government of Porfirio Díaz (1876–1910) showed greater tolerance toward the Catholic Church. His regime, known as the Porfiriato, gave rise to large-scale discontentment and revolutionary ferment.

When the Mexican Revolution began in 1910, political dissidents perceived the Church as a strong institution and a reactionary force that would compete with the revolutionary governments for the people's loyalties by seeking to impose a conservative order. The Mexican Constitution of 1917 codified a series of severe restrictions on the Catholic Church and the practice of religion in general. In the constitution, religious institutions were accorded no legal or juridical recognition, churches could not officially own property or run schools, seminary studies could not be recognized by universities or colleges, places of worship were to be state property, public religious ceremonies were outlawed, and priests and the members of religious orders could not vote or be involved in any political activities.

However, these laws were difficult to apply and their enforcement sparked a popular revolt called the "Cristero War" in the late 1920s. When President Plutarco Elias Calles (1924–8) enforced the constitutional restrictions in 1925, an armed peasant rebellion against the government began in the region of the central-western states, which had a strong presence of the Catholic Church. Many acts of violence took place on both sides of the conflict. A Jesuit priest named José Miguel Agustín Pro and a nun, Mother Concepcion Acevedo, were accused of participating in the assassination of former President Alvaro Obregon in 1928. The priest was convicted of murder and executed by firing squad the same year, and the nun was imprisoned for eleven years. In 1929, negotiations between the Vatican and the Mexican state, with the US diplomatic corps as an intermediary, ended the conflict (Meyer 2008).

The outcome was a so-called "modus vivendi" (Latin for "way of life") between church and state that involved a simulated application of the laws by the government and a passive acceptance by the religious authorities. The state governors and federal presidents learned to apply the restrictions discretely according to their personal inclinations or their political opportunism. Thus, while President Lázaro Cárdenas (1934–40) maintained a strong leftist inclination and applied the restrictions moderately, his successor President Manuel Avila Camacho (1941–7) openly recognized his Catholic faith and did not apply the law. However, changing the Constitution itself was not considered a viable alternative for many years.

Contemporary Events

Remarkably, this church and state arrangement remained in place until 1991, when President Carlos Salinas de Gortari sent the National Congress a proposal to modify sections of the constitution dealing with the official approach toward religion. The result was the Law of Religious Associations and Public Worship (Ley de Asociaciones Religiosas y Culto Público) enacted in 1992. The new law placed all churches under the category of Asociaciones Religiosas (Religious Associations or ARs). Currently, all ARs must register with the Ministry of the Interior to receive official recognition. To register they must present a list of all their clergy and assets; but they are exempt from taxation. Registered religious groups may now own property. Clergy still cannot hold political positions or any post awarded by popular election. ARs cannot own mass media outlets, but they can rent them. Mexico now has more than 9,000 registered ARs, more than 2,000 of which are linked to the Catholic Church (different religious orders and dioceses have their own registers and records).

The uneasy relationship between church and state continues in the twenty-first century. The conservative government of President Vicente Fox (2000–6) challenged the secular tradition of Mexican politics by showing a clear affinity for the Catholic Church. His government made widespread use of Catholic symbols and was reluctant to mediate in the resolution of religious conflicts. This tendency continued under the administration of President Felipe Calderón (2006–12), also of the conservative Partido Acción Nacional (National Action Party), who also favored public expressions of faith. President Enrique Peña Nieto (2012–8) tried to maintain a more liberal orientation during his administration, even attempting to legalize homosexual marriages on a federal level in 2016, a measure that provoked strong protests from conservative Catholics and Evangelicals which resulted in the proposal being retired. The current administration of President Andrés Manuel López Obrador (2018–present) has maintained a distant relationship with the Catholic Church, favoring instead certain Evangelical groups.

In the Catholic Church, divergent pastoral tendencies have developed in order to attend to the spiritual needs of the faithful. The most notable for its social impact was

Liberation Theology which sought a commitment to the so-called "popular" sectors of society, such as the urban poor, migrants, peasants, and Indigenous communities. This theological orientation was expressed in the work of Bishops Sergio Méndez Arceo in the diocese of Cuernavaca, Morelos from 1952 to 1982 and Samuel Ruiz in the diocese of San Cristóbal de las Casas in Chiapas from 1959 to 1999. However, the Liberation Theology was disapproved of by Pope John Paul II (Karol Wojtyla), who considered its practitioners as too independent and close to Marxism. During his long pontificate period (1978–2005), he vigorously replaced its advocates with successors who would be more aligned to the official policies of the Vatican. The unintended result was that many persons in the "popular sector" joined the Evangelical Protestant ranks.

Papal Visits

There have been seven papal visits to Mexico, five by Pope John Paul II, one by Pope Benedict XVI, and one by Pope Francis. The visits allow us to perceive how the Church´s role in country has changed and how Mexican society itself has been transformed. The first visit to Mexico by the head of the Vatican state was by Pope John Paul II during January 1979. He visited Mexico City, Puebla, Oaxaca, Guadalajara, and Monterrey. At the time, public religious ceremonies were not officially permitted by law, but the Pope's visit was considered an exception. President Carlos Salinas de Gortari invited back the Pope, who made his second visit in May 1990. John Paul II emphasized his devotion to the Virgin of Guadalupe by visiting the basilica at Tepeyac and carrying out the **beatification** of Juan Diego, the legendary Indigenous man who was witness to the Guadalupan apparition. On his third visit in August 1993, the Pope visited the state of Yucatan and the shrine of Izamal. By 1993, public religious rituals were legalized and the Pope was openly received by public officials. On his fourth visit in January 1999, John Paul II held a Mass at the Aztec Stadium with a huge audience in attendance. On his final visit from July 30 to August 1, 2002, Pope John Paul II returned to the Basilica of Guadalupe to preside over the **canonization** of Juan Diego Cuauhtlatoatzin as a saint. Now, Karol Wojtyla was received with official honors as a head of state by Conservative President Vicente Fox. On March 2012, Pope Benedict XVI (Joseph Ratzinger) visited the state of Guanajuato, which is part of the Catholic core of Mexico. The ceremonies were carried out under strict security measures, which were more common during the administration of the then president Felipe Calderon. Ratzinger did not visit the Basilica of Guadalupe.

In February 2016, Pope Francis (Jorge Mario Bergoglio) arrived in Mexico City on a flight from Havana, Cuba. He visited the Basilica of Guadalupe and included in his travel itinerary the severely impoverished areas near the capital as well as the city of Morelia, Michoacan and a highly symbolic sojourn at San Cristóbal de las Casas, Chiapas, where he recalled the work of both friar Bartolomé de las Casas and Bishop Samuel Ruiz in defense of Indigenous peoples. Pope Francis ended his tour at the border city of Ciudad Juarez, Chihuahua, speaking in favor of the rights of migrants. His visit signaled a rather different orientation from the Vatican state.

FIGURE 5.4 *At the canonization ceremony of Juan Diego held at the Basilica of Guadalupe, an image of the new saint is carried past Pope John Paul II.* Source: *Joe Raedle/Getty Images.*

FIGURE 5.5 *On his 2016 trip to Mexico, Pope Francis stopped to visit the Cereso no. 3 penitentiary in Ciudad Juarez, a city plagued by violent crime.* Source: *GABRIEL BOUYS/ Getty Images.*

Conclusion

Catholicism has been an important element in Mexico's history and national identity; not only as an element of unity but also of discord. The institution, its clergy, and its followers have faced many changes. Indeed, as Mexican society continues to change, it is now clear that religious pluralism will continue to flourish. A growing number of Catholics now regard many traditional Catholic beliefs critically. The public influence of the institution is often questioned. The challenge for the Catholic Church is to find a place for itself in Mexican society in a role that expresses more clearly the social and spiritual needs of a very complex population that is constantly changing and subject to a growing number of challenges. The future will tell if the Catholic Church is ready to face this challenge and continue to be relevant.

Further Reading

Camp, R. A. 1997. *Crossing Swords Politics and Religion in Mexico.* New York: Oxford University Press.

Blancarte, R. 1993. "Recent Changes in Church State Relations in Mexico. An Historical Approach", *Journal of Church and State* 35 (4): 781–805.

Blancarte, R. 2000. "Popular Religion, Catholicism and Socioreligious Dissent in Latin America: Facing the Modernity Paradigm", *International Sociology* 15 (4): 591–603.

Garma, C. 2010. "Mexico: Religious Tensions in Latin America's First Secular State", *Hemisphere* 19: 13–14.

Norget, Kristen. 2005. *Days of Death, Days of Life: Ritual in the Popular Culture of Oaxaca.* New York: Columbia University Press.

References

Brading, D. 2001. *Mexican Phoenix: Our Lady of Guadalupe: Image and Tradition across Five Centuries.* New York: Cambridge University Press.

ENCREER/RIFREM. 2016. *Religious Beliefs and Practices in Mexico National Survey.* Accessed June 11, 2022. https://rifrem.mx/encreer/resultados/english/.

Meyer, J. 2008. *The Cristero Rebellion: The Mexican People between Church and State 1926-1929.* New York: Cambridge University Press.

Peña, E. 2011. *Performing Piety: Making Space Sacred with the Virgin of Guadalupe.* Berkeley: University of California Press.

Rivera, L.N. 1992. *A Violent Evangelism: The Political and Religious Conquest of the Americas.* Louisville, KY: Westminster/John Knox Press.

Schwaller, J.F. 2011. *A History of the Catholic Church in Latin America: From Conquest to Revolution and Beyond.* New York: New York University Press.

Turner, V. and E. Turner. 2011. *Image and Pilgrimage in Christian Culture.* New York: Columbia University Press.

Glossary Terms

Beatification: In a beatification ceremony, the pope declares a deceased person "blessed" and worthy of veneration. This is often seen as the first step toward canonization.

Canonization: This is the official process of becoming a saint.

Patron Saints: These are saints who fulfill the role of a "patron" on behalf of a person or people group. Patron saints act as intermediaries between humans and God.

Popular Catholicism: This refers to Catholicism as practiced by everyday people. These everyday practices sometimes conflict against the official Church practices, though they can also exist harmoniously or even within official Catholic practices.

Subaltern: The subaltern refers to the dominated people or people group in the circumstance of acute power imbalances.

6

Latinx Catholicism in the United States

Daisy Vargas

Introduction

Latinx Catholicism, as a category encompassing a wide variety of ethnicities, races, and nationalities, refers to the religious practices and devotions of "the descendants of Latin American nations whose racial identifications were forged in the wake of Spanish colonialism and through the ideology of *mestizaje*" (Saldaña-Portillo 2017: 139). As Spanish colonialism was co-sponsored by the Roman Catholic Church, many Latinx communities also descend from the first converts to Christianity in the Americas. Latinx Catholicism is characterized by sacramental and liturgical practices introduced to the Americas through Iberian colonialism. Pilgrimages, processions, saint veneration, and other forms of **lived religion** are found throughout different Latinx Catholic communities and often represent local histories and ancestral customs (Vargas 2022a).

Catholicism serves as a broad category for containing a diversity of Christian practices and beliefs with ties to the Roman Catholic Church. Scholars of lived religion (Orsi 1997), popular religion, and vernacular religion (Primiano 1995) allow for more inclusive considerations of religious life beyond, and sometimes apart from, institutional and ecclesial governance. Instead, Catholicism (and religion more broadly) is understood through the everyday, lived, experiences of practitioners with varying sets of relationships to church hierarchies. Scholars try to capture the multiplicity of Catholic traditions through descriptions of a "sacramental imagination" (Greeley 2001: 1) that distinguishes itself through the belief in supernatural "presence" (Orsi 1997) or as those who engage with discourse on "sacraments, saints, apostolic succession, and [Catholic] self-identification" (Byrne 2019: 224).

Latinx Catholicism has been historically defined through an emphasis on **pre-Tridentine**, **baroque** Iberian devotion and practice. The reworking and refashioning of Christianity by Indigenous communities amidst devastating colonial violence, destruction, and disease transformed Christianity in Latin America. Widely understood to be forms of local syncretism, or false conversions ("idols behind altars," Brenner 1929), more recent scholars (Scheper Hughes 2021) argue for a historical accounting of Indigenous agency in Catholic colonial history. Similarly, scholars of Afro-Latinx and Afro-diasporic religions remind us of African Christian histories predating European colonialism and the Transatlantic slave trade. In the racial milieu of the colonial history of the Americas, the presence of Indigenous and African peoples contributed to Roman Catholicism in Latin America and its legacies today (Iyanaga 2019: 157).

Mestizaje and *mulatez*, different categories of race measured by degrees of racial miscegenation, were elements of the Spanish colonial racial classification system of *castas* (castes). Determined by different degrees of racial mixture between European, Indigenous, and Black peoples, *castas* were flexible categories capable of changed meaning depending on context; the construction of these racial categories was largely dependent on class and wealth. They afforded different forms of social and political influence; though flexible, Indigenous and African descended peoples remained lowest in this system. The casta system was exported and introduced into all new territories of Spanish colonialism. As the Spanish Empire moved north into the frontiers of what is now the United States, this racial order was also used in the classification and subjugation of newly encountered Indigenous peoples. As neophyte Christians and their descendants converted to Catholicism, they often introduced ancestral Indigenous practices. These local practices were often accepted by Church officials and priests as expressions of true Christianity. In other instances, they were rejected as un-Christian, primitive, and defiant. Nevertheless, traditions with elements of pre-Christian African and Indigenous elements continued to be practiced, shaping Latinx Catholicism today. Latinx Catholicism is one of continued conflict and disagreement, and often disengagement, with the hierarchy of the Roman Catholic Church. Many Latinx Catholic communities forged autonomous and independent lived religion and vernacular practices and mutual aid organizations separate from Church leadership; as the following sections demonstrate, they were also met with distrust and repression.

The chapter is organized by a loose chronology to account for Latinx communities in geographic landscapes ceded to the United States and periods of large-scale Latin American immigration into the United States. Though migrants from different parts of Latin America arrived in the United States at earlier times than those noted in these sections, these historical moments account for the largest waves of arrival from these communities. This historical survey concludes with a section on historical continuities in the contemporary period and theoretical and methodological debates in the study of Latinx Catholicism.

"The Border Crossed Us"

Despite the deep historical roots of Catholicism in the United States, Latinx Catholicism is most often characterized as an immigrant religion partly due to the continuous waves of Latin American migration and **transnational** ties that limit older models of assimilation (Jimenez 2009). As historians Timothy Matovina and Gary Riebe Estrella note, "whereas the saga of nineteenth-century European Catholic émigrés is one of seeking a haven in a new land, the story of the first Mexican American Catholics is in large part a tale of faith, struggle, and endurance in their ancestral homeland" (2002: 4). Two places built during the Spanish colonial period represent the longest operating and surviving Catholic churches in the United States. The sixteenth-century Cathedral of San Juan Bautista (1511) in San Juan, Puerto Rico and the San Miguel Mission church (1598) in Santa Fe, New Mexico predate the founding of the United States by almost two centuries. As part of the "Catholic borderlands," they represent "former Spanish territories that had to find their respective places within a growing U.S. sphere of political, economic, and cultural influence" after American occupation (Martínez 2014: 3).

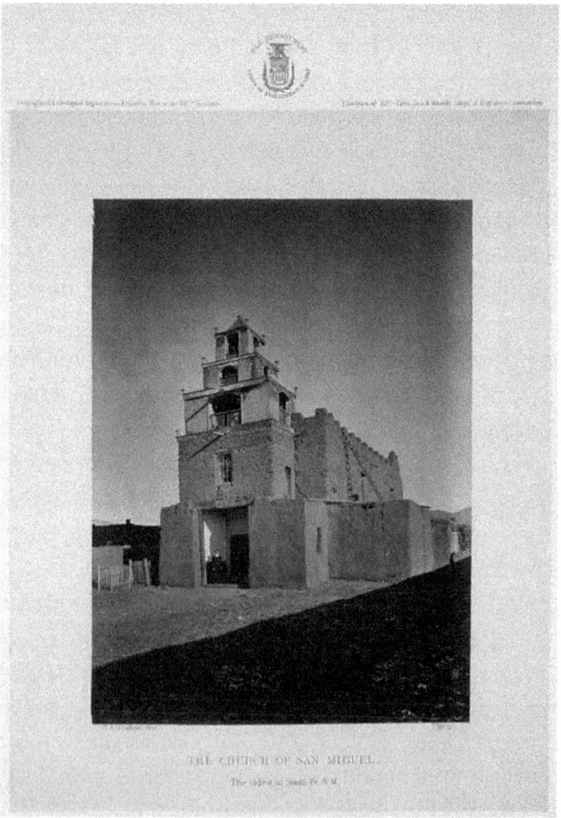

FIGURE 6.1 *The Church of San Miguel, the oldest church in Santa Fe, NM.* Source: *Photo by Timothy H.O'Sullivan/New York Public Library/Flickr.*

In 1845, the Republic of Texas was annexed by the United States after it declared itself independent of Mexico in 1836, and after decades of conflict against the outlawing of slavery in Mexico. In the years following US occupation of the Texas territory, Mexicans experienced political and economic marginalization as Euro-American settlers litigated dispossession of Mexican property. The signing of the Treaty of Guadalupe Hidalgo following the 1846–8 Mexican-American War resulted in the ceding of approximately 55 percent of Mexico's territories—including the region recognized today as the American Southwest (California, Arizona, Nevada, New Mexico, Colorado, Texas, and bordering parts of Wyoming, Oklahoma, and Kansas). Overnight, over 100,000 Mexican citizens became de facto US citizens. The famous phrase, "We didn't cross the border, the border crossed us," reflects the political reality of these new US citizens, now inheritors of a new mode of imperial occupation.

The influx of Euro-American settlers from the Eastern United States into these regions and the increased encroachment on these lands by squatters, missionaries, and settlers positioned Mexican communities as foreigners in their own lands. White settlers carried with them preconceived ideas about race that quickly translated to characterizations of Mexican immorality with respect to their encounters in the Southwest. In the settler imagination, the racist constructions of Mexicans as inheritors of Aztec "brutish superstitions" (Pinheiro 2014: 56) also marked them with immorality, "depravity, and primitivism" (De León 1983: 43–60).

The Roman Catholic Church also sent Church leadership into the New Mexico territories and California to reside over their new bishoprics. The French Catholic Archbishop Jean-Baptiste Lamy arrived in Santa Fe, New Mexico in 1851 and soon set out to eradicate the region of a folk Catholicism practiced by the **confraternity** *Los Hermanos de la Fraternidad de Nuestro Padre Jesūs Nazareno* (The Brotherhood of Our Father Jesus the Nazarene). Though historians disagree on whether the practices of the group originate in pre-Tridentine Spain and were preserved due to clerical scarcity in the region or reflect popular practices found in Central Mexico and continued contact with Northern Mexican clerics from the Durango archdiocese, the *Hermanos Penitentes* (as the confraternity is commonly known) practiced a form of Catholic devotion defined by penitential practices meant to tax and mortify the body. In the mid to late nineteenth century, Euro-Americans sought to eradicate these practices through a series of warnings and, ultimately, prohibition and excommunication of participants. Leaders like Lamy and, Jean Baptiste Salpointe understood their continued practices as explicit defiance against the authority of the Church (Espinosa 1993; Carroll 2002; Vargas 2022b).

The popularity of California as a destination for natural resources after gold was found in the mid-nineteenth century also increased the number of Euro-American settlers in the region. Economic interests and competition led to racially and ethnically motivated violence as speculators and laborers competed over land parcels and potential mineral wealth. The California Gold Rush in 1848 ushered in new waves of violence against Mexican inhabitants. Across the US West, vigilante mobs enacted extra-legal violence in the post Mexican-American War period. Between the years 1880 and 1930, 188

Mexicans were murdered by mob violence (Carrigan and Webb 2003: 415). Vigilantism was not limited to violence against individuals; it also extended to the destruction of institutions representing Mexicanness. In 1855, a Roman Catholic church in California was burned down by an arsonist white mob targeting a local Mexican community (Boessnecker, 1976: 52–28). As in New Mexico, Catholic leadership also restricted Mexican Catholic celebrations; in 1862 bishop of Los Angeles Thaddeus Amat prohibited the celebration of *los pastores,* a traditional Christmas Nativity play, and criticized popular Mexican devotional practices as unruly and irreverent (Matovina 2011: 26).

Despite the racial violence, land dispossession, and religious restriction, Latinx Catholics in the Southwest connected to their ancestral traditions through religious ceremony and devotion and also employed them as tools for political and civic activism in a climate of racial exclusion. The continued celebrations of *La Virgen de Guadalupe, los pastores*, ritual penance, and patron saint festivals were public affirmations of Latinx presence and participation in larger communities, and refusals of erasure (Matovina 2011: 31).

By the end of the nineteenth century, US Manifest Destiny succeeded in the Caribbean and the Pacific Islands. The end of the Spanish-American War and the signing of the Treaty of Paris ceded Puerto Rico, Guam, and the Philippines to the United States, creating new Catholic borderlands.

Migrations

In the years following the 1910 Mexican Revolution and the establishment of the 1917 Constitution, the Mexican government began enforcing a series of anti-clerical laws as a reaction to the Church's association with the Diaz regime and republican oligarchy. These restrictions became more stringent in 1926 with the introduction of the so-called Calles Law, effectively banning Church ownership of property, the public presence and political participation of clergy, and public celebrations of Catholicism. Under the battle cry, "Viva Cristo Rey," Catholic rebel groups, concentrated in the central states of Mexico, retaliated against the federal government by destroying state property and murdering federally employed rural teachers. This effectively set into motion years of violent retaliation and a mass exodus of Mexicans into the United States (Young 2015).

In Puerto Rico, US economic interests in sugar cane accelerated the production and exportation of refined sugar. This period of US occupation also introduced many Protestant missionaries to the island. While Puerto Rico's population identified primarily with Roman Catholicism, the number of Protestant converts increased. Granted citizenship in 1917, many Puerto Ricans left the island for places like New York. The largest influx of Puerto Rican migrants to the US mainland occurred because of "Operation Bootstrap," the post–Second World War economic policy meant to modernize and industrialize the Puerto Rican plantation economy. In the succeeding two decades (1946–64) approximately 600,000 Puerto Ricans migrated to the United

States, primarily establishing communities in the New York City. They transformed formerly Irish and Italian ethnic enclaves and "forc[ed] a degree of mutual integration between Euro-Americans and Hispanics" (Diaz-Stevens 1993: 116). As with Mexican Catholics, Puerto Rican Catholics asserted their presence and influence through public participation in religious and ethnic celebrations, including the patron saint festivities of St. John the Baptist and membership in associated lay confraternities (Matovina 2011: 51).

The Cuban Revolution (1953–9) and the Marxist overthrow of the Batista regime created large-scale migration of Cuba's mostly white, landowning class to the United States. Cuban immigrants created new communities in Miami, Florida. Accompanied by exiled priests and women religious, the Cuban immigrant community quickly organized to form "a plethora of diocesan and lay organizations ... in response to the urgent need for bilingual and ministerial resources" (Padilioni 2020: 89). The Immigration and Nationality Act of 1965 (also known as the Hart-Celler Act) effectively abolished national quotas that limited the number of non-Western European migrants from entering the United States. This historical period coincided with a number of Caribbean and Latin American armed conflicts, followed by war-time refugees.

The Dominican Civil War of 1962 was precipitated by the assassination of Rafael Trujillo, also known as *El Jefe* (The Boss), a violent dictator responsible for the violent suppression of opponents, a "reign of terror," and the racial massacre of the Dominican Republic's Haitian population (Derby 2009; Paredes 2019). His association with the Catholic Church worked to create a racial order in which Catholicism was associated with whiteness and *Dominicanidad*; after the fall of his regime, Afro-Dominican folk Catholicism served to reform "Dominican national-religious identity" (Padilioni 2020: 88). Aided by the teachings of Vatican II and the canonization of the Afro-Peruvian San Martín de Porres, Catholicism in the Dominican Republic, and its diaspora, was revitalized. Dominican immigrants to the United States established enclaves in New York and Miami, sharing devotional sites with other Caribbean Catholic immigrants and incorporating Afro-Catholic folk traditions.

The second large wave of Cuban migration in the 1980s, composed of lower class, mixed race and Black "undesirables," included practitioners of Cuban Afro-religious traditions like Regla de Ocha. Many also identified as Catholic and practiced Yoruba-based Regla (Santeria) in official Catholic places of worship, including the Shrine of Our Lady of Charity in Miami (Tweed 1997: 43–55).

Civil Rights Movements

The reforms of Vatican II and their reverberations across Latin America invigorated a theological movement centered on the "preferential option for the poor." Gustavo Gutiérrez's 1971 book *A Theology of Liberation* articulated a socially conscious vision of Christianity that called attention to the structural inequalities and economic oppression that plagued Latin America in the centuries following European colonialism.

Direct action was necessary, liberationists argued, to liberate the world from sin. Theologians like Gutiérrez, Ernesto Cardenal, and Oscar Romero called for reforming the Catholic Church, scrutinizing its wealth and ties to Latin American oligarchies and repressive regimes.

In the United States, Latinx Catholics fought for social reform and liberation in the same period. In 1968, labor and civil rights leader Cesar E. Chavez penned, "The Mexican-American and the Church," admonishing the leadership of the Church for failing to support Mexican-American farm workers. Chavez's Catholicism was a powerful motivator in his leadership of California field laborers, and during his 1966 march from Delano, California to Sacramento, he deployed the symbolic image of the Virgin of Guadalupe, the sixteenth-century Mexican Marian apparition, to decorate the standard at the front of his caravan. This image, tied to both Mexican identity and Catholic practice, displayed the Virgin as a social justice symbol for farmworker rights and dignity. This image served as a continued symbol of resistance during the United Farm Worker grape boycotts and became a standard part of their marches (León 2014).

Católicos Por la Raza, a group of young Chicano activists in Los Angeles, also questioned the absence of Catholic leadership in social justice support. On Christmas Eve 1969, after almost a year of ignored requests to meet with Catholic leadership to

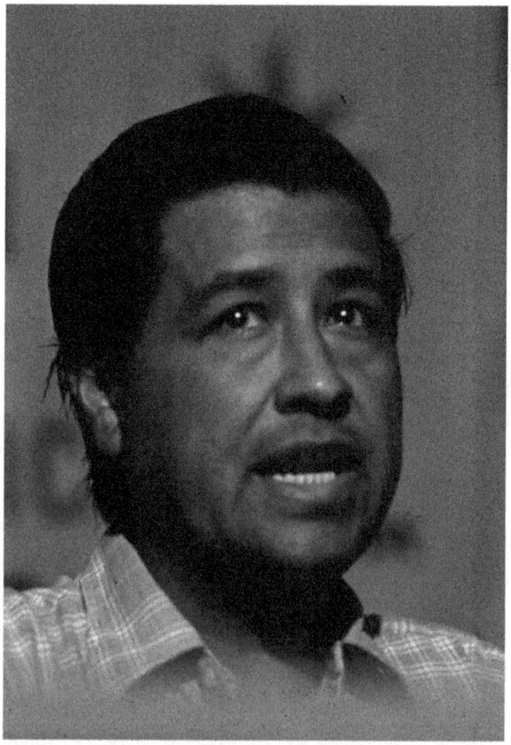

FIGURE 6.2 *Cesar Chavez, 1972.* Source: *Photo by Cornelius M. Keyes/US National Archives and Records Administration/Wikimedia Commons.*

address the disparity between funding for the building of St. Basil's Catholic Church and the Church's failure to address the material and economic needs of the Mexican community, Catolicos Por la Raza disrupted Mass to occupy St. Basil's (García 2008; Hinojosa 2016: 26).

Internal Church movements included the creation of Catholic religious organizations like PADRES—*Padres Asociados para Derechos Religiosos, Educativos y Sociales* (Associated Priests for Religious, Educational, and Social Rights) and Las Hermanas. Inspired by Vatican II and Catholic social teachings, the organizations of priests and women religious used direct action to address the needs of Latinx communities in the United States and fight for Latinx representation in Church leadership (Medina 2004; Martinez 2005). The political activism of members of PADRES and Las Hermanas inspired new Latinx theologies in the United States, including the *mujerista* theology of Ada María Isasi-Díaz (Medina 2004).

War

In the late 1970s and early 1980s, the US backing of the Contra paramilitary group in Nicaragua boosted it to wage a violent battle against the democratically elected (and Liberation Theology-inspired) Sandinista government in an effort to eliminate Marxism from Central America. Similarly, US involvement in the politics of Guatemala included the support of General José Efraín Ríos Montt in the 1980s during his campaign of genocide and ethnic cleansing that targeted the Indigenous Maya community; in El Salvador, the United States also funded the right-wing government in a civil war against leftist rebels.

A mass exodus of Central Americans fled to the United States seeking asylum, only to be denied Temporary Protected Status. Groups of religious activists and congregations helped provide sanctuary to undocumented migrants, aiding in their crossing, transport, and housing. These sanctuary churches were mostly made up of varying Christian denominations. In Los Angeles, the Catholic La Placita Olvera Church led by Father Luis Olivares became a center for assistance (García 2018; Romero 2020; Barba and Castillo-Ramos 2021). By the end of the Guatemalan Civil War (1954–1996), an estimated 200,000 Guatemalans had perished; in El Salvador (1979–1992), the number was 75,000. These numbers do not account for those disappeared.

Catholicism in Central America followed a similar pattern to other Latin American countries—a long history of alliance with oligarchs and ruling elites, with dissenting minorities of clerics calling for reform and liberation. Liberationist clerics, like Bishop Oscar Romero and Bishop Juan Gerardi, were among the many Catholic leaders assassinated for their support of the poor and impoverished. As Central American migrants and refugees travelled north to the United States, they carried with them the memories of these Catholic martyrs, commemorating their presence through public art and supporting the canonization of Romero.

FIGURE 6.3 *Oscar Romero Square, Pico Union District, Los Angeles, CA.* Source: *Photo by Daisy Vargas.*

Continuities

The Immigration Reform and Control Act of 1986 granted amnesty to three million mostly Latinx undocumented migrants in the United States, creating a pathway to legal residency and citizenship. However, the passage of California Proposition 187 in 1994 was followed by a series of restrictive immigration acts at the turn of the twentieth century, including Senate Bill 1070 in Arizona. After the 9/11 terrorist attacks in New York in 2001, nativist and xenophobic policies targeting non-white minoritized communities and the increased militarization of international borders and ports of entry changed strategies of migration from Latin America. The establishment of the Prevention through Deterrence policy in the US-Mexico borderlands by to "funneling undocumented migrants into areas of extreme weather and hostile terrain in the Sonoran Desert" has killed over 3,200 undocumented migrants (largely of Latin American origins) (De Leon 2015). Along the US-Mexico border, Roman Catholic lay groups process saint relics, hold religious services through the border wall, and perform *posadas*, religious re-enactments of the biblical narrative of Mary and Joseph seeking shelter in Bethlehem.

Latinx Catholic communities in the United States continue to express their social and political identities through religious practices and devotions. In 2003, the Guatemalan and Mexican community of St. Cecilia's Church in Los Angeles commissioned a reproduction of *El Cristo Negro de Esquipulas* for the congregation. The image journeyed from Guatemala to the United States on the backs of *cofradia* (confraternity) devotees. When they arrived at the US-Mexico border, the Cristo's companions "hired a Mexican coyote [smuggler] to take them across the U.S.-Mexico border, and in honor of those who crossed before them, renamed the image *El Cristo Mojado*, the Undocumented Christ" (2008: 154). Other churches in Los Angeles also commissioned their own images of El Cristo Negro, including San Raphael's Catholic Church in South Los Angeles. The $4,000, 300-pound image was processed through South Los Angeles in October 2003 before its installation in the church (Hayasaki 2003).

Despite new forms of criminalizing undocumented migrants and the increased militarization and surveillance of the US-Mexico border, Latinx Catholics retain ties to places of origin. Facilitated by new technologies of social media, cell phones, and video-conferencing, Latinx Catholics connect to communities across international borders to form diasporic nationalisms, or identities based on particular locations implying "geopiety, or an attachment to the natal landscape," including "feelings for the natural terrain" and "affection for remembered traditions" (Tweed 2008: 86). Through religious narratives, Latinx Catholic migrant communities strengthen the collective memory of the diaspora, especially in "express[ing] attachment to the natal land, sacraliz[ing] or forming bridges between the two" (Tweed 2008: 86). In the United States, migrant hometown associations form bonds with communities in nations of origin. These hometown associations send remittances and provide capital for community development, public healthcare, and infrastructure (Durell 2020; Muñoz 2019; Orozco 2000). Transnational exchanges also include religious and ritual resources—Latinx Catholic cofradias finance the building of churches and shrines, commission religious images, and sponsor festivals and pilgrimages (Popkin 2005; Peña 2011; Scheper Hughes and Vargas 2014; Bada 2014).

Futures

Though Latinx Catholic communities retain ties to communities of origin, evading normative definitions of assimilation and acculturation through what Tomas R. Jimenez calls "replenished ethnicity" (2009), conversion to Protestantism challenges the centrality of Catholicism in Latinx identity. The success of the Charismatic Renewal Movement in the Roman Catholic Church among Latinx devotees and the conversion of Latinx Catholics to Protestant traditions like Pentecostalism in Central America and the United States reveal a diverse landscape of Latinx Catholicism and a future of imagined possibilities of ethno-national and diasporic attachments that do not rely on Catholic markers of identity.

Renewed debates on the limits of *Latinidad* as an umbrella category representing disparate histories, economic contexts, racial identities, and nationalities also highlight the complexities of Latinx identity. The discourses surrounding the use of terms like "Hispanic" and "Latino" in the mid-twentieth century brought into conversation questions about Spanish language inheritance and gender. "Hispanic," for many critics, too strongly emphasized historical linguistic links to Spain, erasing the mixed-race heritage of Latin

FIGURE 6.4 *Cristo Negro, St. Raphael's Church, Los Angeles, CA.* Source: *Photo by Patrick A. Polk.*

Americans. "Latino" for others also reenforced the categories created by European colonialism and served as another referent for proximity to European centers of power. Though widely adopted as political and legislative identifier, others point out that the use of the term "Latino" also reenforces gender exclusive language. Opting for Latinx or Latine, popularized among leftist activist in Latin American in the early twenty-first century, facilitates more gender inclusivity and neutrality in references to Latinidad.

Still, Latinx and Latinidad as terms and categories that contain and define diasporic communities from regions of Latin America recreate racist and racial hierarchies in Latin American and the United States. Historically, Latinx communities, including the Chicano movements of the 1960s, adopted *mestizaje* as a defining characteristic of Latinidad. For many Indigenous communities, this is a valorization of an imagined

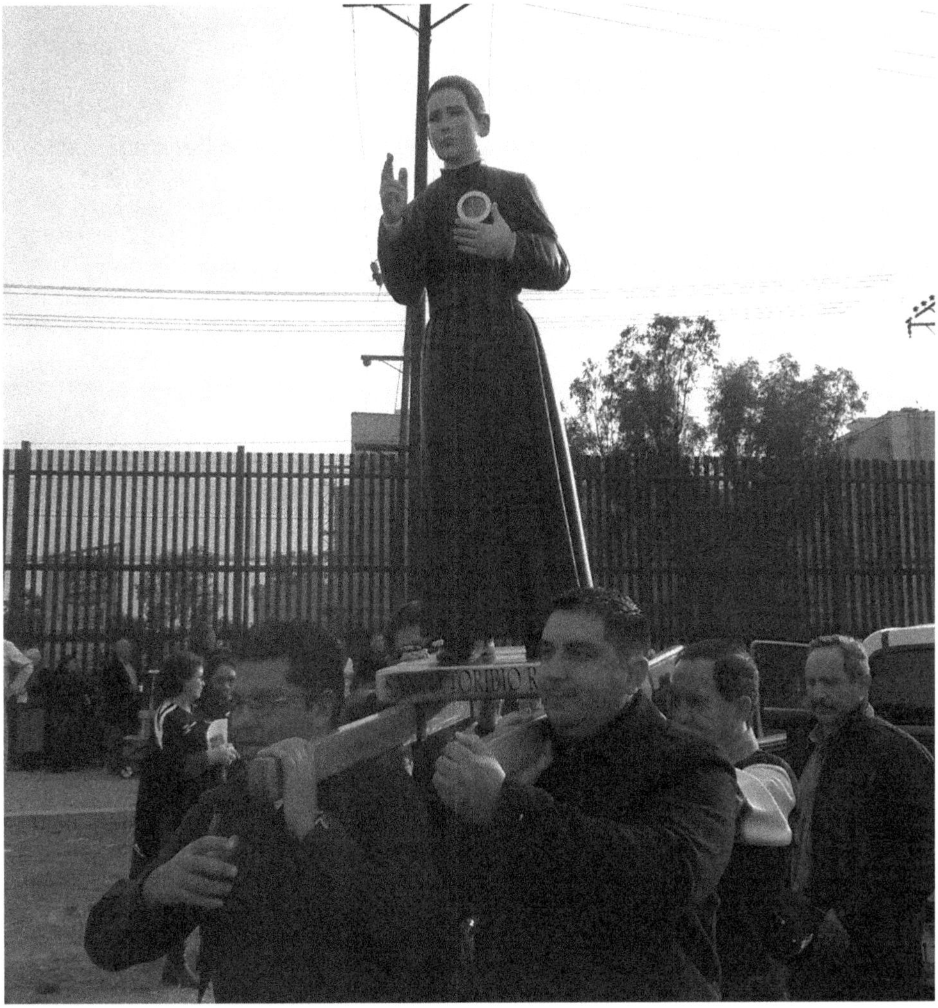

FIGURE 6.5 *San Toribio Romo reliquary at US-Mexico border in Calexico, CA.* Source: *Daisy Vargas.*

Indigenous past that erases Indigenous communities in the United States and Latin America, who continue to face structural and systemic racism, dispossession, and political marginalization. Also, many Indigenous communities hold stronger affinities and ties to "pre-Columbian indigenous culture ... than with any other culture labeled as 'Latino' in the United States" (Solano 2004: 117), speaking Spanish only as a second language and choosing to identify as American Indian or Native American in census materials (Le Baron 2012). Anti-Blackness in the Latinx community also troubles any unifying category of identify, as many Afro-Latinxs struggle to be recognized as Latin Americans in the United States and often face ethnic and cultural erasure (Flores 2021). This reckoning with anti-Indigeneity and anti-Blackness in the Latinx community also provides new possibilities to generate more inclusive consideration of Catholicism in the United States.

Further Reading

Díaz-Stevens, A.M. 1993. *Oxcart Catholicism on Fifth Avenue: The Impact of the Puerto Rican Migration upon the Archdiocese of New York.* South Bend: Notre Dame University Press.
León, L.D. 2014. *The Political Spirituality of Cesar Chavez: Crossing Religious Borders.* Berkeley: University of California Press.
Matovina, T. 2011. *Latino Catholicism: Transformation in America's Largest Church.* Princeton: Princeton University Press.
Peña, E. 2011. *Performing Piety: Making Space Sacred with the Virgin of Guadalupe.* Berkeley: University of California Press.

References

Bada, X. 2014. *Mexican Hometown Associations in Chicagoacán: From Local to Transnational Civic Engagement.* New Brunswick: Rutgers University Press.
Barba, L.D. and T. Castillo-Ramos. 2021. "Latinx Leadership and Legacies in the US Sanctuary Movement, 1980–2020." *American Religion* 3 (1) (Fall 2021): 1–24.
Boessnecker, J. 1976. *Gold Dust and Gunsmoke: Tales of Gold Rush Outlaws, Gunfighters, Lawmen, and Vigilantes.* New York: Wiley.
Brenner, A. 1929. *Idols behind Altars: Modern Mexican Art and Its Cultural Roots.* New York: Biblio & Tannen Publishers.
Byrne, J. 2019. "Catholicism Doesn't Always Mean What You Think It Means." *Exchange* 48 (3): 214–24.
Carrigan, W.D. and C. Webb. 2003. "The Lynching of Persons of Mexican Origin or Descent in the United States, 1848 to 1928." *Journal of Social History* 37(2): 411–38.
Carroll, M.P. 2002. *The Penitente Brotherhood: Patriarchy and Hispano-Catholicism in New Mexico.* Baltimore: Johns Hopkins University Press.
De León, A. 1983. *They Called Them Greasers: Anglo Attitudes Towards Mexicans in Texas, 1821–1900.* Austin: University of Texas Press.
De Leon, J. 2015. *The Land of Open Graves: Living and Dying on the Migrant Trail.* Berkeley: University of California Press.

Derby, L.H. 2009. *The Dictator's Seduction: Politics and the Popular Imagination in the Age of Trujillo*. Durham: Duke University Press.
Díaz-Stevens, A.M. 2003. *Oxcart Catholicism on Fifth Avenue: The Impact of the Puerto Rican Migration upon the Archdiocese of New York*. South Bend: Notre Dame University Press.
Durrell, J. 2020. "Transnational Organizations, Accessibility, and the Next Generation." *Latin American Perspectives* 47 (3): 168–85.
Espinosa, J.M. 1993. "The Origin of the Penitentes of New Mexico: Separating Fact from Fiction." *Catholic Historical Review* 79 (3): 454–77.
Flores, T. 2021. "Latinidad Is Cancelled: Confronting an Anti-Black Construct." *Latin American and Latinx Visual Culture* 3 (3): 58–79.
García, M.T. 2008. *Católicos: Resistance and Affirmation in Chicano Catholic History*. Austin: University of Texas Press.
García, M.T. 2018. *Father Olivares, a Biography: Faith Politics and the Origins of the Sanctuary Movement in Los Angeles*. Chapel Hill: University of North Carolina Press.
Greeley, A.M. 2001. *The Catholic Imagination*. Berkeley: University of California Press.
Hagan, J.M. 2008. *Migration Miracle: Faith, Hope, and Meaning on the Undocumented Journey*. Cambridge: Harvard University Press.
Hayasaki, E. 2003. "A Sacred Symbol Arrives." *Los Angeles Times*, October 20. https://www.latimes.com/archives/la-xpm-2003-oct-20-me-christ20-story.html
Hinojosa, F. 2016. "Católicos Por La Raza and the Future of Catholic Studies." *American Catholic Studies* 127 (3): 26–9.
Iyanaga, M. 2019. "On Hearing Africas in the Americas: Domestic Celebrations for Catholic Saints as Afro-Diasporic Religious Tradition." In *Afro-Catholic Festivals in the Americas: Performance, Representation, and the Making of Black Atlantic Tradition*, edited by C. Fremont. University Park: Pennsylvania State University Press.
Jiménez, T.R. 2009. *Replenished Ethnicity: Mexican Americans, Immigration, and Identity*. Berkeley: University of California Press.
Le Baron, A. 2012. "When Latinos Are Not Latinos: The Case of Guatemalan Maya in the United States, the Southeast and Georgia." *Latino Studies* 10 (1–2): 179–95.
León, L.D. 2014. *The Political Spirituality of Cesar Chavez: Crossing Religious Borders*. Berkeley: University of California Press.
Martínez, A.M. 2014. *Catholic Borderlands: Mapping Catholicism onto American Empire, 1905–1935*. Lincoln: University of Nebraska Press.
Martinez, R. 2005. *PADRES: The National Chicano Priest Movement*. Austin: University of Texas Press.
Matovina, T. 2011. *Latino Catholicism: Transformation in America's Largest Church*. Princeton: Princeton University Press.
Matovina, T. and G. Riebe- Estrella. 2002. "Introduction." In *Horizons of the Sacred: Mexican Traditions in US Catholicism*, edited by T. Matovina and G. Riebe-Estrella, 1–16. Ithaca: Cornell University Press.
Medina, L. 2004. *Las Hermanas; Chicana/Latina Religious-Political Activism in the U.S. Catholic Church*. Philadelphia: Temple University Press.
Muñoz, J. 2019. "Promoting Health from Outside the State: La Comunidad, Migrants, and Hometown Associations." *Migration Letters* 16 (2): 155–64.
Orsi, R. 1997. "Everyday Miracles: The Study of Lived Religion." In *Lived Religion in America: Toward a History of Practice*, edited by D. Hall. Princeton: Princeton University Press.
Orozco, M. 2000. *Latino Hometown Associations as Agents of Development in Latin America*," Inter-American Dialogue.

Padilioni Jr., J. 2020. "A Miami Misterio: Sighting San Martín de Porres at the Crossroads of Catholicism and Dominican Vodú." *US Catholic Historian* 28 (2): 85–111.
Paredes, C.L. 2019. "Catholic Heritage, Ethno-racial Self-identification, and Prejudice against Hatians in the Dominican Republic." *Ethnic and Racial Studies* 42 (2): 2143–66.
Peña, E.A. 2011. *Performing Piety: Making Space Sacred with the Virgin of Guadalupe*. Berkeley: University of California Press.
Pinheiro, J.C. 2014. *Missionaries of Republicanism: Religious History of the Mexican-American War*. New York: Oxford University Press.
Popkin, E. 2005. "The Emergence of Pan-Mayan Ethnicity in the Guatemalan Transnational Community Linking Santa Eulalia and Los Angeles." *International Sociological Association* 53 (4): 675–706.
Primiano, L.N. 1995. "Vernacular Religion and the Search for Method in Religious Folklife." *Western Folklore* 54 (1): 37–65.
Romero, R.C. 2020. *Brown Church: Five Centuries of Latina/o Social Justice, Theology, and Identity*. IVP Academic Press.
Saldaña-Portillo, M.J. 2017. "Critical Latinx Indigeneities: A paradigm drift." *Latino Studies* 15 (2): 138–55.
Scheper Hughes, J. 2021. *The Church of the Dead: The Epidemic of 1576 and the Birth of Christianity in the Americas*. New York: New York University Press.
Scheper Hughes, J. and D. Vargas. 2014. "Traveling Image of the Holy Child of Atocha (Santo Niño de Atocha), Plateros, Mexico." *Object Narrative. In Conversations: An Online Journal of the Center for the Study of Material and Visual Cultures of Religion*. DOI: doi:10.22332/con.obj.2014.35
Solano, J.R. 2004. "The Central American Religious Experience in the U.S.: Salvadorans and Guatemalans as Case Studies." In *Introduction to the U.S. Latina and Latino Religious Experience*, edited by H. Avalos, 116–39. Boston: Brill Academic Publishers.
Tweed, T. 1997. *Our Lady of the Exile: Diasporic Religion at a Cuban Catholic Shrine*. New York: Oxford University Press.
Tweed, T. 2008. *Crossing and Dwelling: A Theory of Religion*. Cambridge: Harvard University Press.
Vargas, D. 2022a. "Latina/o/x Pilgrimage and Embodiment." In *The Oxford Handbook of Latinx Christianities in the United States*, edited by K. Nabhan-Warren. New York: Oxford University Press.
Vargas, D. 2022b. "Is Anti-Catholicism Relevant Where and When We Are?" *American Catholic Studies* 133 (3): 25–30.
Young, J.G. 2015. *Mexican Exodus: Emigrants, Exiles, and Refugees of the Cristero War*. New York: Oxford University Press.

Glossary Terms

Transnational Transnationalism refers to cross-border international exchanges, including goods, information, and culture.

Lived Religion Lived religion refers to religion as it is practiced in everyday contexts by ordinary people.

Baroque Baroque is related to the period of European art and architecture characterized by ornate and lavish detail.

Confraternity A lay Catholic organization, sometimes known as a "brotherhood."

Pre-Tridentine Pre-Tridentine refers to Catholicism's historical period before the Council of Trent (1543–63).

7

US Latina/o Pentecostalism

Erica Ramirez

The Rise of Pentecostalism

Today, Pentecostals number more than 600 million across the globe, a sum so vast that Pentecostalism has come to be referred to as the "third force in Christendom." Such a number is staggering for a movement commonly understood to have begun as recently as 1900. More surprising, Pentecostalism has flourished during a time that many sociologists were expecting highly developed nations like the United States to become increasingly secular. Secular societies are characterized by decreasing religious belief. This process of shedding religious belief is termed by German sociologist Max Weber, in 1918, "disenchantment" (Swatos 1998).

Sociologists of religion were collectively expecting the twentieth century to be marked by a decrease in religiosity and an increase in secularity. But the turn of the twentieth century proved to be one marked by profound *fin-de-siecle* anxieties, meaning, end of the century reflections marked by pessimism, cynicism, the belief that civilization leads to decadence and broadly felt expectations of cataclysmic upheaval (Heffernan 2002). During the 1890s, some of this energy animated cross-continental expectations for a worldwide revival, what some in the period conceptualized as a return of the biblical Pentecost (an event they read about in the New Testament book, *Acts of the Apostles*). This return they expected to be animated by embodied, religious experiences like divine healing, prophetic knowledge, and falling down under the force or "power" of the Holy Spirit. Historian Edith Blumhofer frames this expectation as a kind of "restorationism" (1993: 12–13). In her account of the Assemblies of God (AG), evangelicals of the 1890s felt a desire to return to (or restore) the Christianity of the New Testament, which they took to be purer than the Christianity they witnessed in American churches of the period. They agitated for this return to a better, truer Christianity through recourse to altars, where they hoped revival would break out and change the spiritual composition of people at the altars. Revivals seemed then to spring up across the world, in addition to the United States, in places like India, Ireland, England, and Scotland. Together these worldwide revivals effectively *reenchanted* the world at precisely the time secularization was expected to take hold; Blumhofer's narrative tracks the development of Pentecostalism primarily through European-American lines into one large and influential US denomination, the AG.

In the United States, the restorationism that Blumhofer delineates was matched by another kind of restorationism. US evangelicals of the period wanted a return to the church of the New Testament, but many also wanted a purification of the nation, which they took to be on the wrong path. Such a linking of the fate of the nation and its levels of spiritual fervor was a logic as old as the nation itself. White and Black evangelical populists of the time believed that the period's strained economics, corrupt political parties, and church hierarchies all threatened the gifts of "Christian liberty" and "Jeffersonian democracy," which they believed to be America's special, blessed characteristics and without which America would be lost (Creech 2006: xix). In particular, they feared losing freedoms of conscience in politics and religion, which they believed would cause race wars, class wars, anarchy, and religious "Romanism," a negative reference to a globalized Catholic power. To fight these trends, many evangelicals attempted to emphasize local autonomy in *both* church and state politics, while also encouraging individuals to have transformative spiritual experiences in churches. Both forms of restorationism, toward the New Testament and toward early American ideals, make sense in a context of insecurity about cultural decadence, weakened civilization, and the possibility of cataclysm. At the turn of the twentieth century, a broad array of Americans were anxious for the nation to get on a better course. Many white and Black believers thought the nation would be strengthened through a return to New Testamental religiosity in churches.

This anxious political context is somewhat muted in Grant Wacker's foundational book *Heaven Below* (2001). Therein, Wacker depicts early American Pentecostals as having spiritual "experiences" relatively delinked from the larger context of fears about nation. Instead, like Blumhofer before him, Wacker depicts Pentecostals as primarily concerned with New Testamental Christianity. Wacker suggests that early Pentecostalism was both "primitive and pragmatic," by which he meant that early Pentecostals forwarded a version of "old time religion" that sought to keep the best of what they deemed to be New Testament religiosity (as in Blumhofer's *restorationism*), including more ostentatious forms of religious practice, and at the same time developed a can-do attitude that fostered resilience and practicality in daily affairs. Early Pentecostals put these two contradictory impulses, a primitivism that looked toward the past and pragmatism oriented toward the rapidly changing present, Wacker argues, into a dynamic, creative, "genius" tension (2001: 10). Wacker depicts early Pentecostals as resilient and enterprising.

Like Blumhofer, Wacker foregrounded white experiences in early Pentecostalism. In this way, their authoritative reconstructions of the movement's beginnings proved at odds with adherents' histories of early Pentecostals in which one event, the Azusa Street Mission Revival (1906-1909), played an all-important role and, importantly, featured prominent Black American leadership. When the historiography of early American Pentecostalism returned to beginnings at the Azusa Street Mission Revival, it represented the first real opening for the stories of people of color, including Latin American Pentecostals, to figure prominently in the authoritative history of Pentecostalism.

Finding a Role within Azusa Street Mission's Prominence

Academic historians had been building a narrative that included, but did not center, the Azusa Street Revival, which took place at the Apostolic Faith Mission in Los Angeles, California. In 2006, at the centennial anniversary of the start of the revival, Edith Blumhofer insisted, "Azusa Street has a place in the story of how contemporary Christianity came to be, but its story is but one piece in the narrative of exploding charismatic Christianity, not its prototype" (2006). For insiders, however, the Azusa Street Mission Revival represented the *sine qua non* of Pentecostalism (Creech 2009). A subsequent book, Cecil M. Robeck's *The Azusa Street Mission and Revival: The Birth of the Global Pentecostal Movement* (2006), recentered the Azusa Street Mission and its headlining revival, which drew in thousands of visitors for three years, as the origin of the movement. In his introduction, Robeck pointedly asserts, "'Azusa Street' rightfully continues to function as the primary icon expressing the power of the worldwide Pentecostal movement" (10–11). But tensions between historians persisted. Then in 2014, historian Gastón Espinosa released *William Seymour and the Origins of Global Pentecostalism*, which painstakingly traces the network of churches and missions that grew out of the Azusa Street Mission Revival, to argue that the revival was truly central to the rise and spread of the third force in Christendom; again, the *reenchantment* of the world. Importantly, he depicts an African American, William Seymour, as truly presiding over this ground-breaking revival, which championed love above all else and birthed a worldwide movement (2014: 22–5; Barba 2022a: 132).

In his 2014 book, Espinosa chides prior historians' focus on early Pentecostalism's denominations and institutional networks. "Some make a faulty leap in logic concerning historical agency and the spread of ideas by assuming that the only way a person, center, and ideology can have paradigmatic influence" is to affiliate through institutional or structural ties. Yet, he admonishes, "influence is not solely determined by ongoing institutional or structural ties" (2014: 25). There are

FIGURE 7.1 *The Azusa Faith Mission, Los Angeles, CA*. Source: *Wikimedia.*

important differences in conceptualizing early Pentecostalism as a revival, a set of movements, or denominations. Where historians of the movement have focused on denominations and institutions, they found themselves producing an emphatically white account of early Pentecostalism. Centering Azusa Street Mission as the source of American Pentecostalism renders the tremendously important leadership of Black Americans in the mission visible, and this, during a time when African Americans had few opportunities for religious leadership over ethnically diverse communities, matters.

Centering the history of this movement back on the Azusa Street Revival also means that the epicenter of the movement is placed in southern California, where Mexican migrant workers moved in and out of Los Angeles's burgeoning labor forces. Primary source documents from the revival indeed indicate that Mexican workers were among the first to receive the Holy Spirit there. In one first-person account of Azusa Street, for example, a "rough Indian, an indigenous man from Mexico" laid hands on a Mrs. S. P. Knapp, who was needing healing from consumption (Ramírez 2015: 4–5). Though this detail is modest, it is also revealing: this is an image of a Mexican man praying for a white woman. Such a spiritual connection between people of different races and genders is notable, even today. However, in the United States at this time, such an exchange would usually have been a white person preaching to or praying for a person of color. A Mexican man praying for the healing of a white woman is a striking reversal of these roles!

The most important role that Mexican attendees together achieved, through these early accounts, was that of helping to make Azusa Street Mission Revival a multiracial, multiethnic event. "The work began among the colored people," the mission reported in its newsletter. "Since then, the multitudes have come. God makes no difference in nationality, Ethiopians, Chinese, Indians, Mexicans, and other nationalities worship together" (Espinosa 2014: 88). Mexicans at the mission helped the revival transcend the racial segregation of its day. Such an interracial, international event was *exactly* what the leaders of the mission wanted it to be! Early Pentecostals were enamored with the idea that the Holy Spirit "washed the color line away" and was "no respecter of persons" (Espinosa 2014: 73, 108). Azusa Street gave birth to a Pentecostal vision of the Holy Spirit inflected with radical egalitarian sympathies, one which Mexican converts helped bring to life (Ramírez 2021).

But the continuing story of Latino Pentecostalism illustrates how complicated such a vision is to work into daily life.

Spirit Empowerment for Mexican Believers

Daniel Ramírez's monograph *Migrating Faith* (2015) begins at Azusa Street with early Mexican converts to the movement drawn into Azusa's centripetal pull. They worshipped, sought healing, prayed for sanctification, and received the baptism of the Holy Spirit at Azusa's altars alongside thousands of others. But from there, Ramírez's book charts the quick rooting of the movement into Mexican territorial networks, as early converts shared their testimonies along their paths of migration. The looser border politics of the early twentieth century allowed Mexican converts to missionize while they moved freely back and forth across the border for work. Daniel Ramírez's early leaders spread news of the Los Angeles Pentecost all along their cross-national agricultural routes.

Migrating Faith exemplifies what many authors have noted as the speed with which Pentecostalism "indigenizes," that is, the manner in which the movement was taken over by ethnic minorities who become messengers to their own ethnic demographics (Tarango 2014: 2). In the case of the Azusa Street Mission, this indigenization happened virtually instantaneously, as participants in the mission felt empowered to preach the gospel based on their charismatic gifting from the Holy Spirit. Converts did not feel they needed, for example, a seminary education in order to preach. Instead, the mission forwarded a concept of spirit empowerment in which "[a]nyone could play an active role in worship. No one was ruled out by virtue of gender, color, class or previous condition of servitude" (Robeck 2006: 137). One of the outgrowths of this egalitarian view of the Holy Spirit was that Mexican nationals quickly began preaching and singing about their Pentecostal experiences in Spanish, for example, and on their preferred instruments, like the guitar (as opposed to, say, a pipe organ). Indigenous messengers are often able to share versions of the gospel that are easier for their fellow countrymen to understand given language barriers. Critically, *Migrating Faith* also shows that converts were not only able to share the gospel in their own Spanish language but also how these leaders produced songs that put God on the side of Mexican believers, for example, on the side of people who might be working without citizenship. In Mexican Pentecostal versions of hymns and in their sermons, God was positioned near to vulnerable workers. Indigenized messages can be not only more intelligible but also far more comforting and empowering to believers than messages produced by people from other classes or racial ethnic groups.

Over time, Mexican Pentecostals developed a robust culture that reflected their own language and musical customs, and addressed their own needs. Robeck's account of Azusa Street not only centers the Mission, it also highlights the Black-inflected aesthetics of the Azusa Street Revival, via revival practices that seemed similar to the ring shout and spirit possession of African traditional religions. *Migrating Faith* emphasizes how early Latino Pentecostals produced a version of Pentecostalism that forwarded *Mexican* cultural aesthetics—including tapestries, food, and biblical translations—as sacred (see also Barba 2022b). As early Pentecostalism aimed

FIGURE 7.2 *From renovated theatres (as shown here) to traditional church buildings and storefronts, Latino Pentecostals have proven remarkably pragmatic in their organizational efforts.* Source: *Farragutful/Wikimedia.*

to re-enchant the world, early Mexican converts helped to disentangle its Christian message from white American culture. Tracing early Pentecostal aesthetics, whether within Azusa Street or via Mexican labor circuits, helps to keep the breadth of early Pentecostal diversity in clear view.

Thus, newer histories of the movement clearly demonstrate that early Pentecostalism provided opportunities for Mexican converts to participate in and shape the fledgling movement. They were also able to produce their own version of Pentecostalism that centered their linguistic needs and spiritual aspirations.

The subsequent development of Pentecostal revivals into denominational organizations represents what scholars have long framed as the "routinization of charisma" (Gordon 2007). This period of transition has been one of both obstacles and realized opportunities for Latino Pentecostals, who have faced myriad challenges in channeling their charismatic gifts into institutionalized leadership roles.

Routinization and Latino Pentecostal Transnationalism

Where many can be drawn into a revival because of emotional connection or prophetic gifts like healing, long-term stewardship of such a movement usually requires the development of hierarchies of leadership, formalized roles and affiliations, and other more official methods of organization. Charismatic movements that begin with loosely organized revivals need to transform themselves into more institutional forms to grow and persist. In *Heaven Below*, Wacker (2001) asserts that the unexpected success of American Pentecostalism is owed to the movement's "balance" between the earliest charismatic forces of revival and the pragmatic forces that channel those energies into missions and churches, again, what he calls the "primitive" in productive tension with the "pragmatic." In Ramirez's *Migrating Faith* (2015), early Mexican leaders who experienced visions that called them into the ministry, which we could call a charismatic experience, proved able to find denominations that have since seen magnificent growth.

One such leader was Eusebio Joaquín González, who had a vision in which God rechristened him as an incarnation of the biblical prophet Aarón and called him to restore the Christian faith after "twenty centuries of divine silence and religious apostasy" (Ramírez 2015: 38). This vision became part of the founding folklore of *La Luz del Mundo*/Light of the World (LLDM), today one of Mexico's largest Pentecostal denominations with more than three million believers (Schulson 2014). Like other early forerunners of Mexican Pentecostalism, Aarón won his following with charismatic gifts like preaching, healing, and emotive singing, but the building of LLDM required, as Daniel Ramírez puts it, "institutional sobriety." Fortunately, many of the successful founders of Pentecostal denominations in Mexico had prior experience in mainline Protestantism, like Methodism and Congregationalism, and drew on those experiences to build structures of leadership in their own new Pentecostal denominations (Ramírez 2015: 76).

In Mexican Pentecostalism's infancy, Mexican converts were empowered by the Holy Spirit to (among other things) develop musical traditions that lyricized them as cosmic protagonists who, despite not having US citizenship, already possessed an all-important heavenly citizenship. Their testimonies of their experiences with the Holy Spirit authorized them to create theologies "from below," that is, from oppressed social positions. In their accounts, the Holy Spirit readily became the divine guardian of the vulnerable, the hopeful, and the underpowered. As the movement grew, leaders like Aarón helped to stabilize the faithful into churches and denominations, on both sides of the border. A word like "routinization" may conjure images of boring, bureaucratic processes; but in Ramírez' account, transnational *denominational* ties proved to be life-giving and sustaining, especially in times of political turmoil, as in decades subsequent to the early period of Pentecostal revivals, during which US border policies turned harsh. Mexican Pentecostals have proven able to translate the transnational character of the Azusa Street Revival into churches and denominations that have provided work, friendship, and belonging for new Latinx arrivals to the United States, with and without work permits.

Today, sociologists of religion like Manuel Vasquez point to such powers of transnational religion to shift the focus of the sacred away from the nation. Vásquez writes, "Religion's entwinement with contemporary migration has also led to intense processes of de-and re-territorialization. In the modern imagination, religion has

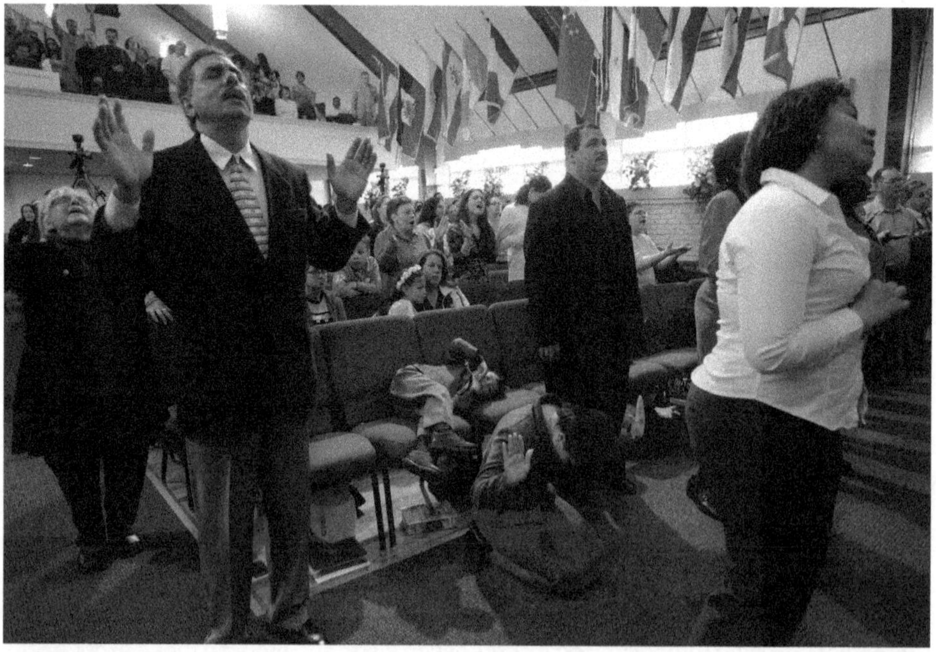

FIGURE 7.3 *A Latino Pentecostal worship service in Brooklyn.* Source: *Robert Nickelsberg/ Getty Images.*

been contained within the space of the nation. Within the nation, religion has been understood ... as the nation's secularized collective conscience, the source of its moral habits. Transnational migration and other globalizing processes have destabilized Western modernity's equation of religion with the nation" (2008: 157–8).

From the earliest days of the movement, the Holy Spirit was believed to have a global agenda, not a mission confined only to the well-being of America. The transnational consciousness of early Mexican Pentecostal songs and denominations has brought early Pentecostal hopes for a Christianity that transcended borders to life.

Denominational Repression

If charismatic believers have proved able to create transnational denominational structures, the career of one of early Mexican Pentecostalism's brightest US-based leaders shows how such a transnational vision was elsewhere stifled. The implementation of structural hierarchies of leadership, a major part of the processes of routinization, often proves to be the occasion of the conscious or unconscious implementation of race, class, and gender hierarchies. Charismatic gifts are often not enough to challenge these structures.

Rev. Francisco Olazábal was the best-known Latin American faith healer within the US circles during the early period of Pentecostal revivalism. His stature as one of a cadre of tent revivalists in early Pentecostalism is measurable in a number of ways: the throngs who claimed to be healed by his spiritual gifts, the thousands who attended his multicity funeral, and the way in which other revivalist notables, like Aimee Semple McPherson, sought to collaborate with him. But Francisco Olazábal was not just a gifted evangelist; he wanted to see US Latino and Latin American Pentecostalism develop denominational structures, staying powers, and political influence. In addition to his healing gift, Olazábal had an imagination for institutional strength.

Born in 1886 in El Verano, Sinaloa, Mexico, Olazábal was the son of a Catholic woman who, upon her conversion to Methodism, began her own itinerant evangelistic campaigns. Following in his mother's ministerial footsteps, he attended the Wesleyan School of Theology in San Luis Potosí, Mexico, from 1908 to 1910, and began conducting his own evangelistic campaigns, sometimes crossing the border into Texas to do so (Espinosa 2004: 180). By 1911, Olazábal was pastoring a small Mexican Methodist church in El Paso, well-placed to begin outreach to the million plus Mexicans who would cross the border seeking respite from the fires of the Mexican Revolution (Ramírez 2015: 294). Owed to these experiences, Olazábal understood the work of preaching campaigns and had valuable experience serving the Mexican population.

In 1912, Olazábal enrolled at Moody Bible Institute in Chicago, where he improved his English and studied under Ruben A. Torrey and James M. Gray. Olazábal then joined Torrey by invitation in Los Angeles, where he ministered to the large Mexican population. In 1914, Olazábal married Macrina Orozco and then began fundraising to build a "massive mission-style" church. Ordained in 1916 with the Methodist Episcopal

Church, he moved north and into the pastorate of two Spanish Methodist churches. Married, ordained, and celebrating successes, Francisco Olazábal could see a bishopric in his future (Espinosa 2004: 182). This period in Olazábal's ministry career strongly suggests he understood the culture and practices of Christian denominations.

Olazábal then had an experience that transformed his ministry; his wife Macrina was physically healed by the prayers of good friends who had converted to Pentecostalism. From that day forward, though he had been a detractor of Pentecostalism before, Olazábal became committed to preaching divine healing and baptism in the Spirit with tongues. He thus relinquished his Methodist credentials, and joined the AG—a majority white, English-speaking Pentecostal denomination formed in Hot Springs, Arkansas, in 1914.

In 1918, Olazábal was invited by Alice Luce, the leader of AG efforts to win Spanish-speakers to the faith, to preach a revival in Los Angeles. Thereafter Luce and Olazábal joined efforts to reach immigrants for Christ. It was as early as 1919 that Olazábal began communicating his vision for a Latino Bible Institute and for indigenous Mexican leadership of the AG's Hispanic district (Sanchez Walsh 2010: 270). But these plans for independence and ethnic self-governance, for Mexican institutional power, were ultimately frustrated by white paternalism. The AG's Caucasian leaders seriously doubted that Mexican believers had the skills or resources to lead themselves.

Tensions between Luce, Olazábal, and another missionary named H. C. Ball erupted into all-out conflict in the fall of 1922, when Ball told Mexican leaders at their annual convention that they would not be able to elect a new president of the Latin District Council. Espinosa notes that, that year, "most believed that Olazábal would be elected over Ball not only because he was ten years older and had formal seminary training, but also because he was the most respected evangelist in the council" (2008: 279). Ball's suspension of the vote upended the democratic processes that many early converts highly valued. Convinced that *gringos*, Spanish for "white people," would not willingly relinquish control over Mexican believers, Olazábal then led a faction of defectors out of the AG into a new denomination, eventually named the *Concilio Latino Americano de Iglesias Cristianas* (CLADIC). In their founding document, denominational organizers laid down that CLADIC considered it a high spiritual privilege to serve the, "in many respects, worthy Mexican people."

After this schism with the AG, Olazábal's healing ministry began to take on genuinely national proportions. Olazábal reached national renown after the reported healing of a "deaf-and-dumb" twelve-year-old Hispanic girl. During the 1920s, Olazábal toured the nation, preaching healing and repentance to thousands of Mexicans in migrant farm labor camps, factories, and inner city *barrios*.

As word of Olazábal's healing campaigns spread, he was invited by a Latino AG minister to speak at the Palace Opera House in Chicago. His visit attracted thousands every night for several weeks; these crowds required police control. Francisco Paz, an AG minister, attended one of Olazábal's healing services in Chicago and asked him to conduct a similar campaign in New York. In the summer of 1931, Olazábal traveled to Spanish Harlem, where one periodical reported: "[p]robably not less than

100,000 different people have attended the Olazábal meetings in New York City since he inaugurated his meetings in New York in August, 1931" (Espinosa 2008: 276).

Olazabal's healing services grew his profile throughout New York so that soon people from its Italian and Anglo-American boroughs were attending. Services grew so large and diverse that Olazábal began holding English-language services on Monday nights and Italian-language services on Thursday evenings and Sunday mornings. He also regularly ministered in Black Pentecostal churches in Harlem and throughout New York City. As his preaching campaigns crossed linguistic and racial boundaries, Olazábal's charismatic preaching and healing gifts helped him rise above the constraints of the white supremacy and segregation of the 1930s.

El Azteca as Charismatic Rhetoric

If he looked to transcend racial differences, Francisco Olazábal did not try to transcend his Latino identity. In 1934, he conducted the first mass Pentecostal, island-wide evangelistic healing and revival crusade in Puerto Rican history. He held services in tents, churches, civic auditoriums, and sports arenas. *El Mundo*, the largest newspaper on the island, dubbed Olazábal the "Mexican Billy Sunday" and claimed that "he converted 20,000 people throughout the island" (Espinosa 2008: 281).

This was not the name that the majority of his followers would have called him. It is unclear when, exactly, Olazábal came to be popularly known as "El Azteca" (Espinosa 2004: 186). What is certain, however, is that for Mexicans "Aztec" has great significance. To be Aztec carries both historical and mythological importance. Aztlan is the mythical origin for all Mexican people, while the Aztec Empire (1427–1519) has come to symbolize Indigenous Mexican power, civilization, and achievement cut short by Spanish colonial invasion. This cultural mythology is still vibrant: the Mexican flag bears Aztec imagery.

Of course, one does not name oneself *The Great Aztec*. Indeed, while Olazábal could and clearly did possess rhetorical prowess, he alone could not have attributed to himself all the weight of Mexican cultural pride. Rather, Olazábal's role as an ambassador of ethnic pride fits what anthropologist Kenelm Burridge terms "the refertilization of the myth-dream." Burridge, whose work analyzes charismatic forms of resistance to colonialism, describes a "myth-dream" as emerging from "the shared repertoire of symbolic resources" of a community (1960: 27).

Burridge describes the development of a myth-dream as one of the most creative and persuasive strategies for resisting colonization. In myth-dream scenarios, the role of a prophet is to "re-fertilize" the myth dream. The prophet, according to anthropologist Thomas Csordas, becomes "swallowed by" the myth and becomes its personification, "ceas[ing] to be an actor," becoming instead "a creature of discourse" (1997: 146). In becoming "El Azteca," Francisco Olazábal, the Pentecostal preacher, was eclipsed into an ethnic myth-dream; he served as a creature of Latin Americans' racial discourse, personifying a version of Mexican identity that made his followers proud in so much as his campaigns were epic. In a 1936 issue of *The Christian Herald*, Spencer Duryee described Olazábal as "The Great Aztec," whose transnational ministry was "one of the most startling stories … in modern religious history." He went on to compare Olazábal to the Apostle Paul, John Wesley, David Livingstone, and William Booth. If Olazábal found his means to institutional power obstructed, Pentecostal revivals provided a setting in which he could fully operate his charismatic power. Mexican Pentecostals found earlier, and often greater, empowerment in charismatic revival circuits than they found in institutional networks.

As Olazábal crisscrossed the nation, ministering to a wide diversity of ethnicities and nationalities, he grew an equally large vision for a network of Christians who could affiliate and advance the kingdom of God together. As CLADIC added churches in Puerto Rico and grew a large congregation in Spanish Harlem, Olazábal was looking for opportunities to collaborate with ministers from across the spectrum of Protestant Christian denominations. But Olazábal's high-profile and growing denomination attracted nervous attention. His visionary attempts to create a transnational Latin American network floundered as his forays to expand into Puerto Rico were eventually met with closed doors: the island's Catholic and Protestant leaders viewed Olazábal's movements with suspicion and with some jealousy. By the time of his untimely death by car crash in 1936, *The Aztec* had healed hundreds of believers and helped to found fourteen denominations; he had brought dreams to life. But among all the bigger, white denominations of the period, none proved to be able to enfranchise Olazábal and CLADIC without trying to subordinate him and his people in a way that would have fallen far short of his vision and hopes—despite many attempts at collaboration and mergers. The routinizing or institutionalizing period of Pentecostalism proved, for Olazábal, one which presented serious challenges.

Staying Powers and Costs

Beginning in the 1930s, American Pentecostalism transformed from collectives animated by laity empowerment, clergy migration, an emphasis on healing, and direct spiritual experiences into denominations that could keep the faithful stable and growing. Historian Lloyd D. Barba describes the period between 1930 and 1965 as a time of testing the movement's abilities to sustain growth *with and without* the charismatic personalities that marked the foundational period of Pentecostalism (2022a: 135). In this period, groups like the Latino AG, CLADIC, and Apostolic Assembly of the Faith in Christ Jesus (AAFCJ) did not cooperate as one; instead, they competed for adherents. As a cohort, they broadly achieved stability in the religious landscape around 1960 with strongholds in New York, Puerto Rico, Texas, and Southern California. From 1966 to the present, Latino Pentecostal denominations have capitalized on this foundation period by expanding, that is, by planting new churches, missions, and educational institutions.

In conceptualizing the growth of Latino Pentecostalism as a whole, it is necessary to keep the pressures of migration in mind as well as Pentecostalism's hallmark commitment to international missions. Waves of Latin American immigration, now from Central America, Cuba, and the Dominican Republic, have since brought groups of indigenized Latin American Pentecostals into the established networks of Latino US Pentecostalism, even while these same networks have seen their base congregations shift from predominantly agricultural and working class laborers to include, now, emerging middle class and professional second and third generations. Latino Pentecostal churches in the United States are often Spanish speaking, while at the same time there are plenty of adherents whose first language is English.

Despite a falling out with Olazábal, Texas proved to be a fortuitous spot from which the AG could launch initiatives into Cuba, El Salvador, and Guatemala in the late 1920s. Later, in 1955, LLDM expanded from its stronghold in Guadalajara into California and then, in 1960, into Texas; these inroads helped Latino Pentecostalism become strong in Texas. Barba highlights that making good on this growth required that Ball relinquish control of the Latin American district of the AG by the end of the 1930s. It also required the development of an *autonomous* pipeline for Latino believers in which, "from elementary age, through adulthood, the Latino AG faithful learned to carry out ministry on their own" (Barba 2022a: 138). These are the very kind of structures that Olazábal long envisioned and from which he was blocked.

Today, the Latino AG is the largest Protestant, Evangelical, or Pentecostal body in the United States, claiming over one million adherents. If Latino adherents of the AG developed some visible autonomy, and if this autonomy helped their districts and churches grow and persist, the question of what effect AG identity has had on their sense of ethnic belonging is still an open one.

The popularity of Donald Trump with conservative voters was the leading story coming out of the 2016 election, but while most analysts centered their criticism on "evangelicals," Pentecostals proved to be some of Trump's earliest adopters and remain among his most loyal supporters. The surprising willingness of Latino conservative voters, in particular, to support Trump as candidate and incumbent, despite his calling Mexicans "bad hombres," "not the best people," animals, rapists, and thugs, can only be explained when their religious commitments are factored in (Molina 2020). Trump certainly appeals to the strain within Pentecostals that has long felt the nation is at risk in established politicians' hands; today these ranks include many Latino believers. Trump may also appeal to Pentecostals, Latino Pentecostals included, who are accustomed to charismatic styles of leadership. Rev. Samuel Rodriguez, an AG minister, served as the highest-profile Latino pastor on Donald Trump's evangelical advisory group (Goldstein 2018).

When *The New York Times* reported on what they called "the rise of the far right Latina" in July of 2022, the article made some mention of religion, but not enough to show the real impact of Pentecostalism on the Latino social imagination.

Close attention to the congressional campaign of Texan Mayra Flores powerfully illustrates the way Latino Pentecostalism now sounds in Texas circles. Flores was born in Mexico, but she migrated to the United States when she was a child and married a border patrol agent. She constantly invokes "God, family, and country" and routinely

FIGURE 7.4 *Donald Trump launched Evangelicals for Trump at a Latino Pentecostal megachurch in Miami, FL.* Source: *Joe Raedle/Getty Images.*

inveighs against illegal Latin American migration. Flores deftly circulates in Texas's Latin American Pentecostal circles. Her pastor, Joshua Navarrete, is connected to AG communities and uses social media to call for Christian principles to be protected through governmental channels (Ramírez 2022). Tejanas like Flores help mobilize Pentecostal politics that prioritize borders and laws over the well-being of Latin American asylum seekers. Perhaps most tellingly, *none* of her rhetoric resonates with Azusa Street, where the vision of the work of the Spirit was one that transcended borders and nations. Something once essential to American Pentecostalism has gone missing during its routinization: a vision for multiethnic and multiracial politics has been lost.

With Samuel Rodriguez and Mayra Flores in the news cycle, there is reason to doubt that the structures of the AG have proven to be beneficial to Latino Pentecostals. What is not in doubt is the reality that Latino Pentecostals have proven to be a real boon to the AG, who are today the *only* denomination that is growing in a US religious landscape otherwise experiencing collective decline.

Political scientist Ryan Burge reflects, "almost no traditional denomination has seen any growth in the past twelve years, so the Assemblies of God is a true outlier. It's difficult to pinpoint just one reason for the increase in membership," but without Latino growth the AG would, too, be in decline (2021).

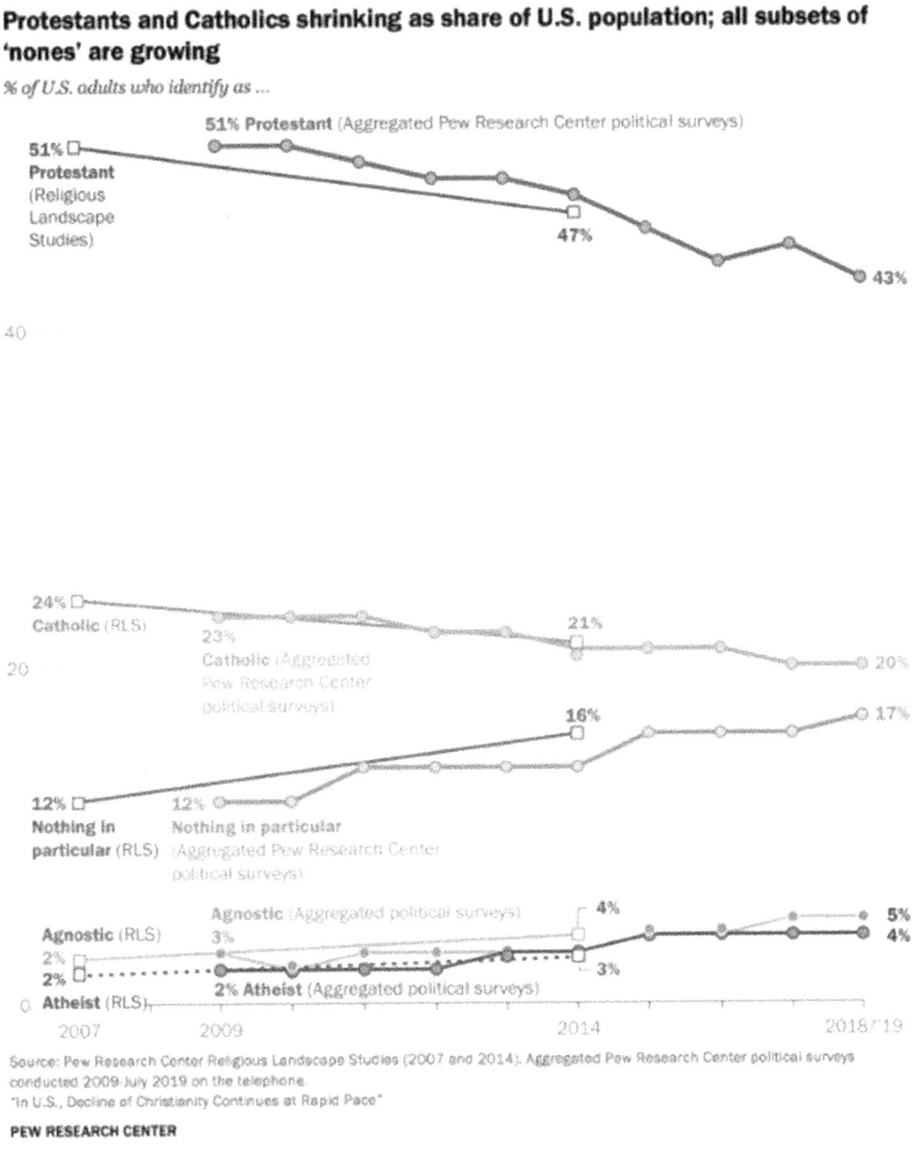

FIGURE 7.5 *As shown in this Pew Research Center study, the percentage of Protestants and Catholics in the United States continues to decline from previous years.* Source: *Pew Research Center.*

At what cost to Latino Pentecostals? US Latino AG leaders seem uninterested in the role they might play in advancing specifically *Latino* well-being. The AG readily tout their diverse constituency and their historical connection to Azusa Street Mission, and the AG is one of the most global forces in Christianity at present. Brazil is now the country with the largest AG population in the world, which means, in one sense at

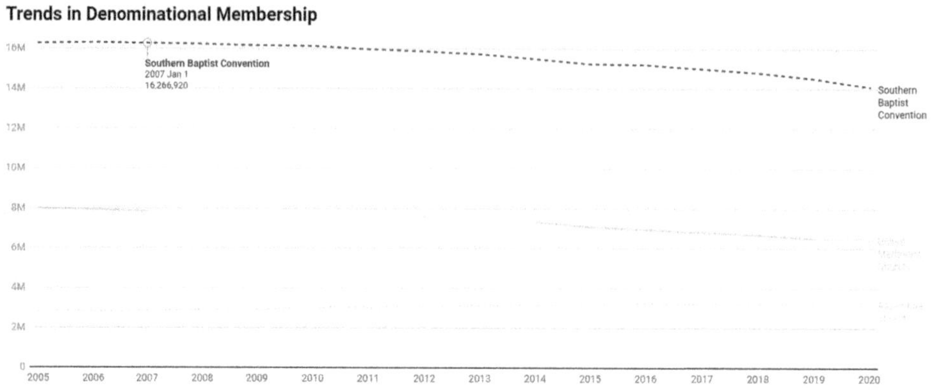

FIGURE 7.6 *Compared to the two largest Protestant denominations in the United States—the Southern Baptist Convention and the United Methodist Church—the Assemblies of God has always been outnumbered. While other denominations have been dropping year-over-year for more than a decade, there have only been three years in the past forty when the Assemblies of God did not report annual growth in adherents.* Source: *Ryan Burge.*

least, it is the epicenter of the AG is in the global South. Yet, if Latino members are to be more than a form of racial capital, that is, a way for white-led institutions to use non-white people to acquire social and economic value, AG leadership will need to decide how to make the movement's multiethnic composition really matter (Leong 2013; Tran 2020). What would it mean for the AG's many adherents, both in the United States and across the world, to develop a transnational consciousness, the sort that Ramírez highlights in *Migrating Faith*?

Seeds of this possibility remain for those who know where to look: Daniel Ramírez highlights that Latin American Pentecostals are still writing songs that place God on the side of the world-weary itinerant laborer, *testimonios desafiantes*: songs that defy the state orders that oppress Latinos who remain at the mercy of labor markets (Ramírez 2021). Any full assessment of Latino Pentecostalism should consider the very real possibility that, despite media optics and marginalization in scholarship, and despite too, the dominance of denominational Pentecostalisms that take little to no interest in their well-being, it is to these kinds of believers that American Pentecostalism may truly belong.

Further Reading

Espinosa, G. 2022. "Latinos Shifting Republican?." *Pneuma* 44 (3–4): 380–414. DOI: https://doi.org/10.1163/15700747-bja10079.

Jackson, N. 2020. "Religion Divides Hispanic Opinion in the U.S." *Public Religion Research Institute*, November 17. https://www.prri.org/spotlight/religion-divides-hispanic-opinion-in-the-u-s/

Lloyd, V. W. 2018. *In Defense of Charisma*. Chichester, New York: Columbia University Press.
Weber, E. 2000. *Apocalypses. Prophecies, Cults and Millennial Beliefs through the Ages*. Cambridge: Harvard University Press

References

Barba, L. 2022a. "Latina/o Pentecostalism." In *The Oxford Handbook of Latinx Christianities in the United States*, 130–50, edited by K. Nabhan-Warren. New York: Oxford University Press.
Barba, L. D. 2022b. *Sowing the Sacred: Mexican Pentecostal Farmworkers in California*. New York: Oxford University Press.
Burge, R. 2021. "Assemblies of God Growing with Pentecostal Persistence." *Christianity Today*. https://www.christianitytoday.com/news/2021/august/assemblies-of-god-grow-us-council-denomination-decline-poli.html
Burridge, K. 1960. *Mambu: A Melanesian Millennium*. London: Methuen.
Calvillo, J. 2018. "Book Review: Latino Pentecostals in America: Faith and Politics in Action, by Gastón Espinosa." *Sociology of Religion* 79 (2): 283–284. https://doi.org/10.1093/socrel/sry009
Calvillo, J. 2020. *The Saints of Santa Ana: Faith and Ethnicity in a Mexican Majority City*. New York: Oxford University Press.
Creech, J. 1996. "Visions of Glory: The Place of the Azusa Street Revival in Pentecostal History." *Church History* 65 (3): 405–24. DOI: https://doi.org/10.2307/3169938.
Creech, J. 2006. *Righteous Indignation: Religion and the Populist Revolution*. Champaign: University of Illinois Press.
Csordas, T.J. 1997. *Language, Charisma, and Creativity: The Ritual Life of a Religious Movement*. Berkeley: University of California Press.
Espinosa, G. 2004. "Francisco Olazábal and Latino Pentecostal Revivalism in the North American Borderlands." In *New Directions in North American Revivalism*, edited by M. McClymond, 172–200. Baltimore: Johns Hopkins University Press.
Espinosa, G. 2008. "Brown Moses: Francisco Olazábal and Mexican American Pentecostal Healing in the Borderlands." In *Mexican American Religions: Spirituality, Activism, and Culture*. Durham, NC: Duke University Press.
Espinosa, G. 2014. *William J. Seymour and the Origins of Global Pentecostalism: A Biography and Documentary History*. Durham, NC: Duke University Press
Goldstein, L. 2018. "'I Know I Will Be Criticized': The Latino Evangelical Who Advises Trump on Immigration." *New York Times*. March 27.
Gordon, R. 2007. "Charisma, Routinization of." In *The Blackwell Encyclopedia of Sociology*, edited by G. Ritzer, 437–8. Malden, MA: Blackwell. https://doi.org/10.1002/9781405165518.wbeosc022
Heffernan, M.J. 2002. "FIN DE SIÈCLE, FIN DU MONDE?: On the Origins of European Geopolitics, 1890–1920." In *Geopolitical Traditions: Critical Histories of a Century of Geopolitical Thought*, edited by D. Atkinson and K. Dodds 27–52. London: Routledge.
Leong, N. 2013. "RACIAL CAPITALISM." *Harvard Law Review* 126 (8): 2151–226. http://www.jstor.org/stable/23415098.
Medina, J. 2022. "The Rise of the Far Right Latina." *New York Times*, July 6. https://www.nytimes.com/2022/07/06/us/politics/mayra-flores-latina-republicans.html
Molina, A. 2020. "Latino Protestants More Conservative, Supportive of Trump Than Latino Catholics, Poll Finds." *Religion News Service*. February 18. https://religionnews.

com/2020/12/01/latino-protestants-more-conservative-supportive-of-trump-than-latino-catholics-poll-finds/

Ramírez, D. 2015. *Migrating Faith: Pentecostalism in the United States and Mexico in the Twentieth Century*. Chapel Hill, NC: The University of North Carolina Press.

Ramírez, D. 2021. "Pilgrims or Settlers? Pentecostal Politics at the Crossroads." *Political Theology Network*. September 9. https://politicaltheology.com/pilgrims-or-settlers-pentecostal-politics-at-the-crossroads/

Ramírez, E. 2022. "The Particularly Pentecostal Flavor of Mayra Flores' Christian Nationalism." *Religion News Service*. July 11. https://religionnews.com/2022/07/11/the-particularly-pentecostal-flavor-of-mayra-flores-christian-nationalism/

Sanchez Walsh, A. 2010. "Alice E. Luce, Henry Ball & Assemblies of God Borderlands." In *From Aldersgate to Azusa Street: Wesleyan, Holiness, and Pentecostal Visions of the New Creation*, edited by H.E. Knight, 266–74. Eugene, OR: Wipf and Stock Publishers.

Schulson, M. 2014. "Like Azusa Street Baptized into Bureaucracy: Mexico's Flourishing LLDM Church Loses Its Apostle." *Religion Dispatches*. December 11. https://religiondispatches.org/like-azusa-street-baptized-into-bureaucracy-mexicos-flourishing-lldm-church-loses-its-apostle/

Tarango, A. 2014. *Choosing the Jesus Way: American Indian Pentecostals and the Fight for the Indigenous Principle*. Chapel Hill, NC: University of North Carolina Press.

Tran, J. 2021. *Asian Americans and the Spirit of Racial Capitalism*. New York: Oxford University Press.

Vasquez, M. 2008. "Studying Religion in Motion: A Networks Approach." *Method and Theory in the Study of Religion* 20 (2): 151–84.

Wacker, G. 2001. *Heaven Below: Early Pentecostals and American Culture*. Cambridge, MA: Harvard University Press.

8

Black Atlantic Religions

Alejandro S. Escalante

Introduction

Formed "in the wake" (Sharpe 2015) of transatlantic enslavement, "Black Atlantic religions" refers to interrelated religious communities birthed in the Caribbean and Latin America that draw inspiration from African practices and theologies. In this colonial context, African-inspired religious practices were eventually formalized as "**Candomblé**," "Espiritismo," "**Ocha**," and "**Palo**." While "Black Atlantic religions" is often used to refer to adaptations of African practices, the term can also be understood to refer to traditions that have been "Africanized," such as "Afro-Catholicism" (Fromont 2019) and "Afro-Islam" (Johnson and Palmié 2018). Moreover, there are still myriad other African-inspired traditions in the Caribbean and Latin America that are still to be properly attended to. Thus, the term "Black Atlantic religions" refers to an aqueous group of practices and theologies that draw variously on African-inspired customs and cosmologies and which are still evolving.

Over the nearly 400 years that the transatlantic slave trade was active, upwards of an estimated 12 million people from a host of African ethnic groups, including the Gbe, Kongo, and Yoruba peoples, were violently trafficked into the Americas by French, Portuguese, and Spanish colonizers. In places that are today known as Brazil, Cuba, Dominic Republic, Haiti, Puerto Rico, and all throughout the Caribbean and Latin America, enslaved people were forced to mine for gold and work on agricultural plantations, growing coffee, sugarcane, and tobacco. Under the grueling conditions of their forced migration, enslavement, and "social death" (Patterson 1982), they remade their homes in settler colonial states and rearticulated their religious lives in the Americas, often borrowing from their colonial settings to produce new versions of their African practices. Variously called "Afro-Latinx religions," "Afro-Atlantic religions,"

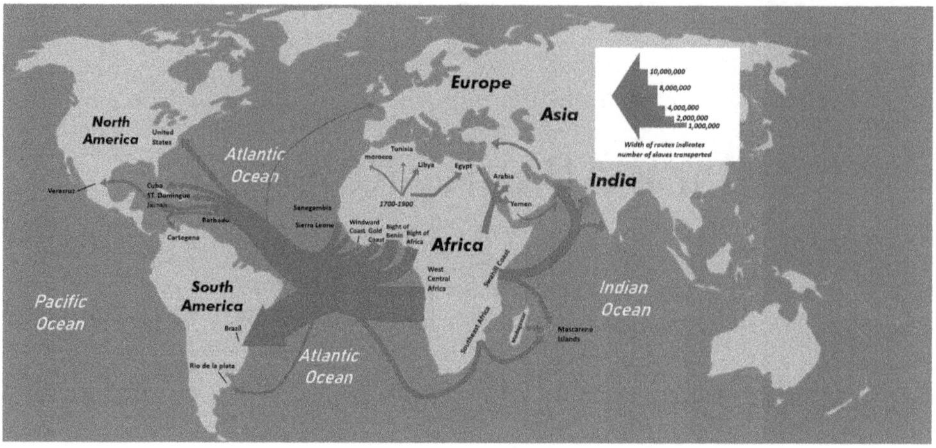

FIGURE 8.1 *Map showing the direction and numbers of enslaved Africans brought to the Americas. This map is adapted from Eltis and Richardson (2015).* Source: *KuroNekoNiyah/ Wikimedia Commons.*

or "Afro-Caribbean religions," Black Atlantic religions have since migrated to other parts of the Americas, including the United States (Greene-Hayes 2021) and back across the Atlantic to Europe and beyond (Matory 2018).

Following this introduction is a brief sketch of the nature and significance of the "**Black Atlantic**" for the study of Afro-Latinx religions, emphasizing its conceptual openness and adaptability. Building on this theoretical openness, the next section cautions readers against reading to find easy answers to complex questions. The penultimate section is comprised of thumbnail sketches of a sampling of some Black Atlantic religions, introducing them in alphabetical order and focusing on their African-inspirations and their cosmological and theological structures. The final section notes two developments in the study of Black Atlantic religions, namely a focus on Christianity and Islam, and gender and sexuality studies. In the conclusion, I revisit the chapter's themes and identify potential areas for new research.

Situating "Black Atlantic Religions"

In designating these religious formations as "Black Atlantic religions," this chapter centers transatlantic slaving as pivotal to the shaping of new religious practices in the Caribbean and Latin America. Secondly, it considers how Afro-Latinx people's religiosity forms part of wider historical and regional discourses about identity, migration, and history. Thus, this term helps us to hold in tension the historical and ongoing realities of coloniality and how sacred practices and knowledge adapt and change to ever-developing contexts.

The term "Black Atlantic" was first coined by art historian Robert Farris Thompson in his highly influential text on the global impact of African art and philosophy, *Flash of the Spirit* (1983). Thompson does not develop this concept fully, though, and it is not until Paul Gilroy's *The Black Atlantic* (1993) that we see a fully developed theory of the Black Atlantic as a theory of "creolization" or cultural development in colonial contexts (Etherington 2020). Gilroy demonstrates slaving's centrality to the development of the Atlantic world, including ideas of "race," "nation," and their reciprocity. Later, J. Lorand Matory (2005) develops Gilroy's Black Atlantic and applies it to Brazilian Candomblé and, in turn, coins "Black Atlantic religion," tracing Candomblé's relationships back-and-forth across the Atlantic, between Brazil and Africa.

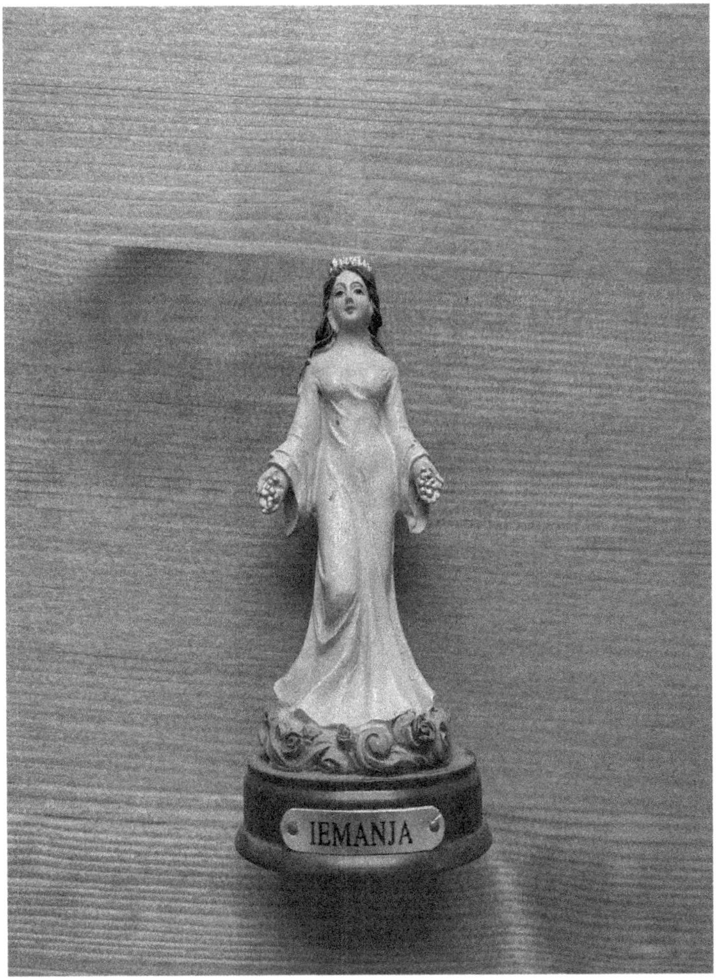

FIGURE 8.2 *Figure of the orixá Iemanja (also spelled "Yemanjá"; see "Candomblé" below) for sale in Porto, Portugal in 2018. Practitioners of Candomblé see Portugal as a new frontier for their religion (Strongman 2019).* Source: *Alejandro Escalante.*

Given the term's rootedness in the legacy of the transatlantic slave trade, "Black Atlantic" also pushes us to consider how religious practices move and develop over time through the processes of migration, both forced and chosen. In considering that Ocha (see below) is now practiced all over Europe, for example, Stephan Palmié (2013), asks us to consider what makes something an "Afro-Cuban religion." Does the practitioner need to be Afro-Cuban themselves for the practice to be considered as such? Or is a practice Afro-Cuban independent of its practitioners? While no easy answer can be given to Palmié's questions, "Black Atlantic religions" helps us to see how these religious practices are not bound to one geographical location, language, or culture. Indeed, as Afro-Latinx people migrate within and beyond the Caribbean and Latin America, they bring their practices along and further extend the boundaries of the Black Atlantic. Likewise, as new initiates join Black Atlantic religious communities, what makes Afro-Latinx religion expands, too (Forte 2010).

Finally, "Black Atlantic religions" destabilizes easy conceptions of "purity." As the enslaved attempted to create new lives in new contexts, they often replicated elements of their African customs and cosmologies in the Americas. Drawing from what was available to them, including colonial Christianity and Indigenous customs, it is perhaps appropriate to talk about "*Africas*" in the Americas (Palmié 2008) given how enslaved Africans extended their ethnic communities in the Americas. The mixture and overlap of the Black Atlantic means that there is not one authentic version of African practices and theologies but many. To avoid any unwarranted hierarchical thinking regarding "originality," scholars use "African-inspired" as opposed to "African-based," which denotes a timeless "Africa" that can be known objectively (Beliso-De Jesús 2015; Crosson 2020; Ochoa 2010b). In this spirit, I use "continuation," "extension," and "rearticulation" and other synonyms in this chapter to mean the same.

Studying Black Atlantic Religions

Two problems initially present themselves when discussing Black Atlantic religions. Firstly, the sets of practices and crafts associated with each are not immutable, which is to say, that practices, theologies, and crafts slightly differ between region and language (Johnson and Palmié 2018: 440). Technological advancements and globalization only intensify the way that these religious forms evolve (Beliso-De Jesús 2015; Romberg 2003). Finally, given the history of anti-Blackness in the region, it is important to note how practitioners often "disidentify" (Muñoz 1999) with certain forms of blackness.

Kristina Wirtz (2007) argues that while community hierarchies exist, there is no meta-level centralizing authority that assigns orthodoxy, making religious authority localized. Therefore, it is better to think about Black Atlantic religions as "decentralized network of lineages, cults, and disparate public and private ritual practices that readily intermingle across definitional boundaries with other religions" (Wirtz 2007: 28). In some cases, practitioners will mix different religious formations into what Raquel Romberg calls "laissez-faire spirituality," a buffet-like approach to religious life wherein practitioners practice whatever works. Furthermore, as Ochoa has shown, ritual hierarchies differ between Havana and Cuba's countryside (2003: 81ff, 2010b, 2020). In Havana, he argues, rituals are highly regulated by recognized a religious authority called *babalawos* ("father of mysteries," Ocha ritual experts). By contrast, in Sierra Morena, such hierarchies dissolve and rituals are regularly overseen by laity. Thus, great care and nuance is required when studying Black Atlantic religions, as they are not timeless.

Race and racialization are highly charged topics in the Caribbean and Latin America, especially as Black Atlantic religions are racialized and policed in ways that other religions are not (Crosson 2020; Román 2007). Many national myths operate under the guise of "racial democracy," a theory of racialization that posits everyone to be a blend of three archetypal historical lineages: African, European, and Indigenous (Alberto and Hoffnung-Garskof 2018). No one is *only* Black or white; everyone is mixed. Therefore, racism is said not to exist. Racial democracy, however, ignores the ongoing anti-Black racism by eliding the obvious problem of racialization and racial hierarchies in the region (see Gillam 2022, for example). Because of the historical and contemporary negative associations with Blackness, practitioners are often wary of being associated with African practices. As such, African-inspired crafts are often called by different names in certain contexts to "disidentify" (Muñoz 1999), to take advantage of ambiguity so as to avoid negative stereotypes and harassment (Crosson 2020; Hayes 2011; Romberg 2009).

Candomblé

Due to importing more enslaved Africans than any other country, Brazil is now home to one of the largest diasporic African populations in the Americas. In turn, this means that Brazil is likewise home to a host of African-inspired religious formations, including its largest community: Candomblé, a West and west Central African-inspired practice that shares cosmology, history, and linguistic inheritances with Cuban Ocha and Palo (below). And like its Cuban counterparts, Candomblé "emerged out of, or at least in near proximity to, Catholicism" (Johnson and Palmié 2018: 448). This means that it is a "redaction of west African religions recreated in the radically new context of a nineteenth-century Catholic slave society" (Johnson 2002: 41). The origins of the word "Candomblé" are debated; however, some scholars argue that it is derived from the "African Kongo-Bantu *Kandombele*, meaning 'musical festival'" and was used by Portuguese slavers to describe African religious practices they witnessed (Murrell 2010: 167).

Candomblé can be divided into different *nacões* (nations) that refer to different ethnolinguistic groups that were reshaped in Brazil: Nagô, Jeje, and Angola. Each nation draws inspiration from different African ethnic communities for its practice and theology. Nagô, for example, refers to a "nation avowing Yorùbá origins" (Matory 2005: 5). Jeje, on the other hand, refers to Gbè-inspired traditions, tracing their lineage to Yoruba neighbors, the Ewe and Fon (Matory 2005: 23). Finally, Angola nations claim

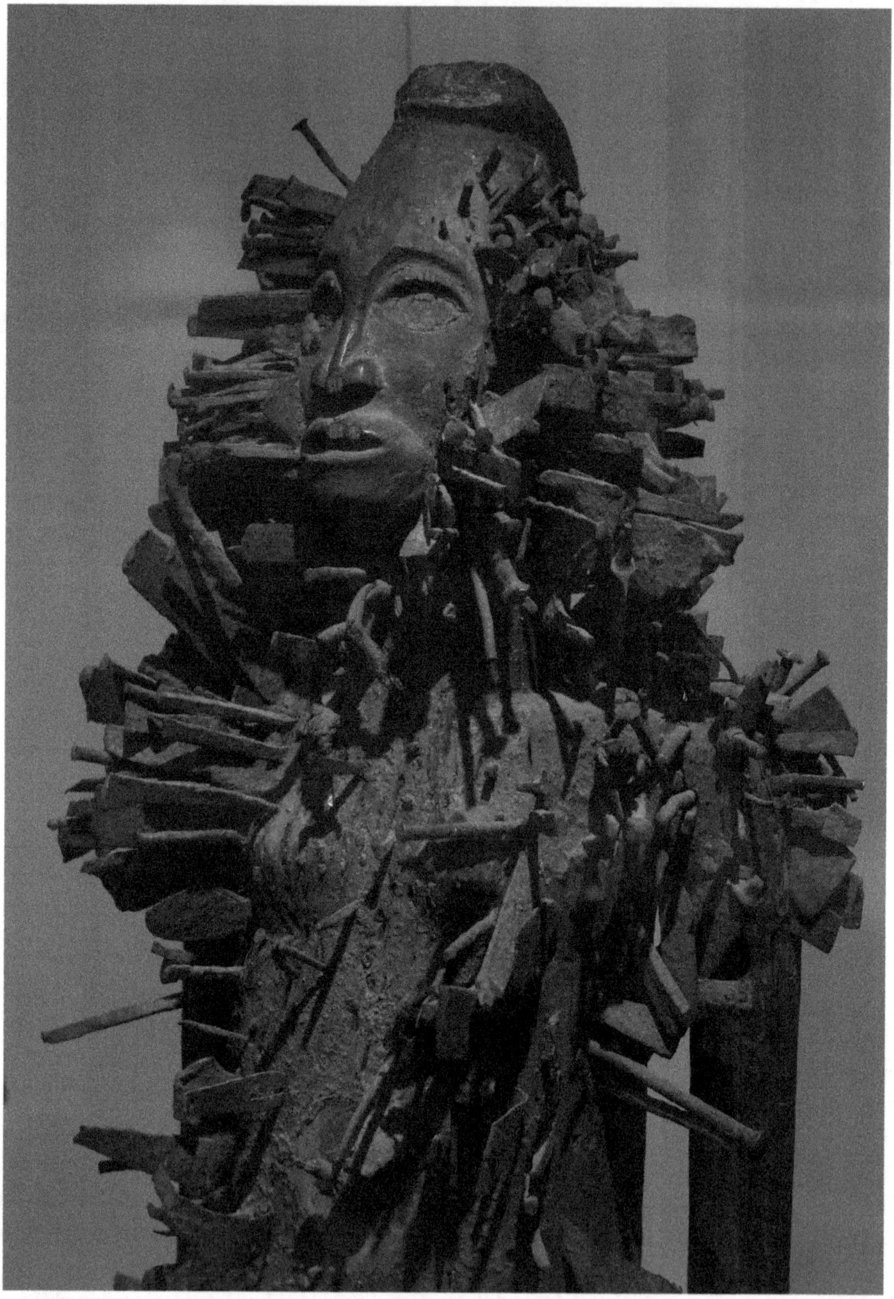

FIGURE 8.3 *Nineteenth-century BaKongo* nkisi, *a west Central African divinity, on display at the British Museum.* Minkisi *(plural of nkisi) are material powers constructed "to benefit clients of the owner-operator, the* nganga *[the ritual specialist], by identifying and punishing wrongdoers supposed to have caused misfortunes, sickness, and death, or by providing benefits such as fertility of crops and women" (MacGaffey 2014: 149).* Source: *Vassil/Wikimedia Commons.*

west Central African lineages, including Kongo (Matory 2005: 24). Nations are not mutually exclusive, though. Indeed, the historical mutual reliance between the Jeje and the Najô, for example, reveals that these national boundaries are somewhat porous, leading scholars to refer to them as "Jeje-Nagô" (Matory 2005: 24). Finally, nations can be further divided into even more specific African lineages and even down to the specific *terreiros* (temples) where practitioners gather to dance, sing, and hear from the gods.

In addition to ethno-linguistic differences, each nation likewise attends to different divinities and combinations thereof. The Nagô nation's pantheon is headed by Olorun (sometimes also called "Olodumare"), who is distant and does not receive devotional attention. Instead, the *orixá*, who are Brazilian continuations of Yoruba *òrìṣà*, act as divine intermediaries between Olorun and human beings (Johnson 2002: 14). The orixá have dominion over specific areas, such as the sea (Iemanjá, see Figure 8.2), metallurgy (Ogun), or thunder (Xangô). The orixá were further reconceptualized through their cross filiation with Catholic saints who shared similar characteristics or areas of sovereignty. Ogun, for example, is aligned with Catholic saints Anthony and George (Johnson 2002: 204). Jeje and Angola nations devote themselves to other African divinities that were likewise transported to Brazil and reconfigured there. The *inquice*, from the Kikongo word "nkisi" (Figure 8.3; see "Palo" below), are the Kongo-inspired divinities who fill Angola terreiros (Matory 2005: 25). The *vodun*, meaning "gods," are Gbè-inspired divinities that are principally found in Jeje Candomblé (Matory 2005: 76).

Candomblé rituals generally take place in a terreiro that belongs to a particular nation and were historically formed in proximity to Catholic churches (Johnson and Palmié 2018: 448). A terreiro is the place that contains *axé*, from the Yoruba "*àṣẹ*" (see "Ocha" below). Axé is the vital energy that underlies the cosmos and is found in all living creatures. It is concentrated and transferable in animal blood, making animal sacrifice an important element of ritual life in Candomblé (Matory 2005: 123). In the terreiro, the orixá make themselves known physically both through their likenesses (for example, see Figure 8.2) and through spirit possession as they are "danced, fed, dressed, and sung into tangible presence" (Johnson 2002: 14). Therefore, Nathaniel Samuel Murrell (2010: 167) can neatly summarize Candomblé as "a signifying act of exchange in which gods ride humans, humans feed gods, and gods empower the weak through axe [*sic*]." Murrell's language of "ride" points to the equestrian language used to describe possession, in which the practitioner is likened to a horse and the orixá, the rider. Notably, though, the equestrian language is overlaid with gendered conceptions indicating that to be possessed is to be feminine and to ride (to mount, to possess) is masculine (Johnson 2002: 44).

Espiritismo

In the mid-nineteenth century, French Spiritism was making its way around the Black Atlantic and was being developed by practitioners into its own distinct form, Espiritismo. In fact, as early as 1860, copies of Allan Kardec's founding text, *Le livre des esprits*

(The Spirits's Book, 1857), were already being circulated in Brazil (Johnson and Palmié 2018: 454). Not a "religion" per se, Kardec's Spiritism was a "religious metaphysics" that possessed a body-mind dualistic view of the world and emphasized the ability to communicate with the dead via mediumship (Edmonds and Gonzalez 2010: 116). In the Caribbean, Spiritism was infused with other Black Atlantic religious formations and developed into **Espiritismo cruzado** or "mixed Spiritism," an Africanized version (Johnson and Palmié 2018: 454). Such distinctions, though, between "orthodox" and "Africanized" were usually made by social elites to differentiate themselves from perceived Others (Román 2007). Diana Espírito Santo further clarifies that such

FIGURE 8.4 *Brazilian stamp featuring Allen Kardec, founder of Spiritism, celebrating "the Codification," the five books that make up the essential Spiritist doctrine, on the centenary of the publication of the final book of the Codification,* L'Évangile Selon le Spiritisme *(The Gospel According to Spiritism, 1876 [1864]).* Source: *Etat brésilien/Wikimedia Commons.*

divisions are disingenuous to the reality, where practitioners often mixed elements from other practices and theologies (2015: 5).

In Espiritismo, the material and immaterial world are linked together such that each can influence the other, with spirits and humans acting as guides for one another. This is because the spirits of the dead are hierarchically categorized from the ignorant to the enlightened, from those still attached to the material world and to those who are *espíritus de luz* or spirits of light (Edmonds and Gonzalez 2010: 116). Through séance-like rituals conducted around tables, practitioners summon the dead, who give and receive messages from the living. The tables are typically covered with a white tablecloth, along with "images of saints, flowers, cigars, and other ritual objects" that help channel the spirits (Edmond and Gonzalez 2010: 119). During these *misas* (masses), participants commune with the spirits of the dead to learn from them and in turn help them along in their evolutionary journey toward pure spirit (Fernández Olmos and Paravisini-Gebert 2011: 207).

Though possessing metaphysical elements, Kardecian Spiritism was ostensibly a scientific and "secular-transcendental practice" (Romberg 2009: 15). Conceived of as a moral philosophy of life rather than a "religion," Spiritism was, therefore, seen as complementary to religious practices, including Catholicism, though not without qualification (Edmonds and Gonzalez 2010: 117). In the Caribbean, this complementarity meant that Spiritism was often practiced alongside other Black Atlantic religions, including Candomblé, Ocha, and Palo. Like other Black Atlantic religions, Espiritismo cruzado is a network-like assemblage that does not necessarily have a centralized leadership and community, per se. Indeed, Diana Espírito Santo (2015: 9) found that mediums in Havana, for example, "were disparate and heterogenous." Likewise, Raquel Romberg (2003; 2009) found that *espiritistas* in Puerto Rico worked as *ad hoc* healers and diviners, with some consistent clientele but no one standardized ritual schedule. Moreover, theologies and cosmologies are made flexible such that espiritistas (practitioners of Espiritismo) will recapitulate other practices as part of their Spiritism. One does not, therefore, need to pledge allegiance to one tradition; instead, one can create multiple filiations, finding whatever works (Jacobson 2007; Romberg 2003). Illustrating this point, Romberg (2003: 20) notes that an espiritista's altar contained "African, Catholic, and Spiritist ritual objects side by side, erasing any hierarchical order." Moreover, other Black Atlantic religious formations have subsequently been affected by Espiritismo such that "virtually all more obviously African-derived Cuban ritual traditions have absorbed elements of spiritist doctrine" (Johnson and Palmié 2018: 455).

Ocha

Regla de Ocha ("rule" or "law of Ocha"; sometimes "Santería," "Lucumí," or simply "Ocha") is a Yoruba-inspired ritual system that took shape in the "areas of western Cuba around the end of the nineteenth century" (Wirtz 2007: 30). So, while Spanish colonists trafficked enslaved Africans into Cuba for decades, Ocha was not fully systematized until much later. Developed in *cabildos* (African societies modeled on Spanish Catholic fraternal societies), Ocha can be described as an uneven mixture of Yoruba and Catholic traditions, with Yoruba practices retaining a slight advantage (Wirtz 2007: 29). The term "Ocha" itself is derived from the word "*oricha*," the Spanish word for the Yoruba "òrìṣà" (see "Candomblé" above). There is also some discussion regarding the appropriateness of the term "Santería" ("way of the saints"), which was initially used pejoratively to describe ostensibly inappropriate devotion to the saints (De La Torre, 2004). However, the term has been adopted by some as their chosen designation for their ritual practices, sometimes for the sake of legitimation as a "religion" (Palmié 2013). Still others contend that practitioners prefer "Regla de Ocha" (Wirtz 2007).

The Ocha pantheon is headed by Olodumare, who is often described as "God" in a Christian sense of the word (Murrell 2010: 107) or more generally as the "Supreme Being" (Lawal 2004: 292). However, *santeros* (practitioners of Ocha) do not generally engage with him; instead, they interact with the oricha, his emissaries, to whom he delegated the maintenance of the earth (Lawal 2004: 292). Each oricha has several *caminos* (manifestations) that are based on traditions about them and are sometimes contradictory, underscoring their evolving, multifaceted, and often capricious personalities. Chief among the oricha is Elégua (sometimes "Eleguá" and "Eleggua"), who was tasked with serving as messenger of the oricha. His domains are the cemetery, the crossroads, and, therefore, transitions more generally. Rituals begin by acknowledging and making the appropriate sacrifices to him as he can divert supplications one way or the other. Elégua has at least twenty-one caminos (Beliso-De Jesús 2015), seeing him manifest as a respected old man or as a mischievous child. Furthermore, the oricha are cross identified with the Catholic saints with whom they are coequally identified (Figure 8.5). Changó (Yoruba "Ṣàngó"), for example, who is sovereign over thunder, fire, and masculine virility, is associated with Santa Bárbara (St. Barbara), who is associated with the "thundering Spanish artillery cannons" (Fernández Olmos and Paravisini-Gebert 2011: 43).

In Ocha, *aché* (from Yoruba "àṣẹ"; see "Candomblé" above) constitutes and holds the world together (Clark 2007: 11). Aché is the vital, creative force of the universe through which all things happen and is the power to make things happen (Thompson 1983). Mary Ann Clark (2007: 11) continues: "[Aché] is without beginning or end; it cannot be enumerated or exhausted. It is not a particular power but Power itself." Finally, she argues, that such an understanding means that the cosmos itself is "monistic," made of one substance: aché (Clark 2007: 11). As the creative energy of all things, aché likewise constitutes humanity and moves through humans, giving us the energy and the motivation to complete tasks and make things happen in the world. Aché, therefore, can be felt corporeally, in and on our bodies, like the tingling of electrical currents (Beliso-De Jesús 2015).

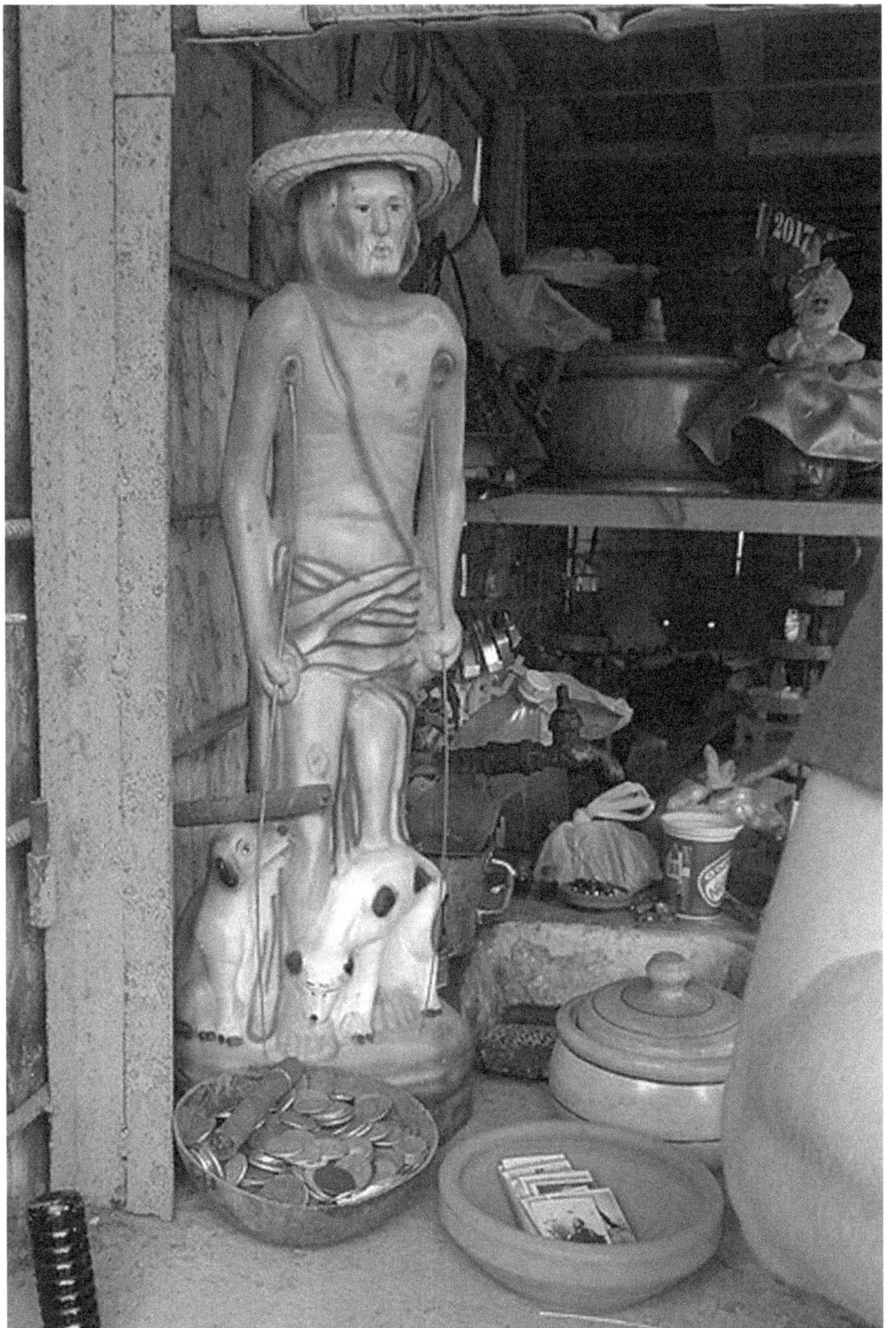

FIGURE 8.5 *Statue of San Lazaro-Babalú Ayé in Havana, Cuba. In Ocha, San Lazaro (St. Lazarus) and Babalú-Ayé are cross identified, sharing sovereignty over curative powers (see Ochoa 2020)*. Source: *RG72/Wikimedia Commons*.

Palo

Palo is a Kongo-inspired religious formation that took shape in Cuba around the same time as Ocha. In Cuba, the "*Reglas de Congo*" (often simply "Palo") and Ocha are often spoken about as the "left" (hot, harming) and "right" (cool, healing) hands of Cuba's African-inspired ritual systems, with Palo being the left and Ocha the right (Ochoa 2010a: 389). This is often the result of Palo's affiliation with the dead and with forms of negation (punishment and affliction) to accomplish a practitioner's goal (Ochoa, 2010b). Perceptions of negativity and witchcraft, though, are largely based on readings of Palo from the vantage point of Ocha, which is considered more refined than Palo (Palmié 2002). Palo's supposed "unruliness" is further evidenced by its multiple *ramas* (branches), which means that there is not one "regla" de Congo but multiple "*reglas*" de Congo (Fernández Olmos and Paravisini-Gebert 2011: 89; Johnson and Palmié 2018: 463).

Though the different ramas of Palo are extremely idiosyncratic, *prendas* help unify Palo's different ramas (Johnson and Palmié 2018: 463). Prendas (Figure 8.6) draw inspiration from BaKongo nkisi (Figure 8.2; see "Candomblé" above) and are called "*enquiso*" or sometimes "*nganga*," the word for a ritual specialist (Ochoa 2010b; Palmié 2002). As Todd Ramón Ochoa argues "prenda," "nganga," and "enquiso" are mutually constituting forces (2010a: 499). Therefore, to choose one over the other is to flatten their relationality. Thus, he writes them as "prenda-nganga-enquiso" to emphasize their relationality but he also notes the ubiquity of simply using "prenda" (Ochoa 2010a, 2010b). Most typically, a prenda refers to clay or metal cauldrons into which sticks (*palos*), dirt, and human remains are packed into, and which are then used to power the prenda to accomplish their goal. Each prenda is dedicated to a *mpungu*, Kongo-inspired divinities that characterize each cauldron. For example, three-footed iron prendas are dedicated to Zarabanda (sometimes "Sarabanda"), who has sovereignty over hard work and physical strength, and who is often associated with aggression and power (Bettelheim 2001). The human remains, *nfumbe*, are what power the prenda, turning these material constructions into active forces (Ochoa 2010b). Thus, more than objects, prendas are ritual powers that are versions of the dead (*kalunga*), making them subjectivities who can influence the material world (Espírito Santo 2018).

Nzambi (variously spelled "*Nsambi*" or "*Zambi*") is often regarded as "God" given his creative, self-sustaining, and omniscient attributes (Murrell 2010). Such theological complementarity to Christianity is likely the result of Portuguese missionary efforts in west Central Africa prior to the transatlantic slave trade (Fernández Olmos and Paravisini-Gebert 2011: 94; Johnson and Palmié 2018: 444). However, Ochoa argues that in Cuban practice Nzambi does not possess a categorical difference in the way that "God" implies and that other subjectivities, such as kalunga, are talked about similarly (Ochoa 2010b: 267n2). Nzambi is distant from the day-to-day activities of the humans and does not receive sacrifices or prayers. Instead, it is the mpungu and the dead (kalunga) who are called upon as fate changers. Just as the oricha have dominion and cross affiliation

FIGURE 8.6 *A Zarabanda prenda in Havana, Cuba. This prenda is packed tight with an assortment of ritual matter, including a femur bone, just below the drawing of an eye.* Source: *Cyberesque/Wikimedia Commons.*

with Catholic saints, so do the mpungu. Mama Chola, for example, shares sovereignty of the fresh water and likeness with the oricha Ochún and the Catholic saint *La Virgen del Cobre* (Bettelheim 2001; Schmidt 2015). As Ochoa (2007: 482) argues, "kalunga" is a flexible Kikongo loanword that refers to the place where the dead reside, the constitution of this place, and the dead themselves. Kalunga, like the oricha, are corporeal subjectivities that are felt both on and in the body, often as "chills, goose bumps, or fluttering the chest or stomach" (Ochoa 2007: 492). It is through the dead that *paleros* (practitioners of Palo) accomplish their various undertakings, namely the healing of clients and the afflicting of their respective enemies. Most typically, the use of the dead to accomplish one's goals is related to the history of enslavement wherein slavers used the enslaved to perform certain tasks; likewise, the dead are enlisted in Palo to perform the tasks of the living (see Figure 8.6; Matory 2008; Ralph, Beliso-De Jesús, and Palmié 2017; Routon 2008).

Developments in Black Atlantic Religions

While most research has focused on the so-called "stars" (Johnson 2018: 34) of Black Atlantic religions, namely Candomblé and Ocha, there has been increasing attention to Christianity as a "Black Atlantic religion" (Thornton 2021). This shift in attention considers how Christianity is shaped by African-inspired practices. Beginning in the late fifteenth century, for example, Portuguese missionaries were already Christianizing portions of west Central African communities, many from there were subsequently brought to the Americas via the transatlantic slave trade (Fromont 2019). This emphasis is further seen in scholarly attention to how enslaved Africans and their descendants in the Black Atlantic adapted Christianity to meet their needs. In Puerto Rico, for example, Black Catholics in Loíza have made space for celebrating their Africanness (Figure 8.7) during the city's major annual religious festivals, *las fiestas tradicionales en honor a Santiago Apóstol*, the Catholic festival in honor of St. James (Alegría 1954; Escalante forthcoming). Similarly, scholars are increasingly interested in the role of Charismatic and Pentecostal Christianity in the Black Atlantic, noting how these affiliations change our understanding of Evangelical Christianity beyond prevailing conceptions of it as a white and North American phenomenon (Thornton 2016).

Researchers are also interested in the role of Islam in the Black Atlantic (Chitwood 2021; K. Khan 2020). It is estimated that over the course of the transatlantic slave trade, "as many as '480,000 [enslaved African Muslims] could have landed in the Caribbean.' However, these totals are only estimates and represent only what is documented about the ships, the number of Africans aboard, and their final destinations" (Escalante 2019a: 182). Once in the Americas, African Muslims "were isolated and inserted in small communities with a weak religious life .... In other words, there were Muslims but no Muslim institution building" (Delmonte 2015: 191–2). Since that time, however, stronger networks developed in the Caribbean and Latin America, leading to a robust Islamic life in Brazil and Cuba (Johnson and Palmié 2018), Mexico (Chitwood 2021),

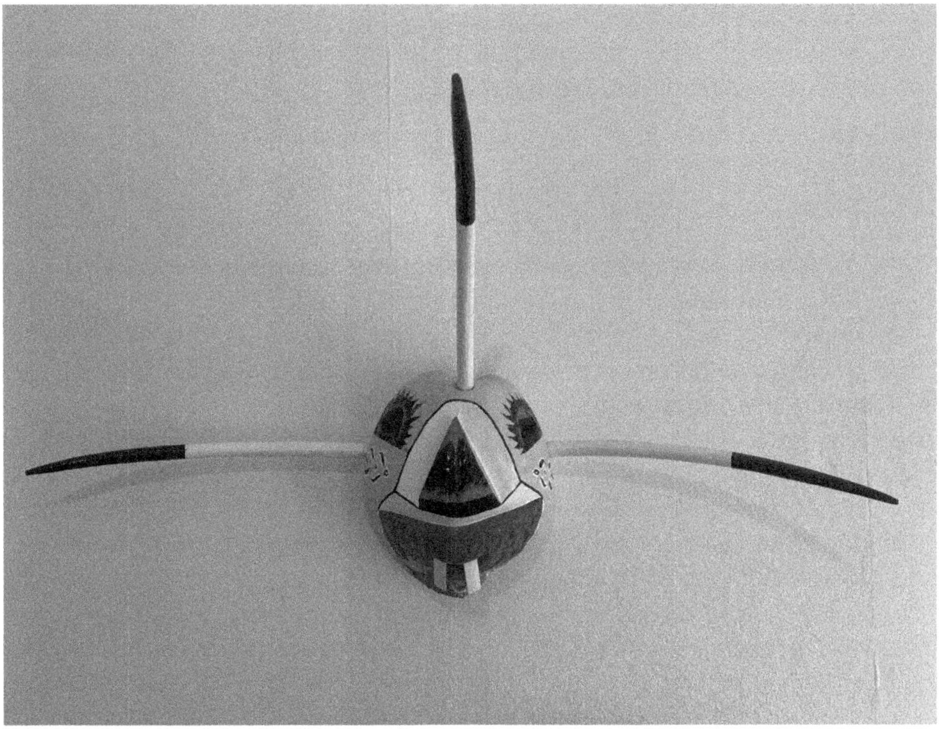

FIGURE 8.7 *A* vejigante *mask made by Raúl Ayala, master mask maker in Loíza, Puerto Rico. The* vejigante *is an African-inspired, carnivalesque persona that residents of Loíza take on during* las fiestas tradicionales en honor a Santiago Apóstol. *See Alegría (1954).* Source: *Alejandro Escalante.*

Martinique (Kuczynski 2015), and Trinidad (Kassim 2015). This has led to a retheorization of the Black Atlantic as the "Muslim Atlantic," a nuancing of Gilroy's concept that draws attention to the diasporization of African Muslims in the Americas (A. Khan 2020).

Finally, feminist and queer theorizations of Black Atlantic religions have further added to our understanding of these communities. Though gender had already been a framework for understanding Black Atlantic religions (Brown 1991; Matory 2005), in recent years, queer readings of Black Atlantic religions have highlighted the undertheorized homophobia implicit and explicit in scholarship and practice. Here, Omise'eke Natasha Tinsley's (2008) work is particularly important for thinking about the role of gender and sexuality in Gilroy's "Black Atlantic." Her work critically traces how queer, nonnormative relationships were formed in the hold of the slave ships and beyond. Since Tinsley, scholars have followed three general streams: (1) the queerness of Black Atlantic divinities (Wilcox 2018), (2) practitioners' queerness (Beliso-De Jesús 2013b; Pérez 2016), and (3) the queer relationships between divinities and humans (Escalante 2019b). Scholars sometimes blend all three of these streams in developing an overall theory of queerness within Black Atlantic religions. Roberto

Strongman's *Queering Black Atlantic Religions* (2019) is one such example that offers a unique reading of Black Atlantic religions, including Candomblé and Santería (Ocha), by analyzing ethnographic research and media studies.

Conclusion

While attending to some minor literatures of Black Atlantic religions, this chapter has still been necessarily limited. In an increasingly globalizing world, "Black Atlantic religions" are constantly taking on new valences, new caminos. Because of this, new areas of research constantly present themselves. Omar Ramadan-Santiago's 2019 work, for example, on "spiritual blackness" in Puerto Rican Rasta communities highlights the need to critically reflect further on racialization in the Caribbean. Likewise, scholars theorizing the African influence on Afro-Latinx Pentecostalism (Cruz 2005) push us to consider the deep ties between Africa and the Americas. And still other Black Atlantic religious communities, such as Brazilian Umbanda and Quimbanda (Carvalho and Bairrão 2019; Hale 2009; Hayes 2011; Hess 1992) and Dominican vodú or vudú (Davis 2007; Tallaj 2018), form a small portion of Black Atlantic religious practices that could not be traced here but deserve our consideration. Much research is still to be conducted with these communities and others while maintaining an ethical and responsive presence that does not fall into the trap of viewing them from the vantage point of so-called "neutrals."

Furthermore, future researchers would do well to maintain Gilroy's transnationalist theorization of the Black Atlantic as we think about "Afro-Latinx religion." This is particularly the case as the boundaries of the Black Atlantic are in flux, just as the waters of the Atlantic are constantly in motion. Through migration, Black Atlantic religions have made their way to major US cities like New York (Beliso-De Jesus 2013b), Chicago (Pérez 2016), and Los Angeles (Wilcox 2018). With practitioners of Candomblé in Italy (Golfetto 2018) and Germany (Bahia 2014), the Black Atlantic reminds us that practices and theologies are constantly evolving—and like the ocean, cannot be contained.

This chapter situates Black Atlantic religions fluidly, attending to how Afro-Latinx people in the Caribbean and Latin America have extended African practices and theologies in new contexts, developing new religious formations in the wake of transatlantic slavery. Given the overall surfeit of scholarship on Candomblé and Ocha, I have sought to augment the picture of Black Atlantic religions by focusing on additional, lesser studied practices. Moreover, in pointing to developments in Afro-Christianity and Afro-Islam, I likewise push the boundaries of what is considered "Afro-Latinx" religion. The Black Atlantic's aqueous nature allows me to attend to all these facets at once, noting their complexity and ambiguity. In the context of thinking about Afro-Latinx religions, "Black Atlantic religions" helps us see not only how Afro-Latinx religions take shape in the Caribbean and Latin America but also how these religious groups move between and outside of these contexts and how that movement might further nuance our understanding of Afro-Latinx religions. Therefore, the answer to the question "what makes something an Afro-Latinx religion?" is still unfolding and demands constant revision.

Further Reading

Johnson, S. 2015. *African American Religions, 1500–2000: Colonialism, Democracy, and Freedom*. New York: Cambridge University Press.

The Slave Voyages Consortium. https://slavevoyages.com.

Thornton, J. 1998. *Africa and Africans in the Making of the Atlantic World, 1400–1800*. Cambridge: Cambridge University Press.

Trost, T. L., ed. 2007. *The African Diaspora and the Study of Religion*. New York: Palgrave Macmillan.

References

Alberto, P. L., and J. H. Garskof. 2018. "'Racial Democracy' and Racial Inclusion: Hemispheric Histories." In *Afro-Latin American Studies: An Introduction*, edited by A. d. l. Fuente and G. R. Andrews, 264–316. Cambridge: Cambridge University Press.

Alegría, R. 1954. *La fiesta de Santiago Apóstol en Loíza Aldea*. Madrid: Artes Gráficas.

Bahia, J. 2014. "Under the Berlin Sky: Candomblé on German Shores." *Vibrant* 11 (2): 327–70.

Beliso-De Jesús, A. M. 2013a. "Yemayá's Duck: Irony, Ambivalence, and the Effeminate Male Subject in Cuban Santería." In *Yemoja: Gender, Sexuality, and Creativity in the Latina/o And Afro-Atlantic Diasporas*, edited by S. Otero and T. Falola, 43–84. Albany: State University of New York Press.

Beliso-De Jesús, A. M. 2013b. "Religious Cosmopolitanisms: Media, Transnational Santería, and Travel between the United States and Cuba." *American Ethnologist* 40 (4): 704–20.

Beliso-De Jesús, A. M. 2015. *Electric Santería: Racial and Sexual Assemblages of Transnational Religion*. New York: Columbia University Press.

Bettelheim, J. 2001. "Palo Monte Mayombe and Its Influence on Cuban Contemporary Art." *African Arts* 34 (2): 36–49.

Brown, K. M. 1991. *Mama Lola: A Vodou Priestess in Brooklyn*. Berkeley: University of California Press.

Carvalho, J. B. B., and J. F. M. H. Bairrão. 2019. "Umbanda and Quimbanda: Black Alternative to White Morality." *Psciologia USP* 30: 1–11.

Chitwood, K. 2021. *The Muslims of Latin America and the Caribbean*. Boulder: Lynne Reinner Publishers.

Crosson, J. B. 2020. *Experiments with Power: Obeah and the Remaking of Religion in Trinidad*. Chicago: University of Chicago Press.

Cruz, S. 2005. *Masked Africanisms: Puerto Rican Pentecostalism*. Dubuque: Kendall Hunt Publishing.

Davis, M. E. 2007. "*Vodú* of the Dominican Republic: Devotion to 'La Vientuna División'." *Afro-Hispanic Review* 26 (1): 75–90.

De La Torre, M. 2004. *Santería: The Beliefs and Rituals of a Growing Religion in America.* Grand Rapids, MI: William B. Eerdmans Publishing Company.

Delmonte, L. M. 2015. "Cubans Searching for a New Faith in a New Context." In *Crescent over Another Horizon: Islam in Latin America, the Caribbean, and Latino USA*, edited by M. d. M. L. Narbona, P. G. Pinto and J. T. Karam, 190–205. Austin: University of Texas Press.

Fernández Olmos, M., and L. Paravisini-Gebert. 2011. *Creole Religions of the Caribbean: An Introduction from Vodou and Santería to Obeah and Espiritismo*, 2nd edn. New York: New York University Press.

Edmonds, E., and M. A. Gonzalez. 2010. *Caribbean Religious History: An Introduction.* New York: New York University Press.

Eltis, D., and D. Richardson. 2015. *Atlas of the Transatlantic Slave Trade.* New Haven: Yale University Press.

Escalante, A. S. 2019a. "The Long Arc of Islamophobia: African Slavery, Islam, and the Caribbean World." *Journal of Africana Religions* 7 (1): 179–86.

Escalante, A. S. 2019b. "Trans* Atlantic Religions: Gender Ideology and Spirit Possession in Cuban Santería." *TSQ: Transgender Studies Quarterly* 6 (3): 386–99.

Escalante, A. S. forthcoming. "Playful Masculinity: Rest and Transgression in Loíza, Puerto Rico's Fiesta de Santiago." In *Religions in the Américas: Transcultural and Transhemispheric Approaches*, edited by C. Tirres and J. Delgado, Albuquerque: University of New Mexico Press.

Espírito Santo, D. 2015. *Developing the Dead: Mediumship and Selfhood in Cuban Espiritismo.* Gainesville: University Press of Florida.

Espírito Santo, D. 2018. "Assemblage Making, Materiality, and the Self in Cuban Palo Monte." *Social Analysis* 62 (3): 67–87.

Etherington, B. 2020. "Creolization." *Oxford Research Encyclopedia of Literature*, Accessed June 14, 2022. https://oxfordre.com/literature/view/10.1093/acrefore/9780190201098.001.0001/acrefore-9780190201098-e-1054.

Forte, J. R. 2010. "Black Gods, White Bodies: Westerners' Initiations to Vodun in Contemporary Benin." *Transforming Anthropology* 18 (2): 129–45.

Fromont, C., ed. 2019. *Afro-Catholic Festivals in the Americas: Performance, Representation and the Making of Black Atlantic Tradition.* Pennsylvania: Pennsylvania State University Press.

Gillam, R. 2022. "Latent Blackness: Afro-Brazilian People, History, and Culture in São Paolo, Brazil." *Journal of Latin American and Caribbean Anthropology* 26 (3–4): 451–67.

Gilroy, P. 1993. *The Black Atlantic: Modernity and Double Consciousness.* Cambridge: Harvard University Press.

Golfetto, T. 2018. "Candomblé Ketu in Italy: Dialogues in Adaptations." *Studia Religiologica* 51 (4): 265–78.

Greene-Hayes, A. 2021. "Black Atlantic Religions in America." *Bloomsbury Religion in North America.* London: Bloomsbury Academic, 2021. Theology and Religion Online. Web. December 10, 2021. http://dx.doi.org/10.5040/9781350970540.002.

Hale, L. 2009. *Hearing the Mermaid's Song: Umbanda Religion in Rio de Janeiro.* Albuquerque: University of New Mexico Press.

Hayes, K. E. 2011. *Holy Harlots: Femininity, Sexuality, and Black Magic in Brazil.* Berkeley: University of California Press.

Hess, D. J. 1992. "Umbanda and Quimbanda Magic in Brazil: Rethink Aspects of Bastide's Work." *Archives de Sciences Sociales de Religions* 37 (79): 135–53.

Jacobson, C. J., Jr. 2007. "'¿Espiritus? No. Pero la Maldad Existe': Supernaturalism, Religious Change, and the Problem of Evil in Puerto Rican Folk Religion." *Ethnos* 31 (3): 434–67.
Johnson, P. C. 2002. *Secrets, Gossip, and Gods: The Transformation of Brazilian Candomblé*. Oxford: Oxford University Press.
Johnson, P. C. 2018. "The Dead Don't Come Back Like the Migrant Comes Back: Many Returns in the Garifuna Dügü." In *Passages and Afterworlds: Anthropological Perspectives on Death in the Caribbean*, edited by M. Forde and Y. Hume, 31–53. Durham: Duke University Press.
Johnson, P. C., and S. Palmié. 2018. "Afro-Latin American Religions." In *Afro-Latin American Studies: An Introduction*, edited by A. d. l. Fuente and G. R. Andrews, 438–85. Cambridge: Cambridge University Press.
Kardec, A. 1857. *Le livre des esprits*. Paris: Édouard Dentu.
Kardec, A. 1876 [1864]. *L'Évangile Selon le Spiritisme*. Paris: Librairie Spirite.
Kassim, H.-S. 2015. "Forming Islamic Religious Identity among Trinidadians in the Age of Social Networks." In *Crescent over Another Horizon: Islam in Latin America, the Caribbean, and Latino USA*, edited by M. d. M. L. Narbona, P. G. Pinto and J. T. Karam, 225–254. Austin: University of Texas Press.
Khan, A. 2020. "Realising the Muslim Atlantic." *Critical Muslim* 35: 11–26.
Khan, K. 2020. *Far from Mecca: Globalizing the Muslim Caribbean*. New Brunswick: Rutgers University Press.
Koss, J. D. 1977. "Social Process, Healing, and Self-Defeat Among Puerto Rican Spiritists." *American Ethnologist* 4 (3): 453–69.
Kuczynski, L. 2015. "Muslims in Martinique." In *Crescent over Another Horizon: Islam in Latin America, the Caribbean, and Latino USA*, edited by M. d. M. L. Narbona, P. G. Pinto and J. T. Karam, 206–24. Austin: University of Texas Press.
Lawal, B. 2004. "Reclaiming the Past: Yoruba Elements in African American Arts." In *The Yoruba Diaspora in the Atlantic World*, edited by T. Falola and M. D. Childs, 291–324. Bloomington: Indiana University Press.
MacGaffey, W. 2014, "Franchising Minkisi in Loango: Questions of Form and Function." *RES: Anthropology and Aesthetics* 64 (65): 148–57.
Matory, J. L. 2005. *Black Atlantic Religion: Tradition, Transnationalism, and Matriarchy in the Afro-Brazilian Candomblé*. Princeton: Princeton University Press.
Matory, J. L. 2008. "Free to Be a Slave: Slavery as Metaphor in Afro-Atlantic Religions." In *Africas in the Americas: Beyond the Search for Origins in the Study of Afro-Atlantic Religions*, edited by S. Palmié, 351–80. Leiden: Brill.
Matory, J. L. 2018. *The Fetish Revisited: Marx, Freud, and the Gods Black People Make*. Durham: Duke University Press.
Muñoz, J. E. 1999. *Disidentifications: Queers of Color and the Performance of Politics*. Minneapolis: University of Minnesota Press.
Murphy, J. 1993. *Santería: African Spirits in America*. Boston: Beacon Press.
Murrell, N. S. 2010. *Afro-Caribbean Religions: An Introduction*. Philadelphia: Temple University Press.
Ochoa, T. R. 2007. "Versions of the Dead: Kalunga, Cuban-Kongo Materiality, and Ethnography." *Cultural Anthropology* 22 (4): 473–500.
Ochoa, T. R. 2010a. "Prendas-Ngangas-Enquisos: Turbulence and the Influence of the Dead in Cuban-Kongo Material Culture." *Cultural Anthropology* 25 (3): 387–420.
Ochoa, T. R. (2010b), *Society of the Dead: Quita Manaquita and Palo Praise in Cuba*. Berkeley: University of California Press.

Ochoa, T. R. 2020. *A Party for Lazarus: Six Generations of Ancestral Devotion in a Cuban Town*. Berkeley: University of California Press.
Palmié, S. 2002. *Wizards and Scientists: Explorations in Afro-Cuban Modernity and Tradition*. Durham: Duke University Press.
Palmié, S., ed. 2008. *Africas in the Americas: Beyond the Search for Origins in the Study of Afro-Atlantic Religions*. Leiden: Brill.
Palmié, S. 2013. *The Cooking of History: How Not to Study Afro-Cuban Religion*. Chicago: University of Chicago Press.
Parés, L. N. 2004. "The 'Nagôization' Process in Bahian Candomblé." In *The Yoruba Diaspora in the Atlantic World*, edited by T. Falola and M. D. Childs, 185–208. Bloomington: Indiana University Press.
Patterson, O. 1982. *Slavery and Social Death: A Comparative Study*. Cambridge: Harvard University Press.
Pérez, E. 2016. *Religion in the Kitchen: Cooking, Talking, and the Making of Black Atlantic Traditions*. New York: New York University Press.
Ralph, M., A. Beliso-De Jesús, and S. Palmié. 2017. "Saint Tupac." *Transforming Anthropology* 25 (2): 90–102.
Reis, J. J., and B. G. Mamigonian. 2004. "Nagô and Mina: The Yoruba Diaspora in Brazil." In *The Yoruba Diaspora in the Atlantic World*, edited by T. Falola and M. D. Childs, 77–110. Bloomington: Indiana University Press.
Ramadan-Santiago, O. 2019. *Dios en carne: Rastafari and the Embodiment of Spiritual Blackness in Puerto Rico*. Ann Arbor: ProQuest Dissertation Publishing.
Román, R. 2007. *Governing Spirits: Religion, Miracles, and Spectacles in Cuba and Puerto Rico, 1898–1956*. Chapel Hill: University of North Carolina Press.
Romberg, R. 2003. *Witchcraft and Welfare: Spiritual Capital and the Business of Magic in Modern Puerto Rico*. Austin: University of Texas Press.
Romberg, R. 2009. *Healing Dramas: Divination and Magic in Modern Puerto Rico*. Austin: The University of Texas Press.
Routon, K. 2008. "Conjuring the Past: Slavery and the Historical Imagination in Cuba." *American Ethnologist* 35 (4): 632–49.
Schmidt, J. A. 2015. *Cachita's Streets: The Virgin of Charity, Race, and Revolution in Cuba*. London: Duke University Press.
Sellers, A. P. 2013. "Yemoja: An Introduction to the Divine Mother and Water Goddess." In *Yemoja: Gender, Sexuality, and Creativity in the Latina/o and Afro-Atlantic Diasporas*, edited by S. Otero and T. Falola, 131–52. Albany: State University of New York Press.
Sharpe, C. 2016. *In the Wake: On Blackness and Being*. Durham: Duke University Press.
Strongman, R. 2019. *Queering Black Atlantic Religions: Transcorporeality in Candomblé, Santería, and Vodou*. Durham, NC: Duke University Press.
Tallaj, A. 2018. "Religion on the Dance Floor: Afro-Dominican Music and Ritual from Altars to Clubs." *Civilisations* 67: 95–109.
Thornton, B. J. 2016. *Negotiating Respect: Pentecostalism, Masculinity, and the Politics of Spiritual Authority in the Dominican Republic*. Gainesville: University Press of Florida.
Thornton, B. J. 2021. "Refiguring Christianity and Black Atlantic Religion: Representation, Essentialism, and Christian Variation in the Southern Caribbean." *Journal of the American Academy of Religion* 89 (1): 41–71.
Thompson, R. F. 1983. *Flash of the Spirit: African and Afro-American Art and Philosophy*. New York: Random House.
Tinsley, O. N. 2008. "Black Atlantic, Queer Atlantic: Queer Imaginings of the Middle Passage." *GLQ: A Journal of Lesbian and Gay Studies* 14 (2–3): 191–215.

Wilcox, M. 2018. "Religion Is Already Transed; Religious Studies Is Not (Yet) Listening." *Journal of Feminist Studies in Religion* 34 (1): 84–8.

Wirtz, K. 2007. *Ritual, Discourse, and Community in Cuban Santería: Speak a Sacred World.* Gainesville: University Press of Florida.

Glossary Terms

Black Atlantic: a theory of relationality that traces cultural connections across the Atlantic ocean, centering the role of slaving in the formation of modernity and in subsequent conceptualizations of "race" and "nation."

Candomblé: an African-inspired religious formation that took shape in Brazil. Practitioners draw variously from Ewe, Fon, Gbe, Kongo, and Yoruba comsologies and practices forming different nations that attend to different divinities through dance, song, and sacrifice.

Espiritismo cruzado: an "Africanized" continuation of Spritism that emphasizes communion with the dead through senace-like rituals and trance possession. Aspects of Espiritismo can be found in nearly all Black Atlantic religions.

Ocha: a Yoruba-inspired religious formation that took shape in Cuba and is often characterized as a cooling practice that works through healing. Practitioners attend to the oricha through song and sacrifice.

Palo: a Kongo-inspired religious formation that took shape in Cuba that is often characterized as a harming practice that works through affliction. Practitioners attend to the mpungu and kalunga through song and sacrifice.

9

Muslims in the Latinx United States and Latinx Americas

Ken Chitwood

Latinx Muslims in the United States and the Americas

Over the last few years, Wilfredo Amr Ruiz has become a bit of a media darling. As communications director for the Council on American-Islamic Relations (CAIR) in Florida and founder of CAIR *en Español,* the Puerto Rican convert to Islam has appeared on television and radio, in print, and on podcasts ranging from *Newsweek* to NBC News, CNN to *The Orlando Sentinel.* His visible presence in the news media has made him one of the most prominent **Latinx** Muslim faces in the country. That, as it turns out, is quite the accomplishment given the number and frequency of stories appearing about Latinx Muslims over the last three decades.

In the early 1990s, the media began to take notice of Latinx Muslims living in the United States. They chronicled their stories of "reversion" (the often preferred term of Latinx Muslims, who view conversion as a return to "Latino" or "Hispanic" roots as well as the state of purity in which Muslims believe humans were born in). Over 30 years later, the themes covered by the media remain largely the same. Typical articles begin with a hook about the comparative peculiarity of a Latinx Muslim, often playing on superficial cultural tropes like eating tamales without pork. Most articles then continue with a discussion of Latinx Muslim demographics before explaining why they convert to Islam. Common elements of these Latinx Muslim testimonies include: interacting with Muslims at work or in urban neighborhoods, marriage to a Muslim, questioning the complexity or corruption of Catholic and/or Protestant Christianity, inquiring into Islam following 9/11, Islam's familiar cultural focus on family, and the simplicity of Islamic faith and practice. In addition, most stories mention the centuries-long history of Moorish Spain, when Islamic culture dominated the Iberian Peninsula and influenced Spanish civilization. The stories also highlight the reverts' experience of ostracism by their families of origin and their *comunidad*.

These themes are important to document and the Latinx Muslim story is a vital narrative to integrate into our wider understanding of American religion. Nonetheless, this relatively unchanged and unimaginative coverage has produced, and reproduced, what scholar Harold Morales called "predictable and relatively uniform scripts" about the Latinx Muslim experience (2018: 10). These hackneyed discourses about Latinx Muslims lack both critical context and a scale that encompasses the wider linkages and lineages that constitute Latinx Muslim life. The following is an attempt to provide a deeper contextualization and broader description of Latinx Muslims in the United States and the broader Americas. Beginning with an overview of the historical junctures that helped make contemporary communities across the region what they are, it then provides snapshots of socialities in the United States, Cuba, Mexico, and Puerto Rico, as well as some of the networks that exist between, and across, them.

Historical Junctures

The expansive, crisscrossing history of Latinx Muslims can be divided into four overlapping categories: (1) Muslim Spain and the making of the **Latinx Americas**, (2) enslaved Muslims from North and West Africa, (3) migration and movement from Muslim-majority lands, and (4) contemporary conversions and community **dawah**.

Muslim Spain and the Making of the Latinx Americas

Latinx Muslim history does not begin in New York, Mexico City, Havana, or San Juan. Instead, its roots stretch all the way back to the *Hejaz*, a western region bordering the Red Sea in what is now Saudi Arabia, which includes the cities of Mecca and Medina, and from whence Islam emerged in the seventh century to spread across the Middle East and North Africa to places like India and Spain. By 711 CE, the Arab-Islamic Umayyad Empire achieved its first victory over the Visigothic Kingdom of Hispania. The Umayyads, a series of successor kingdoms and subsequent dynasties (the Almoravids, Almohads) and emirates (e.g., Marinids and Nasrids) would rule either all—or at least part—of the Iberian Peninsula until January 2, 1492, which marked the fall of Nasrid Granada and the end of the *Reconquista* (reconquest), of Spain by Catholic forces under Isabella's Crown of Castille and Ferdinand's Crown of Aragon. Nonetheless, for eight centuries, Islam and Muslims shaped Iberian imaginaries, history, language, religion, and polity alongside Jewish, Christian, and other influences through cross-cultural encounter, conflict, and collaboration. Those presences and influences are still felt in Spain today, especially in the south of the country.

Thanks to Spain's colonial ambitions, that influence came to impact the making of the Americas as well and continues to live on in Latinx Muslim memory to the present day. Just ten months after the fall of Granada, Christopher Columbus set foot in what is now the Bahamas, sparking what became the colonial subjugation of the Americas by Spain and ensuing European colonial empires. The confluence of these two historical moments—the *Reconquista* and the initial European encounter with the Americas—should not be overlooked. Their convergence points to not only how Muslims came to the colonial Americas in the early years of Spanish conquest but also to how their influence on Spanish culture and dominion played a role in shaping *Nueva España*'s laws, architecture, rituals, and other aspects of its culture, such as its understanding of race and religion.

For example, ***Moriscos***—former Muslims who were forcibly converted to Catholicism following Spain's reconquest of the Iberian Peninsula—came to the Americas as part of the Spanish Empire's expanding colonial commercial complex. Though they had to remain outwardly Catholic, these "new Christians" maintained ties to their former cultural and religious traditions. In the Americas, they even

FIGURE 9.1 *A statue of Santiago Apóstol (St. James) vanquishing los Moros (the Moors) related to the Fiesta de Santiago Apóstol in Loíza Aldea, Puerto Rico.* Source: *Photo by Ken Chitwood.*

used this to their economic advantage. As historian Karoline P. Cook wrote, there is substantial evidence that moriscos in Mexico became known as particularly potent healers, selling talismans, amulets, and curatives for a variety of customers in the "New World" (2016).

Otherwise, beyond physical presence, the legacy of **al-Andalus** lived on in the Spanish Americas through language, architecture, and ritual. The Spanish language contains over 3,000 words directly loaned from—or influenced by—Arabic, including *pantalones* (pants), *azúcar* (sugar), *aceite* (oil), and *ojála* (let's hope). Buildings across the Americas bear the imprint of Andalusian and neo-Andalusian (or neo-Mudejar) architectural elements, including vaulted ceilings and painted ceramic tiles (*azulejos*), iron grating, and lavish landscaping. In rituals, Spanish soldiers sometimes transferred the image of the Moorish enemy (*los Moros*) onto American Indigenous peoples in festivals and parades like *la Fiesta de Santiago Apostól* in Loíza, Puerto Rico (Figure 9.1) or the Corpus Christi celebrations in Cusco, Peru (Dean 1999; Escalante 2019; Chitwood 2021). In these ways and more, the centuries-long Islamic influence on the Iberian Peninsula was transferred to the Latinx Americas along with Spanish Catholic power.

Enslaved Muslims from North and West Africa

Early Muslim presence in the Americas came not only from Spain but also from North and West Africa. Following the decimation of Indigenous American peoples from disease and conflict, insatiable colonial coffers began to look elsewhere for bodies to bolster their economic aspirations and to meet existing trade quotas. This time, they looked to West Africa, where between the sixteenth and nineteenth centuries, some 10–12 million individuals were forcibly enslaved and transported across the Atlantic to labor in the Americas. Anywhere from 10 to 20 percent of them were Muslim. According to historian Greg Grandin, the transatlantic trade of enslaved persons came to be the "back door" by which many Muslims arrived in the Americas (2014: 190).

These enslaved Muslims arrived in multiple ports of call across the Americas, including Brazil, Cuba, and Mexico (Diouf 2013; Domingues da Silva et al. 2018; Gomez 2005). Depending upon the place and period, their presence could be quite significant. Some enslaved African Muslims became leaders of maroon communities and rebellions. Others became prominent public figures. For example, in January 1835 in the city of Salvador de Bahia, Brazil, a company of enslaved and free Africans rebelled. Inspired by a core group of Muslim leaders, the rebellion became known as the Mâle Revolt (Reis 1993). Although the revolt was quickly quashed, its symbolic meaning endured. It remains an example of not only how Muslims could serve as leaders among the enslaved but also their lasting relevance to Black people in the Americas resisting ongoing racism and structural oppression today. There was also Mahommah Gardo Baquaqua. Literate in Arabic, Baquaqua was captured in West Africa and brought to Brazil around 1845. He escaped captivity and fled to New York in 1847. Published by Samuel Moore in 1854, his autobiography—the only known written account by an enslaved African in Brazil—helped make his story known (Law and Lovejoy 2006). It is a testament not only to the difficulties faced by enslaved Muslims in Brazil but also to the networks that existed between the Atlantic and American worlds, which are central to the story of Muslims in the Americas.

Migration and Movement from Muslim-majority Lands

Due to sociopolitical pressures to convert to Christianity and a lack of Islamic infrastructure (schools, teachers, mosques, leaders, texts, etc.), both Muslims from Spain and Muslims from West Africa who came to the Americas were not able to pass their religion on to future generations. Eventually, it appears as if the practice of Islam died out in the nineteenth century, even if its legacy lived on in music, language, or hybrid religious practices (Diouf 2013; Khan 2015). However, starting in the middle of the nineteenth century, Muslims started to arrive in the Spanish-speaking Americas from the Middle East and North Africa.

From the 1860s onward, migrants from what is now Palestine, Lebanon, Egypt, Jordan, and Morocco arrived in places as diverse as Argentina, Canada, Chile, Colombia, Ecuador, Honduras, Mexico, Puerto Rico, and the United States. Though most of the early immigrants were Christian, some were Muslim. Over the years and through a process of chain and circular migration, the Arab Muslim community grew. Beyond Arab Muslims, there are also other Muslim migrants who have settled in the Latinx Americas from Malaysia and Indonesia, Senegal, and the Philippines. Through both voluntary and involuntary migration, these Muslims came to establish themselves economically and socially, building Islamic centers, *madrasahs* (schools), *halāl* certification associations, and other institutions that helped establish and propagate Islam across the Latinx Americas. They also came to influence Latin American politics, music, culture, and economics. There have been presidents and vice presidents of Arab ancestry or descent in Argentina, Brazil, Chile, Colombia, the Dominican Republic, Ecuador, El Salvador, and Honduras. Beyond politics, Muslim migrants have established themselves with successful businesses, built transregional economic partnerships (e.g., through Brazil's trade in *halāl* meat products, which is the largest in the world), and succeeded in the realms of literature and art (Chitwood 2021).

FIGURE 9.2 *The Muslim community in Jayuya, Puerto Rico may be small, but it proudly supports a musallah located downtown near this local cafeteria.* Source: *Photo by Ken Chitwood.*

Contemporary Conversions and Community Dawah

Thanks in part to the influence of Muslim migrants, the number of converts to Islam in the Latinx Americas appears to have increased in recent years. There are significant communities in places like San Cristóbal de las Casas, Mexico, where hundreds of locals converted to Islam beginning in the 1990s, or in Mexico City, where there is a sizable Sufi order with links to New York and Turkey (Khan 2015; Cirianni Salazar 2015). There have also been significant efforts by transnational missionary movements and dawah organizations to draw more local converts in the Spanish-speaking Americas (see Figure 9.3). Among them are the Tablighi Jamaat, a proselytizing movement started by Deobandi Muslims in India in the 1920s, who established the **Mezquita** as-Salaam in Santiago, Chile (Perez and Ingalls 2021) and the relatively new group ISLAm en Puerto Rico, whose stated mission is "to (re)discover & cultivate" Islamic heritage on the Puerto Rican archipelago, "providing educational, historical and religious resources for those in search for a mutual understanding" (ISLAm en Puerto Rico 2020).

Latinx Muslim in the United States

The leaders of ISLAm en Puerto Rico are Muslims with significant links that connect towns like Aibonito and Vega Alta with cities as diverse as Houston, Texas, Atlanta, Georgia, and New York City. It is the latter locale, perhaps, that is the most significant point on the map for the contemporary Latinx Muslim community in the United States. It was there that the first significantly Latinx Muslim communities coalesced in the 1970s and 1980s. Both before and after, Latinx Muslims have been a part of the Muslim landscape in the United States, situated between Black Muslim groups and umbrella Islamic organizations, sometimes founding their own groups in urban centers across the United States and online.

According to the "Latino Muslim Survey," there are approximately some 50,000–70,000 Latinx Muslims in the United States. They are spread across "California (19%), Texas (15%), New York (12%), New Jersey (11%), Florida (7%), Illinois (5%), Georgia (4%), and Pennsylvania (3%)" (Espinosa, Galvan, and Morales 2017: 15). Latinx Muslims are also to be found in Arizona, Maryland, Massachusetts, Michigan, Ohio, and Virginia. Dispersed across such a wide geographical range, it is sometimes hard to speak of a Latinx Muslim "community" in any real sense. Nonetheless and despite the distances that divide them, there is a palpable, shared identification between Latinx Muslims, maintained by a network of online platforms; significant nodes in places like Houston and Union City, New Jersey; and shared experiences of ostracism and opportunity.

Latinx Muslims do not share a single pathway to conversion, nor does the demographic only consist of adult converts. With that said, there are some shared experiences and common sentiments frequently expressed by Latinx Muslims when it comes to why they chose Islam. Many describe a period of spiritual wandering, wherein they sought answers to some of their most vexing religious questions in different traditions and practices (e.g., Buddhism, agnosticism, mysticism, New Age, meditation, and various Christian denominations). Many Latinx Muslims also express some form of dissatisfaction with their former religion or worldview. For example, those raised with Catholic influence often talk about struggling with the concept of the Trinity (that God is one but at the same time "Father, Son, and Holy Spirit"), Jesus's divinity, or the veneration of Mary, his mother, or dissatisfaction with having to appeal to God through intermediaries like saints and priests. These are not universal experiences, but they point to how some Latinx Muslims find answers in Islam with its doctrine of the absolute oneness of God (*tawhid*), respect for Jesus and Mary without any deification, and direct access to Allah through prayer (both obligatory and voluntary) (Chitwood 2015; Martínez-Vásquez 2010). After decades of Latinx individuals converting to Islam, there are now some second- and third-generation Latinx Muslims born into Islam.

These Latinx Muslims are the descendants of converts who found Islam through groups such as the Ahmadiyya, the Nation of Islam (NOI), or the Five Percent Nation (FPN) in the early and mid-twentieth centuries. According to Patrick Bowen, there

FIGURE 9.3 *Dawah materials and related paraphernalia at a Latinx Muslim event in New York City.* Source: *Photo by Ken Chitwood.*

is evidence of Latinx converts as early as the 1920s (2010; 2013). It was not until the 1960s and 1970s, however, that significant numbers started to discover Islam. Largely through contact with Black Muslims and related organizations (e.g., NOI and FPN) in the United States urban centers, Latinx Muslims began to appear more frequently in the historical record. Struggling to find their place between Black Muslim activism on the one hand and large, immigrant-driven Islamic organizations on the other (e.g., the Islamic Party of North America [IPNA] or the Islamic Society of North America [ISNA]), they began to seek out their own spaces and initiatives. The first clear example of this is Bani Sakr, founded in the 1970s with "Hajj Hisham Jaber, who led Malcolm X's funeral prayer, as their spiritual guide" (Ocasio 2016). Lacking any distinct Latinx institutional presence or other guidance, Latinx converts in the Newark area turned to neighbors who had already embraced Islam to found their own spiritual community. With an eclectic group of Puerto Ricans and Haitians, Yemenis, and Black American Muslims, they came together for prayer and to support one another in an environment of racism and ethnocentrism toward both Latinx people and Muslims.

Individuals who later went on to found the first Latinx Muslim-specific organization in the United States—Alianza Islámica—were inspired by groups like Bani Sakr. Writing of his visit to Bani Sakr in 1974, Ramon Francisco Ocasio noted:

> For the first time since we entered Islam, we were among other Muslims unashamedly Latino, proudly sporting names like Yusuf Padilla and Bilal Arce. A wedding there was a delight, feasting on sumptuous *arroz con pollo* to the pulsing percussive rhythms of a conga's *tumbao*, an expression of ourselves that no longer looked foreign or alien, something our mothers could relate to. We now had a glimpse of what was possible and were determined to make it a reality.
>
> (Ocasio 2016)

Thus motivated, Ocasio, Ibrahim Gonzalez, and Yahya Figueroa sought out partners to establish the United States' first Spanish-speaking mosque in 1979. Working with a "pan Latino group representing Costa Rica, Puerto Rico, Panama, and Brazil" they wanted to launch a *masjid* (mosque) for Spanish-language *khutbahs* (Friday sermons) and religious instruction. The project met resistance and ran out of steam.

It would not be until 1987 that Ocasio, Gonzalez, and Figueroa were able to make their dream come true, at least in part. Founded along with other New York-born Puerto Ricans, Alianza Islámica was based first in East Harlem (*el Barrio*) and then the Bronx. They provided instruction and conducted not only dawah outreach to friends, families, and neighbors but also social programs such as drug rehab, AIDS awareness campaigns, GDP prep, and anti-gang peace initiatives (Aidi 2003; Aidi 2014; Morales 2018). The organization became a beacon for other Latinx Muslims in the New York City area, and in the mid-1990s established *La Mezquita del Barrio* (The Mosque of the Barrio), the long-hoped-for Spanish-language mosque community, "just 10 blocks away" from the Islamic Cultural Center of New York (Ocasio 2016). By 2005, a series of infrastructural, financial, and other issues forced Alianza Islámica to close.

Nonetheless, Alianza Islámica inspired several other organizations that emerged over the ensuing years, creating a dense and diverse Latinx Muslim organizational ecosystem that has helped the community grow and consolidate. Among them are organizations like the Latino American Dawah Organization (LADO), *La Asociación Latino Musulmana de América* (LALMA, originally the Los Angeles Latino Muslim Association), or *La Propagación Islamica para la Educación de Ala el Divino* (PIEDAD, Islamic propagation for education on and devotion to Allah) (Essa 2010; Morales 2018). There are also regional hubs like the Ojalá Foundation in Chicago; the North Hudson Islamic Education Center (NHIEC) and its annual National Latino Muslim Day in Union City, New Jersey; IslaminSpanish in Houston and Atlanta; CAIR en Español in Miami, Florida; and the Centro Islámico mosque, also in Houston, Texas. In addition, there are also specific initiatives like #TacoTrucksInEveryMosque in Orange County, California; the Three Puerto Rican Imams project organized in the wake of Hurricane María in 2017; the publishing house Hablamos Islam, Inc.; and or the refugee center and transitional shelter run by the Latina Muslim Foundation in Tijuana, Mexico.

FIGURE 9.4 *Latinx Muslims claim various identifications and heritages from places like Puerto Rico, the Dominican Republic, Peru, Argentina, Mexico, Colombia, and beyond.* Source: *David Grossman/Alamy Stock Photo.*

Latinx Muslims' corresponding experiences—and the ecosystem of organizations they have founded—helped to create what researchers Gaston Espinosa, Juan Galvan, and Harold Morales call a shared sense of *Islamidad*. This ***Islamidad*** is the product of the Latinx Muslims' distinct conversion pathways (and subsequent testimonies) and historical factors related to their "dreams of al-Andalus," wherein they draw on the memory of Andalusian Spain to ground both aspects of their dual identifications as *Latinx* and *Muslim* in the history of Islam and Spanish language and culture (Espinosa, Galvan, and Morales 2017; Chitwood 2021). With significant concentrations in places like the New York City metro area, Chicago, Southern California, Texas, and Florida, Latinx Muslims can bind together to carve out a space of their own amid the more general diversity of Muslim populations in the United States. Even if they do not have their own organizations, they may form a more representable cohort in local communities or play a more visible role in mosque leadership as board members or imams.

Within this broader Latinx Muslim community, there are also regional differences and accents according to specific ethnic identifications or histories. As evidenced above, there is immense diversity under the umbrella term "Latinx Muslims." Latinx Muslims draw on heritages from various countries across North America, South America, Central America, and the Caribbean. Half identify as either Mexican (31 percent) or Puerto Rican (22 percent). Others claim South American (12 percent),

Central American (9 percent), Dominican (5 percent), or Cuban (3 percent) heritage. A further 12 percent claim a multi-country identity, while 34 percent identify at least in part with Mexico and 27 percent with Puerto Rico (Espinosa, Galvan, and Morales 2017). These countries each have richly diverse cultures, governments, languages, and geopolitical struggles that shape the contours of Latinx Muslim identities across the United States. Beyond their own identifications, many Latinx Muslims are married to people of multiple backgrounds, Muslim and non-Muslim alike. This further influences the expression of their own Islamidad in the context of everyday life.

At the same time, Latinx Muslims share in being *quadruple minorities*—Latinx among Muslims, Muslims among Latinx, and *both* Latinx *and* Muslim in the context of American empire. They experience discrimination and misunderstandings, police profiling and racial bias, complicated colonial relationships with the United States, and many have migration histories that significantly shaped their present lives. The above factors, and Latinx Muslims' multiple marginalizations in each community they claim membership in, might give us a clue to why Islamidad

> is characterized by high levels of religious practice, moderate levels of religious tolerance toward other religions and racial-ethnic groups, and high levels of theological and moral, but not necessarily political and social conservatism. For example, although most Latino Muslims affirm traditional Patriarchal relations, gender roles, and support traditional marriage, they tend to vote Democrat and oppose President Trump's 90-day ban, building the wall, and immigration legislation. Latino Muslims also express a desire to see their religious leaders and organizations get more involved in politics.
>
> (Espinosa, Galvan, and Morales 2017)

Increasingly, Islamidad is also shaped by a complex interconnection with other Muslim communities across the globe, specifically in the broader Spanish-speaking Americas. Whether it be Muslims collaborating across the US-Mexico border, imams in the northeastern United States organizing aide for Puerto Ricans in the wake of Hurricane María, or dawah initiatives initiated by both sides to call more Latinx people to Islam, there are shared histories, concerns, and programs that connect Latinx Muslims with other Muslims beyond their borders.

Muslims across the Latinx Americas

At an event at the Muslim American Society's Ibn Sina Center in Queens, New York in October 2017, *both* those interconnections *and* Latinx Muslims' multiple, specific ethnic heritages were on display (see Figure 9.5). As various Latinx Muslim luminaries shared the stage to relate histories of early conversions, raise funds for particular projects, or otherwise address issues shared among them, numerous flags from

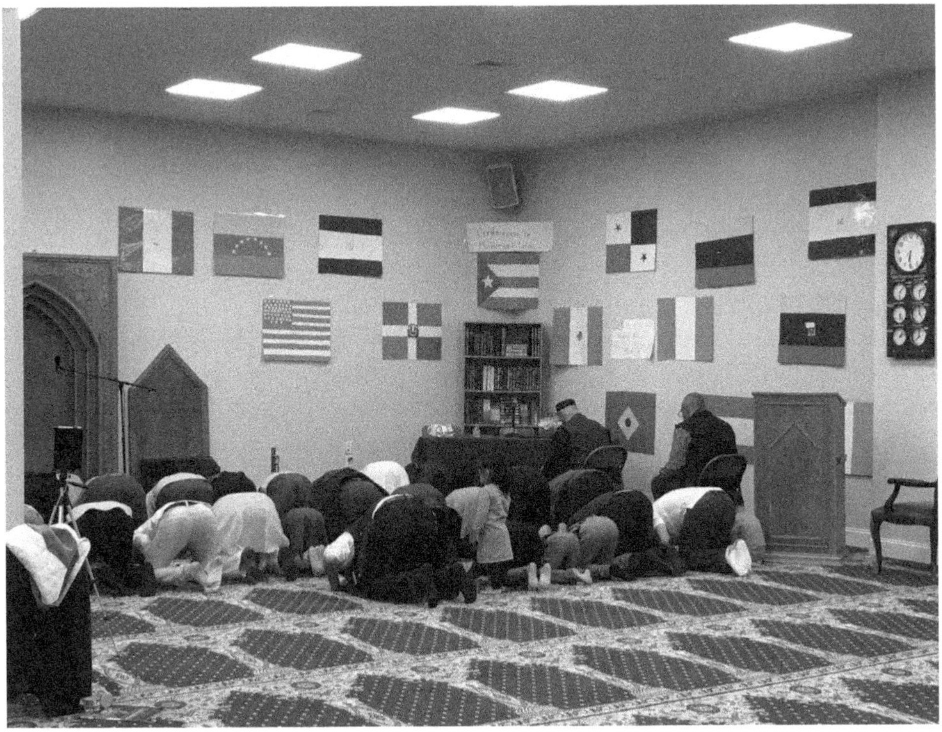

FIGURE 9.5 *Latinx Muslims gather for prayer at Muslim American Society's Ibn Sina Center in Queens, New York.* Source: *Photo by Ken Chitwood.*

across the Americas hung behind them. The standards of Panama, the Dominican Republic, Mexico, Brazil, El Salvador, Ecuador, and elsewhere hung behind them as they implored visitors to donate to Hurricane María relief in Puerto Rico, a well-building project in Haiti, and dawah efforts in Houston.

Speaking to Vilma Santos, a graphic designer born and raised in Puerto Rico, during one of the breaks, we talked about how connections between Latinx Muslims in the United States and Muslims elsewhere in the Americas animate discourses, debates, and philanthropic activity in, across, and between *el Norte y el Sur* (the North and the South). "What is happening in Puerto Rico concerns me," she said, "what's happening in Mexico or Ecuador concerns me. We may have resources to share, they may have stories to share, we have an exchange. We never forget where we come from and will always relate to our brothers and sisters in places beyond our borders."

With those connections in mind, the following is an all-too-brief introduction to a few, select communities in the Latinx Americas, some of their own unique features, as well as some of the networks that connect them with one another and the Latinx Muslim community in the United States.

Cuba

Made up of a mix of students, expatriots, diplomates, local converts, and business entrepreneurs, the Muslim community in Cuba remains relatively small. Estimates range between 3,000 and 9,000, and the real number could be even smaller. Despite Cuba being an officially "atheist" state for over three decades, locals have been converting to Islam in more recent years, especially since the "Special Period," a time in the 1990s that brought about an economic crisis and during which the government abandoned its official atheism and declared itself a "secular state." Today, various external religious organizations and national governments regularly send money in the form of humanitarian aid and supplemental support for the nascent Islamic organizations in Cuba (Delmonte 2011; Chitwood 2021).

One of the most significant moments for the local Muslim community occurred in June 2015, when the nation's first mosque was founded thanks to funding from the Kingdom of Saudi Arabia (see Figure 9.6). Located in Vieja Havana next to a museum known as "The Arab House," which used to function as a prayer room for Muslim diplomats, the mosque is a symbolic accomplishment for Cuba's Muslims and their international partners. There is also a small *mezquita* in the southern city of Santiago

FIGURE 9.6 *Muslims gather for jumaah (Friday communal) prayers at Mezquita Abdallah in Havana, Cuba.* Source: *Photo by Ken Chitwood.*

de Cuba. Saudi Arabia began building an even larger, purpose-built, mosque after Mezquita Abdallah was established in 2015. When complete, it will be one of the largest mosques in the Americas. Today *La Liga Islámica de Cuba* (The Cuban Islamic League), presided over by Imam Yahya Pedro, oversees much of Islamic religious life on the island in conjunction with imams from outside the island. There are reports of some Muslim communities beyond Havana, including in Playa de Rosario—in the west of the country—where some estimate that up to 40 percent of the population is Muslim (Hines 2016).

Mexico

Besides populations in Brazil and Argentina, the Muslim population in Mexico is probably one of the most well-known and thoroughly researched. Beginning with moriscos during the period of Spanish colonization, Muslims have played a role in Mexican public spheres (Cook 2016). Starting with this phase, sociologist Arely Medina outlines five stages of Islamic history in Mexico: *taquiyya* (dissimulation and/or concealment) during the colonial era, controlled and diplomatic migration in the nineteenth century, Arab migration in the nineteenth and early-twentieth centuries, "re-Islamization" and local conversions in the late-twentieth century and early-twenty-first, and a proliferation of local groups in more recent years in places as diverse as Mexico City, Merida, Puebla, Guadalajara, Aguascalientes, San Luis Potosí, Torreón, Monterrey, Chihuahua, and Tijuana (Medina 2021).

Among those more recent groups have been three that have attracted significant international attention: the conversion of hundreds of Tzotzil Maya near San Cristóbal de las Casas in Chiapas, a vibrant Sufi order in Mexico City, and a Salafi organization also in the capital. First, in 1995, the head of the Sufi-inspired *Movimiento Murabitun Mundial* (Murabitun World Order or MMM), then based in Spain, Shaykh Abdalqadir as-Sufi, sent two missionaries with the aim of converting the leader of the *Ejército Zapatista de Liberación Nacional* (Zapatista Army of National Liberation, EZLN or Zapatistas), Subcomondante Marcos, based on what he thought was the two groups' shared anti-capitalist agenda. While unsuccessful in converting Marcos, the missionaries remained and were able to convert many Tzotzil Maya in one of the *campos* (fields) outside San Cristóbal de las Casas (Cañas Cuevas 2015; Gallardo 2018). Since those initial conversions, the community has flowered and diversified, with mosques representing various Islamic traditions, including Sunni *madhab,* the MMM, and the Ahmadiyya. Second, Shaikh Amina Teslima al Yerrahi is the leader of a Sufi *tekke* (lodge) in the country's capital, which is descended from the Nur Ashki Jerrahi Sufi order in Turkey through the tutelage of Lex Hixon (a.k.a. Nur al-Anwar al-Jerrahi). They are marked by their interreligious engagement, significant female leadership, and their participation in popular Mexican traditions such as *conchero* dances and the popular Catholic feast *el Día de la Virgen de Guadalupe* on December 12 each year (Cirianni Salazar 2015). They have received criticism for these practices, with some Muslims interpreting them as dangerous innovations (*bida*). Among them is Abdullah Ruiz, who founded Al Markas as Salafi, a Salafi mosque in 2004, which professes to offer adherents a more purified form of Islamic faith and practice.

Puerto Rico

In Puerto Rico, there are mosques—or *mezquitas*—across the main island. The first Islamic center was built in 1981 in the heart of the Río Piedras market district, where many Arab—predominately Palestinian—immigrants had established their businesses. The first purpose-built mosque was completed in 1992 in the town of Vega Alta, west of San Juan. It is also the largest of Puerto Rico's mosques, with space for over 1,200 individuals. There are other mosques in Hatillo, Aguadilla, Montehiedra, Ponce, Fajardo, and Jayuya (see Figures 9.2 and 9.7). In addition, numerous Muslims across Puerto Rico pray at home or gather with small groups at local residences for *jumaah* prayers and holidays (Caraballo-Resto 2019; Ramadan-Santiago 2015). For *Eid al-Fitr* (the feast marking the breaking of the Ramadan fast), the island's Muslims gather at the San Juan Convention Center for joint *takbir,* prayer, the collection of *zakat,* and a large communal meal along with special activities for the kids, music, and entertainment (Chitwood 2018).

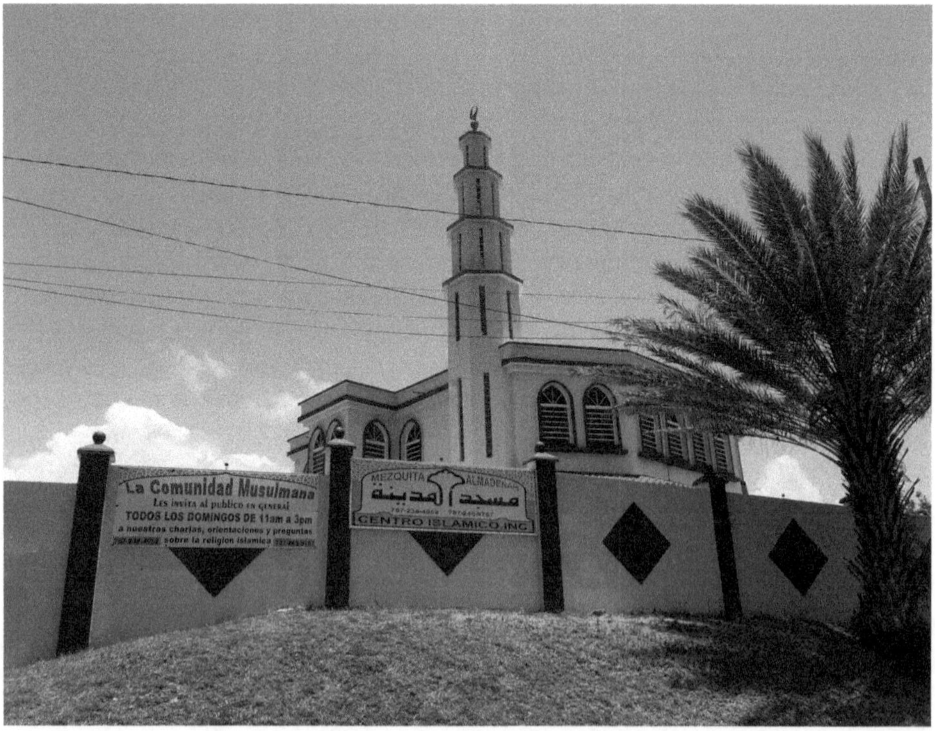

FIGURE 9.7 *Mezquita Almadenah in Hatillo, Puerto Rico.* Source: *Photo by Ken Chitwood.*

In the United States, Puerto Ricans represent an outsized proportion of the Latinx Muslim community. They make up around a quarter of the overall Latinx Muslim population (Espinosa, Galvan, and Morales 2017) and, as outlined above, played a critical role in the formation of its earliest institutions and organizations (Aidi 2003; Aidi 2014; Bowen 2010; Bowen 2013; Chitwood 2019). Still today, Puerto Ricans are at the forefront of important Latinx Muslim initiatives and feature, like Amr Ruiz, in news reports on the population. Perhaps more than other subsets of the Latinx Muslim community, they maintain meaningful ties with Puerto Rico and express concern for the archipelago's population. Organizations and initiatives such as *ISLAm en Puerto Rico* or the Three Puerto Rican Imams project testify to this fact.

Elsewhere in the Latinx Americas

Beyond the three locations outlined above, there are also notable, growing, or otherwise significant Muslim populations in places like Argentina, Belize, Brazil, Chile, Costa Rica, Colombia, the Dominican Republic, Ecuador, Panama, and elsewhere. Although space does not allow for a further exploration, these populations are each marked with their own specific histories, contextual contours, and networks with other groups, communities, and institutions in Latin America, the broader Americas, and locales across the world. Each deserves more careful attention as their populations continue to change and grow in the years to come thanks to evolving political, cultural, economic, and religious conditions.

Conclusion and Areas for Further Consideration

Thus, there is much research still to be done on Latinx Muslim populations in the United States and the broader Americas. Already, however, a few themes are evident from the above: that Latinx Muslim communities in the Americas are networked with one another and with various other locales and populations across global Islam; that Latinx Muslims occupy a tenuous, contested space in American public spheres; and that their minoritization has created a range of different political, religious, and social adaptations, practices, and reactions, crafting what some have called a distinct Latinx Islamidad in the process. Future research will continue to refine our understanding of these connections, contested identifications, and community sentiments as well as expand our appreciation for the variety and vibrancy of Latinx Muslim lifeworlds in the United States and beyond.

Further Reading

Chitwood, K. 2021. *The Muslims of Latin America and the Caribbean*. Boulder: Lynne Rienner.

Espinosa, G., J. Galvan, and H. Morales 2017. "Latino Muslims in the United States Reversion, Politics, and Islamidad." *Journal of Race, Ethnicity, and Religion* 8 (1): 1–48.

Maytorena Taylor, J. 2009. New Muslim Cool, PBS media.

Molina, A. 2022. "Centro Islámico, a hub for Latino Muslims near and far, breaks ground on expansion during Ramadan." *Religion News Service*.

Morales, H. 2018. *Latino and Muslim in America: Race, Religion, and the Making of a New Religious Minority*. New York: Oxford University Press.

References

Aidi, H. 2003. "Let Us Be Moors: Islam, Race, and 'Connected Histories'." *Middle East Report* no. 229: 42–53.

Aidi, H. 2014. *Rebel Music: Race, Empire, and the New Muslim Youth Culture*. New York: Pantheon Books.

Bowen, P. 2010. "The Latino American Da'wah Organization and the 'Latina/o Muslim' Identity in the United States." *Journal of Race, Ethnicity and* Religion 1 (11): 1–23.

Bowen, P. 2013. "U.S. Latina/o Muslims since 1920: From 'Moors' to 'Latino Muslims'." *Journal of Religious History* 37 (2): 165–84.

Cañas Cuevas, S. 2015. "The Politics of Conversion to Islam in Southern Mexico." In *Islam and the Americas*, edited by A. Khan, 163–85. Gainesville: University Press of Florida.

Caraballo-Resto, J. F. 2019. "¿Islam *en* Puerto Rico o Islam *de* Puerto Rico?: Prácticas Identitarias entre Conversos/as al Islam en Puerto Rico." *Revista Ámbito de Encuentros* 12 (2): 7–29.

Chitwood, K. 2015. "Islam en Español: The Narratives, Demographics, & Reversion Pathways of Latina/o Muslims in the U.S." *Waikato Islamic Studies Review* 1 (2): 35–54.

Chitwood, K. 2018. "A Peek into the Lives of Puerto Rican Muslims and What Ramadan Means Post Hurricane Maria." *The Conversation*.

Chitwood, K. 2019. "Muslim AmeRícans: Puerto Rican Muslims in the USA and the Need for More Cosmopolitan Frames of Analysis in the Study of Islam and Muslim Communities in the Americas." *International Journal of Latin American Religions* 3 (2): 413–34.

Chitwood, K. 2021. *The Muslims of Latin America and the Caribbean*. Boulder: Lynne Rienner Publishers.

Cirianni Salazar, L. 2015. "Fusion and Disruption: A Sufi Pilgrimage to the Basilica of Guadalupe." In *The Study of Culture through the Lens of Ritual*, edited by Logan Sparks and Paul Post, 259–72. Amsterdam, Netherlands: Netherlands Studies in Ritual and Liturgy.

Cook, K. P. 2016. *Forbidden Passages: Muslims and Moriscos in Colonial Spanish America*. Philadelphia: University of Pennsylvania Press.

Dean, C. 1999. *Inka Bodies and the Body of Christ: Corpus Christi in Colonial Cuzco, Peru*. Durham: Duke University Press.

Delmonte, L. M. 2011. "Musulmanes en Cuba: entre necesidades espirituales y materiales." *Revista de Historia Internacional* XII 45: 44–75.

Diouf, S. 2013. *Servants of Allah: Muslims Enslaved in the Americas*. New York: New York University Press.
Domingues da Silva, D. B., D. Eltis, N. Khan, P. Misevich, and O. Ojo. 2017. "The Transatlantic Muslim Diaspora to Latin America in the Nineteenth Century." *Colonial Latin American Review* 26 (4): 528–45.
Escalante, A. 2019. "The Long Arc of Islamophobia: African Slavery, Islam, and the Caribbean World." *Journal of Africana Religions* 7 (1), Special Issue: East African and Indian Ocean Perspectives: 179–86.
Essa, Y. 2010. "Interview with LADO/Piedad." *MBMuslima Magazine*.
Espinosa, G., J. Galvan, and H. Morales. 2017. "Latino Muslims in the United States: Reversion, Politics, and Islamidad." *Journal of Race, Ethnicity, and Religion* 8 (1): 1–48.
Gallardo, M. R. 2018. "Allah Made Me Indian: Narratives of Divine Determination of the Self among Muslim Tzotzils in Southern Mexico." *Religion and Power Conference*, University of Florida, March 17.
Gomez, M. 2005. *Black Crescent: The Experience and Legacy of African Muslims in the Americas*. London: Cambridge University Press.
Grandin, G. 2014. *The Empire of Necessity: Slavery, Freedom, and Deception in the New World*. New York: Metropolitan Books.
Hines, S. 2016. "The Muslims of Cuba: How a New Crop of Neighbourhood Entrepreneurs Are Helping Spread Awareness about a Fledgling Religious Community." *Al Jazeera* English.
ISLAm en Puerto Rico. 2020. "ISLAmenPuertoRico." May 31, 2020. https://www.facebook.com/ISLAmenPuertoRico.
Khan, A. 2015. *Islam in the Americas*. Gainesville: University Press of Florida.
Law, R., and P. E. Lovejoy. 2006. *The Biography of Mahommah Gardo Baquaqua: His Passage from Slavery to Freedom in Africa and America*. Markus Wiener Publishers.
Martínez-Vásquez, H. 2010. *Latina/o Y Musulmán: The Construction of Latina/o Identity among Latina/o Muslims in the United States*. Eugene: Wipf & Stock Publishers.
Medina, A. 2021. "Islam in Mexico: Diversity, Accommodations and Perspectives on Approach." Latin America and Caribbean Islamic Studies Association Colloquium. Berlin.
Morales, H. 2018. *Latino and Muslim in America: Race, Religion, and the Making of a New Minority*. New York: Oxford University Press.
Ocasio, R. F. 2016. "Alianza Islamica: The True Story." *The Islamic Monthly*.
Perez, M. V., and M. Ingalls. 2021. "Chile Has a Growing Muslim Community—But Few Know about It." *The Conversation*.
Ramadan-Santiago, O. 2015. "Insha'Allah/Ojalá, Yes Yes Y'all: Puerto Ricans (Re)examining and (Re)imagining Their Identities through Islam and Hip Hop." In *Islam and the Americas*, edited by A. Khan, 115–38. Gainesville: University of Florida Press.
Reis, J. J. 1993. *Slave Rebellion in Brazil: The Muslim Uprising of 1835 in Bahia*. Baltimore: The Johns Hopkins University Press.

Glossary Terms

Al-Andalus: Area(s) of the Iberian Peninsula (including Portugal and Spain) that were ruled by a series of Islamic states from the seventh century to the fifteenth century.

Dawah: Literally, the "call to Islam," it can refer to either internal or external appeals to individuals and communities to adhere to the tenets of Islam.

Islamidad: A shared sense of Latinx Muslim experience, political orientation, and practices.

Latinx: A gender-neutral term sometimes used to refer to people of Latin American culture or ethnic origin in the United States, in favor of Latino, Latina, Latina/o, or Hispanic. Originally created by activists in the Latinx queer community, it is used here to denote the wide range of identifications among Latinx Muslims.

Latinx Americas: Here used to refer to a cultural region of the Americas made up of nation-states that predominately speak languages derived through Spanish or Portuguese colonial influence. "Latin America" can also refer to nations with French-language heritage as well.

Mezquita: The Spanish term for mosque (Arabic, *masjid*), a public space for communal prayer. Despite rumors, it is not a derogatory term derived from the Spanish word for mosquito.

Moriscos: Former or secret Muslims who were forcibly converted to Catholicism following Spain's reconquest of the Iberian Peninsula.

10

Latinx Jews in the United States: Remaking the Jewish Mainstream

Laura Limonic

Introduction

The United States has a rich history of Jewish life and Jewish culture that can be traced back to the large migration stream of Jews who settled in the United States, first from Germany in the 1800s, joined by eastern European coreligionists at the turn of the twentieth century and followed by Sephardic (Jews with origins in the Iberian Peninsula) and Mizrahi Jews (from the North African region) in the following decades. While Jewish migration essentially ceased during the 1930s and through the Second World War, after the war thousands of refugees from Europe made their way to American shores. In the following decades Jews from other parts of the world also made the United States their home (Diner 2006). Contemporary Jewish immigrants who arrived to the United States during the postwar era have had a tremendous impact on the development of modern American Jewish life and cultures, much as their predecessors did during their assimilation into American society. While the largest group of postwar Jewish immigrants hail from the former Soviet Union, thousands of Jews from the Middle East, North Africa, Europe, and Latin America have settled in the United States over the past six to seven decades. Latin American Jewish immigrants, or Latinx Jews, comprise one of the largest groups to migrate to the United States in recent times. This chapter details where the majority of Latinx Jews come from and the Jewish history of their countries of origin as well as where Latinx Jews settle in the United States and the ways in which Latinx Jews are redefining Jewish life and Jewish identity in the United States.

Jewish Migration to Latin America

Jewish people are found all over the globe, and Latin America is no exception. Latin America has a long history of Jewish migration to the region, dating back to the time of the Spanish and Portuguese Inquisition in the late fifteenth century. The Tribunal of the Holy Office of the Inquisition (most commonly known as the Spanish Inquisition) essentially forbade the practice of any religion except Catholicism. A royal decree was issued prohibiting the practice of Judaism and Islam and forced all non-Catholics to convert to Catholicism or face expulsion from the region. During this period, Jews who settled in areas under Iberian rule, which at the time included the colonies of what is today Latin America and the Caribbean, were forced to convert to Catholicism. Among those who converted, "crypto Jews" continued to practice Judaism in secret, essentially maintaining their Jewish faith, yet many chose to fully embrace the Catholic faith. Regardless of their practices and beliefs many converted Jews (*conversos*) were persecuted for "Judaizing" (secretly observing and maintaining Jewish customs and rituals) and were ostracized from their communities or faced even worse fates. In Lima, Peru, for example, the church-affiliated government persecuted an entire community of converted Jews under a charge of Jewish treachery; some of those convicted were burned at the stake while others died in prison. Nonetheless, there were time periods in which Jews managed to establish communities and practice freely in Latin America; this was particularly true in countries ruled by the Dutch. By the mid-seventeenth century, Jews had established vibrant communities in Brazil, Suriname, Curaçao, Haiti, Jamaica, Barbados, and St. Croix. Jews and their descendants who had originally settled in these colonies later expanded into Central America and the Spanish-speaking Caribbean (Costa Rica, the Dominican Republic, Puerto Rico) (Elkin 2014). However, due to the difficult history of integration and persecution Jews faced under Spanish colonial rule, only few Jewish people in Latin America today can link their history to the period of the Inquisition and these aforementioned communities.

Contemporary Jewish communities in Latin America trace their roots to more recent migration trends. During the nineteenth and twentieth centuries, millions of Jews left Europe, Africa, and the Middle East—escaping pogroms, wars, and economic downturns. While the largest number of Jewish migrants found new homes in the United States, during the 1920s the United States Congress passed the Immigration Act of 1924 more commonly known as the Johnson-Reed Act, which imposed quotas on the number of immigrants from Asia and Eastern and Southern Europe who were able to legally enter the United States. As a result, many Jews who might have migrated to the United States settled in countries like Mexico, Colombia, Cuba, and Argentina instead. Oftentimes neighbors and families from Eastern Europe ended up split across the continent—one brother might migrate to New York and the other to Buenos Aires or Sao Paolo. Where Jewish immigrants settled and the cultural, social, and political climates of the nation-states they migrated to greatly influenced the kind of Jewish communities that evolved.

Jewish Communities across Latin America

While Jewish communities exist in every country within Latin America, the following section concentrates on the history of those communities with some of the largest Latin American Jews in the United States today.

Argentina

The largest contemporary Jewish community in Latin America is found in Argentina. Jews from Eastern Europe first arrived to Argentina in the late 1800s, when Argentina enacted national policies that encouraged European immigrants to settle there. Argentina was also one of the primary sites for the planned Jewish agricultural communities sponsored by the Jewish Colonialization Association (the JCA). The JCA was a Jewish resettlement program that sought to assist Jews who were facing rising antisemitism and violence in Eastern Europe and resettle them in agricultural villages. Argentina had a number of these communities—colloquially termed "*Colonias de Baron Hirsch*" (Baron Hirsch's colonies), named for Maurice de Hirsch the founder and funder of these programs. The colonies were agricultural districts where Jews lived and created a Jewish life and community, many working as farmers and *gauchos* (the term for an Argentine cowboy). Over the following decades thousands of other Jews immigrated to Argentina, primarily settling in the capital city of Buenos Aires. Jewish immigrants from Eastern Europe established tight-knit neighborhoods and founded synagogues, community centers, loan associations, and schools. Throughout the early to mid-twentieth century, Sephardic Jews joined their coreligionists in Argentina and also built strong, interconnected communities. Over the following century, the children and grandchildren of these immigrants forged a path to the middle class, with a majority maintaining strong networks within the larger Jewish community as well as subethnic (Ashkenazi and Sephardic) groups. Today there are around 200,000 Jewish people in Argentina, close to 100 synagogues, a number of cultural and athletic centers, one of the largest networks of Jewish day schools and, more recently, a growing presence of Orthodox and Chabad organizations and houses of worship.

Mexico

Mexico was not at the top of the list for Jews fleeing persecution, violence, and economic crisis at the turn of the twentieth century. Throughout the early years of the twentieth century, Mexico did not have a legal separation of Church and state and, as a result, the few Jews who did migrate to Mexico during this period were not able to freely practice their religion, build houses of worship, or establish burial grounds or schools. It was not until 1917, when the Mexican Revolution brought about

FIGURE 10.1 *Maurice de Hirsh funded and facilitated Jewish migration to the Americas.* Source: *Remi Jouan/Wikimedia Commons.*

constitutional changes and religious freedom was granted to non-Catholics, that Mexico became a destination for Jews looking to escape the economic downturns, wars, and violence of their lands across the ocean.

Jews in Mexico primarily settled in the capital city of Mexico City, forming entrenched ethnoreligious communities with mutual aid organizations, burial societies, and synagogues. Due to national restrictions that left Jews unable to fully participate in the economic life of the nation, most Jews in Mexico worked as merchants or peddlers of small goods, and a small minority was engaged in the import-export trade of goods from/to their region of origin. Over time, as economic restrictions lifted, Jews found their way into the middle class and some to the

FIGURE 10.2 *Celebration of the Jewish harvest festival (sukkot) in Buenos Aires, Argentina.* Source: *Ilene Perlman/Alamy Stock Photo.*

wealthier upper classes. Today the Mexican Jewish community, with around 40,000 to 50,000 members, is one of the most tight-knit in Latin America and comprises several subethnic (i.e., from different regional origins, such as Eastern Europe, the Middle East, and North Africa) and subnational (for example, Jews from Syria or Turkey) groups and maintains strong institutions, including schools, synagogues, universities, and social-athletic centers.

Venezuela

Jews first arrived in Venezuela via the Caribbean island of Curaçao in the seventeenth century, but the contemporary Jewish community that, until recently, thrived in Venezuela was founded by Moroccan Jews and joined by their Eastern Europe coreligionists in the 1920s. Over the following decades, other Jews from North Africa, the Middle East as well as Holocaust survivors and refugees migrated to Venezuela and built one of the most diverse Jewish communities in the Americas. Similar to the Jewish populations of other Latin America countries, the majority of Venezuela's Jews settled in the capital city of Caracas. Over time a large part of the Jewish population of Venezuela achieved high socioeconomic status and contributed to the construction

FIGURE 10.3 *The interior of Mexico City's Synagoga Historica de Justo Sierra 71*. Source: *Mexch/Wikimedia Commons.*

of strong Jewish institutions—including Jewish day schools, synagogues, and a large cultural-athletic center.

The Jewish population of Venezuela has fallen dramatically in recent years—in 2018, there were an estimated 6,000 Jews in Venezuela, down from a high of 25,000, when Hugo Chávez came to power in 1999 (DellaPergola 2022). The recent out-migration of Jews from Venezuela to the United States and Israel is felt across the entire community and has had a particularly high toll on membership in Jewish communal organizations. Synagogue and school attendance is down, as is membership in the capital's Jewish community center (JCC).

Cuba

The Cuban Revolution spurred the outmigration of a large sector of the Cuban middle and upper classes from Cuba—among them, Cuban Jews. The Jewish population in Cuba prior to the Cuban Revolution of 1959 is estimated to have been around 15,000. While some Jewish settlers on the island likely arrived during the period of the Spanish Inquisition, the first synagogue was founded in 1906 by a group of American (US) Jews who were living in Cuba at the time. Following this period, Jews from places as

FIGURE 10.4 *Jewish Cuban youths sing at Temple Bet Shalom in Havana, Cuba.* Source: *Sven Creutzmann/Mambo Photo/Getty Images.*

near as the United States and as far as Turkey, Middle East (Sephardic), and Eastern Europe (Ashkenazi) made Cuba their home and eventually climbed the economic ladder—in similar fashion to the Jews of other Latin American countries (Kaplan 2005). In 1959, the Cuban Revolution set the stage for the outmigration of thousands of middle-class Cubans. Almost 95 percent of Cuban Jews left the island—while some fled the perceived antisemitism or lack of religious freedom, many more likely counted economic factors as the major migration push. At the time of the revolution, Jews in Cuba had a lot to lose—small enterprises, commercial stores, and private property. The majority of Cubans (Jewish and non-Jewish) who left their homes found their way to Miami, Florida. In Miami, Cuban Jews founded a thriving community with their own synagogues, athletic and cultural centers, and lived for decades within a tight-knit community.

Latin American Jews Migrate

The peak of Jewish migration to Latin America occurred during the first half of the twentieth century. It was during this period that Jewish immigrants built strong Jewish communities and supporting institutions such as synagogues, Jewish day schools, mutual aid societies, and athletic and cultural institutions. Jewish communities thrived in Latin America, and many Jews experienced considerable upward mobility and elevated social-class status. But throughout the latter half of the twentieth century, countries across Latin America underwent a series of political, financial, and social crises. One of the first groups to migrate to the United States were the Jews of Cuba who left following the Cuban Revolution of 1959 and were allowed easy entry to the United States as a result of Cold War policies that designated them as political refugees. In 1965, the United States revised its immigration policy through the enactment of the Hart-Celler Act, which paved the way for thousands of new immigrants to enter the country. Latinx Jews are among the almost 59 million immigrants who have made the United States their home since 1965.

Today there are approximately 300,000 Jewish adults and children who identify as Hispanic or Latino ("Jewish Americans in 2020" 2021). The majority of Hispanic or Latinx Jew are immigrants or children of immigrants from Latin America who immigrated to the United States as a result of the myriad of crises that hit the region, but a number of Latinx Jews are children of a non-Hispanic Jewish parent and a non-Jewish Hispanic parent.

Where Do Latinx Jews Settle in the United States?

While Latinx Jews are found all over the United States, most tend to cluster in areas where they have connections or networks, a pattern that social scientists call chain migration. Urban cities such as New York and Boston attract large numbers of Latinx Jews through opportunities such as education or work. California has one of the largest Mexican populations—both Jewish and non-Jewish. Other large cities such as Houston and Chicago are also popular destinations for Jews migrating from Latin America. The largest population of Latinx Jews is found in Miami—a city with strong Jewish, Latinx, and now Latinx Jewish influence.

Where Latinx Jews settle has important implications for the possibility of forming new communities, identities, and prospects for assimilation and integration. Miami, for example, has experienced a constant flow of Latinx Jews and therefore is ripe with opportunities to meet, socialize, form networks, and even create families with Jewish people who are originally from Latin American countries such as Mexico, Argentina, Peru, or Venezuela. Many Latinx Jews have strong Jewish cultural and ethnoreligious identities. In Latin America, Jews were accustomed to belonging or having the opportunity to belong to a myriad of Jewish institutions such as schools, community centers, sports teams, and country clubs—many of these organizations are culturally and ethnically Jewish but not necessarily religious in nature. The high rates of affiliation with Jewish institutions among Jews in Latin America foster entrenched networks and social identities in which Jewishness is a core factor in how people construct their sense of self in relation to others. In other words, because so much of life for many of the affiliated Jews in Latin America revolves around Jewish institutions, their sense of who they are is deeply rooted in Jewish life. Latin American Jewish immigrants bring this sense of Jewish identity with them when they migrate. But, oftentimes, when they arrive to the United States they find that those factors that gave them a strong Jewish network and identity are absent in Jewish life in the United States.

Experiencing Jewish Life in the United States

Jewish life in the United States is markedly different from that in Latin America. First, whereas institutional affiliation in Latin America is likely to revolve around nonreligious organizations, formal affiliation to Jewish life in the United States often happens through the synagogue. While JCCs, day schools, and scholarly and cultural organizations exist in the United States, they are not the locus around which Jewish community is constructed. Among the millions of Jews in the United States who do not identify as Orthodox, most have little connection to organized Jewish life—they may visit the synagogue only a few times per year or sporadically attend an event at the JCC. Nonetheless their individual sense of Jewish identity is salient and strong, regardless of how often they participate in organized Jewish events.

Because Jewish life in the United States is noticeably different than it is in Latin America—Latin American Jewish immigrants as well as Latinx Jews born in the United States grapple with assimilating into the US Jewish community. They may find that their Jewishness is questioned either due to their accents, or their appearance. One recent study by the organization Jews of Color Initiative found that youngest Latinx Jews did not feel accepted in Jewish spaces and their identities as Jews was constantly questioned (Belzer et al. 2021). Some Latinx Jews do not resemble the larger white Ashkenazi group that comprises the majority of Jewish people in the United States; others have cultural practices that diverge considerably from the mainstream Jewish American institutions; and still others come from or inhabit socioeconomic classes that deviate from the larger Jewish American norm. Another important issue is that Latinx Jews have different ways of practicing Judaism and identifying as Jews. For example, in a recent study, Jews in the United States who identified as Latinx /Hispanic reported lower levels of ritual observances or practices associated with Jewish religiosity—such as fasting on Yom Kippur, lighting candles on Shabbat, or attending a Passover Seder. Yet, many of them continue to claim Jewishness as central to their sense of social and individual identity, which emanates from their strong sense of communal ties fostered in their home countries (Limonic 2020).

Defining an Ethnic Identity

How do Latinx Jews reconcile the differences in how they understand their Jewish identity and how Jewish identity is defined in the United States? Some might assimilate into existing communities and join synagogues, or attend Jewish schools or local community centers. Some seek community with other Latinx people and have a stronger connection with their national ethnic identity (i.e., Mexican, Puerto Rican, Argentine, etc.). And many find that their identity as Jews or as Latinx depends on the situation they find themselves in (what is termed "situational identity") and highlight different aspects of their complicated ethnicity depending on what group they are interacting with.

Latinx

It goes without saying that Jewish Latinx people are both Jewish *and* Latinx. Upon arrival to the United States, Latin American Jewish immigrants find that they share characteristics with various ethnic and ethnoreligious groups. The same is true for children of Latinx and Jewish parents and **Jews by choice**. The term "Latinx" (a relatively new term that seeks to be inclusive of all genders), or Hispanic or Latino is an imperfect category that encompasses all people who were born in Latin America or are descendants of Latin Americans. This definition includes an immense group of people whose racial, religious, subethnic, subnational, class, and immigration status vary widely. The Latinx population in the United States is almost 19 percent of the US population, and Mexicans make up the majority of this group (Jones et al. 2021).

Jewish Latinx people in the United States are a small minority of the larger Latinx population. Not only does their Jewish faith and ethnic identity separate them from the larger Latinx demographic group, their socioeconomic class and racial status is also distinct from much of the Latinx population. Important questions arise surrounding how Latinx Jews identify and the salience of their Latinx cultural attributes. Latinx Jews have strong connections to Latinx culture through food, language, and music. Moreover, for many Latinx Jews—their Jewish and Latinx identities are inherently tied. For example, Mexican Jewish traditions and cultural practices such as food and language are closely related—not only can one find kosher tacos at the famed Klein's taqueria in Mexico City, but the matzah ball soups with roots in Eastern Europe takes on distinctive Mexican flavors when it is spiced with local chilies. In Argentina, soccer has is both the national sport and pastime as well as a way highlight one's ethnic identity. Jewish soccer fans cemented their identities as both Jewish and Argentine through their support of the local neighborhood soccer team, Atlanta. These are but two examples that show how closely tied the cultural identities of Latinx Jews are with their home countries. Ethnicity comprises cultural building blocks—language, food, norms, behaviors—and for many Latinx Jews these diverge from those of their American coreligionists.

Becoming Latinx Jews

One way that Latinx Jews traverse the conflict inherent in mixed ethnic identities is to redefine how they think about their own ethnic identity. For Latinx Jews, this often involves forming a new ethnic group—in this case, an ethnoreligious one. Sociologists Mary Waters and David Mittelberg (1992) found that when immigrants or ethnic minorities do not seamlessly slot into one existing ethnic group—as is the case for Latinx Jews—they engage in a process called ethnogenesis, defined as the formation of a new ethnic group. Latinx Jews are both Jewish and Latinx—and many do find an "ethnic home" within these groups, yet most find that they do not *fully* belong to either of these ethnic groups. As a result, Latinx Jews, when given the opportunity, engage in the process of ethnogenesis and construct identities that are both Latinx and Jewish at the same time. Latinx Jews often take common pillars of ethnicity, such as language and food, that are shared across members of the group and incorporate them into the building blocks of a new ethnic group.

However, in order for ethnogenesis to occur—opportunities must exist for Latinx Jews to meet, network, and form new social ties as well as create stories and history together. What are these opportunities and how is this new ethnic group formed? For this group of immigrants, it depends on where they locate or arrive to, the possibilities for meeting other Jewish people from Latin America and the existence of institutions that can support community building and ethnic group construction. Latin American Jewish immigrants as well as Latinx Jews by choice or children of Jewish and non-Jewish Latinx parents are found across the United States. Yet, similar to the Jewish population as whole—Jews of Latin American descent are more likely to be concentrated in large, urban areas with significant Jewish communities. Latin American Jewish immigrants are likely to migrate for jobs, education, as well as business opportunities to cities such as Los Angeles, San Diego, New York, or Miami.

Miami: A Haven for Latinx Jews

One area where ethnogenesis has taken place is in Miami, Florida. Miami has the largest Latinx population in the United States. Not only was it the first home for Cuban Jewish and non-Jewish Cuban refugees in the 1960s, thousands of Latin American immigrants from across the continent began to call Miami home after 1965. Latinx Jewish individuals and families began to settle in large numbers in Miami Beach and later in the small city of Aventura in Miami-Dade county beginning in the 1980s. Peruvians, Argentines, Mexicans, Colombians, and Venezuelans are among some of the Jewish immigrants that congregate in close proximity to one another in the Miami area. Over time, as the Latinx population of Miami grew, more people followed. Miami is not only close to Latin America which makes the cost of travel more affordable, but since Spanish is widely spoken, Latin American immigrants feel very much at home in the sprawling city. Moreover, the large informal economy that exists in the area allows for job and financial opportunities for immigrants who might not have the documents or skills needed to succeed in the formal economy. Miami offers newcomers, particularly Latin American immigrants who possess some modicum of social and financial capital, an easier cost of entry into the United States. All of these factors work together to

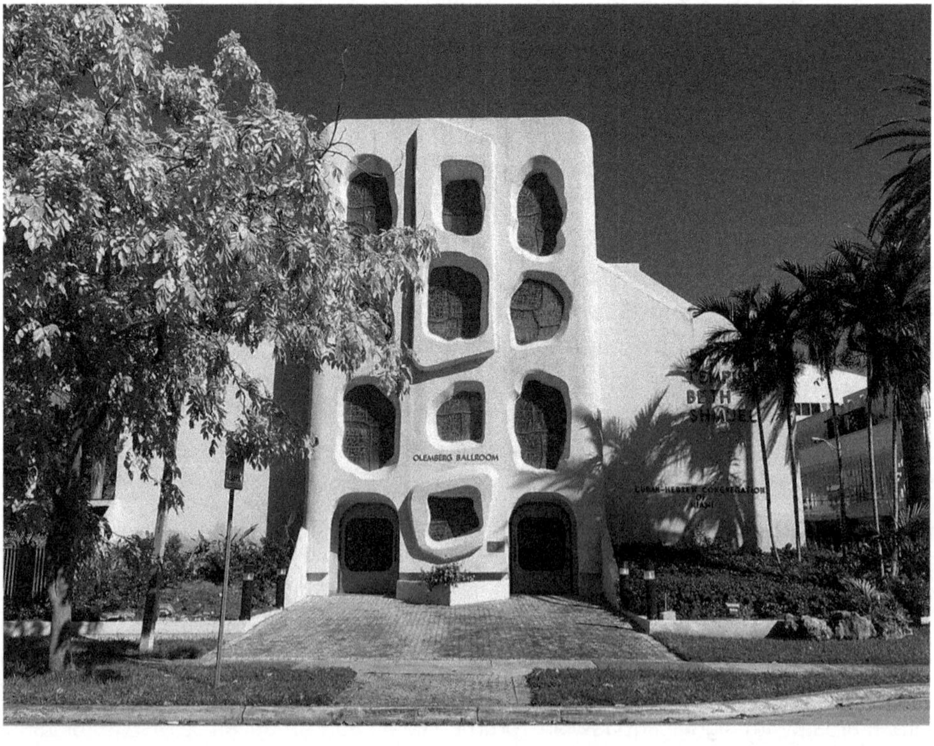

FIGURE 10.5 *Temple Beth Shmuel, Cuban-Hebrew congregation in Miami, FL.* Source: *Phillip Pessar/Wikimedia Commons.*

make Miami an inviting place for Latinx immigrants to migrate to and stay. Yet, it is not only the language, proximity to Latin America, and existing networks that foster a welcoming environment for Latinx Jews—the Jewish communal and religious institutions have also played a role in creating a hospitable atmosphere for new Latinx Jewish immigrants.

South Florida has been a destination for Jewish families and retirees since the end of the Second World War. Thousands of retirees made their way to Miami to escape the colder climates of the northeastern United States. The population of Jews in Miami peaked in the 1970s and has since been slowly declining. Today, immigrants are an increasingly large portion of the Jewish population in Miami, and Latinx Jewish immigrants are one of the largest immigrant groups to make Miami their home. Jewish Latinx immigrants account for 15 percent of all Jewish people in Miami, the largest representation of Latinx Jews across the United States (Sheskin 2015).

As the population of Jewish retirees declined in the Miami area—due to both an aging population and a preference for other retirement locales (such as Palm Beach or Boca Raton), Jewish institutions found themselves in need of members and supporters. Synagogues such as the Beth Torah Temple or Skylake Synagogue, both in North Miami Beach, made concerted efforts to offer support to new Latin American immigrants through Spanish-language services, job referrals, networking events, and, in some cases, visa sponsorship. In addition, synagogues offered financial support through free or reduced-cost memberships and scholarships to affiliated schools and camps. This type of support was instrumental in building community and worked to both strengthen existing institutions in the Miami area that were losing membership while also constructing ties among a new sector of the Jewish population.

In Miami, Latin American Jewish immigrants found themselves in the position to recreate certain aspects of their own Jewish communities back home. They formed new networks with Jews from across Latin American and have begun the process of ethnogenesis—through networks comprising Jews from across the Latin American continent. The Jewish community in North Miami Beach (where the majority of Latin American Jews have settled) has a distinctly "Latin" flavor. The local JCC has a youth program modeled after those in Latin America. The Hebraica program at the JCC offers overnight trips and leadership courses for youth, most of whom are first- or second-generation immigrants from Latin America. Community members from Argentina, Mexico, Venezuela, Mexico, Peru, and Colombia find themselves conversing over coffees at the center's snack bar and creating new communities centered on the shared aspects of their cultural and ethnic identities—Latinx and Jewish. In this way, their national identities (Argentine, Venezuelan, Mexican, etc.) are subsumed and their panethnic (Latinx Jewish) is highlighted. Moreover, Latinx Jewish identities and sense of group belonging among the youth who participate in these programs is firmly rooted within the Latinx Jewish community and culture.

Latinx Jews Are American Jews

Much in the same way that Jews from Germany, Eastern Europe, North Africa, and the Middle East defined the meaning of Jewishness and constructed an American Jewish community at the time of their arrival and eventual assimilation into American life, contemporary immigrants as well as Jews by choice are doing the same. Latinx Jews are part of a larger group of diverse Jews—from Latin America, the former Soviet Union, Israel, or Iran, as well as Jews by choice and offspring of Jewish and non-Jewish children who are redefining what it means to be an American Jew. Latinx Jews bring with them a strong sense of community and support for cultural Jewish institutions as well as new foods, dances, languages, and songs. As Latinx Jews become more integrated into existing Jewish communities—we can expect to see salsa dancing at Bar Mitzvahs, kosher taco bars, and jalapeño spiced brisket to become much more commonplace in the American Jewish experience.

Further Reading

Bettinger-López, C. 2000. *Cuban-Jewish Journeys: Searching for Identity, Home, and History in Miami.* Knoxville, TN: University of Tennessee.

Elkin, J.L. 2014. *The Jews of Latin America*, 3rd edn. Boulder, CO: Lynne Rienner Publishers.

Limonic, L. 2019. *Kugel and Frijoles: Latino Jews in the United States.* Detroit, MI: Wayne State University Press.

Mays, D. 2020. *Forging Ties, Forging Passports: Migration and the Modern Sephardi Diaspora. Forging Ties, Forging Passports.* Stanford University Press.

References

Belzer, T., T. Brundage, V. Calvetti, G. Gorsky, A.Y. Kelman, and D. Perez. 2021. "Beyond the Count: Perspectives and Lived Experiences of Jews of Color." *Jews of Color Initiative.* https://jewsofcolorinitiative.org/wp-content/uploads/2021/08/BEYONDTHECOUNT.FINAL_.8.12.21.pdf. Accessed September 17, 2022.

DellaPergola, S. 2022. "World Jewish Population, 2020." In *American Jewish Year Book*, vol. 120, edited by A. Dashefsky and I.M. Sheskin, 273–370. Cham: Switzerland, Springer.

Diner, H.R. 2006. *The Jews of the United States, 1654 to 2000.* Berkeley: University of California Press.

Elkin, J.L. 2014. *The Jews of Latin America*, 3rd edn. Boulder, CO: Lynne Rienner Publishers.

Jones, N., R. Marks, R. Ramirez, and M. Rios-Vargas. 2021. "2020 Census Illuminates Racial and Ethnic Composition of the Country." *US Census.* https://www.census.gov/library/stories/2021/08/improved-race-ethnicity-measures-reveal-united-states-population-much-more-multiracial.html. Accessed September 17, 2022.

Kaplan, D.E. 2005. "Fleeing the Revolution: The Exodus of Cuban Jewry in the Early 1960s." *Cuban Studies* 36 (1): 129–54. https://doi.org/10.1353/cub.2005.0036

Limonic, L. 2020, "Jewish Identity among Contemporary Jewish Immigrants in the United States." In *Wandering Jews: Global Jewish Migration*, special issue *The Jewish Role in American Life An Annual Review*, edited by S.J. Ross, S.J. Gold, and L. Ansell, 1–32. West Lafayette, IN: Purdue University Press.

Mittelberg, D., and M.C. Waters. 1992. "The Process of Ethnogenesis among Haitian and Israeli Immigrants in the United States." *Ethnic and Racial Studies* 15 (3): 412–35. DOI: 10.1080/01419870.1992.9993755

Sheskin, I. 2015. "The 2014 Greater Miami Jewish Federation Population Study: A Portrait of the Miami Jewish Community." *Greater Miami Jewish Federation*. http://www.jewishdatabank.org/Studies/downloadFile.cfm?FileID=3225. Accessed September 17, 2022.

Pew Research Center. 2021. "Jewish Americans in 2020." https://www.pewresearch.org/religion/2021/05/11/jewish-americans-in-2020/. Accessed September 17, 2022.

Glossary Term

Jew by Choice: A Jew by choice is someone who has adopted or converted to Judaism, instead of a person born to a Jewish mother.

PART III

Devotional, Material, and Textual Cultures

11

Latinx Devotional Stuff and Material Religion

Alyssa Maldonado-Estrada

Introduction: Stuff, Sensations, and Substances

To study the materiality of religion is to explore all of the stuff, sensations, and substances of religious life. The stuff of religion includes deliberately designed and prepared objects—statues, altars, candles, ritual clothing and food offerings, and the places and sites of religion.

People come to be part of religious communities, interact with divine figures, and even become ethical and disciplined religious subjects through embodied feeling and action (Mohan and Warnier 2017; Mahmood 2004). To study material culture is to explore how aural, olfactory, tactile, visual, and gustatory sensations are essential to religious ways of knowing. Being part of a religious community is often about cultivating a certain sensorium, and becoming attuned to certain sights, sounds, and tastes, and to be *in touch*, literally and figuratively, with sacred spaces, gods, spirits, ancestors, and the dead.

But material culture also includes the manipulation of substances that have their own affordances, capabilities, and properties that exceed their human makers/users. While humans make and invest objects and materials with meaning, substances also have forces, trajectories, and tendencies of their own (Bennett 2010: viii, 61).

Sacred, special, efficacious things can be mass-produced consumer goods and handmade artisanal creations alike. But for the purposes of studying material culture, it is important to explore how stuff *becomes* sacred, holy, special, protective, and powerful. A material culture approach helps us explore how objects, sites, and bodies can become worthy of veneration and capable of acting and transmitting divine power.

Snapshots of Latinx Material Culture

Lower East Side, New York

When I was a little girl, my grandma had an altar on the top shelf of her closet. She lived in the projects, the carbon copy brick buildings that lined the Lower East Side along the East River. A statue of *San Lázaro* (St. Lazarus), a saint associated with poverty, illness, and affliction, presided over the mess of nineties fashion and the pastel plastic hangers in her cramped closet (Murphy 2017; Penagos 2021). In the shadowy space on the top shelf he stood, frozen in a limp, balancing on his crutches, his tan body covered in sores. This statue was often accompanied by a clear glass of water. She also kept a cup of water with a cube of *alcanfor* (camphor) behind the thick, metal front door of the apartment to pick up any negative energies that attempted to pass this threshold. With this protective measure, she would watch out for when the water was filled with air bubbles, which was her sign to change and freshen the water.

In my great-aunt Tita's apartment, the bedroom was full of saintly and spiritual characters. But there was no designated altar to speak of. Statues of Our Lady of Fatima and a framed image of St. Martin de Porres sat on the shelves next to bobblehead chihuahuas and ivory Buddhas and elephants. Statues of Santa Barbara, golden Buddhas, and Coney Island souvenirs crowded her dresser. There was a spirit of accumulation in this small apartment: photos of the Twin Towers, Puerto Rican flags, and Beanie Babies decorated the house alongside brooding portraits of Jesus.

Chimayó, New Mexico

The Santuario de Chimayó is a pilgrimage site outside of Santa Fe and is one of the most important Catholic sites in the United States. Chimayó is famous for housing a miraculous crucifix that was discovered in 1810 in a hole along the Santa Cruz River. Every time the crucifix was moved to the altar of a Catholic church, it miraculously and independently returned to the hole in the ground. Today, thousands of pilgrims travel to Chimayó to visit the hole, called the *pocito*, to collect holy dirt. In a low-ceiling shrine room, they kneel over this aperture in the ground and use a little shovel to gather fine, sandy earth. The shrine room is crowded with objects that are testaments to the miraculous power of the earth in Chimayó. Crutches hang together on the walls, and every surface is crowded with photographs—so many eyes peer out from the glossy pictures, each one a personal story of hope and gratitude. Prayers are materialized everywhere at Chimayó. Even the chain-link fences that lead into the site are covered with crosses scribbled with sharpie, plastic rosaries, envelopes stuffed with handwritten notes, and even pregnancy tests in Ziploc bags (see Figure 11.1).

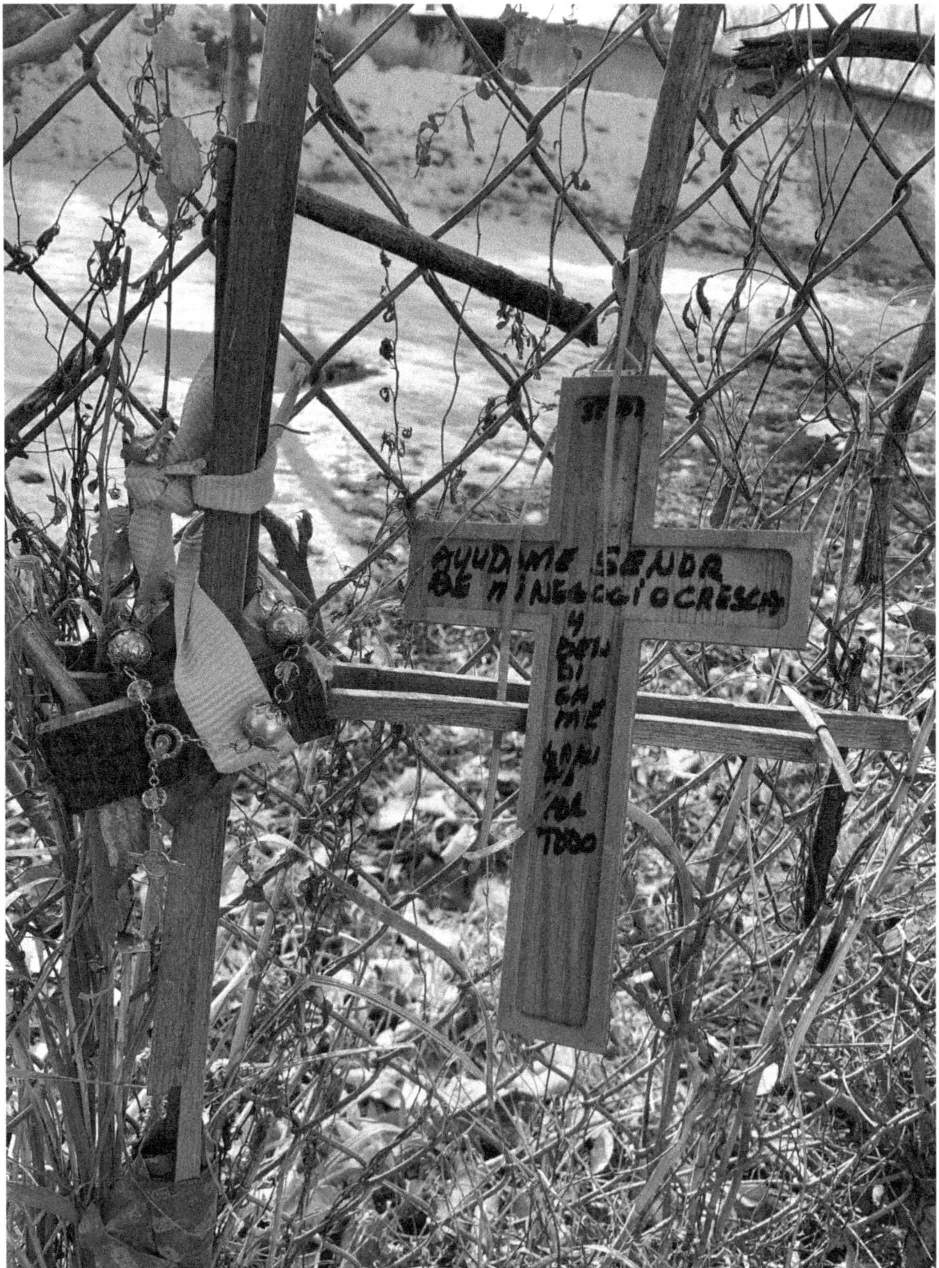

FIGURE 11.1 *Wooden cross with petition in Spanish on a fence at the Santuario de Chimayó. The devotee prays for help growing their business.* Source: *Photo by Alyssa Maldonado-Estrada.*

San Miguel de Allende, Mexico

In the Templo de Nuestra Senõra de la Salud, a statue of el Niño Jesús de la Salud sits with a little, coy smile behind glass (see Figure 11.2). He is surrounded by toys, so much so that only his head and torso peek out from the pile of plastic trucks and cars, baby dolls, Play-Doh sets, soccer balls, and plush rabbits. The playful plastic aesthetic of childhood mixes with the baroque aesthetics of the church. On a velvet-lined bulletin board next to his shrine, a long braid of hair, photos of loved ones, and little metal offerings, called *milagritos*, in the shape of eyes, people kneeling in prayer, and legs, are safety pinned to the velvet. These personal touches and bodily fragments coexist with the consumer objects.

FIGURE 11.2 *El Niño Jesus de la Salud surrounded by toys.* Source: *Photo by Alyssa Maldonado-Estrada.*

Across these examples we can explore themes that unify Latinx material culture: (1) the spirit of additivity and acquisition, (2) eclectic and pragmatic actions and assemblages, and (3) the importance of reciprocity.

Additivity and Acquisition

The aesthetics and assemblages of Latinx material culture often refuse and contradict neat distinctions between religious traditions and "spiritual commodities." In my grandmother and Tita's apartments, the stuff of Catholicism coexisted with folk ritual objects, consumer goods, and the objects of other religious traditions. It is no contradiction to have Buddha alongside Catholic saints. As Raquel Romberg, anthropologist of Puerto Rican religion, argues "the foreign origins of many [icons] does not limit their ritual efficacy ... on the contrary, the **translocal** specifics of their essential powers are drawn into a comprehensive spiritual world, regardless of their or their devotees' gender, national, or ethnic identity—proof of the nondiscriminatory power of spiritual commodities" (2003: 85). Latinx religious material culture is not monolithic but contextual and relational, and Romberg has argued that there is a cosmopolitan spirit to Puerto Rican material religion. In the Lower East Side, a neighborhood historically composed of Jewish, Puerto Rican, and Chinese communities, the Buddhas make sense next to their more overtly Catholic things. Indeed in botánicas, the spiritual goods stores found in Latinx neighborhoods, New Age, African-inspired, Catholic, and Southeast Asian religious objects are often sold side by side, creating a "comprehensive spiritual world" from "ritual commodities" (Romberg 2003: 85).

Eclectic and Pragmatic

In these examples, we find Latinas working with substances that are potent and protective, even if they seem ultramundane—dirt and water. The assemblage of a clear glass, the *alcanfor*, and the clean water is not just a symbolic combination of elements, but a combination that *works*. In various Caribbean traditions water is a powerful substance. A glass of water can "quench the thirst of the dead so they might not torment the living," water can work to "separate good spirits from evil ones," and water can act as a "spiritual conduit" for communicating with the spirits (Viarnes 2009: 333). Across traditions like **Espiritismo** and **Santería**, water "is a primary conductor of spiritual energy" (33). With this pragmatic combination of ingredients, my grandmother ensured that any "bad energy ... would dissolve and evaporate, just as camphor and water do" (Romberg 2003: 152).

The dirt at Chimayó too has been long used as a powerful healing substance. In *The Healing Power of the Santuario de Chimayó*, religious studies scholar Brett Hendrickson explores the testimonies of people who have experienced healing they attribute to the *Santuario*—from chronic pain and cancer remission to fertility issues and insomnia (2017: 184). Clerics insist that the dirt cannot heal in and of itself and encourage devotees to place their faith in God rather than the dirt. Brochures on site warn visitors against ingesting the dirt. According to Catholic officials, "the holy dirt, by its own, has no inherent healing properties. It works, so to speak, only through faith in God's power and love." Yet pilgrims gather the dirt into all sorts of vessels to carry this special, benevolent substance away with them (Hendrickson 2017: 186).

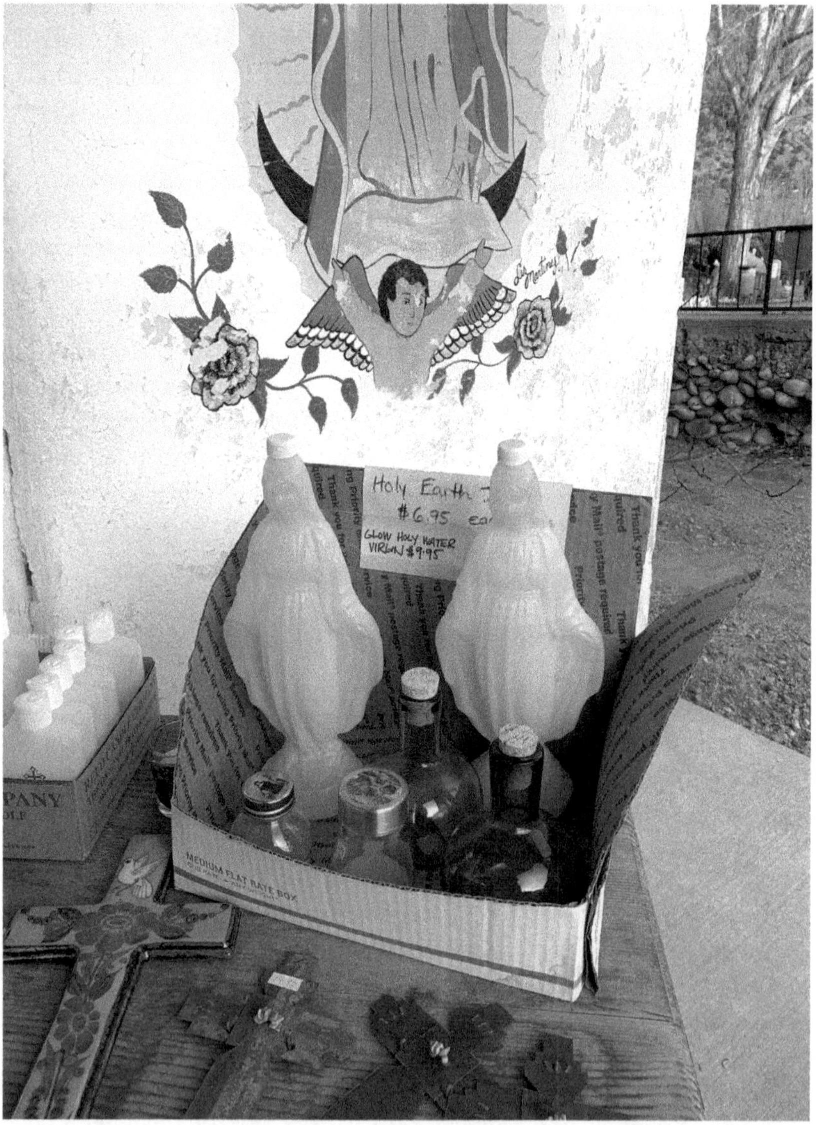

FIGURE 11.3 *Jars and vessels for sale at the Santuario de Chimayó.* Source: *Photo by Alyssa Maldonado-Estrada.*

So, by eclectic, I mean that in Latinx religious material culture we find people pursuing wellness, healing, and protection from objects and substances beyond the bounds of traditional religious orthodoxy. They work to better their circumstances and deal with the stresses of everyday life. This pragmatic spirit means that many value practices and objects that *work* and prove to be efficacious in the domains of health, romance, and family life.

Reciprocity

In much Latinx material religion we see relationships of reciprocity and exchange between humans, saints, and spirits. In the *milagritos*, photos, and toys piled around the Niño Jesús, we see that gifts, no matter how humble or playful, are essential in maintaining relationships with divine figures. These offerings express gratitude for intervention or the hope of intervention. According to religious studies scholar Frank Graziano, "petitionary devotion consists primarily of making miracle requests together with promises to offer something in exchange" (2015: 392). When a Hasbro toy or a braid of hair are placed at a shrine, they become public testaments to a saint's powerful presence and intervention in the life of a devotee and broadcast the possibility of that intervention to others. In these objects we see the love, hope, loss, and need with which people approach the sacred and evidence of the action and responses of divine beings and forces.

Further Reading

Durand, J., and D. S. Massey. 1995. *Miracles on the Border: Retablos of Mexican Migrants to the United States.* Tuscon, AZ: University of Arizona Press.
Morgan, D. 2021. *The Thing about Religion: An Introduction to the Material Study of Religions.* Chapel Hill, NC: University of North Carolina Press.
Murphy, J. M. 2015. *Botánicas: Sacred Spaces of Healing and Devotion in Urban America.* Jackson, MS: University Press of Mississippi.

References

Bennett, J. 2010. *Vibrant Matter: A Political Ecology of Things.* Durham, NC: Duke University Press.
Graziano, F. 2015. "Votive Exchange in Mexican Petitionary Devotion." *Material Religion* 11 (3): 392–4.
Hendrickson, B. 2017. *The Healing Power of the Santuario de Chimayó: America's Miraculous Church.* New York: New York University Press.
Mahmood, S. 2004. *Politics of Piety: The Islamic Revival and the Feminist Subject.* Princeton, NJ: Princeton University Press.

Mohan, U., and J-P. Warnier. 2017. "Marching the Devotional Subject: The Bodily-and-Material Cultures of Religion." *Journal of Material Culture* 22 (4): 369–84.

Murphy, J. M. 2017. "The Many San Lázaros of Hialeah: Material Practice in the Celebration of a Cuban-American Saint." *Material Religion* 13 (4): 482–513.

Penagos, E. 2021. "How We Heal: Genealogical Narratives of Healing among San Lázaro Devotees." *Genealogy* 5 (1): 18. DOI: https://doi.org/10.3390/genealogy5010018

Romberg, R. 2003. *Witchcraft and Welfare: Spiritual Capital and the Business of Magic in Modern Puerto Rico.* Austin, TX: University of Texas Press.

Viarnes, C. 2009. "Muñecas and Memoryscapes: Negotiating Identity." In *Activating the Past: History and Memory in the Black Atlantic World*, edited by A. Apter and L. Derby, 319–69. Newcastle upon Tyne, UK: Cambridge Scholars Publishing.

Glossary Terms

Espiritismo: Influenced by the nineteenth-century French philosopher Allan Kardec (1804–69) and various folk traditions, Espiritismo is a system of healing and spirit communication practiced in Puerto Rico and Cuba. Espiritismo contends that the spirit world and the material world are in constant contact and spirits can interact with humans and intervene in their everyday lives. Spirit mediums, or espiritistas specialize in communicating with and discerning these spirits in order to help spiritually cleanse and heal people.

Santería: Also known as Lucumí and Regla de Ocha, Santería is an African diasporic religion that emerged in Cuba during the transatlantic slave trade. It is centered on a pantheon of Yoruba-inspired deities, called orishas, each with its own domain over sectors of life and forces of nature. Altars, feeding and nourishing the orishas, initiation, divination, and spirit-possession, are key ways humans engage with the orishas and their spiritual power and energy.

Translocal: It is the concept of "translocality," which helps us think about connections *between* places. Thinking about religion translocally helps to consider how media, technology, movement of peoples, commerce, and other global forces shape and challenge the geographic boundedness of practices, traditions, and communities.

12

The Bible and Latinxs

Jacqueline M. Hidalgo

Introduction

Just as Latinxs are a diverse group—encompassing many different races, ethnicities, and religions, among other social identities—so too the Bible has a complex and diverse set of histories and engagements within Latinx contexts. The Bible itself is not a straightforward, singular document (Beal 2012). It is a compendium of different texts that vary among communities, and even within Western Christian traditions, the texts that constitute the Bible are not the same in Roman Catholic and Protestant contexts. There are books in the Roman Catholic Bible that are not present within the Protestant Bible, for instance, Judith or Sirach. There are many different translations of biblical texts, many varied forms that a Bible might take—whether as Torah scrolls, illuminated manuscripts, magazines (Harding 2010), virtual sites (Bible Gateway), musical theater productions, or podcasts to name a few examples—and many different sorts of relationships with the Bible that get practiced, even within one religious tradition. Yet, the Bible, often imagined as a singular leather-bound book, has long held a special, iconic public role in **Abya Yala**/the Americas at large and the United States in particular (Marty 1989: 141). In this brief chapter, I share a few key examples that speak to the Bible's iconic associations with colonialism as well as its diverse and divergent receptions in different Latinx contexts.

The Bible and Colonization

Many retellings of Francisco Pizarro's 1532 ambush of the Inca Atahualpa at Cajamarca describe a moment when a Spanish priest, Vicente de Valverde, accompanying Pizarro's violent mission moves to speak with Atahualpa just prior to the ambush. A popular

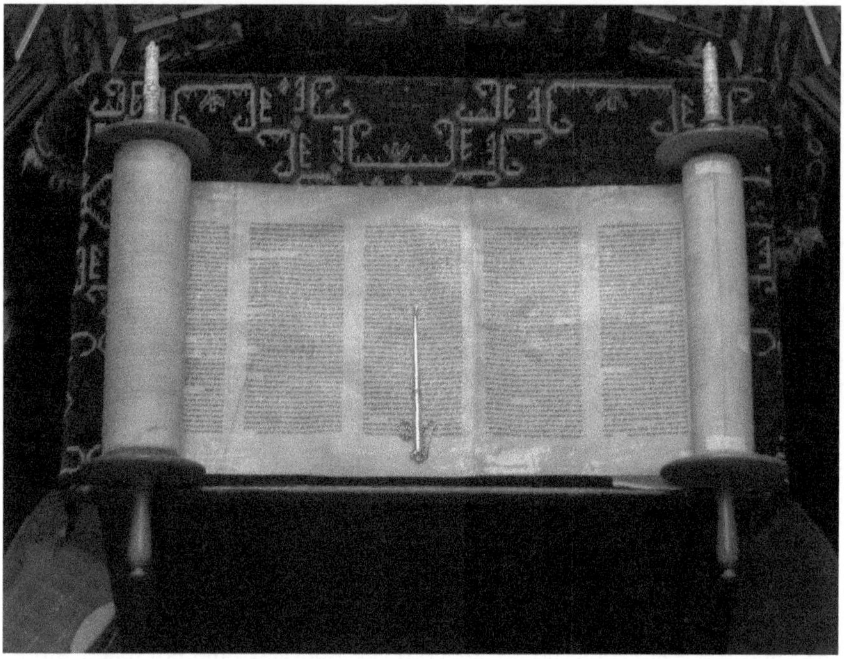

FIGURE 12.1 *An open Torah scroll. Jewish communities throughout the world, including Latin American and Latinx ones, engage in ritual readings from Torah scrolls.* Source: *Lawrie Cate/Wikimedia Commons.*

FIGURE 12.2 *The St. John's Bible, completed in 2011, stands out as among the most famous and recent examples of an illuminated manuscript.* Source: *MediaNews Group/Reading Eagle via Getty Images/Contributor/Wikimedia Commons.*

FIGURE 12.3 *We commonly imagine the Bible as this leather-bound text, seen here in the hands of a minister during a moment of public prayer in front of the US Supreme Court.* Source: *Mark Wilson/Getty Images.*

retelling captured in Eduardo Galeano's modern classic *Memory of Fire: Genesis* depicts Valverde advancing toward Atahualpa while Pizarro and Spanish soldiers hide, waiting for the right moment to ambush the Indigenous leader. Valverde attests to his faith in one, true god, and Atahualpa asks Valverde how he knows this. Valverde replies, "'The Bible says it.'" Atahualpa asks to hear from this Bible, so he holds it, shakes it, tries to get this object to speak to him, but replies to Valverde, "It says nothing. It's empty." Atahualpa then tosses the Bible down (Galeano 1985: 88). This dropping of the Bible is perceived as a violation of its sacred nature, and it serves as a pretext for Pizarro and the soldiers to spring into action, attack the Quechua soldiers, and seize Atahualpa.

Valverde may not have had a Bible, and Atahualpa may not have questioned the Bible's power, but the imagination of this moment has left a lasting memory of the Bible as an iconic symbol of Christianity's role in violent and genocidal conquest. This particular story not only encapsulates the appearance of the Bible as iconic but also demonstrates the very different ways of relating to *writing* that have structured ongoing power dynamics in the Americas (Wimbush 2012). In this narrative, we see Valverde taking for granted that this object can "say" anything at all. Meanwhile, for the Inca, embedded in a Quechua

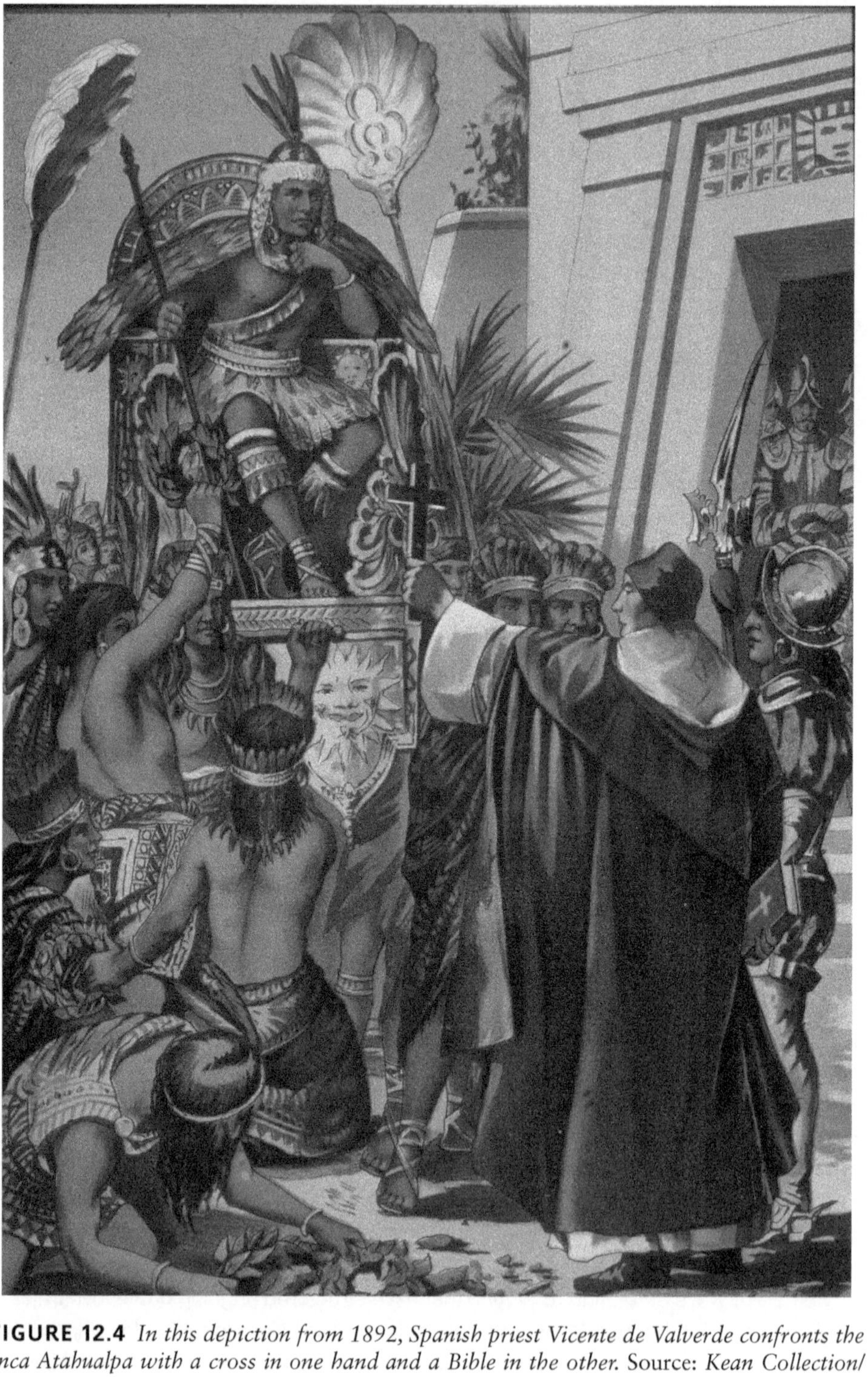

FIGURE 12.4 *In this depiction from 1892, Spanish priest Vicente de Valverde confronts the Inca Atahualpa with a cross in one hand and a Bible in the other.* Source: *Kean Collection/ Getty Images.*

context where writing in the form of **quipu** looks nothing like the objects Europeans tend to associate with writing, especially in contrast to the clothbound sets of paper we call a book, this assumption seems ridiculous. How can this strange, paper object speak? It produces no sound. As many contemporary Latinx biblical scholars would remind us, the Bible does not speak on its own. Instead, we must examine the ways human beings derive meaning from their interactions with the Bible, and we must turn to what those humans are saying when they say the Bible speaks.

Nearly 500 years after Valverde, a group in Peru identifying themselves as "Indians of the Andes and the Americas" returned the Bible to Pope John Paul II. They said,

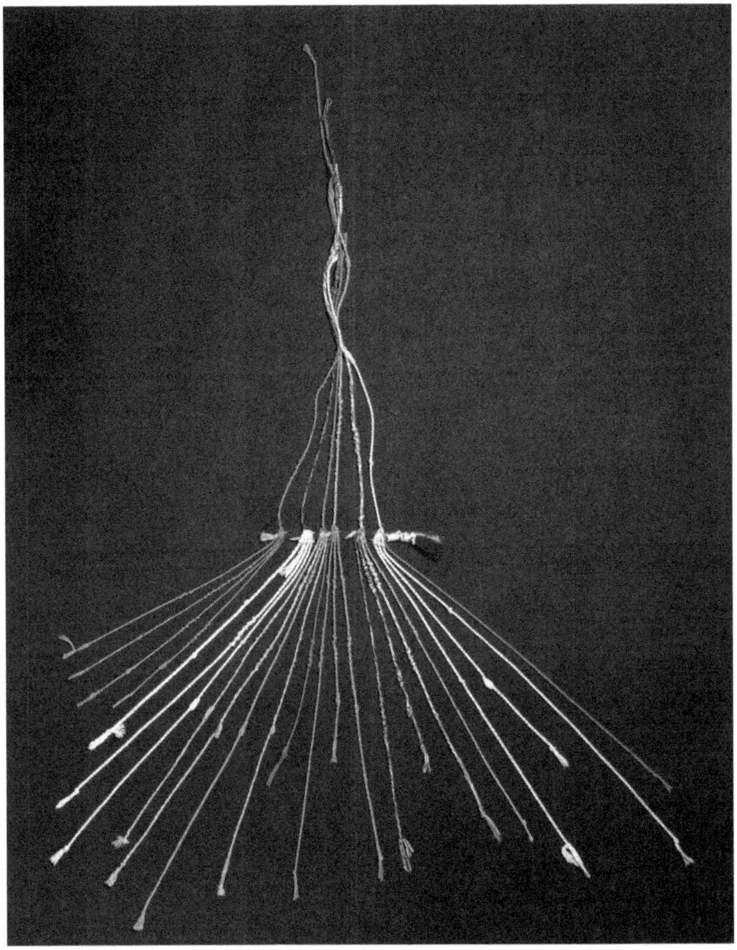

FIGURE 12.5 *In this replica of a* quipu, *we can see how this form of recording an account is visually and physically distinctive from the forms of "writing" found in the Bibles depicted above.* Source: *SSPL/Getty Images.*

"Please take your Bible and give it back to our oppressors, because they need its moral precepts more than we ... It was the ideological arm of the colonial assault" (Richard 1992: 45–6; Tamez 2006: 18). Many Latinxs in the USA have echoed this sentiment. In particular, many ethnic Mexican and Puerto Rican communities associate the Bible not only with Spanish conquest and colonization but also with US conquest, conquests that are related historically but "not identical" (Maldonado 1995: 10). The Bible took on a distinctive role as icon and ideological partner of conquest in US **Manifest Destiny** amid the annexation of northern Mexican territories following the US-Mexican War in 1848 and the annexation—and ongoing colonial occupation—of Puerto Rico following the US-Spanish War in 1898. Writing in the wake of celebrations of 500 years of Christopher Columbus's arrival in the Caribbean (1492), Chicana author Cherríe Moraga associated Christianity with histories of conquest. She looked beyond Christian sources for other forms of "sacred texts," toward Indigenous Nahua traditions as well as other contemporary lived sources, such as the **mural art** of "barrio walls" or to recipes and cooking practices, all of which she identified as part of a "Chicano codex" (1993: 187–90). One Latinx response to the Bible is to identify it as a symbol of colonialism that must now be rejected.

FIGURE 12.6 *Murals are an important form of art in many ethnic Latinx contexts in the United States. This image of Paul Botelló's "The Wall That Speaks, Sings, and Shouts" is an example of a mural that has special—even sacred—value for some ethnic Mexicans.* Source: *Photo by Anne Cusack/Los Angeles Times via Getty Images.*

The Bible as a Healing and a Homing Device

Despite the fraught histories that surround the Bible in Abya Yala, many Latinxs embrace the Bible as a sacred text and as a resource for navigating the world after colonization and for healing its ills, though, again there is no singular way Latinxs relate to the Bible as sacred. Many Latinxs relate to the Bible as sacred but without sitting and reading the book. For many Catholics, the Bible long-held space as an iconically powerful text, seen to be of sacred import and treated in special ways, but, as in my own family, it was not a text often read at length or with great attention outside of short passages heard in church. In my family's daily life, the Bible was mostly engaged through pieces of story and song found in prayers, religious rituals, and art. For many Protestant communities, the Bible also holds iconic stature, sometimes used in healing rituals in which a sick person's body is touched with the Bible or as a way of demarcating sacred space within the home by laying open to Psalm 23 (Jiménez 1997: 67).

The Bible also holds an important place in many non-Christian and not exclusively Christian traditions and practices. Of course, the first part of many Christian bibles ("the Old Testament") overlaps significantly with the central contents of Jewish bibles (the "Tanakh" or "Hebrew Bible"). And many Latinx Muslims see the Bible as an important text even if its stature is not equal to that of the Qur'an. Many Afrodiasporic and Indigenous traditions also turn to the Bible and particular biblical texts, stories, and images in their own rituals and practices. For instance, popular Cuban Catholic and Santería devotions often combine different figures under the moniker San Lázaro. There are two different Lazaruses in the gospels: Lazarus of Bethany, whom Jesus resurrects (John 11:1–46) and a poor Lazarus covered in sores that dogs would lick, who dies (Luke 16:19–31), with this sickly version of Lazarus popularly represented in statues on home altars. San Lázaro is also an avatar of the Lukumí orisha Babalú Ayé, a divine figure associated with disease and healing (Escalante 2023).

Rituals related to San Lázaro and the stories of his miraculous healing powers can become sacred tales themselves. For instance, Elaine Penagos, a scholar of religion, describes her grandmother's devotion to San Lázaro as a form of familial sacred story. Penagos contextualizes her grandmother's devotion in relationship to other key facets of her grandmother's life: her migration from Cuba, her hard work in a factory job, the severe injuries she suffered to her feet, the surgery that was required, and the constant prayers to San Lázaro, who was also worn around her grandmother's neck and significantly emplaced in a home altar. Eventually, her grandmother was healed, a healing the grandmother and the family attribute to San Lázaro. Stories about San Lázaro's role in healing constitute familial histories and act not only as stories about individual healing but as forms of communal continuity and healing within the families that share these stories (Penagos 2021).

For some Jewish, Catholic, and Protestant communities, their Bibles are read daily, and the active reading of them forms a central part of religious engagement. From 2003 to 2006, I spent time with one such community of Latinx Protestants at

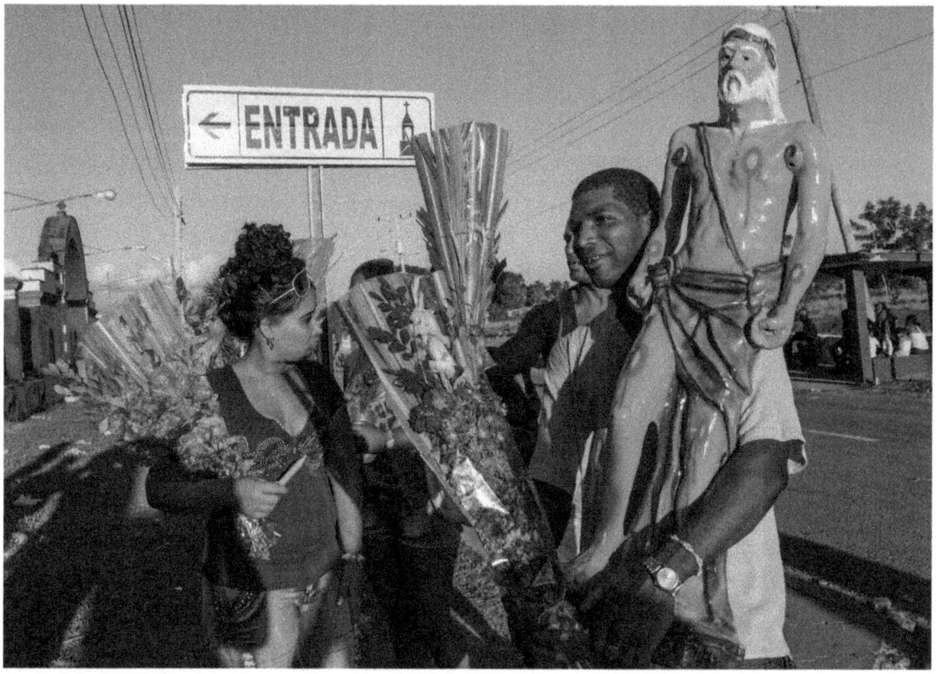

FIGURE 12.7 *A devotee carries a statue of Saint Lazarus in Cuba.* Source: *AFP/Stringer/ Getty Images.*

a Calvary Chapel in Claremont, California (Hidalgo 2018). The pastor, his wife, and many members of the community came from Cuban backgrounds, though there were also some ethnic Mexican as well as non-Latinx members of the community at the time. In that context, the Bible was regularly read, studied, and cited in practice and conversation.

During my time with the community, I saw the Bible acting as a homing device, as an object through and around which congregants sought and made homes. Most members of this community experienced some form of political exile from the nation they felt was their home, even if they were highly critical of that nation. They also often experienced the world as a harsh place. Many of them were quite critical of the racism they witnessed in the outside world, and their community's opposition to racism drew them into Calvary Chapel. One congregant saw most of the world as so broken that she would not read any text besides the Bible, even commentary on the Bible, because all other texts were the product of human hands whereas the Bible offered more direct access to the divine. For the pastor, Marco Álvarez, feeling unhomed within the world was remedied through a strong relationship with the Bible. He depicted specific biblical texts as providing guidance "so that we may live as citizens of the Kingdom of heaven in a hostile and difficult world" (Álvarez as quoted in Hidalgo 2018: 30). The Bible was engaged for the access it gave to a better home beyond the ills of this world even as it provided guidance for how to make home in this difficult world. Yet those ways of making home often encoded a strong gender hierarchy and an exclusionary sexual ethic that denied full humanity to LGBTQIA+ Latinxs.

Biblical Multivalence

Although the Bible at Calvary Chapel was part of an ongoing struggle to make home in a world of ongoing migration and displacement, quests for home in and around the Bible can remain fraught for many because of the historical ways the Bible has been used to dominate and exclude. Biblical scholar Angela N. Parker recently distinguished between the Bible as an "authoritarian" text and the Bible as an "authoritative" text, and Parker demonstrates the ways that biblical authoritarianism has been deeply entangled with white supremacist authoritarianism historically. Communities that treat the Bible as an authoritarian text often treat it as having a commanding power with a true meaning that must be submitted to; to enact an authoritarian relationship with the Bible is to venerate the Bible for its power over others, a form of domination that has been deeply intertwined with the histories of European and Euro-North American colonizing and enslaving domination over others. In this approach, the Bible cannot be the start of a conversation, but it is instead "a conversation ender" (Parker 2021: 45). By contrast, to engage the Bible as authoritative is to still hold it as sacred and to enter into a conversation with it and with other readers, a conversation that is relational and necessarily involves exchange and fluidity. In that relationship the Bible's meaning is not presumed to be fixed but is instead perceived to be open to change.

Both ways of relating to the Bible have been part of different Latinx traditions. So too have other ways of relating to the Bible as a shared set of stories, neither authoritative nor authoritarian, but always present as part of the world, informing art, music, and the making of daily life. Yet the Bible is not always determinative of daily life. Many Latinxs also turn to myriad other traditions and to their own lived experiences as a source of revelation (Hidalgo 2016; Ruíz 2021). And many Latinxs reject any sort of sacred relationship with the Bible, even if they also still draw on biblical narratives and phrases in making art or discussing family histories. It is important to distinguish between different ways of relating to the Bible as sacred. It is equally important to recognize that for many Latinxs the Bible may be a socially important and powerful compendium of texts, but it is not sacred.

There is no one way of relating to the Bible, and a student of the Bible in Latinx communities must reckon with a broad range of bibles, by which I mean that Latinxs do not all mean the same thing when they utter the phrase *la Biblia* or the Bible. Among its many roles, the Bible has been a part of Iberian and US conquests: some Latinxs have experienced it as an agent of white supremacist domination over others; some Latinxs have seen the Bible as a text that has also supported other forms of unjust domination (misogyny, homophobia, transphobia, ableism, classism, xenophobia, etc.); some Latinxs have turned to the Bible as a source of healing in the wake of suffering; some Latinxs have seen within the Bible a promise of freedom; and some Latinxs have employed the Bible as a homing device for making communal belonging in the face of displacement. For Maldonado (1995: 25), this diversity signals a hopeful multivalence; if we see the Bible as open to many different meanings, we may broaden our own abilities to see the equal dignity of human diversity. Yet such multivalence is perilous if we forget the fraught and violent histories within colonialism that have also shaped the Bible that Latinxs encounter in daily life.

Further Reading

Isasi-Díaz, A. M. 1996. *Mujerista Theology: A Theology for the Twenty-First Century.* Maryknoll, NY: Orbis Books.

Ruiz, J. P. 2011. *Reading from the Edges: The Bible and People on the Move.* Maryknoll, NY: Orbis Books.

Sánchez, D. A. 2008. *From Patmos to the Barrio: Subverting Imperial Myths.* Minneapolis, MN: Fortress Press.

Segovia, F. F., and F. A. Lozada, eds. 2014. *Latino/a Biblical Hermeneutics: Problematics, Objectives, Strategies.* Atlanta, GA: Society of Biblical Literature.

Wimbush, V. L., et al., ed. 2015. *MisReading America: Scriptures and Difference.* New York: Oxford University Press.

References

Beal, T. 2012. *The Rise and Fall of the Bible: The Unexpected History of an Accidental Book.* San Francisco, CA: HarperOne.

Escalante, A. S. 2023. "Black Atlantic Religions." In *Bloomsbury Religion in North America,* edited by L. D. Barba. London, UK: Bloomsbury Academic, 2023. Online DOI: http://dx.doi.org/10.5040/9781350898806.001

Galeano, E. 1998/1985. *Memory of Fire: Genesis (Part One),* translated by Cedric Belfrage. New York: Norton.

Harding, S. 2010. "The Transevangelical Zone." *Anthropology Now* 2 (3): 10–18.

Hidalgo, J. M. 2016. *Revelation in Aztlán: Scriptures, Utopias, and the Chicano Movement.* New York: Palgrave Macmillan.

Hidalgo, J. M. 2018. "The Bible as Homing Device among Cubans at Claremont's Calvary Chapel." In *Latinxs, the Bible, and Migration,* edited by E. Agosto and J. M. Hidalgo, 21–42. New York: Palgrave Macmillan.

Jiménez, P. A. 1997. "The Bible: A Hispanic Perspective." In *Teología En Conjunto: A Collaborative Hispanic Protestant Theology,* edited by J. D. Rodríguez and L. I. Martell-Otero, 66–79. Louisville, KY: Westminster/John Knox.

Maldonado, R. D. 1995. "*¿La Conquista?* Latin American (*Mestizaje*) Reflections on the Biblical Conquest." *The Journal of Hispanic/Latino Theology* 2 (4): 5–25.

Marty, M. E. 1989. *Religion and Republic: The American Circumstance.* Boston, MA: Beacon Press.

Moraga, C. 1993. *The Last Generation: Prose and Poetry.* Boston, MA: South End Press.

Parker, A. N. 2021. *If God Still Breathes, Why Can't I? Black Lives Matter and Biblical Authority*. Grand Rapids, MI: William B. Eerdmans

Penagos, E. 2021. "How We Heal: Genealogical Narratives of Healing among San Lázaro Devotees." *Genealogy* 5 (1): 18. https://doi.org/10.3390/genealogy5010018 Accessed August 13, 2022.

Richard, P. 1992. "Hermenútica biblica india: Revelacíon de Dios en las religiones indígenas y en la Biblia (Después de 500 años de dominación)." In *Sentido histórico del V Centenario (1492–1992)*, edited by G. Meléndez, 45–62. San José, Costa Rica: CEHILA-DEI.

Ruiz, J. 2021. *Revelation in the Vernacular*. Maryknoll, NY: Orbis Books.

Tamez, E. 2006. "The Bible and the Five Hundred Years of Conquest." In *Voices form the Margin: Interpreting the Bible in the Third World*, edited by R. S. Sugirtharajah, 13–26. revised edition. Maryknoll, NY: Orbis Books.

Wimbush, V. L. 2012. *White Men's Magic: Scripturalization as Slavery*. New York: Oxford University Press.

Glossary Terms

Abya Yala: In the language of the Dule/Guna peoples, who are Indigenous to the nations we call Panama and Colombia, this term refers to the land mass we call North and South America. Certain Latinx and Indigenous peoples prefer to use Abya Yala because it is an Indigenous name for this land, instead of being a name like "New World" or "the Americas" that European colonizers placed on this land.

Manifest Destiny: A phrase first coined in 1845, this term refers to a broader belief in a divine mandate for the United States—specifically white Protestant US culture—to dominate North America and the larger hemisphere.

Mural Art: Murals are generally understood to be large images painted on the exterior walls of buildings. They have often been understood as a more popularly accessible form of art because of their availability within daily life in neighborhoods instead of being locked away inside museums or private homes.

Quipu: A transliteration from Cusco Quechua, also spelled *khipu*, these Indigenous forms of record-keeping, found among peoples in the region we commonly term "the Andes," consist of strings and knots. As in many cultures with different forms of writing, especially before the advent of the printing press, a specialist, a *quipucamayoc*, was charged with interpreting the meanings encoded in *quipu* and relaying those meanings to others.

13

The Virgin of Guadalupe as a Symbol of Resistance

Tatyana Castillo-Ramos

Introduction

The historiography of religion in Latin America indicates a well-documented relationship between religion and resistance. Religion, specifically **popular Catholicism**, is widely regarded as a weapon of the weak to combat power structures by drawing on divine support as a higher form of authority than that of the state and the institutional church. For the greater portion of Latin American history, the church and state have operated hand in hand. In this arrangement, *La Virgen de Guadalupe* (The Virgin of Guadalupe) stands out as the premier symbol of resistance to social and political domination. While Catholicism has also been a tool for oppression, a study of how Guadalupe has been appropriated for various causes sheds light on how many have leveraged her image to resist oppression by the church and state.

Origins: Thus It Is Told

In 1521, Hernán Cortéz conquered the Aztec Empire in central Mexico with the support of both the Spanish Monarchy and the Catholic Church. However, only ten years later, one of the most widely venerated saints in Mexican history emerged: the distinctly Mexican Marian apparition, the Virgin of Guadalupe. According to the *Nican Mopohua* ("Thus It Is Told") on December 9, 1531, the Virgin Mary appeared to an Indigenous man named Juan Diego and requested that he construct a chapel in her honor at Tepeyac Hill. However, the bishop of Mexico, Juan de Zumárraga, doubted Diego's account, so on December 12 Guadalupe instructed Diego to climb the Tepeyac Hill to collect roses and other flowers in his *tilma* (a cloak-like garment) and take the flowers to the bishop. Diego did as he was told, and when he dumped the flowers out for the bishop, an image of the Virgin Mary appeared on his tilma. This was only the first of many miracles that would be attributed to the Virgin of Guadalupe that would help cement her status as the patroness of Mexico and later the patroness of all of the Americas (Brading 2001: 55–7; Matovina 2019: 3).

In Guadalupe's apparition story alone at least three subversive aspects merit attention. First, she appeared to an Indigenous person, not a Spaniard or even the local bishop. Second, she spoke to Diego in Nahuatl, the Aztec language, rather than Spanish. In fact, the *Nican Mopohua* was written in Nahuatl. Although her race is not specified in the *Nican Mopohua*, devotees of Guadalupe commonly regard her as brown-skinned and appearing as an Indigenous or **mestizo** Mexican (Matovina 2005: 12). Third, the location for her requested chapel is important because Tepeyac was already a sacred site for the Aztec goddess Tonantzin, the mother of the gods and generally the deity of motherhood and fertility (Brading 2001: 2). The location only further linked the two divine mothers. These aspects of her origin story convinced many that her chosen people were not the colonizing Spaniards but the Indigenous peoples of Mexico and their descendants. In this way she is truly a *mestiza* apparition that combines both Spanish Catholic and Indigenous Mexican influences.

Mexican Independence

The Virgin of Guadalupe was an essential symbol in the Mexican War of Independence from Spain (1810–21). Mexican priests proved important as leaders in the fight for independence, and historians credit this war as one where Catholicism became inextricably tied with Mexican national identity. As D. A. Brading states, "No aspect of the Mexican insurgency more impressed foreign observers than its emphasis upon religion" (2001: 229). Father Miguel Hidalgo y Costilla's famous call to action to fight for independence known as *El Grito de Dolores* (The Cry of Dolores) exemplifies this link. Although accounts vary, most remember his battle cry as

> My children: a new dispensation comes to us today. Will you receive it? Will you free yourselves? Will you recover the lands stolen three hundred years ago from your forefathers by the hated Spaniards? We must act at once ... Will you not defend your religion and your rights as true patriots? Long live our Lady of Guadalupe! Death to bad government! Death to the *gachupines*!
>
> (Meyer and Sherman 1995: 287–8)

Independence fighters fittingly carried banners of Guadalupe into battle (Brading 2001: 228). Spaniards, however, also used Guadalupe alongside other Catholic saints as symbols in their efforts to repress the war for independence (Matovina 2005: 12). Her appropriation for the war prefigured her use as a symbol of military and political resistance.

Mexican Revolution and the Cristero War

From the nineteenth to the early twentieth century, Catholicism in Mexico would at various points become both the target of government regulations and an accomplice to the government due to dramatic shifts in power and political instability. A variety of regulations passed from 1854 to 1876, a period known as *La Reforma* (The Reform), established the separation of church and state and aimed to limit the Catholic Church's power (Young 2015: 21). It was not until the aftermath of the Mexican Revolution (1910–20) that these tensions between church and state erupted. In 1926, President Plutarco Elías Calles added further penal code reforms to the anti-clerical laws essentially dating back to *La Reforma* and the new 1917 Constitution. These anticlerical codes called the *Ley Reglamentaria* (more commonly known as the *Ley Calles*-Calles Law) outlawed religious orders, forbade people from taking religious vows, and banned any public religious acts outside of churches, among various other restrictions (Young 2015: 25–6). The Catholic populace was outraged, particularly in west-central Mexico, and ultimately organized a military force that revolted against the federal government in the Cristero War (1926–9). The Catholic rebels were branded "Cristeros" for their battle cry of "*Viva Cristo Rey!*" (Long live Christ the King!) and organized under Catholic rhetoric and symbols. However, although religion deeply mattered in this conflict, it was not the only driving factor in the revolt (Butler 2004: 3–10). Cristeros used both images of Christ and the Virgin of Guadalupe, and they even flew a modified Mexican flag with Guadalupe in the place of the eagle on one side as their symbol (J. Meyer 1976: 186). She was their protectress, a symbol of resistant Mexican Catholicism (Young 2015: 27).

Cesar Chavez and the United Farm Workers Movement

Guadalupe was used as a symbol of resistance not only in Mexico but also in the United States by Mexican Americans. In the civil rights movements in the 1960s, farm labor activist Cesar Chavez gained popularity for his spiritual approach to the fight for farmworkers' rights. Chavez and his essential comrade Dolores Huerta were leaders of the National Farm Workers Association (NFWA) and later the United Farm Workers (UFW) movement. The NFWA was founded in 1962 in Delano, California, and in focusing on specifically Mexican-American farmworkers, they decided that "Our Lady of Guadalupe would be the patron saint, Spanish would be the language, and nonviolence would be the union's central virtue" (Garcia 2012). Chavez in particular carried this religious framework throughout his activism, even after merging with another mainly Filipino activist group in 1966 called the Agricultural Workers Organizing Committee to eventually form the UFW. He utilized several tactics that involved public displays of religion, such as the 1966 *peregrinación* (pilgrimage), which included marching to the California State Capitol while parading banners of Guadalupe, marking this march as not just a secular act of protest but an act of sacred resistance. Later, when Chavez fasted as an act of protest, he surrounded himself with Catholic paraphernalia, particularly with images of Guadalupe (Lloyd-Moffett 2008: 109). Chavez consistently drew on sacred rhetoric and imagery in his activism and throughout all of this he kept Guadalupe as his patron of choice to oversee the UFW's fight against abusive farm corporations (León 2015).

Immigrant Rights and the US Sanctuary Movement

Beyond farm worker rights, US Latinx populations have integrated the symbol of Guadalupe into the struggle for immigrant rights.

The 1980s Sanctuary Movement began as a religious effort to help Central American refugees who were being categorically denied asylum by the Reagan administration (Barba and Castillo-Ramos 2019). Father Luis Olivares, a social justice veteran also involved with the UFW, launched Los Angeles' most robust Sanctuary Movement effort (García 2018: 13). On December 12, 1985, the feast day of the Virgin of Guadalupe, he declared the famous "La Placita" Church (Our Lady Queen of the Angels Church) to be a sanctuary for Central American refugees. The declaration was themed around the Virgin of Guadalupe, with references of her made in the declaration itself and prolific usage of her image throughout the church (García 2018: 320). A poem included in the service program equated Central Americans with Juan Diego, implying that they should receive her favor, as both are oppressed yet virtuous people worthy of her divine, motherly protection (García 2018: 323–4).

In 2006, Elvira Arellano entered Sanctuary at Adalberto United Methodist Church in Chicago, effectively launching the New Sanctuary Movement, a new iteration of the Sanctuary Movement that fought to prevent the deportation of undocumented people, particularly those who were part of mixed citizenship-status families and who were established in the United States. Arellano, along with her son Saul, made public appearances alongside images of the Virgin Mary, specifically the Virgin of Guadalupe, which some argue was a strategic move to associate her with sacred motherhood (Pallares 2015: 51). In more recent years, Latinx immigrants have found community, belonging, and empowerment through Guadalupan devotion and consequently appeal to her when making claims for political and social rights (Gálvez 2009).

FIGURE 13.1 *A mural in Chicano Park in San Diego, California painted by artist Sal Barajas in 2018 and commissioned by the Border Angels. The Border Angels are a humanitarian nonprofit that is pro-migrant rights and participates in efforts such as leaving containers of water in the desert for migrants attempting to circumvent immigration checkpoints. The mural features the Virgin of Guadalupe in the center, holding a jug of water and a cross that reads "No Olvidados" ("Not Forgotten") in remembrance of migrants who perished attempting to cross.* Source: *Photo by Tatyana Castillo-Ramos.*

Conclusion

The Virgin of Guadalupe has been and continues to be a powerful symbol of resistance. Although her apparition has origins in the colonial era, Mexican and US Latinx political and social movements have strategically (re)claimed her as a unifying symbol of resistance. For these reasons, she continues to be among the most ubiquitous symbols of religious resistance in the Americas.

Further Reading

Brading, D. A. 2001. *Mexican Phoenix: Our Lady of Guadalupe: Image and Tradition across Five Centuries*. New York: Cambridge University Press.

León, L. D. 2015. *The Political Spirituality of Cesar Chavez: Crossing Religious Borders*. Oakland, CA: University of California Press.

Gálvez, A. 2009. *Guadalupe in New York: Devotion and the Struggle for Citizenship Rights among Mexican Immigrants*. New York: New York University Press.

Matovina, T. 2019. *Theologies of Guadalupe: From the Era of Conquest to Pope Francis*. New York: Oxford University Press.

References

Barba, L., and T. Castillo-Ramos 2019. "Sacred Resistance: The Sanctuary Movement from Reagan to Trump." *Perspectivas* (16): 11–36.
Brading, D. A. 2001. *Mexican Phoenix: Our Lady of Guadalupe: Image and Tradition across Five Centuries*. New York: Cambridge University Press.
Butler, M. 2004. *Popular Piety and Political Identity in Mexico's Cristero Rebellion Michoacán, 1927–29*. New York: Oxford University Press.
Gálvez, A. 2009. *Guadalupe in New York: Devotion and the Struggle for Citizenship Rights among Mexican Immigrants*. New York: New York University Press.
Garcia, R. A. 2012. "United Farm Workers of America." In *The Oxford Encyclopedia of American Social History*, edited by L. Dumenil and P. Boyer. New York: Oxford University Press.
García, M. T. 2018. *Father Luis Olivares, a Biography: Faith Politics and the Origins of the Sanctuary Movement in Los Angeles*. Chapel Hill, NC: University of North Carolina Press.
Matovina, T. 2005. *Guadalupe and Her Faithful: Latino Catholics in San Antonio, from Colonial Origins to the Present*. Baltimore, MD: Johns Hopkins University Press.
Matovina, T. 2019. *Theologies of Guadalupe: From the Era of Conquest to Pope Francis*. New York: Oxford University Press.
Meyer, J. 1976. *The Cristero Rebellion: The Mexican People between Church and State, 1926–1929*. New York: Cambridge University Press.
Meyer, M., and W. Sherman. 1995. *The Course of Mexican History*. New York: Oxford University Press.
León, L. D. 2015. *The Political Spirituality of Cesar Chavez: Crossing Religious Borders*. Oakland, CA: University of California Press.
Lloyd-Moffett, S. 2008. "Holy Activist, Secular Saint: Religion and the Social Activism of César Chávez." In *Mexican American Religions: Spirituality, Activism, and Culture*, edited by G. Espinosa and M. García. Durham, NC: Duke University Press.
Pallares, A. 2015. *Family Activism: Immigrant Struggles and the Politics of Noncitizenship*. New Brunswick, NJ: Rutgers University Press.
Young, J. 2015. *Mexican Exodus: Emigrants, Exiles, and Refugees of the Cristero War*. New York: Oxford University Press.

Glossary Terms

Mestiza/o: A person of mixed race. In colonial Latin America this term referred to people of mixed Spanish, Indigenous, and African descent.

Popular Catholicism: Also known as folk Catholicism describes everyday or ordinary practices of Catholics that fall beyond institutional approval and at times work within the institution.

14

La Santa Muerte—Saint Death

Francisco Peláez-Díaz

Introduction

The veneration of Saint Death is one of the fastest-growing religious phenomena in the first decades of the twenty-first century with an estimated 10 to 12 million followers of primarily Mexican and Central American origin (Chesnut 2017). Devotees of Saint Death are concentrated mostly in Mexico and the United States. Saint Death or *Santa Muerte* is a Mexican folk saint that personifies death and is considered to have powers of healing, love magic, protection, and revenge against enemies.

The Name and Visual Representation of *Santa Muerte*

The Spanish name *Santa Muerte* could be translated as Holy Death or Saint Death. If translated as Holy Death, it refers to the sacred quality of death, while the translation Saint Death refers to the personification of the death. The translation in this case become almost interchangeable because the common usage applies fluidly both meanings. The suffix "a" in the word *Santa* indicates that this is a female figure.

The visual representation of *Santa Muerte* strongly resembles that of the female Grim Reaper who is holding a scythe in one hand and a globe in the other. The attire of Saint Death varies greatly according to personal preference, occasion, and function attributed to it. Her attire usually includes a robe and a dress that could be that of a bride, queen, nun, or the widely venerated Virgin Mary.

Origin and Trajectory of Saint Death

The first specific reference to Saint Death known so far appeared in a 1797 document from the archives of the Inquisition. In this document, there is a description of how Saint Death was considered not only a miracle worker for the purpose of obtaining or keeping political power but also an entity capable of doing harm to other people upon request (Perdigón Castañeda 2008: 33–4). The Inquisition condemned the rituals involving *Santa Muerte* and destroyed the small chapel where this practice was taking place. As Andrew Chestnut has documented, Saint Death's next reference appeared 150 years later in the 1947 book *Treasury of Mexican Folkways*, written by Francis Toor (Toor 1947; Chesnut 2012: 23). Subsequent references made by other anthropologists occurred in 1958 and 1961 (Aguirre Beltrán 1958; Lewis 1961; Chesnut 2012: 33). The context in which Saint Death is mentioned in these works shows that the veneration of this saint was part of the religious experience of both people in urban and countryside environments, and, in any case, among people on the margins. In all these cases, Saint Death appears in her role as a love sorceress. In the 1990s, Saint Death made the headlines thanks to the capture of the dangerous criminal Daniel Arizmendi López, *El Mochaorejas* (the Ear Chopper), whose *modus operandi* consisted of kidnapping

FIGURE 14.1 *One of many public Santa Muerte shrines in Santa Ana Chapitiro, Pátzcuaro, Michoacán.* Source: *Alejandro Linares Garcia/Wikimedia Commons.*

people and requesting ransom by cutting off the ears of his victims and sending them as a message to the victims' relatives. When arrested, it was discovered that Arizmendi had an altar to Saint Death in his home (Chesnut 2012: 15–16). This was just the beginning of a series of other cases in which criminals, and particularly drug traffickers, were reported as devotees of Saint Death (Lomnitz-Adler 2005: 492–3). In these cases, a different role of Saint Death came to light, namely as a protector from dangers even when the devotee's actions were criminal or against the law. All these references indicate that the devotion to Saint Death was being practiced privately.

The public expressions of devotion to Saint Death as they are known today started in the Mexico City neighborhood of Tepito on October 31, 2001. Enriqueta Romero, known now as the godmother of these devotional public practices, was instrumental in transforming the private and out-of-sight veneration of Saint Death into a very public act of devotion (Fragoso Lugo 2007: 15; Reyes Ruiz 2010: 92, 96). Once the open and public devotion started, its expansion soon reached many of the major Mexican cities and towns and also, due to migratory flows, the United States. By 2007 there were already reports of public expressions of Saint Death devotion in New York, Houston, Los Angeles, and Chicago (Gray 2007). A palpable proof of Saint Death's devotion's expansion is the availability of paraphernalia in grocery stores in mid-size and small towns throughout the United States.

FIGURE 14.2 *Procession at the Santa Muerte Temple in the Mexico City neighborhood of Tepito.* Source: *Future Publishing/Getty Images.*

Some Features of the Public Devotion to Saint Death

This **lived religion** was born outside of official Catholicism, but it built a significant part of its worship and devotional practices on Roman Catholic elements. The devotion to Saint Death draws heavily from Catholic rituals. These include masses, **novenas**, rosaries, and offerings. A detailed description of symbols, along with instructions as to how to practice the devotion to Saint Death, including full prayers, has been collected in *La Sagrada Biblia de Nuestra Señora Santísima de la Muerte* (The Holy Bible of Our Lady Most Holy of Death) ("Sagrada Biblia de Nuestra Señora Santísima de la Muerte").

One of the distinct features of some of the prayers to Saint Death is the petition to cause harm to those who are perceived of as or considered enemies. The practice of including this kind of petition can also be found in Afro-Cuban **Santería** and witchcraft, both of which have been linked to the origins of the devotion to Saint Death (Chesnut 2012: 180).

The other important element in the veneration of Saint Death is the use of different colors in the dresses of the statues and in the votive candles. Each color has a meaning and has to be utilized according to the desired result. Gold represents economic power, success, and money. The natural bone color is believed to promote peace and harmony. The color red is associated with love, passion, and emotional stability. White represents purification and defense against negative energy, particularly in situations where there is envy among relatives. Blue is used to improve mental concentration and represents wisdom. Green is used to help people with legal problems and represents justice. Yellow is used for healing from diseases. Purple is also used to attract good health and reject any disease, natural or provoked. Black represents protection against black magic and hostile spirits associated with Santería, Palo Mayombe (parallel to the Afro-Cuban religion Santería), and Voodoo. Black is also used to cause harm to enemies or to scare away people who are of bad influence or troublemakers ("Sagrada Biblia de Nuestra Señora Santísima de la Muerte").

A Fluid and Adaptive Faith

The devotion to Saint Death emerged originally from segments of the Mexican population that faced increased levels of pressure to meet basic needs, as well as a context of violence, insecurity, and a great sense of uncertainty about the future.

The main reason that devotees provide for turning to Saint Death is the favors they have received from her and the hope and strength that come with this responsiveness. Rejection by the Catholic Church is not necessarily an obstacle for Saint Death's devotees who continue to consider themselves Catholics. In most cases, they continue sharing their loyalty between the two. Additionally, there is no known disciplinary action on the part of the Catholic Church against devotees of Saint Death. It is known that many

FIGURE 14.3 *Santa Muerte votive candles for sale at grocery stores in suburban Washington D.C.* Source: *T. Carter Ross/Wikimedia Commons.*

saints and other sacred figures such as the Virgin of Guadalupe have traditionally been considered as miracle workers. But apparently something changed that made the rise of the devotion to Saint Death one of the fastest and broadest in the first decade of the twenty-first century. There seems to be a combination of elements that have led to the expansion of this devotion. First of all, the cultural environment in Mexico related to the notion of death seems to play a role. This cultural environment embraces the idea of death in festive, playful, and friendly terms in songs, food, decorations, funerals, and holidays (Paz 1994: 47–64; Lomnitz-Adler). But more importantly, there was a dramatic change in the conditions of violence, job insecurity, and the deteriorating prospect of the future that occurred around the same time of the proliferation of the public devotion to Saint Death. The levels of violence and insecurity in Mexico reached the highest point between 2006 and 2012, when a war on drug cartels left over 100,000 people violently killed. This prevalent violence, combined with the effects of the economic policies adopted in the 1990s, put extraordinary pressure on large portions of the population. As a result, many people migrated to the United States, and many others were caught up in the drug trafficking business, which was fueled by the incessant demand in the United States and some significant changes in the configuration of the dominance of drug cartels in the Southern Hemisphere, particularly in Colombia in the 1990s ("Mexico's Drug Cartels" 2007). Many others simply fell into the dramatic reality of uncertainty and the constant search for ways to overcome it, oftentimes outside of the law. The difference that Saint Death represents in comparison with other saints and sacred figures is that she is not judgmental. Saint Death only demands loyalty. This explains, to some degree, the fact that many people whose activity is criminal or outside of what are considered predominant moral standards have found in Saint Death an advocate, an ally, and a refuge.

Further Reading

Bastante, Pamela, and Brenton Dickieson. 2013. "Nuestra Señora de Las Sombras: The Enigmatic Identity of Santa Muerte." *Journal of the Southwest* 55 (4): 435–71. https://doi.org/10.1353/jsw.2013.0010

Chesnut, R.A. 2012. *Devoted to Death: Santa Muerte, the Skeleton Saint*. New York: Oxford University Press.

Perdigón Castañeda, K. 2008. *La Santa Muerte, Protectora de Los Hombres*, 1st edn. México, D.F: Instituto Nacional de Antropología e Historia.

References

Aguirre Beltrán, G. 1958. *Cuijla, esbozo etnográfico de un pueblo negro*. México: Fondo de Cultura Económica.

Chesnut, R.A. 2012. *Devoted to Death: Santa Muerte, the Skeleton Saint*. New York: Oxford University Press.

Chesnut, R.A. 2017. "Santa Muerte: The Fastest Growing New Religious Movement in the Americas." Lecture, University of Portland, October 16, 2017. https://www.up.edu/garaventa/archives/lectures-and-readings/2017-2018-lectures-and-readings/andrew-chesnut-lecture.html. Accessed June 14, 2022.

Fragoso Lugo, P.O. 2007. "La muerte santificada: El culto a la Santa Muerte en la Ciudad de México." *Revista de El Colegio de San Luis*, Vetas, IX (26–27) (May 2007): 9–37. https://colsan.repositorioinstitucional.mx/jspui/bitstream/1013/1152/1/La%20muerte%20santificada.pdf. Accessed: 14 January 2015.

Gray, S. 2007. "Santa Muerte: The New God in Town." *Time*, October 16, 2007. http://content.time.com/time/nation/article/0,8599,1671984,00.html. Accessed December 18, 2014.

Lewis, O. 1961. *The Children of Sánchez: Autobiography of a Mexican Family*. New York: Random House.

Lomnitz-Adler, C. 2005. *Death and the Idea of Mexico*. Brooklyn, NY, Cambridge, MA: Zone Books.

"Mexico's Drug Cartels." *United States Congressional Research Service*, Report for Congress, October 16, 2007, CRS1–17. http://www.fas.org/sgp/crs/row/RL34215.pdf. Accessed January 5, 2015
Paz, O. 1994. "The Day of the Death." In *The Labyrinth of Solitude: The Other Mexico, Return to the Labyrinth of Solitude, Mexico and the United States, the Philanthropic Ogre*, Underlining edn. New York: Grove Press.
Perdigón Castañeda, K. 2008. *La Santa Muerte, Protectora de Los Hombres*, 1st edn. México, D.F: Instituto Nacional de Antropología e Historia.
Reyes Ruiz, C. 2010. *La Santa Muerte: Historia realidad y mito de la niña blanca, Retratos urbanos de la fe*. México, D.F.: Editorial Porrúa.
"Sagrada Biblia de Nuestra Señora Santísima de La Muerte."
Toor, F. 1947. *A Treasury of Mexican Folkways*. New York: Crown Publishers.

Glossary Terms

Lived religion religion as practiced and experienced by people in everyday life, not only as is practiced and defined in institutional settings.

Novenas a series of prayers recited during nine consecutive days, usually performed for special or difficult situations.

Santería Afro-Cuban religion that incorporates elements of the Yoruba religion (which is practiced by the Yoruba people in parts of the African countries of Nigeria, Togo, and Benin), Roman Catholicism, and Spiritism. It is used for purposes of healing, divination, and mediumship.

PART IV

Immigration and Transnationalism

15

Oaxacan Religious Transnationalism

Daniel Ramírez

Introduction

Santa Maria, California. By the two-hour mark, the funeral service has included most of the elements one would expect in a Pentecostal homecoming celebration. A eulogy describes labor migration from Oaxaca to Baja California to Santa Maria and, importantly, the deceased's conversion at the midpoint. The tearful testimonials are capped by a grateful granddaughter recounting her guardian's care since her arrival to the United States at age twelve (in the absence of her parents), and his determination—even while on dialysis treatment—that she excel in school and college. In his sermon the pastor folds in three songs to the five already rendered by the praise team; all but one of the eight hymns are original Spanish-language compositions. Finally, the officiating minister introduces the newly arrived "*banda mixteca*" (Mixtec band) from the borrowed temple's host congregation. The ten-member ensemble files onto the platform, carrying typical instruments of the "wind band" tradition of Oaxacan towns and villages: tuba, trombone, trumpets, baritone horns, and two drum sets, one of these a bass drum capped with cymbals. After the requisite condolences, a drummer taps out the requisite triple percussive introduction, and the *banda* launches into the funeral standard, "*Más Allá del Sol*" (Beyond the Sun). After eight decades, the weepy dirge about hope amidst tears and poverty is sung throughout the hemisphere in **Evangélico** and *Católico* (Catholic) funerals alike. The brass rendering adds an additional sonic layer. The tuba and baritone horns carry a syncopative load, while the trombone and single trumpet tend to the melodic task; all the while the remaining trumpeters and the bass drummer/

cymbalist await the final measure of each verse and chorus to wrap up with a full-throated harmonic and percussive explosion. The same treatment is accorded to three additional hymns: "*Vanidad de la Vida*" (Vanity of Life), "*Soy Peregrino*" (I Am a Pilgrim), and yet another universal favorite, "*Un Día a la Vez*" (One Day at a Time). The nostalgic repertoire may have been created in other places, but tonight it comes wrapped in distinctly Oaxacan musical frames. The final icing on the mourning cake is provided by a keyboard player offering choruses in **Mixteco**. After the benediction, the guests are invited to recess for the requisite repast: *pan dulce y chocolate* (sweet bread and chocolate).

This vignette, set in a farmworker community on the central California coast, shows the durability of homeland ties, the reworking of ancestral traditions, and the tensile strength of teleologies in distant sites of anomic labor. It captures many of the features of **transnational** immigrant life and culture today, much as do border-straddling Catholic devotions. The added layer (or depth) of Indigenous identity and experience in the case of "**Oaxacalifornia**," however, invites an interrogation of the presentism of much contemporary scholarship on the intensified challenges wrought by neoliberal economic arrangements and modernizing forces; these represent points of stress for ancestrally anchored communities in remote Indigenous zones of Oaxaca, one of Mexico's most topographically variegated states. This essay contests the notion of a tabula rasa, focuses on the Pentecostal story, and offers a contextualizing frame that allows for an appreciation of similar and different processes over the long course of Oaxacan history.

Oaxaca's demographic changes over the last half-century merit attention. So does the considerable upsurge in international migration that began in the decade of the 1970s, after the dismantling of the Bracero guestworker program and the creation of the Immigration and Nationality Act of 1965, and before the Immigration Reform and Control Act of 1986. The expanded migratory flow through irregular channels was intensified by the implementation of the North American Free Trade Agreement in 1994, a neoliberal arrangement that devastated traditional agriculture and uprooted millions of subsistence farmers in southern Mexico. During the same period, the state registered a remarkable and steady rise in the percentage of non-Catholic believers, especially Evangélicos, from 1.5 percent in 1970 to 4.4 percent in 1980, 7.3 percent in 1990, 10.1 percent in 2000, and 13.3 percent in 2020. Importantly, the latest figure contrasts with the national one of 9.1 percent, and is surpassed by even more impressive figures in other (also heavily Indigenous) southern states like Chiapas and Quintana Roo (INEGI 2000; INEGI 2010; INEGI 2020). In other words, *evangelicalismo* continues to realize significant inroads in Indigenous Mexico, at rates well above the national (mestizo) average. The most forceful Evangélico option is Pentecostalism. It is also the least missionary-directed. Its ubiquity in the labor diaspora can be explained partially by its presence in rural towns and indigenous-speaking villages with high rates of socio-

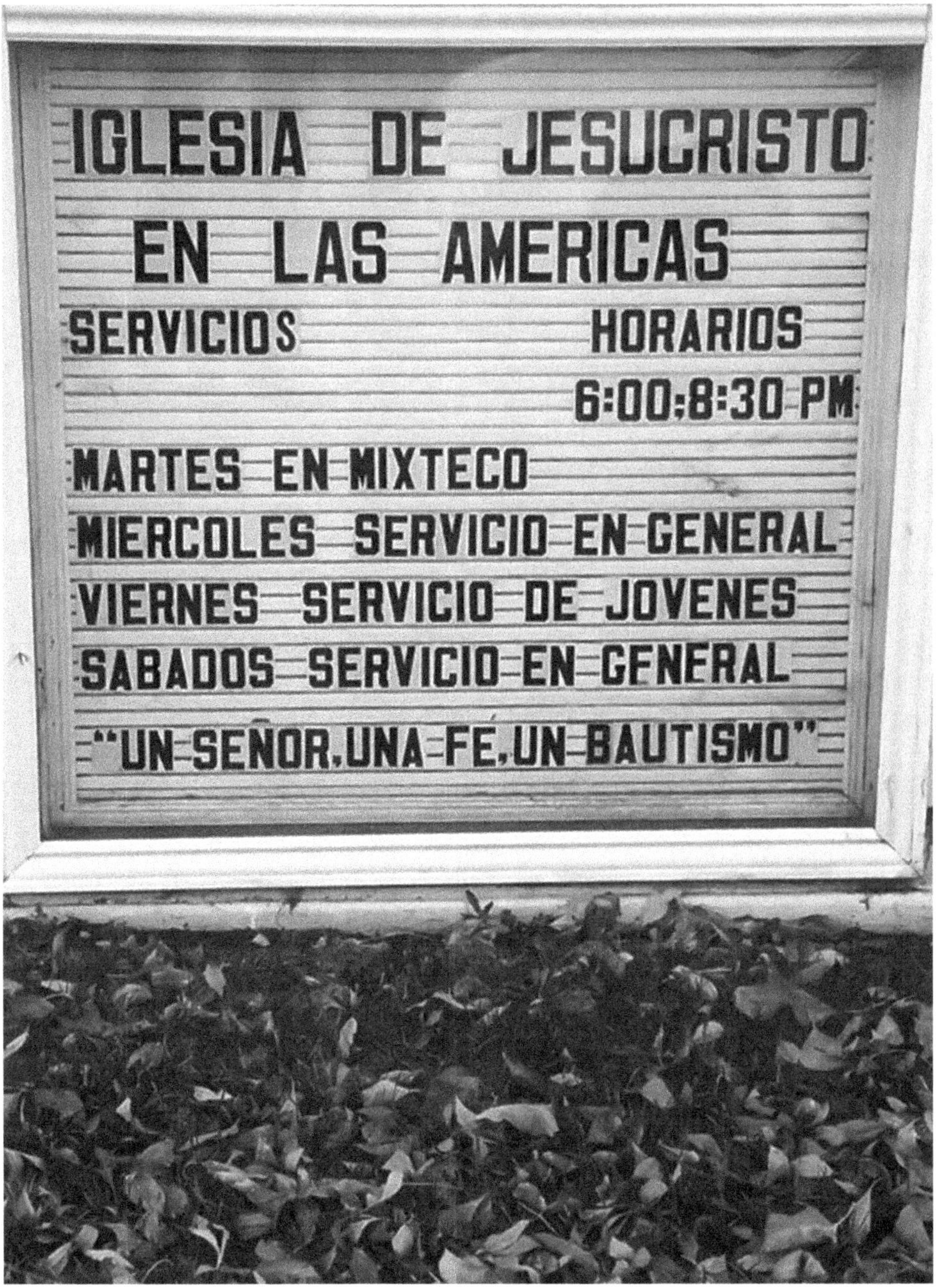

FIGURE 15.1 *US congregations ministering to Oaxacan migrant communities, like Iglesia de Jesús de las Américas in Santa Maria, California, often advertise services in Indigenous languages. Photo by Ana Alemán Barbosa.*

economic marginalization. Pentecostals migrate with their *paisanos* and *paisanas* (countrymen); and they also return, sometimes forcibly through deportation, but usually eager to proselytize.

Religious Transnationalism as Problem

The concern over religious cultural changes and modernizing stresses on ancestral ways and customs often centers on the exponential growth of Pentecostalism and other non-Catholic traditions. This is understandable. First, in their initial attempt at evangelization, the religious and civic agents of Spanish expansion had to settle for a fusion. The resulting hybrid cosmology of Indigenous communities forged traditional practices (*cargos* and *tequios*) that safeguard the reciprocity between communities and sacred beings. The careful custody of saints' feast days assures continued favor and abundant rain and harvests. The gradual ascension into prestigious leadership roles binds generations. Individual compliance with collectively assigned tasks ensures communal harmony and life. Alcohol lubricates ritual, social, and civic intercourse. Extravagant expenditures redistribute wealth and level out economic disparities. Since feast sponsors often must borrow to meet financial commitments, the fundraising thickens the web of reciprocity and expectations. The very welfare of the communities, then, depends on the maintenance of the structure. Remove one brick, and the structure weakens. Reciprocity—vertical between humans and sacred beings and horizontal between community members—provides the mortar holding the structure in place. Finally, the maintenance (and revival) of indigenous languages also has proven central to the survival of indigenous identities.

Modern globalization and heightened migration flows have introduced influences that can fracture the vulnerable ecosystem of indigenous culture. In the battle for the indigenous soul, sectarian proselytism is seen as a piece with Coca Cola's predatory marketing practices and American agribusiness's nefarious transgenic food research. Even tongues-talking, miracle-wielding, premodern, and migrating Pentecostals are implicated in the ripping of the sacred canopy (Berger 1967).

Religious Transnationalism in Historic Perspective

It is a mistake, though, to think of Oaxaca as a pristine region. Historically, it represented—along with Puebla, Mexico City, and Michoacán—an important node in colonial expansion and administration. Indeed, the Spanish merely built upon the prior dominance of the Aztec Empire over Mixteco and Zapoteco kingdoms. The Antequera Diocese was founded in 1535, and remained chiefly a Dominican province throughout the colonial period, with a smaller presence of Augustinian and Jesuit orders, and tied administratively to the **colonial Audiencia** in Mexico City and the Consejo de Indias (Council of the Indies) in Seville, Spain. Thus, rather than an isolated redoubt, Oaxaca emerged as a key stage for the imperial and colonial drama. Dominican friars undertook an impressive project of Indigenous language translation and ministry, especially for the two principal groups, Mixtecos and Zapotecos.

The Independence and Republican periods provided clear examples of Oaxacan protagonism on the national and international stage. After Guanajuato curate Miguel Hidalgo's capture and execution in Chihuahua in 1812, his fellow liberators continued the struggle in the south, with several key battles in Oaxaca led by fellow priests José María Morelos, Mariano Matamoros, Valerio Trujano, and Vicente Guerrero. Antequera bishop Antonio Bergosa y Jordán, a key mover in the inquisitorial court, provided stabilizing ecclesial leadership for royalist forces in Oaxaca and Mexico City, before returning to his native Spain. Perhaps no other Oaxacan figures would mold the nation as much as native sons Benito Juárez (of Zapoteco lineage) and Porfirio Díaz. The former's herculean fight to separate the church from its privileges, lands, and monopoly (he instituted civil birth and marriage registries and municipal cemeteries) earned him the hierarchy and Rome's enduring enmity. The latter effected a rapprochement with the church. His three-decade rule, ultimately despotic, allowed for Mexico's modernization and industrial development. The turn of the twentieth century saw the steady rise of anti-reelection agitation, led by, among others, anarchists brothers Ricardo and Enrique Flores Magón, Oaxacan natives. The initial thrust of the Partido Liberal Mexicano's ideological spear was a renewed anti-clericalism. The platform expanded to include labor rights and agrarian reform; several of the most articulate spokesperson were Oaxacan Methodist ministers, active outside of the state. Perennially harassed by the regime, the Flores Magón brothers took their crusade abroad. They continued to exert a catalytic ideological influence from such cities as San Antonio, St. Louis, Toronto, San Francisco, and Los Angeles; at the height of their influence their *Regeneración* periodical counted 20,000 subscribers and a broad network of allied newspapers that reprinted *Regeneración* articles. In the end, Francisco Madero's more moderate anti-reelection program won the day and toppled the Díaz regime in May 1911. But his subsequent assassination and the Revolution's implosion made for a protracted and bloody civil war up through 1917. The Constitution of 1917 enshrined labor and agrarian reform, and incurred the opposition of Catholic prelates for its harsh but delayed anti-clerical measures. As with the earlier Wars of Independence, Reform, and French Intervention, the national and transnational narratives would be incomplete without the inclusion of the expansive projection of Oaxacan protagonism.

The history of religious dissidence in Oaxaca leading up to contemporary Pentecostal expressions is similarly a case of the relationship between native protagonists and would-be external allies and sponsors. As early as 1828, British and Foreign Bible Society agent James Thompson scouted the state's linguistic diversity and began the Bible-seeding project. In the Benito Juárez era, restive liberal priests formed the proto-Anglican Iglesia de Jesús; a Oaxaca City chapter was convened by ex-priest José Peña in 1861. The Methodist Episcopal Church, South encountered the nucleus a decade later. By 1912 there were thirty-eight Methodist congregations in the Oaxaca district. By that time, several second-generation Oaxacan Methodists, as noted, had enlisted in the liberal cause against the reelection of Porfirio Díaz. Others remained active in church work (Bastian 1989). In 1934, native son Sixto Avila was elected as the second presiding bishop of the newly nationalized (1930) *Iglesia Metodista Mexicana*.

During that period, Cameron Townsend's Summer Institute of Linguistics (SIL) cast its eyes on polyglot Oaxaca. By 1950, missionary linguists were working and living among at least eight of the state's principal ethnic groups, rescuing and alphabetizing Indigenous languages for school curriculum under the auspices of the national Public Education Secretariat—the trade-off was the SIL's freedom to produce and distribute translations of New Testament scriptures. A decade later, critic Pedro Rivera (a Jesuit) counted thirty sites of SIL activity. In 1979 Mexican anthropologists, leveling conspiratorial charges, succeeded in pressuring the Education Secretariat to sever the nearly four-decade-long working relationship with the SIL (Colegio de Etnólogos y Antropólogos

FIGURE 15.2 *Benito Juárez, twenty-sixth president of Mexico (1858–1872), is revered in Protestant memory for decoupling church and state and enshrining religious liberty through his liberal Reform project.* Source: *Wikimedia Commons.*

1979). By then, the linguists had produced twenty-two Scripture translations; by the century's end, a total of fifty-six translations in all of Oaxaca's languages and their regional dialects represented a corpus of work that superseded the early Dominican one of the sixteenth and seventeenth centuries (Gutiérrez 2001). The terrain, thus, was well seeded for cultivation at the hands of whoever arrived—or returned—to take up the plow. When opportunities and challenges uprooted the faithful into the migratory stream, they had symbolic navigational tools for the journey. Together with parallel projects of hymn translation, the SIL was arguably the most consequential precursor to Pentecostal growth. The workers' reliance on Native informants and collaborators can be seen as akin to the method employed by the sixteenth-century Franciscan Bernardino de Sahagún for the creation of his monumental *La Historia General de las Cosas de Nueva España* (General History of the Things of New Spain) and *Psalmodía Cristiana* (Christian Psalmody), resources that scholars plumb today for a window into sixteenth-century Nahua religion and culture.

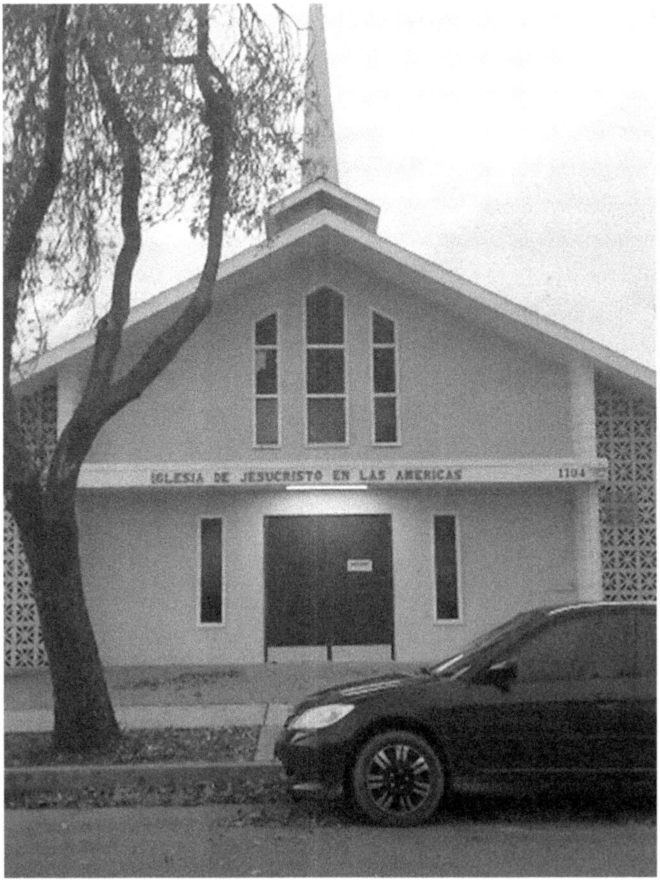

FIGURE 15.3 *La Iglesia de Jesucristo en las Americas exemplifies transnational religious exchanges between the United States and southern Mexico's indigenous populations. Photo by Ana Barbosa.*

Pentecostalism in Oaxacalifornia: A Case Study in Religion and Transnationalism

The neighboring congregations in Santa Maria belong to the **Oneness** variant of Pentecostalism, and exemplify the broader movement's ability to maximize transnational connections. There are at least five Apostolic denominations active in the homeland. The first to arrive was Mexico's *Iglesia Apostólica de la Fe en Cristo Jesús* (IAFCJ) at mid-century and in tandem with its expansion into northern Chiapas. In 2000, the IAFCJ reported twenty-seven congregations in Oaxaca. The Iglesia's US counterpart, the Apostolic Assembly of the Faith in Christ Jesus (AAFCJ), a historically Mexican American denomination, had established about eighteen congregations by that time (again, connected by return and circular labor migration). The geographical distribution overlapped only slightly. Even combined, both churches seem to have been matched in size by the Guadalajara-based *Luz del Mundo* church and surpassed in size and scope by the Iglesia de Jesucristo en las Américas, the denomination of the host congregation for the Santa Maria funeral (the bereaving family belonged to the neighboring Apostolic Assembly congregation). The result of a traumatic schism in the Apostolic Assembly (1970–2), the Iglesia de Jesús's breakaway congregations could be found at that time in San Diego County, Tijuana, Salinas and Watsonville on California's central coast, and other points of the new and unfolding Oaxacan labor diaspora—ready sites for proselytism. The repercussions in the homeland were immediately felt. From bases in Juxtlahuaca and Oaxaca City, preachers and laypersons—many of them returned migrants—fanned out to many points of the compass. Juxtlahuaca emerged as a spiritual center for the group owing to its role as a site of refuge from intolerance in the surrounding Mixteca region. Importantly, the group's expansion was entirely devoid of missionary strategy; rather, it was the convergence of unexpected developments: schism, labor opportunities, new and circular migration, and the catalytic impact of **religious remittances** and resources, many of these forged in earlier periods.

Religious Transnationalism and Flux in Oaxaca

The case of the Santa Maria Pentecostal Mixteco *banda* speaks directly to the anthropological alarm over religious dissident growth in the towns and villages of the Oaxacan homeland. Simply put, scholars fear that *Evangélico* musicians will desist in playing for saints' days, fiestas, and other events where, in the eyes of the *Evangélicos*, idolatry runs rampant and alcohol flows too freely. Increased conversion rates may sound like the death knell of rich, longstanding musical traditions such as Oaxaca's ubiquitous wind orchestras. Most probably, though, the Oaxacan countryside will not fall silent. New and re-worked sounds are mixing with older ones to create hybrid musics. After all, such was the case in the fusion of musics represented by the *banda* tradition itself, which built on instrumental elements brought to Oaxaca during the colonial period and which adapted similarly imported martial and other European musical forms during the nineteenth-century presidencies of Benito Juárez and Porfirio Díaz. The *banda* secular repertoire now includes John Phillips Sousa numbers and "New York, New York," along with the state's century-old de facto anthem, "*Dios Nunca Muere*" (God Never Dies). In the same manner, Pentecostals the length of Oaxacalifornia are busily refashioning a religious musical culture to call their own. What has remained constant in both cases is flux. That flux demands a similar nimbleness of mind and method in our critical appraisal.

Further Reading

Cruz-Manjarrez, A. 2013. *Zapotecs on the Move: Cultural, Social, and Political Processes in Transnational Perspective*. New Brunswick, NJ: Rutgers University Press.
Fox, J. and Rivera-Salgado G. 2004. *Indigenous Mexican Migrants in the United States*. La Jolla: Center for U.S.-Mexican Studies, University of California, San Diego.
O'Connor, M. 2016. *Mixtec Evangelicals: Globalization, Migration, and Religious Change in a Oaxacan Religious Group*. Boulder: University Press of Colorado.
Ramírez, D. 2015. *Migrating Faith: Pentecostalism in the United States and Mexico in the Twentieth Century*. Chapel Hill: University of North Carolina Press.
Stephen, L. 2007. *Transborder Lives: Indigenous Oaxacans in Mexico, California, and Oregon*. Durham: Duke University Press.

References

Bastian, J-P. 1989. *Los disidentes. Sociedades protestantes y revolución en México, 1872–1911*. México, D.F.: El Colegio de México.
Berger, P. 1967. *The Sacred Canopy: Elements of a Sociological Theory of Religion*. Garden City: Doubleday.
Colegio de Etnólogos y Antropólogos. 1979. *Dominación ideológica y ciencia social: el I.L.V. en México: Declaración José Carlos Mariátegui del Colegio de Etnólogos y Antropólogos, A.C.* México, D.F.: Nueva Lectura.
Gutiérrez, G. R. 2001. *La evangelización de Oaxaca. Una perspective evangélica*. Oaxaca: Arbol de Vida.
INEGI—Instituto Nacional de Estadística y Geografía, "Censo de Población y Vivienda," 2000.
INEGI—Instituto Nacional de Estadística y Geografía. 2010. "Censo de Población y Vivienda."
INEGI—Instituto Nacional de Estadística y Geografía. 2020. "Censo de Población y Vivienda."

Glossary Terms

Colonial Audiencia: The Audiencia, together with the Viceroy, administered the entire colony of New Spain.

Evangélico: The historic term does not equate to "Evangelical" in the strictly North American sense, but rather denotes Protestants in general in Spain and Latin America.

Mixteco: Comprises one of the two largest Indigenous groups in Oaxaca and neighboring states of Puebla and Guerrero. The 2020 census reported over a half-million Mixteco speakers in Mexico; nearly one-third of Oaxaca's population (over five years old) speaks an indigenous language. The 2000 census finding that nearly two out of every ten Pentecostals speak an Indigenous language—a rate three times the national average—underscores the growth of Pentecostalism in Indigenous Mexico.

Oaxacalifornia: The term was coined by binational Indigenous activists to reflect a transnational sphere of life and activism.

Oneness: This heterodox variant—also interchangeably referred to as "Apostolic"—insists on the unity of the Godhead, and rejects Trinitarian paradigms, including in baptismal practice. In Mexico and among Mexican Americans, it is estimated to comprise about one-half of Pentecostal groups.

Religious Remittances: Symbolic goods sent or brought home by migrants to prompt or maintain their relatives and friends' conversion and new religious identity.

Transnational: A reference to communities tied by life, affect, and action to homelands and sites of migration and settlement.

16

Brazilian Migrational Christianity in North America

João B. Chaves

Introduction

Brazilian religions—and the religions of Brazilians—are peculiarly **transnational** commodities. From the growing appeal of Ayahuasca retreat centers across the globe, to the international practice of Santo Daime, and the success attained by the now-infamous Brazilian healer John of God, the diasporic spread of Brazilian religions both transcends and complexifies Brazil's role in the global dissemination of its most popular religion, Christianity (Vásquez and Rocha 2013). It is the multilayered history of Brazil that has helped shape the country's diverse religious traditions that colonial powers, various waves of immigration, and the slave trade introduced into the country. The Christian and other of religious traditions that joined the diversified indigenous cultures in Brazil included those that Portuguese colonists and transnational migrant laborers brought, the latter mostly from Germany, Italy, Spain, Japan, and the Middle East (Engler and Schmidt 2016). As the destination of the largest number of enslaved Africans, and the last nation to abolish slavery, Brazil has the second largest Black population in the world (Gomes 2020). The Afro-Brazilian religions that developed and adapted partially from the country's violent history of anti-Black racism can now be found in places like Lisbon, Montreal, Tokyo, and New York City (Saraiva 2013; Meintel and Hernandez 2013; Arakaki 2013).

This diversity of Brazilian **diasporic religions** notwithstanding the country's Christianity, in its different versions, remains its predominant commodity in the global religious market. Globally, Brazil is the country with the largest number of Roman

Catholics and the largest number of Pentecostals, and Brazilians' global dissemination of expressions of Christianity continues to grow. The United States, by far the most common destination for Brazilian immigrants, is a central part of this story. The complex historical relationship between Brazilian and US religious networks is an important aspect of the insertion of Brazilian Christianities in the United States. Missionary initiatives, geopolitical dynamics, and migratory patterns have all been important foundations for the formation of Brazilian enclaves in North America.

Early Roots of Brazil-US Religious Networks

Though the development of Brazil-US religious networks has multifaceted beginnings, all those beginnings are deeply connected to migration dynamics. Migrants from the United States had a central place in the development of Protestantism in Brazil (Mendonça 1996). Among different migrant groups White Americans from the US South who went to Brazil after the American Civil War, played a particularly key role in Brazilian Protestantism. They also helped establish transnational connections whose endurance continued to inform the complex motions of transnational Christianity in the Americas. The Brazil-US connections that were established in Brazil certainly transcended the groups of disgruntled Confederates that migrated to Brazil partially because of Brazil's longstanding commitment to slavery. Migrants and missionaries from across the United States joined forces with Brazilians in several distinct enterprises. For example, American Anglicans founded the *Igreja Episcopal Anglicana do Brasil*, and Presbyterians from the United States started Presbyterian churches in the country before the end of the Civil War. The Southern Baptist Convention also sent missionaries to Brazil before Confederate exiles arrived (Silva 2011). Yet the role of enclaves of former Confederates in Brazil is nonetheless a central—and sometimes overlooked—element in the genealogy of Brazil-US religious networks and, consequently, in the development of important streams of "Brazilian Migrational Christianity" in the United States (Rosa 2021).

When the American Civil War ended in 1865, Southerners migrated in large numbers to Brazil for several reasons, many of which connected to dispositions that, in retrospect, can be interpreted as an alignment of different White supremacist, Christian imaginations present in the two countries. On the US side, former Confederates who desired to escape the conflicting traumas of the Southern loss imagined the reconstruction of the antebellum South in Brazil because of Brazil's slaveholding status (Simmons 1982; Silva 2015). Simultaneously, the Brazilian Empire encouraged immigration from the United States and Europe partly out of a conviction that White immigrants would strengthen the Brazilian race through miscegenation, infusing what Brazilian officials perceived as the Whites' stronger

FIGURE 16.1 *Even in more modern times, Confederate flags decorate graves in Santa Bárbara d'Oeste, Brazil.* Source: *Solange_Z/Getty Images.*

blood into the darker local population. Miscegenation was commonly practiced in slaveholding Brazil, to the dismay of many White immigrants from the US South. Southerners who desired to escape the racial fluidity of slaveholding Brazil therefore formed Confederate colonies. These colonies became the hub of several churches from different denominations as well as an important center for missionary activity (Harter 2006; Goldman 1972; Horne 2007). Among Christian Confederates, Southern Presbyterians, Methodists, and Baptists were prominent, with Baptists becoming the most successful among these in terms of both numerical growth and the development of Brazil-US religious networks (Barbosa 2008; Chaves 2021). For the purposes of this assessment, I will mostly follow the Baptist thread of Brazil-US religious networks to show how such networks were introduced, developed, and maintained, bearing in mind that the general dispositions of Baptist transnational networks were broadly shared. Other denominations' narratives of Brazilian Migrational Christianity (BMC) in the United States and other forms of nondenominational Christianity followed similar contours. The Baptist thread of this generally broader story takes us back to the missionary enterprises of the Southern Baptist Convention (SBC) in the late 1800s.

FIGURE 16.2 *A church affiliated with the Brazilian Baptist Convention in Rio Grande, Brazil.* Source: *Eugenio Hansen, OFS/Wikimedia Commons.*

The Baptist Thread of Brazilian Migrational Christianity in the United States

Although Southern Baptists already in the early years of the denomination considered Brazil a suitable mission field, Southern Baptist missionaries consistently began arriving in Brazil 1881 onward (Chaves 2022). Eventually, missionaries distanced themselves from the general dispositions of traditional Confederate exiles, who did not show a concern for evangelizing locals. In 1882, SBC missionaries began forming churches with the objective of converting Brazilians to the Baptist faith. Unsurprisingly, Baptists in Brazil not only proliferated but also organized according to the Southern Baptist model. With the indispensable help of local leaders, missionaries first organized churches, then regional and state conventions, and finally, by 1907, a national convention. Furthermore, missionaries established theological seminaries and denominational publications, controlling these and other central denominational institutions for most of the history of Baptists in Brazil (Chaves 2022).

At the same time that immigrants and missionaries from the United States were furthering their agendas in Brazil, Brazilians were also arriving in the United States as a result of missionary efforts and connections. Two reasons for the arrival in the United States of individuals who were introduced to Protestant Christianity by immigrants and missionaries in Brazil stand out: first, the missionaries' perceived need to send Brazilian converts to the United States for theological and ministerial training; and second, the desire of US denominations to use Brazilians in their efforts to convert and minister to both European immigrants and Spanish-speaking populations in the United States. The Baptist case is once again illustrative of broader dynamics in this regard, as other denominations, particularly Methodists and Presbyterians, engaged in similar enterprises.

The story of the Italian-born former Roman Catholic priest Giuseppe Piani, for example, shows how, at times, these aforementioned reasons that undergirded the arrival in the United States of religious workers once rooted in Brazil could happen simultaneously. Piani converted to the Baptist faith in Brazil, and Southern Baptist missionaries of the early 1900s saw in him not only the symbolic value of having a former Catholic priest among their ranks, but also the symbolic value of having a well-educated individual who could help them advance their religious agendas. Missionaries helped Piani attend William Jewell College in Liberty, Missouri, and later the Southern Baptist Theological Seminary in Louisville, Kentucky. Piani, who later changed his name to Joseph Plainfield, eventually joined the SBC's Home Mission Board. As a highly educated, multilingual convert from Catholicism, Piani became an influential voice in Southern Baptist life in the United States. Piani's work on the Home Mission Board focused on the SBC's efforts to convert/Americanize European—particularly Italian—immigrants to the United States (Plainfield 1938; Pruitt 2021; Chaves 2021).

Among Brazilian intellectuals whose history is grafted into that of US missionaries in Brazil, Gilberto Freyre's case stands out. Freyre's father taught at the missionary-controlled North Brazil Baptist Theological Seminary in Recife, and his Baptist connections landed him a scholarship at Baylor University in 1918 (Chaves 2020). After attending Baylor, Freyre studied anthropology at Columbia University and became one of Brazil's leading intellectuals. He left the Baptist ranks while studying at Baylor because of his negative impression of how Southern Baptists treated African Americans, but his Baptist affiliation facilitated his presence in the United States. In short, before Brazilians began migrating in large numbers to the United States in the 1980s and 1990s, forms of Brazilian Migrational Christianity in the United States already existed, although most examples of this earlier form of migrant Christianity did not involve influential intellectuals such as Freyre. Rather, such examples involved ministers whose names have, unlike Freyre's, mostly been forgotten both in the United States and in Brazil.

FIGURE 16.3 *Brazilian intellectual Gilberto Freyre arrived at Baylor University from Brazil in 1918*. Source: *Arquivo Nacional/Wikimedia Commons.*

Brazil-US Religious Networks before the 1980s

Under missionary influence and support, many Brazilians came to the United States specifically to attend seminaries; some subsequently stayed to work for denominational institutions and local churches as music ministers, youth pastors, and even senior pastors. Before the first large waves of Brazilian migrants arrived in the 1980s and 1990s, the Brazilian Baptist presence in the United States took a variety of forms. Many of the stories of Brazilian religious workers in the United States were recorded in denominational periodicals. In the case of Baptists, the periodical *Jornal Batista*—the flagship denominational publication—was the main vehicle through which transnational religious workers were memorialized (Azevedo 1983; Chaves 2020). A few examples of Brazilian religious workers who had careers in the United States before the first waves of Brazilian migrants arrived will illustrate earlier forms of Brazilian insertions into US religious life.

Évio Oliveira, for instance, had been a music minister in the southern US South since 1951; in 1968, while serving as music minister of Eastside Baptist Church in Marietta, Georgia, he released an album entitled *He Leadeth Me*. Pastor Valdeci Alves da Silva also ministered in the United States, but unlike Oliveira, he served as lead pastor in Mexican churches in the Corpus Christi area between 1967 and 1971, when, upon graduating from Corpus Christi University, he planned to attend Southwestern Baptist Theological Seminary for his master's degree. In the 1960s, Brazilian minister Dylton Francioni pastored the Spanish-speaking Misión Bautista in Itasca, Texas, while pursuing his master's degree at Southwestern Seminary. He then moved to New Orleans to pursue a doctorate at New Orleans Baptist Theological Seminary. While in New Orleans, Francioni founded the Spanish-speaking Iglesia Bautista Latino Americana, which he pastored until 1972. In 1974, he was called to pastor the Portuguese Evangelistic Baptist Church in Fall River, Massachusetts. When he visited the church, he preached in Portuguese and English, but he ultimately declined the invitation to pastor the community. Instead, he pastored two English-speaking churches in Louisiana—New Hope Baptist Church in Folsom and First Baptist Church in Abbeville. When Francioni returned to Brazil to pastor Igreja Batista Dois de Julho in 1980, he had accumulated a number of honorary titles: honorary citizen of New Orleans, honorary citizen of New Iberia, and honorary colonel of the state of Louisiana (Chaves 2021). Brazilian Migrational Christianity was very often a multilingual, cross-cultural enterprise and one appreciated by many in the United States.

Brazilian Baptist pastors, at times, toured the United States, preaching in churches and conducting evangelistic crusades. In 1969, Ben Pitrowsky reported various evangelistic efforts by seven Brazilian Baptist pastors. The *Jornal Batista* published eight reports authored by Pitrowsky, who understood their preaching events in the United States as returning the favor of evangelism to the Southern Baptists who had done missions work in Brazil. He wrote that the seven Brazilian Baptist preachers "entered the United States to preach the same Gospel that, around eighty years ago, was announced to us for the first time by a North American." Nilson Fanini, a famous Brazilian denominational leader, was mentioned in a number of reports in the *Jornal Batista* that told stories to the Brazilian Baptist audience of his experiences in the United States. In one of these reports, correspondent Daniel Paixão, then a doctoral student at Southwestern Seminary, wrote of an event at which Fanini was the keynote speaker, during which seminary president Robert Naylor proclaimed that Brazil was the new Antioch, the place from where missionaries were going out to evangelize the world. At the same time, Fanini was involved in helping form and develop initiatives that would open room for later forms of Christian Nationalism in both Brazil and the United States. Fanini became a president of the Baptist World Alliance and a transnational leader whom the Southern Baptist Convention admired; yet he also nurtured close relationships with the military dictatorship in Brazil, as did many other denominational leaders (Cowan 2021).

Nilson Dimárzio, who authored a number of reports on Brazilian pastors in the United States published in the *Jornal Batista*, pastored a church in Port Lavaca, Texas. Dimárzio mentioned the presence of Dr. Ivan Pitzer de Souza, a pastor and professional counselor who had a counseling practice in Mobile, Alabama, and often preached to sailors in town. Souza was far from the only example of Brazilian Baptists performing functions outside traditional church ministry in the United States. The couple Denise and Olavo Feijó, for instance, worked in educational institutions. They arrived in Texas in 1961, and Denise worked as a librarian at Southwestern Seminary while Olavo worked on his doctorate in education. He later taught at Texas Wesleyan College from 1964 to 1966, when he was hired by Weatherford College to teach psychology and philosophy. The *Jornal Batista* also mentioned pastor Amélio Giannetta, whom East Texas Baptist College in Marshall, Texas hired in 1978 to teach evangelism and missions.

That the success of Brazilian pastors in the United States as students, itinerant evangelists, senior ministers, music ministers, and college teachers was portrayed in the *Jornal Batista* certainly had an effect on the imagination of Brazilian Baptists who were considering doing missionary work in the land of the Southern Baptists. The examples of ministers such as Évio Oliveira, Dylton Francioni, Nilson Dimárzio, and others emboldened Brazilian Baptists' sense of potential in regard to their performance in the United States. In addition, reports of the significant Portuguese immigrant communities became a constant feature of the *Jornal Batista* after the late 1960s. Beyond the mention of Portuguese in the reports of pastors such as Francioni, and Dimárzio, other articles highlighted the presence of Portuguese immigrants in general and in the East Coast and California regions in particular. Before the1980s, however, the success of Brazilian denominational workers in the United States was particularly evident in SBC ministries focused on Anglo-American and Hispanic-American (non-Brazilian, Spanish-speaking) parishioners. Brazilian mass migration to the United States in the 1980s changed all that.

Brazil-US Religious Networks after the 1980s

According to the US Census and the American Community Survey, there were 80,485 Brazilian immigrants living in the United States in 1990, most of them on the East Coast. This number grew to 212,428 by 2000 and to 359,149 by 2009, the peak year of Brazilian immigration to the United States (Castro and Castro 2017). These estimates, however, are highly contested. The number of undocumented Brazilian immigrants in the United States makes it difficult to provide an official count, and researchers sometimes significantly underestimate the presence of Brazilian immigrants. The Inter-American Development Bank and the Brazilian Ministry of Foreign Relations estimate that there are between 800,000 and 1.4 million Brazilians in the United States. In 2014, the Ministry of Foreign Relations declared the states of Florida, Massachusetts, New York, New Jersey, and California as having the largest concentration of Brazilian immigrants; more than 60 percent of Brazilian immigrants live in these states (Castro and Castro 2017). In addition to the complications involved in these estimates, however, one must not lose sight of the fact that Brazilian immigrants also return to their home country in largely unknown numbers. That they do not account for returning immigrants complicates estimates both of the number of Brazilian immigrants in the United States and of Brazilian Baptists in the country even though returning immigrants are an indispensable part of the religious networks and interactions they energize (Chaves 2021).

FIGURE 16.4 *Just outside of Boston, the First Brazilian Baptist Church in this photograph shares a building with the Korean congregation All Nations Mission Church.* Source: *Ed Johnston/Wikimedia Commons.*

FIGURE 16.5 *First Brazilian Baptist Church of Greater Boston.* Source: *Photo by João B. Chaves.*

The most important aspect of wider Brazilian immigration for Brazilian Baptists is that the influx of Brazilian immigrants into the United States resulted in the formation and development of US-based immigrant churches by and for Brazilians, which came to characterize the history of the group (Margolis 2009). The history of Brazilian Baptist churches in the United States, however, did not start with a focus on forming churches for Brazilian immigrants. As in the case of other groups, Brazilian Baptist presence in the United States began with the Brazilian Baptist Convention's (BBC) traditional "sending" of Brazilian missionaries to reach the Iberian Portuguese populations on the East Coast and in California (Chaves 2021). The influx of Brazilian immigrants in the 1980s and 1990s, however, shifted the way in which Brazilian immigrant churches formed, as churches were established via diversified means and without formal denominational oversight. In this setting, the religious entrepreneurial spirit of Brazilian religious workers in the United States mostly replaced what was traditionally understood as the responsibility and monopoly of denominational bodies, such as missionary agencies and state and national conventions. Instead of traditional denominationalism, it was Brazilian ethnic solidarity that primarily informed the institutional imagination of these immigrant churches, even when such solidarity was practiced from within the resources and language provided by the traditional denominations. Such ethnic denominationalism shaped the self-understanding of leaders and members who named their religious initiatives "Baptist"—or "Methodist," "Presbyterian," "Pentecostal," etc. How immigrant churches developed in the United States also blurred the long contested and sharply delineated categories of "missionary" and "migrant" (Hanciles 2021).

Generally speaking, the ways in which Brazilian Baptist churches in the United States were launched take one of five forms: (1) at the initiative of the missionary agency of the Brazilian Baptist denomination in partnership with a US-based church; (2) spontaneously, that is, a group is formed without formal leadership, and only after it is well established does it hire a pastor and become Baptist; (3) a group of Brazilians become members of a predominantly Anglo-American, African American, or Hispanic American church, and the host church helps structure the Brazilian congregation; (4) as a mission or congregation of another Brazilian Baptist church; and (5) as a division of another immigrant church. The history of Brazilian Baptists in the United States, therefore, is neither bounded by an easily identifiable genealogy nor limited by a uniform affiliation to institutional structures. It is, however, a function of broader migration dynamics that, beginning in the 1980s, resulted in great numbers of Brazilian people moving to the United States (Rodrigues 2016). When Brazilian Baptist immigrant churches were organized, they by and large became part of the denominational structure of the Southern Baptist Convention through the communities' affiliation to SBC-related associations and state conventions. A significant number of these churches, however, were not particularly satisfied with this common Baptist arrangement. The particular migration patterns and experiences that informed their daily struggles opened space for adaptations that, in turn, encouraged forms of practicing Christianity centered around immigrant living. In other words, migration pushes Christian forms and functions toward new arrangements and imaginations. Brazilian Migrational Christianity provides a particular example of how this general insight can take on particular shapes.

Characteristics of Brazilian Migrational Christianity: A Conclusion

The aspects of immigrant living that affected the corporate dynamics of Brazilian Christians in the United States varied, but for Brazilian immigrant churches, the major characteristics are clear: these Baptists have a particular way of practicing their immigrant religion, but some of these characteristics overlap with other immigrant churches (Madrazo 2021; Lin 2020; Calvillo 2020). Although Baptists in Brazil are historically akin to the SBC institutionally and ideologically, and although Brazilian Baptist immigrant churches become affiliated with the SBC while in the United States, the struggles of immigrant living pushes these communities toward developing ways in which they can minister effectively to their constituencies. The pastoral and theological implications of immigrant living distance these immigrant churches from the general *modus operandi* of their transnational denominational bodies and ideologies. In the particular context of Brazilian Baptist immigrant churches in the United States, this meant: (1) developing an ethnic denominationalism that functioned as the *de facto* center for denominational practice, while the SBC remained the official denominational connection for most of these immigrant churches; (2) fostering a pastoral approach to immigration policy that sides with undocumented parishioners, and presumably is at odds with the SBC; (3) providing an open space for the ordination of women, which is, again, contrary to the stance of the official denomination with which these churches are affiliated; and (4) encouraging or accepting Pentecostal practices and beliefs in unprecedented ways, particularly when these churches are compared to Baptist churches in Brazil and in the United States.

Such stances are, of course, directly influenced by the way in which migration dynamics affect Brazilian parishioners and faith communities. Ethnic denominationalism, for example, developed as a response to the sense of unbelonging often experienced by Latin American immigrants to the United States. It was also an attempt to deal with the perceived need to fulfill deeper denominational connections in light of the perceived inadequacies of the SBC to meet the expectations of immigrant faith communities fully. More broadly, ethnic denominationalism illustrates the fact that immigrant faith communities often have ambiguous relationships with US-based host communities and denominations.

Another notable contextual challenge illustrated in these communities is the role that immigrant churches play in facilitating immigrant adaptation to the United States. Unlike churches whose membership is composed primarily of Anglo-Americans, Brazilian Baptist churches in the United States occupy a central place in the lives of immigrants who see in them a mechanism of religious, social, and legal relief directly connected to their status as immigrants—especially for undocumented parishioners.

Besides that, the political sensibilities of Brazilian immigrant church leaders, which are heavily informed by their roles pastoring undocumented immigrants as well as by their churches' dependence on the financial contributions of undocumented parishioners and their voluntary work, are important in at least two major interconnected ways. First, the distancing of several Brazilian immigrant church leaders from traditional evangelical support of the Republican Party reveals a rift between Southern Baptist ideological commitments and the well-being of many immigrant churches' constituents. Second, the ambiguity of immigrant evangelicals regarding their relationship to the traditional political leanings of US evangelicals problematizes a simplistic characterization of these communities. On one hand, these immigrant churches often have official relationships with religious bodies that are undeniably evangelical (such as the SBC); on the other hand, the churches, upon closer inspection, do not fit the same theopolitical mold of the evangelical world to which they may ambiguously and uncomfortably belong. My claim is that, in the case of Brazilian Protestant immigrants to the United States, and presumably other immigrant religious networks, their difference from US evangelicalism is often not directly imported; rather, such difference is generated from within migrant dynamics experienced in the United States. It is oftentimes the journey of immigrant churches in the United States that distances them from the theopolitical leanings of US evangelicalism that have been effectively introduced, strengthened, and maintained in the evangelical churches of the Global South—particularly Brazil.

When it comes to **pentecostalization**, Brazilian Baptist immigrant leaders have responded to the influx of members from Pentecostal backgrounds in a variety of ways. In general, however, Brazilian Baptist immigrant churches are more open to Pentecostal beliefs and practices than are churches of the Brazilian Baptist Convention (BBC). The militant anti-Pentecostalism found in significant sectors of the BBC (although increasingly diminishing owing to the growing influence of Pentecostalism in Brazil) is virtually non-existent in these immigrant Baptist churches. Primarily disembodied theological reflections on the part of Baptist immigrant pastors do not account for this difference. Rather, it is a direct result of migration dynamics. As immigrants from different denominational backgrounds have flocked to Brazilian immigrant churches primarily out of a sense of ethnic solidarity, churches have had to develop ways to avoid alienating their diverse membership, and, in the process, many communities have welcomed practices and beliefs associated with Pentecostalism. Practices such as speaking in tongues, prophesying, healing prayers, and others that would not be officially accepted by either the BBC or the SBC are commonplace in many Brazilian Baptist immigrant churches. Similarly, the broader acceptance of the ordination of women also sets Brazilian Baptist immigrants apart from the denominations with which they are associated. Although the BBC accepts the ordination of women—in that it recognizes the authority of state denominational bodies to decide on the confirmation of their women pastors—immigrant Baptist pastors agree that women's leadership is more prominent in their churches than in Baptist churches in Brazil. The example of Brazilian Migrational Christianity, despite its particularities, also offers general insights into immigrant faith communities of the Latinx diaspora, specifically that such churches are sites in which traditional theological notions are often disrupted.

Immigrant churches open space for incipient theologies that are born out of the need for new theological maps, which emerge when particular groups of people deem old maps to be inadequate. Yet these pastoral and theological anxieties that spring from within the context of the Latinx diaspora are not articulated as academic, univocal, or even consistent formal theologies. The truth is that these immigrants, much like academic theologians, are still trying to figure out how to understand God and practice their religion in a complex, always-changing world. Yet unlike the world of academics, who may feel safe within the confines of their departments and careers, the on-the-ground immigrant theologians of the Latinx diaspora are pastors and parishioners for whom theological systems have never been sufficient. Brazilian Migrational Christianity in the United States certainly shows the perennial precariousness of theological systems when they are seen from below. These churches offer a strong case study for how the struggles of oppressed peoples in the US context reveal the cracks that continue to characterize traditional theologies and denominations—which continue to decline among white populations in the United States and Europe.

Further Reading

Calvillo, J. 2020. *The Saints of Santa Ana: Faith and Ethnicity in a Mexican Majority City.* New York: Oxford University Press.

Chaves, J. B. 2021. *Migrational Religion: Context and Creativity in the Latinx Diaspora.* Waco, TX: Baylor University Press.

Chaves, J. B. 2022. *The Global Mission of the Jim Crow South: Southern Baptist Missionaries and the Shaping of Latin American Evangelicalism.* Macon, GA: Mercer University Press.

Lin, T. 2020. *Prosperity Gospel: Latinos and Their American Dream.* Chapel Hill: University of North Carolina Press.

Madrazo, T. 2021. *Predicadores: Hispanic Preaching and Immigrant Identity.* Waco: Baylor University Press.

References

Arakaki, U. 2013. "Japanese Brazilians among Pretos-Velhos, Caboclos, Buddhist Monks, and Samurais: An Ethnographic Study of Umbanda in Japan." In *The Diaspora of Brazilian Religions*, edited by C. Rocha and M. Vásquez, 249–70. Leiden: Brill.

Azevedo, I. B. 1983. *A Palavra Marcada: Teologia Política Dos Batistas Segundo O Jornal Batista.* Recife: Seminário Teológico Batista do Norte do Brasil.

Barbosa, J. C. 2008. *Slavery and Protestant Missions in Imperial Brazil: "The Black Does Not Enter the Church, He Peeks in from Outside."* Lanham, MD: University Press of America.

Calvillo, J. 2020. *The Saints of Santa Ana: Faith and Ethnicity in a Mexican Majority City.* New York: Oxford University Press.

Castro, A. E., and A. L. Castro. 2017. *Brasileiros nos Estados Unidos: Meio Século (Re) Fazendo a América (1960–2010).* Brasília: Fundação Alexandre de Gusmão.

Chaves, J. B. 2021. *Migrational Religion: Context and Creativity in the Latinx Diaspora.* Waco, TX: Baylor University Press.

Chaves, J. B. 2020. *O Racismo na História Batista Brasileira: Uma Memória Inconveniente do Legado Missionário*. Brasília: Novos Diálogos.
Chaves, J. B. 2022. *The Global Mission of the Jim Crow South: Southern Baptist Missionaries and the Shaping of Latin American Evangelicalism*. Macon, GA: Mercer University Press.
Cowan, B. A. 2021. *Moral Majorities across the Americas: Brazil, the United States, and the Creation of the Religious Right*. Chapel Hill: University of North Carolina Press.
Engler, S., and B. E. Schmidt. 2016. "Introduction." In *Handbook of Contemporary Religions in Brazil*, edited by B. E. Schmidt and S. Engler, 1–29. Leiden: Brill.
Goldman, F. 1972. *Os Pioneiros Americanos no Brasil: Educadores, Sacerdotes, Covos e Reis*. São Paulo: Pioneira.
Gomes, L. 2020. *Escravidão: Volume 1*. Rio de Janeiro: Globo Livros.
Hanciles, J. 2021. *Migration and the Making of Global Christianity*. Grand Rapids, MI: Eerdmans.
Harter, E. 2006. *The Lost Colony of the Confederacy*. College Station: Texas A&M University Press.
Horne, G. 2007. *The Deepest South: The United States, Brazil, and the African Slave Trade*. New York: New York University Press.
Lin, T. 2020. *Prosperity Gospel: Latinos and Their American Dream*. Chapel Hill: University of North Carolina Press.
Madrazo, T. 2021. *Predicadores: Hispanic Preaching and Immigrant Identity*. Waco: Baylor University Press.
Margolis, M. 2009. *An Invisible Minority: Brazilians in New York City*. Gainesville: University Press of Florida.
Meintel, D., and A. Hernandez. 2013. "Transnational Authenticity: An Umbanda Temple in Montreal." In *The Diaspora of Brazilian Religions*, edited by C. Rocha and M. Vásquez, 222–48. Leiden: Brill.
Mendonça, A. G. 1996. "A History of Protestantism in Brazil: An Interpretive Essay." *International Review of Mission* LXXXV 338: 367–87.
Plainfield, J. F. 1938. *The Stranger within Our Gates*. Atlanta, GA: Home Mission Board of the Southern Baptist Convention.
Rodrigues, D. 2016. *O Evangélico Imigrante: O Pentecostalismo Brasileiro Salvando a América*. São Paulo: Fonte Editorial.
Rosa, W. 2021. *Por Uma Fé Encarnada: Uma Introdução a História do Protestantismo Brasileiro*. Vitória: Editora Unida.
Saraiva, C. 2013. "Pretos Velhos across the Itantic: Afro-Brazilian Religions in Portugal." In *The Diaspora of Brazilian Religions*, edited by C. Rocha and M. Vásquez, 197–222. Leiden: Brill.
Silva, C. A. 2015. "Confederate and Yankees under the Southern Cross." *Bulletin of Latin American Research* 34 (3): 270–304.
Silva, M. M. 2011. "A Chegada do Protestantismo No Brasil Imperial." *Protestantismo em Revista* 26: 113–212.
Simmons, C. W. 1982. "Racist Americans in a Multi-Racial Society: Confederate Exiles in Brazil." *The Journal of Negro History* 67 (1): 34–9.
Vásquez, M., and C. Rocha. 2013. "Introduction: Brazil in the New Global Cartography of Religion." In *The Diaspora of Brazilian Religions*, edited by C. Rocha and M. Vásquez, 1–44. Leiden: Brill.

Glossary Terms

Diasporic Religions: Religions or forms of religions practiced by groups that have been dispersed—voluntarily or compulsorily—outside their traditional or originating homeland.

Pentecostalization: The process, increasingly common in Latin America and other regions, of traditional denominations adopting—officially or not—beliefs and practices associated with Pentecostal forms of Christianity.

Transnational: Transcending nation-states and operating freely across and between geographical borders.

PART V

Current and Future Considerations

17

Latinx Conversions and Religious Change in the United States

Aida Isela Ramos

US Latinx Religion and Religious Change

US Latinx, also known as Latina/os, Hispanics, or Latine, among others, is the name we give individuals whose descendants are from Latin America and the Spanish-speaking Caribbean. These identities were formed out of an intersection of US governmental and cultural forces (Mora 2021; Ramos, Martí, and Mulder 2022). While traditionally, Latinx have been identified as racially white, a spectrum of race/ethnic identities exists within (Dowling 2014; Ramos, Martí, and Mulder 2020). The racial/ethnic diversity within the group is challenging to quantify, but a majority are mixed Indigenous, Black, and European, and a smaller minority of Asian and South Asian, with most preferring to identify as Hispanic, Latino, or with their country of origin (e.g., Nicaragua or Cuba) (Pew Research 2021). The US Census reported 62.1 million Latinos (of any race) in 2020, comprising about 18 percent of the US population. Knowing the demographic landscape, when you think of Latinx in the United States—what comes to mind regarding *religion*? Take a moment to assess your experiences and thoughts. What sights, sounds, and scenes do you see?

Perhaps you hear the gentle guitars and Spanish singing in a Catholic mass in North Carolina? Or the soft rock and melodies of a nondenominational Latinx church in El Paso? Maybe you feel the energy and movement at a bilingual English-Spanish Charismatic service in Portland? What about hearing laughter after Friday prayers at a Muslim community center in San Antonio? Maybe Portuguese is being sung over communion at an Anglican service in Miami? Or Buddhist monks explaining meditation practices in Spanish in Houston? What about Christian prayers in Quechua or Nahuatl at a church service in Austin? What about Latinx who have decided on no religion—what do you imagine their "spiritual" practices are like—if any?

FIGURE 17.1 *Picture of a Latinx Protestant congregation in the Texas-Mexico borderlands.* Source: *Photo by Aida Isela Ramos.*

There is no wrong answer here; all of these scenes represent the religious realities of Latinx in the United States in some way. Still, because of the outsized influence of Catholicism in these communities, their conversions offer a unique lens to study what religious change means and why it happens. Estimates indicate that in 2019, 47 percent of Latinx identified themselves as Catholic, followed by Protestants (primarily evangelical) at 24 percent and the rapidly growing non-Christian, religious unaffiliated Latinx (23 percent) (Pew Research 2019). The rest belong to other Christian-affiliated religions (e.g., Mormon, Jehovah's Witnesses, and Orthodox Christian) and non-Christian religions (Islam, Judaism, Buddhism).

Measuring Religious Conversion

There is extensive literature on religious conversion in various disciplines. In sociology, we situate conversion in relation to social forces influencing people's decisions to "change religion." Consider a family member or friend that converted to a religion different from what they grew up in. How and when did their religious conversion occur? Was it after meeting a friend who invited them to a religious event? Or marrying someone who was of a different faith? After moving to a place with a different religious culture? Maybe after facing a challenging life event or experiencing dissatisfaction with their current religious community? Sociologists do not evaluate the stated theological or spiritual reasons cited by people for their conversion but instead look at how social context shapes a person's decision to convert.

Religious conversion is a complex social behavior with various expressions and can impact identity. For social scientists, conceptualizing what conversion is and how to identify a convert in a population is not easy. While in your typical evangelical Christian Protestant church, you may hear people saying they are "born again" as a signal of conversion at one point, other Christian traditions would see conversion as a lifelong process. A Latina Muslim convert would use completely different language to describe her acceptance of Islam (Morales 2018), while a Latino Buddhist would probably reject the term "conversion" altogether (Cherry et al. 2018). Conversion entails several changes to behaviors and perceptions on behalf of the convert in various combinations depending on context. To measure these concepts in a given population (operationalization), quantitative sociologists choose variables that represent these aspects of conversion, such as religious membership status, acts of religious piety, and even measures that directly ask survey-takers if they left a religious faith for another one or dropped their religion altogether. Qualitative researchers pay attention to the experience and context surrounding conversion, focusing on the patterns in circumstances and motivations that shape people's decisions to leave or adopt another religious identity.

Latinx Catholic to Protestant Switching

So why do some Latinx convert from Catholicism to Protestantism? Falling in line with other theories of conversion, some have argued that Protestantism may be a way to assimilate into a majority Protestant culture of the United States. These theories are in tension with the history of "homegrown" Protestantism in Latin America. While Latin American Protestants still had white American missionary roots, multiple studies confirm a unique Latin American Protestant identity. Still, there is some (but limited) statistical evidence in national data that indicates that Latinx who prefer English are more likely to convert (Ramos, Woodberry, and Ellison 2017), and other scholars have found that Latinx Catholics prefer Spanish (Calvillo and Bailey 2015) which deeply informs ethnic identity preferences (Calvillo 2020; 2022). A stronger relationship appears to be seen in Latino ethnic identity, with Puerto Rican and Central American Latinx being more likely to convert due to the long legacies of Protestantism in their history—we call this the *national origin hypothesis* of US Latinx conversion (Ramos

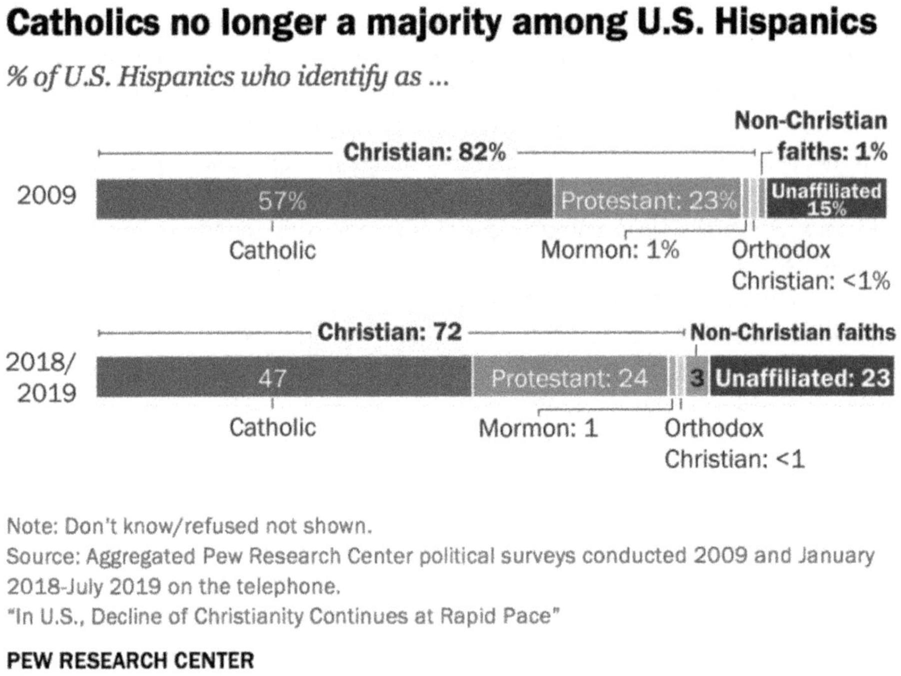

FIGURE 17.2 *A comparative study of Pew Research Center data from 2009 to 2018–2019 showed important changes for US Hispanics. The most significant were the decline of Catholic affiliation and the rise of the unaffiliated.* Source: *Pew Research Center.*

Woodberry, and Ellison 2017). Other statistical analyses (Pew Reseach 2007) showed that Latinx are more likely to say they converted because of a desire for a closer, direct experience of God compared to other reasons (Pew Research 2007). These findings should be taken with caution though, as the dataset used in this work is now dated. More recent Latinx conversion data is needed.

More recent qualitative in-depth interviews and ethnographic research ask Latinos directly why they left Catholicism for Protestantism (Mulder, Ramos, and Martí 2017; Ramos 2022a). Three main themes emerged: first, Latinx who left Catholicism explained feeling disconnected from their Catholic faith. This disconnection manifested in a lack of Catholicism's salience in their lives; in other words, Catholicism did not feel personal or their own, but simply a description of who they were as Latinx. As one study participant said, "It's just a normal part of your existence like you have brown hair, you have brown eyes, it's an identifying characteristic of who you are as a person." When there was a historical line of Catholicism in their families, adherence to the faith was seen as primarily a cultural/national identity rather than a religious one.

Second, Latinx converts cited Protestantism's theology about direct access to God without intercessors (i.e., priests or saints) as a reason for conversion. Catholicism was cast as "religion," a "man-made" institution concerned primarily with following rules, while Protestantism provided them a "relationship" with God. It is important to remember that these interpretations of the conversion experiences are subject to bias. For example, how can we be sure these retellings of the conversion experiences are not influenced by an Evangelical "script" or "talking points" that critique Catholicism?

While not a direct reason for switching from Catholicism to Protestantism, Latinx indicated they encountered tensions in identity with Catholic family and friends. Theories on the "social costs" of conversion indicate that greater tensions are to be expected in religions that are "quasi-ethnic" in nature, that is, religions in which ethnic identity is closely linked to religious identity (Sandomirsky and Wilson 1990). These "social costs" include disapproval, shunning, and exclusion from family gatherings—particularly those tied to Catholic celebrations. Some felt as though they had betrayed their families and their culture by abandoning their long-standing traditions. On the other hand, being in a majority Latinx Protestant congregation eased some of the tension they encountered.

Closing Thoughts

Latinx have, in the present in North America, shaped the United States' religious dynamics in profound ways for centuries—from the wrestling with indigenous understandings and imposed Catholic and Protestant belief systems during colonization to the current debates around Latinx evangelical Protestants as the new right-wing (Martí 2022). Their religious life will continue to have an essential role in the religious terrain of the United States. How will the 2024 election shape how we think about US Latinx religion? What will New Age spirituality on Instagram, growing Native American/Indigenous interpretations of scripture, and religious critiques of immigration policy bring (Guzman 2019; 2016)? In turn, do these religious patterns inform Latinx racial identity in the United States more broadly (Ramos, Martí, and Mulder 2020; Ramos 2022b)? In these everyday ways, Latinx religious conversion continues apace.

Further Reading

Dias, E. 2013. "The Latino Reformation." *Time Magazine*. https://nation.time.com/2013/04/04/the-rise-of-evangelicos/. Accessed July 15, 2022.

Mora, G. C. 2021. *Making Hispanics*. University of Chicago Press.

Mulder, M., A. Ramos, and G. Martí 2017. *Latino Protestants in America: Growing and Diverse*. Lanham, MD: Rowman and Littlefield.

Ramos, A.I., R.D. Woodberry, and C.G. Ellison. 2017. "The Contexts of Conversion among US Latinos." *Sociology of Religion* 78 (2): 119–45.

References

Calvillo, J.E. 2020. *The Saints of Santa Ana: Faith and Ethnicity in a Mexican Majority City*. New York: Oxford University Press.

Calvillo, J. 2022. "Christianities and the Construction of Latinx Ethnoracial Identities." in *The Oxford Handbook of Latinx Christianities in the United States*, edited by K. Nabhan-Warren. New York: Oxford University Press.

Calvillo, J.E., and S.R. Bailey. 2015. "Latino Religious Affiliation and Ethnic Identity." *Journal for the Scientific Study of Religion* 54 (1): 57–78.

Cherry, S.M., K. Budak, and A.I. Ramos. 2018. "Latina/o Conversion and Miracle-seeking at a Buddhist Temple." *International Journal of Latin American Religions* 2 (1): 50–71.

Dias, E. 2013. "The Latino Reformation." *Time Magazine*. https://nation.time.com/2013/04/04/the-rise-of-evangelicos/. Accessed July 15, 2022.

Dowling, J.A. 2014. *Mexican Americans and the Question of Race*. Austin, TX: University of Texas Press.

Guzman Garcia, M. 2016. "Spiritual Citizenship: Immigrant Religious Participation and the Management of Deportability." *International Migration Review* 52 (2): 404–29.

Guzman Garcia, M. 2019. "Mobile Sanctuary: Latina/o Evangelicals Redefining Sanctuary and Contesting Immobility in Fresno, CA." *Journal of Ethnic and Migration Studies* 47 (19): 4515–33.

Martí, G. 2022. "Latinx Protestants and American Politics." *Sociology of Religion* 83 (1): 1–11.

Morales, H.D. 2018. *Latino and Muslim in America: Race, Religion, and the Making of a New Minority*. Oxford University Press.

Mulder, M., A. Ramos, and G. Martí. 2017. *Latino Protestants in America: Growing and Diverse*. Lanham, MD: Rowman and Littlefield.

Pew Research. 2007. "Changing Faiths: Latinos and the Transformation of American Religion." https://www.pewresearch.org/hispanic/2007/04/25/changing-faiths-latinos-and-the-transformation-of-american-religion/. Accessed July 25, 2022.

Pew Research Center. 2019. "In U.S., Decline of Christianity Continues at Rapid Pace." https://www.pewresearch.org/religion/2019/10/17/in-u-s-decline-of-christianity-continues-at-rapid-pace/. Accessed July 25, 2022.

Pew Research. 2021. "Measuring the Racial Identity of Latinos." https://www.pewresearch.org/hispanic/2021/11/04/measuring-the-racial-identity-of-latinos/. Accessed July 25, 2022.

Ramos, A.I. 2022a. "A Matter of the Heart: Understanding Reasons for Latinx Catholic to Protestant Conversion." Manuscript under review.

Ramos, A.I. 2022b. "Faith on the Frontera: Religion, Racialization, and Identity in Texas-Mexico Borderlands." Manuscript under review.

Ramos, A.I., G. Martí, and M.T. Mulder. 2020. "The Strategic Practice of 'Fiesta' in a Latino Protestant Church: Religious Racialization and the Performance of Ethnic Identity." *Journal for the Scientific Study of Religion*, 59 (1): 161–79.

Ramos, A.I., R.D. Woodberry, and C.G. Ellison. 2017. "The Contexts of Conversion among US Latinos." *Sociology of Religion* 78 (2): 119–45.

Ramos, A.I., G. Martí, and M.T. Mulder. 2022. "Latino/a Protestantisms." In *The Oxford Handbook of Latinx Christianities in the United States*, edited by K. Nabhan-Warren. New York: Oxford University Press.
U.S. Census. 2021. "2020 Census Illuminates Racial and Ethnic Composition of the Country." https://www.census.gov/library/stories/2021/08/improved-race-ethnicity-measures-reveal-united-states-population-much-more-multiracial.html#:~:text=The%20Hispanic%20or%20Latino%20population,origin%20grew%204.3%25%20since%202010. Accessed July 25, 2022.

18

Latinx Religious Nones

David Flores

Introduction

Latinx communities have long had to untangle the idea that they are a homogenous population. There are no shortages of stereotypes or oversimplifications to try and box Latinidad into a single category, whether it is that Latinos all speak Spanish, are all brown, or are all immigrants. The reality is, we would be much harder pressed to find commonalities that all Latinx communities can agree upon. Even the term "Latinx" is a hotly debated issue. As such, the theme here challenges another stubbornly persistent Latinx stereotype: that we are all Catholic or religious. Indeed, while a significant majority of the Latinx population is religiously affiliated, namely Christian (Morales, Rodriguez, and Schaller 2021), there is a surprising group that complicates the Latinx religious narrative: *nones*.

The *nones* fall under the broad category of the religiously unaffiliated, people who describe themselves as **atheists**, **agnostics**, or nothing in particular. They are a recent and growing phenomenon in the United States and surprisingly, *nones* are now the fastest growing "religious" group in the country. In 2007, *nones* were only 16 percent of the general population, but by 2021 they had ballooned to 29 percent, translating to nearly three out of every ten adults (Smith 2021). To put that into perspective, social scientist Ryan P. Burge states, the *nones* are "now the same size as both Roman Catholics and evangelical Protestants. That mean[s] that the religiously unaffiliated [are] statistically the same size as the largest religious groups in the United States" (2021: 2). While religious studies scholars have focused on the decline of religious participation in the United States, the rise of *nones* has received much less attention.

Similarly, Latinx religion and spirituality has also largely escaped academic examination, even though eight out of ten Latinxs identify with one religious group or another (Pew Research Center 2014; Chao Romero, Hidalgo, and Flores 2022). Early on, sociologist Ana Maria Diaz-Stevens and religious studies scholar Antonio M. Stevens Arroyo lamented, "Although we admire the many university-based Latino and Latina scholars engaged in Chicano, Puerto Rican, and Cuban American Studies who have greatly enriched the knowledge of Latino experiences, we note with disappointment that most of them have afforded only limited and superficial importance to religion" (1998: 2). Indeed, today, in most metropolitan or urban areas with large Latinx populations, there are departments, colleges, and schools dedicated to the study of all things Latinx, yet, as historians Gastón Espinosa and Mario García observed in 2008, "almost forty [now fifty] years after the founding of the first Chicano studies programs, it is still difficult to find many courses that specifically focus on Chicano religion" (2008: 14). As such, if Latinx religion and spirituality as a whole has been overlooked by scholars, the rise and significance of Latinx *nones* is even further neglected. The lack of academic publications and monographs on Latinx *nones* further indicates the need to advance in this area of research.

First, this chapter examines how religious the Latinx population is, then it explores how Latinx *nones* might contend with their pious counterparts. According to the Pew Research Center, about 80 percent of the US Latinx population still identifies with a religion. The vast majority are Christians (77 percent) and more than half are Catholic (55 percent), although the percentage of Latinx Catholics continues to fall. Buddhists, Jews, Muslims, Hindus, and/or adherents of other faith traditions make up a small minority of the Latinx religious community, all hovering around 1 percent. The final group are the *nones*, which now make up a meaningful 20 percent of the US population. One out of every five Latinxs now identifies with no religion (see Figure 18.1; Pew Research Center 2014).

Interestingly, *nones* are separated into three groups, atheist, agnostic, and nothing in particular. While atheists are the most popular of the group, defined by their certainty that there is no God, they only make up 4 percent of the Latinx religiously unaffiliated. Agnostics are not as confident in their rejection of the idea of a higher power, they simply believe that God cannot be proven and thus claim that they do not know if God exists. Latinx agnostics are also at 4 percent, another minority of the unaffiliated. The final, and overwhelming majority of Latinx *nones* are the "nothing in particulars," representing over 90 percent of Latinxs that do not identify with any religion.

Like all things Latinx, the "nothing in particulars" are also not a uniform group. Yet examining the "Latinos who are unaffiliated" data, a general portrait surfaces (Pew Research Center 2014). For one, a considerable majority of Latinx *nones* are younger; 46 percent are between the ages of 18 and 29, and another 41 percent are between 30 and 49, while those over 50 make up only 13 percent. Income distribution and educational outcomes also play a role in who identifies as a Latinx *none*. Those earning less than $30,000 make up almost half of the group, while Latinxs who make over $100,000 are just 11 percent. As for education, over half of Latinx *nones* have a high school degree or less, and those who have graduated from college represent just 17 percent. As such, younger working-class Latinx without a college degree are more

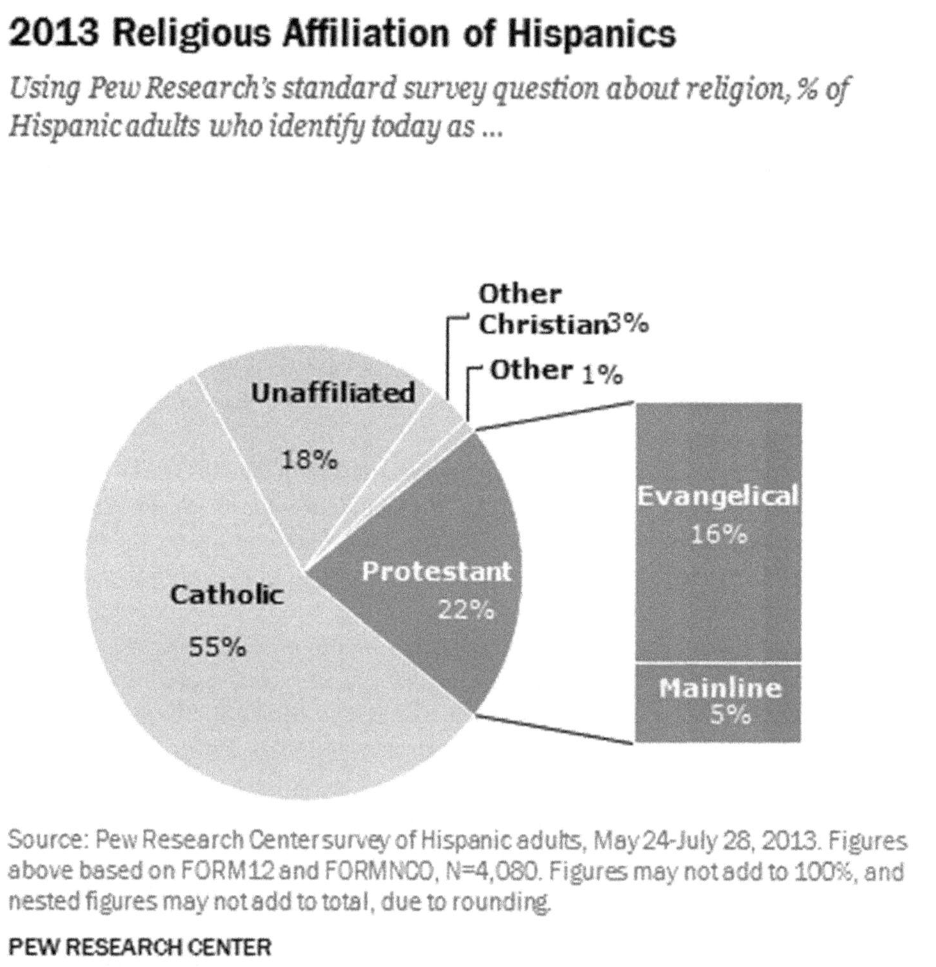

FIGURE 18.1 *Religious affiliation of Hispanics, 2013.* Source: *Pew Research Center.*

likely to identify as a religious *none*, closely mirroring *nones* of the general public. This suggests that the Latinx religiously unaffiliated have staying power and will continue to represent the younger generations of Latinxs in the United States for decades to come.

While Latinx religious dis-identification may seem uncharacteristic of the population as a whole, there are some interesting nuances that complicate the matter even further. For instance, a quick assumption of the *nones* is that they reject all things religious or spiritual, however, that is far from the truth. Over half of Latinx *nones* are at least fairly certain that God exists, with 36 percent of those absolutely certain. And over 50 percent of Latinx *nones* state that religion is at least somewhat important in their life, with a quarter stating that religion is very important. This suggests that Latinx *nones* who have rejected religious affiliation appear to have some dissatisfaction with the dogmas and/or traditional orthodoxy of religious institutions, but not in their personal spiritual identities or beliefs. In fact, the top two reasons the "nothing in particular" group identifies as *none* is that they question religious teachings and dislike positions churches have taken on social or political issues (Pew Research Center 2018). As such, the biggest concerns for *nones* are the policies, character, and political positions of institutional religions, rather than the spiritual teachings of their founders.

Whatever the reason for the dissatisfaction, Latinxs are leaving one of their most trusted institutions in droves (Pew Research Center 2014). Fortunately, for religious institutions, the dramatic rise in the religiously unaffiliated has slowed as of late (Public Religion Research Institute 2020). Yet there is no doubt that religious institutions will have to deal with a significant portion of their flock questioning, in larger numbers, their longstanding membership, particularly Latinxs. For example, even though Latinx Catholics are declining, if population trends hold, "a day could come when a majority of Catholics in the United States will be Hispanic, even though the majority of Hispanics might no longer be Catholic" (Pew Research Center 2014).

The growing number of Latinx *nones* suggests that this is a transitory moment for Latinxs in the United States. In the 1512 opening statement of the Fifth Lateran Council, the Giles of Viterbo stated, "Men must be changed by religion, not religion by men" (Alberigo 2006). It may be precisely the attitude of the Giles of Viterbo that has caused religious institutions to fall behind in responding to the shifting patterns of society, and particularly growing number of Latinxs in the United States. Without serious reflection from religious institutions, signs point to the country heading in the direction of what many European nations have already experienced, **secularization** (Burge 2021).

In the field of Chicanx studies, there is a common theoretical framework that applies well here, ***Nepantla*** (2012). Cultural theorist Gloria Anzaldúa states, "Nepantla is the Náhuatl word for an in-between state, that uncertain terrain one crosses when moving from one place to another, when changing from one class, race, or sexual position to another, when traveling from the present identity into a new identity" (Anzaldúa 2009: 180). The current phenomenon that is the Latinx *nones*, specifically those who largely maintain a spiritual but not religious identity, affirm their belief in God and show an unsatisfaction with the religious options available, can be considered to be in nepantla, searching for something new, different, or something that speaks to the Latinx religious or spiritual experience in the twenty-first century (see Figure 18.2). Cultural historian Edwin Aponte states, while the religiously unaffiliated are not a new group in the history of the United States, "it is becoming more and more common for people who claim that they are 'not religious' to begin a quest for spirituality or 'soul'" (2012: 5).

Recent research has even begun to label a new group of the unaffiliated in the nepantla of the secular and non-secular, calling them the *dones*. Sociologists Josh Packard and Todd Ferguson suggest that the *dones* are a religiously active community

FIGURE 18.2 *Chicano at a Guadalupe mural.* Source: *Author. Mural by Hello Stranger.*

that practice their faith largely outside of religious institutions (2019). How will these new nonreligious religious groups and spiritual seekers fare in the future of the religious marketplace? Will religious institutions be forced to fold and modify *their* orthodoxy under the pressure of the growing *nones* and *dones*? Only time will tell. However, scholars of religion will certainly keep a closer eye on the direction of one of the largest religious groups in the United States, the *nones*.

Further Reading

Aponté, E. D. 2012. *Santo!: Varieties of Latino/a Spirituality*. Maryknoll: Orbis Books.

Burge, R. P. 2021. *The Nones: Where They Came from, Who They Are, and Where They Are Going*. Minnesota: Fortress Press.

Chao Romero, R., J. Hidalgo, and D. Flores, eds. 2022. *Dossier: Rethinking the Role of Religion in Chicanx and Latinx Studies*. Los Angeles: UCLA Chicano Studies Research Center Press.

Pew Research Center. 2014. "The Shifting Religious Identities of Latinos in the United States." *Aztlán: A Journal of Chicano Studies* 47 (1): 131–241. May 7. Accessed May 5, 2022. Available online: https://www.pewresearch.org/religion/2014/05/07/the-shifting-religious-identity-of-latinos-in-the-united-states/

References

Alberigo, G. 2006. *A Brief History of Vatican II*. Translated by Mathew Sherry, Maryknoll: Orbis Books.

Anzaldúa, G. 2012. *Borderlands: La Frontera*, 4th edn. San Francisco: Aunt Lute Books.

Anzaldúa, G. 2009. "Border Arte: Nepantla, el Lugar de la Frontera." In *The Gloria Anzaldúa Reader*, edited by AnaLouise Keating, 176–86. Durham: Duke University Press.

Aponté, E. D. 2012. *Santo!: Varieties of Latino/a Spirituality*. Maryknoll: Orbis Books.

Burge, R. P. 2021. *The Nones: Where They Came from, Who They Are, and Where They Are Going*. Minnesota: Fortress Press.

Chao Romero, R., J. Hidalgo, and D. Flores, eds. 2022. *Dossier: Rethinking the Role of Religion in Chicanx and Latinx Studies*. Los Angeles: UCLA Chicano Studies Research Center Press.

Diaz-Stevens, A. M., and A. M. Stevens-Arroyo. 1998. *Recognizing the Latino Resurgence in U.S. Religion: The Emmaus Paradigm*. New York: Routledge.

Espinosa, G., and M. T. García. eds. 2008. *Mexican American Religions: Spirituality, Activism, and Culture*. Durham: Duke University Press.

Morales, A., C. L. Rodriguez, and T. F. Schaller. 2020. "Latino Political Attitudes: Myths and Misconceptions." *Society* 57 (6): 692–7.

Packard, J., and T. W. Ferguson. 2019. "Being Done: Why People Leave the Church, but Not Their Faith." *Sociological Perspectives* 62 (4): 499–517.

Pew Research Center. 2014. "Latinos Who Are Unaffiliated (Religious 'Nones')." *Society* 57: 693–7. Accessed May 5, 2022. https://www.pewresearch.org/religion/religious-landscape-study/religious-tradition/unaffiliated-religious-nones/racial-and-ethnic-composition/latino/#demographic-information

Pew Research Center. 2014. "The Shifting Religious Identities of Latinos in the United States." May 7. Accessed May 5, 2022. Available online: https://www.pewresearch.org/religion/2014/05/07/the-shifting-religious-identity-of-latinos-in-the-united-states/
Pew Research Center. 2018. "Why America's 'Nones' Don't Identify with a Religion." Accessed April 28, 2022. https://www.pewresearch.org/fact-tank/2018/08/08/why-americas-nones-dont-identify-with-a-religion/
Public Religion Research Institute. 2020. "The American Religious Landscape in 2020." Accessed June 28, 2022. https://www.prri.org/research/2020-census-of-american-religion/
Smith, G.A. 2021. "About Three-in-Ten U.S Adults Are Now Religiously Unaffiliated." Accessed April 10, 2022. https://www.pewresearch.org/religion/2021/12/14/about-three-in-ten-u-s-adults-are-now-religiously-unaffiliated

Glossary Terms

Agnostic: A belief that God or a Higher Power cannot be proven. It is neither a belief or a disbelief in God.

Atheists: Those who maintain a rejection of the belief in God.

Dones: Those that maintain a religious identification and active religious practice, such as praying and studying the Bible, but outside of traditional religious institutions.

Nepantla: A theoretical framework developed most extensively by Gloria Anzaldua, but others as well. Nepantla is often theorized as a middle space, an in-betweenness, or in transition.

Secularization: To have no religious or spiritual basis.

Index